THE YEAR THAT BROKE POLITICS

THE YEAR THAT BROKE POLITICS

Collusion and Chaos in the
Presidential Election of 1968

LUKE A. NICHTER

Yale

UNIVERSITY PRESS

New Haven and London

Published with assistance from the foundation established in memory
of Calvin Chapin of the Class of 1788, Yale College.

Copyright © 2023 by Luke A. Nichter.
All rights reserved.

This book may not be reproduced, in whole or in part, including
illustrations, in any form (beyond that copying permitted by Sections
107 and 108 of the U.S. Copyright Law and except by reviewers for the
public press), without written permission from the publishers.

Yale University Press books may be purchased in quantity for
educational, business, or promotional use. For information,
please e-mail sales.press@yale.edu (U.S. office) or
sales@yaleup.co.uk (U.K. office).

Set in Janson type by Newgen North America.

Printed in the United States of America.

Library of Congress Control Number: 2023931112
ISBN 978-0-300-25439-6 (hardcover : alk. paper)

A catalogue record for this book is available from the British Library.

This paper meets the requirements of ANSI/NISO Z39.48-1992
(Permanence of Paper).

10 9 8 7 6 5 4 3 2 1

To all those who generously shared their memories
of 1968 but did not live to see the result:
Nash Castro
Anna Chennault
Bui Diem
George "Ed" Ewing
Don & Arvonne Fraser
Leslie Gelb
Charles Hill
Tom Hughes
Alva Hugh Maddox
Walter Mondale
Edward Nixon
Rufus Phillips
Raymond Price
John Sears
Katherine Westmoreland

Contents

Introduction

"THIS IS TREASON."[1]

President Lyndon Johnson's remark to Republican Senator Everett Dirksen on the eve of the 1968 presidential election has been widely seen as a reaction to Richard Nixon's effort to sabotage the peace talks in Paris between the United States and North Vietnam. Johnson, after inheriting the conflict in 1963, had begun escalated military involvement in 1965, eventually overseeing a war effort that killed 36,956 Americans—and many more Vietnamese—by the end of 1968.[2] The war reduced American credibility around the world and made it almost impossible for Johnson to advance his remaining domestic agenda. He was desperate to leave office as a peacemaker; there had been a breakthrough in the talks, and his time was short. On November 5, voters would elect either Vice President Hubert Humphrey, former Vice President Richard Nixon, or former Alabama Governor George Wallace to succeed him.

But we need to take a fresh look: at what Johnson said, at what Nixon was doing, at the relations among Johnson, Humphrey, Nixon, and Wallace, and at the entire dynamics of the 1968 presidential campaign. Nothing was as it seemed. Lyndon Johnson should be restored to the central place he occupied. His withdrawal from the election was not a withdrawal from politics. Feeling bitterly rejected by some in his own party, he was eager to influence the choice of his successor—who would bear directly on his own legacy. Nixon correctly perceived that the votes of millions of moderates who supported Johnson over Barry Goldwater in a landslide in 1964 could be in play in 1968. Sworn political enemies, when not facing each other on the ballot Johnson and Nixon had much less to disagree about—and discovered they needed each other.

The year 1968 was one of the most tumultuous in American history.[3] The nation's population passed 200 million for the first time; the war in Vietnam exceeded the Revolutionary War as the nation's longest military conflict; the nation was more divided than at any point since the Civil War.[4] The twentieth-century years 1914, 1929, 1939, and 1991 and the revolutionary years 1789, 1848, and 1989 were pivotal, defined by some political, economic, social, or military event, but 1968 included all four types of events. Americans saw the nation challenged from abroad and from within. We were forced to reconsider what we stood for, where we were going, and whether the fabric of society was strong enough to contain the range of passions our differences evoked.[5] Some of those differences were generational, seen in nationwide campus unrest and the Democratic National Convention in Chicago. *Time* magazine called it "the biggest year for students since 1848."[6] It was a coming-of-age for the younger generation, which was defined by it.[7]

"In 1968," Theodore White wrote in one of the earliest and most famous chronicles of the year, "it was as if the future waited on the first of each month to deliver events completely unforeseen the month before."[8] There was almost too much tragedy and drama to list briefly: the capture by North Korea of the *USS Pueblo*; the Tet Offensive; Senator Eugene McCarthy's stunning performance in the New Hampshire primary; Senator Robert Kennedy's late entry into the race; Johnson's withdrawal on March 31; Dr. Martin Luther King Jr.'s assassination; Kennedy's assassination; Nixon's almost uncontested clinching of the Republican nomination in one of the greatest political comebacks in U.S. history; the Soviet invasion of Czechoslovakia; Humphrey's nomination at the culmination of a historically chaotic convention in Chicago; the inevitable break between Johnson and Humphrey in the fall; and Johnson's cliffhanger peace effort and bombing halt on the eve of the election.

The nation was fractured. Socially, our communities were divided in response to racial upheaval in our cities. We struggled to find the right balance between allowing protest and maintaining law and order. The United States seemed to have reached the limit of its means to pay for both social progress and the war. The economic warning lights, including slower growth and rising inflation, were blinking red. Our armed forces were spread around the world, and few issues were more divisive than the draft that forced our young into combat. The old politics seemed to have run out of answers. The Cold War had reached a turning point, headed toward an unknown destination. The postwar era of American dominance was ending, and the West was being eclipsed by the rise of a hostile and threatening East.

It has taken more than a half century to see 1968 with the distance needed for a more dispassionate assessment.[9] The year was examined even before it was over, with the first published works hastily written in the weeks after Election Day. Campaign memoirs poured out over the next few years. The focus has been on the rebellious actions of young people, the campaigns of Robert Kennedy or Eugene McCarthy, and Vietnam. Few have considered the political history of the entire campaign.[10] Some chroniclers were at the beginning of their careers in 1968, and their choice of subject was shaped by their personal experiences and political commitments.[11] The flood of quickly published works has led to the assumption that we know everything there is to know about that year. By the time historians turned to it, decades later, the conventional wisdom was firmly established—and largely impervious to the new evidence that usually shifts our understanding of people and events.

"The history of the time will require a considerable perspective," British journalists Lewis Chester, Godfrey Hodgson, and Bruce Page predicted with a surprising amount of professional distance in the immediate wake of the election.[12] The intervening years allow for fresh analysis by those with no stake in the outcome or legacy to defend. A great opening of archival materials now permits a fuller discussion, because, despite all that has been written, we have lacked many rigorously researched historical accounts.

Despite the many books about 1968, until now the story of the presidential campaign has been told in solos: political memoirs, campaign biographies, and Cold War histories. This work brings the participants together, reflecting the complexity of the eight-month contest and the high stakes it represented for America and the world. An overemphasis on the actions of Americans has subordinated events in Moscow, Paris, and Saigon that greatly influenced the election's outcome. This work attempts to rebalance the scales of history, taking a broad look while bringing in new voices and perspectives that have been overlooked.

The Democratic consensus, found in many accounts, is that Nixon stole the 1968 election by committing treason and violating the Logan Act. The Republican consensus is that Johnson, by creating the illusion of a sudden change in the status of the war, made a last-minute effort to steal the election for Humphrey, which failed. Each interpretation has perpetuated myths that distort our understanding of the campaign and election result. This book rejects both. Instead, it attempts to offer a better understanding of what motivated Johnson, who, while not on the ballot, remained very much politically alive; how Humphrey closed the gap and almost defeated Nixon; the true basis of Wallace's appeal, which involved much more than racist statements made years earlier; and what really motivated Americans to vote as they did.

PART I

Spring Optimism

CHAPTER ONE

Johnson

"WHEN I TOOK THE oath as President in January 1965 to begin my first full term in office, I felt that it would be my last," Lyndon Johnson wrote in his memoirs.[1] Yet he was tempted by the idea of throwing his hat into the ring for another term. His hero, Franklin D. Roosevelt, had said it was his "firm intention" to step down in 1940, but he ended up running anyway. Johnson waited as long as he could to make a decision, and his health played a bigger role than most people realized.[2] He never acknowledged this during his lifetime.

During his Senate days, he smoked three packs of cigarettes a day and drank like a fish. His heart attack on July 2, 1955, at the age of 46, was far more serious than recognized at the time. Throughout his presidency he was in almost daily pain from angina and popped nitroglycerin tablets like jelly beans.[3] Lady Bird bought a black funeral dress in 1965 in case her husband died suddenly.[4] "Two hospitalizations for surgery while I was in the White House had sharpened my apprehensions about my health," he wrote in his memoirs.[5] His father, Samuel Ealy Johnson Jr., had died at sixty, having suffered a stroke a decade earlier. Johnson would reach that age on August 27, 1968.

Anyone could see how much he had aged in office. He was arguably the hardest-working president of the modern era, and no one could drive Johnson harder than he drove himself. If you met him, you might describe him as a force of nature, an egomaniac, untrustworthy, coarse, mean of spirit, and unforgiving.[6] He understood how the presidency had drained the health of Democratic heroes Woodrow Wilson and Franklin D. Roosevelt. People of Johnson's generation, born in the early twentieth century, remembered how Wilson declined during his second term and was eventually incapacitated, his left arm and leg paralyzed for the last five years of his life. His "family's history of stroke and heart disease" concerned Johnson greatly. While he felt he could run again and win, he worried he would be unable to finish his second term.[7] "This is a terrible strain and men in my family have died early from heart trouble," he said. "I'd like to live a little bit longer."[8]

Something else also kept him from running. "I think what was uppermost—what was going over and over in Lyndon's mind," Lady Bird wrote in her diary, "was what I've heard him say increasingly these last months: 'I do not believe I can unite this country.'"[9] She saw the strain her husband was under from "the growing virus of the riots, the rising list of Vietnam casualties, criticism from your own friends, or former friends, in Congress"—and noted that "most of the complaining is coming from Democrats."[10] Kennedy Democrats, resentful that Johnson was in the Oval Office, never gave him credit after he ensured passage of Kennedy's stalled legislative agenda. Liberals predictably criticized him over Vietnam, but what especially burned him was their growing belief, as seen in the final report of the Kerner Commission, that the Great Society had overpromised and underperformed and had divided the nation more sharply in the 1960s than at any point since the 1860s.

Johnson and his intimates had discussed his retirement as far back as the 1964 campaign, and these conversations grew more frequent and intense after August 1967, when Secretary of Defense Robert McNamara announced his resignation.[11] Lady Bird said that Johnson was stung by every staff departure, but when McNamara left, on February 29, 1968, it was one of the hardest of his entire presidency. Johnson lost not just an anchor in his cabinet but a confidant. "The sense of loneliness and separation is deep," he told Texas Governor John Connally.[12]

Lyndon Baines Johnson arrived in Washington in 1931 at the age of twenty-three, and never really left. He was born on August 27, 1908, in Stonewall, Texas, in Gillespie County. It was a poor, rural borderland, about as far southwest as you could go and remain in the United States. New Mexico and Arizona had not yet joined the union. Texas was a part of the Old Confederacy, but due to a concentration of German immigrants, Gillespie County had always been more opposed to slavery and secession—and more open to outsiders—than much of the South. The people Johnson encountered as a young man were among the nation's poorest, especially in Cotulla, about halfway between San Antonio and Laredo, where he accepted his first teaching position after graduating from Southwest Texas State Teachers College. He was not a likely candidate to become one of America's greatest experts on the machinery of government.[13]

Johnson wanted to make a difference, and inspired by his father's political career and connections made in college, he believed he *could* make a difference. First elected to the House of Representatives in 1936, after cutting his teeth as a congressional staffer and Texas leader of the New Deal's National Youth Administration, he moved up to the Senate in 1949 and became both Senate Democratic Whip and Leader while still in his forties. Johnson learned legislation like no one else—not only the procedures and rules, but the personalities and the art of persuasion.[14] He rose to prominence during the Eisenhower administration as the leader of the opposition. In the opinion of his chief Republican rival, Vice President Richard Nixon, among all those vying for the Democratic nomination in 1960, Johnson was most qualified to become president.[15] His ability to talk to all different kinds of Texans served him well. He learned about loyalty—when it was due, how to show it. "Dear Jack," he wrote in a Christmas letter to President Kennedy in 1961, "where you lead, I will follow."[16] While Johnson did not have the pedigree of an Eastern Establishment that looked down on him, he had the ability to outwork everyone else. In 1960, he rode Kennedy's coattails into the vice presidency while doing his part to hold the South in one of the closest presidential elections in American history.[17]

No one could have predicted that Johnson would become an accidental president. When Kennedy was slain in Dallas on November 22, 1963, Johnson instantly inherited national trauma and the unfulfilled anticipation of his predecessor's leadership. He also inherited the client state of South Vietnam and its "dynastic rivalries, deep clan hatreds, rank betrayals, as well as fortitude in adversity, shining heroism, and deep love of country," as Bernard Fall wrote; "all appear at regular intervals and sometimes simultaneously."[18] Johnson and the nation had little understanding of what they were getting into. Included in this inheritance was the presence of 16,732 Americans engaged in combat, even though, officially, they were there only as military advisors.[19] Had Johnson not inherited the problem,

with his less than sure footing in foreign affairs, he might not have gone in
search of adventure in Vietnam.[20]

Johnson had come of age in Washington as a witness to the powerful
New Deal programs that transformed lives and the nation, and he must
have concluded that he could achieve both Roosevelt's and Kennedy's unfinished goals. By building sufficient consensus in Congress, where Kennedy had stalled out, Johnson also sought to build consensus in the nation.[21] He understood drama and emotion, how to attract the right kind
of press attention at the most opportune time, and how to capitalize on a
moment. Many of his Great Society programs focused on issues such as
civil rights, education, poverty, Medicare, and the environment.[22]

It is hard to choose Johnson's greatest achievement during his presidency: perhaps the Civil Rights Act of 1964, the Voting Rights Act of
1965, or Medicare and Medicaid, which were part of the Social Security
Amendments of 1965. Johnson himself publicly said it was civil rights.[23]
But while he was certainly a visionary on that score, he was not the first.
One could point to the Civil Rights Act of 1957, the first such legislation
since Reconstruction, or Truman's 1948 order to desegregate the armed
forces. Johnson's emphasis on using legislation to effect change meant that
he was often an initiator or architect of change, but not its builder. That
took a collaborative effort, whether for civil rights or the Great Society
more generally.[24]

A less conventional answer might be that Johnson's greatest contribution was simply what he represented—the rise of the New South. The
label incorporates more than the acceptance and promotion of civil rights.
While the Eastern Establishment and national media made fun of his ac-
cent and humble origins, he brought an earthiness and a work ethic to the
White House that had not been seen since the time of Andrew Jackson.[25]
By demonstrating that a Southern president could be more than a gadfly
focused on race and regional issues, Johnson paved the way for future
Southern and Southwestern leaders, changing the way Americans thought
about the South and bringing an additional degree of national healing a
century after the Civil War. Four of the next seven presidents came from
states that had been part of the Confederacy.

Johnson faced great challenges with energy and resourcefulness, but
the experience of governing during the turbulent 1960s seemed to drain
him. Beginning in the summer of 1967, the violence, arson, rioting, looting, and crime across the nation were almost nonstop. "The traditional

standards of American conduct and behavior were, beyond any doubt, changing," Theodore White wrote.[26] Johnson's hold on Congress was slipping, and the political mood in Washington was turning against him.[27] For a generation, the goals of white liberals and Black leaders had been peaceful integration. In June 1966, Stokely Carmichael coined a new slogan: Black Power. He meant Black people having control over their own communities, an appreciation for Black culture and values, Black police officers to secure these communities, and Black businesses serving as their backbone of commerce. But by 1968, some whites equated Black Power with hate, and Carmichael was doing little to counteract that impression. "If a white man tries to walk over you, kill him," he said. He urged followers to become "urban guerillas" who would "fight to the death" while "smashing everything western civilization has created."[28]

Johnson had transformed himself from a Southerner who came of age with typical views regarding race into a champion of equal opportunity. But it was not clear whether, after thirty-five years in Washington, he was up to a new set of challenges. Lady Bird, his sounding board, editor, cheerleader, and chief critic, reflected, "I admire him fiercely. I want to see him spend himself, give whatever it takes, against this miasma of despondency, this ugly virus that is infecting our country."[29] That miasma seemed to be beyond the reach of Congress.[30] Maintaining consensus in the House and Senate was no longer enough to maintain consensus in the nation.[31] Americans misconstrued race as a Southern problem, but the explosion of race riots and urban violence awakened the nation to the fact that Jim Crow did not reside only south of the Mason-Dixon Line.[32]

Lady Bird was discreet, even in her diary, but a close eye can tell when things that bothered her must have irritated her husband too. "Lady Bird had a strength and dignity that were never adequately portrayed to the American people," Billy Graham wrote.[33] "I seriously doubt if any couple could love each other more than these two. I thought about their years together, the battles they had gone through together, the joy and sorrows they had had. I thought about the tremendous impact this couple had had on American life and history."[34] Not only was Lady Bird the closest figure to Johnson to keep a diary, but her thoughts often included his. "I think the most frustrated I've been lately is reading a speech that Senator Fulbright made in which he indicated that the country is damned because we are spending so much in Vietnam instead of spending it here to take care of the poor and underprivileged," she wrote. "This from a man who has never voted for Civil Rights measures and who even voted against Medicare in 1964."[35]

Johnson seriously considered using his 1968 State of the Union address, the least hopeful and most defensive of his annual messages, to announce that he would not run again.[36] He had spoken with Texas Governor John Connally about whether he should seek another term. "You ought to run only if you look forward to being President again—only if you *want* to do it," Connally advised. "You also ought not to run just to keep somebody else from being President." Lady Bird remembered the conversation. "We spoke of the possibility of announcing the decision at the end of the State of the Union Message. . . . John made one grim statement that went something like this: 'The only way to answer all of those arguments is to die in office.'"[37] She signaled her wishes but tried to let the final decision be his. "Lyndon's decision is never far from my thoughts," she wrote in her diaries. "I cannot condone the outcome, though I will have some effect on it."[38] As for his daughters, Johnson wrote, "Luci did not want me to run. She insisted that she wanted a living father. Lynda's response was more complex. As a daughter, she said, and the more reserved of the two, she would prefer that I not run, but as a citizen she hoped I would."[39]

"Well, what do you think? What shall I do?" Johnson asked Lady Bird on the day of the address. The speech was ready; the question was whether to append a final line: "Accordingly, I shall not seek and I will not accept the nomination of my party for another term as your President."[40] She read it over and judged it to be beautifully written. "Lyndon handed me a piece of paper, a letter from John Connally with his recommendations that he go with the statement tonight," she wrote in her diary, "because he would never have a bigger audience . . . the occasion of the State of the Union was a noble time to make an announcement. Lyndon had to weigh this against the fact that the whole 1968 program of action would thereby be diluted, if not completely ignored."[41] He did not make the announcement. Some aides were surprised, since it had been discussed and vetted by his speechwriters in advance. But the timing did not feel right.

After the State of the Union, Johnson labored on, keeping his friends and close aides guessing as to his intentions. His approval rating dipped to 36 percent in March, from 48 percent in late January.[42] His stiff demeanor on television did little to help sell his war policy to the American people or bridge the gap between his generation and younger Americans.[43] "Television has ruined me," he told Billy Graham.[44] Night after night of battles broadcast into the living rooms of Americans made it difficult to tell the winners from the losers.[45] Johnson convened a series of briefings on Vietnam in late March in the Cabinet Room with the "Wise Men," an informal group of advisors whom Walt Rostow and Clark Clifford had originally assembled to serve as a bipartisan sounding board.[46] The group held out little hope for progress in Vietnam until after the presidential election.[47] This consensus challenged one of the nation's most enduring myths, that we can accomplish anything as a people if we set our minds to it.[48]

The war became more personal for the Johnsons on March 31, when Lynda's husband, Chuck Robb, was deployed to Vietnam. That was also the day Johnson decided to announce he would not seek reelection. Lady Bird's unpublished diaries provide a more frank view of the day than the version of her diaries published in 1970.[49] "When I went back into Lyndon's room, he was crying," the unpublished version says. "It's the first time since Mrs. Johnson died that I have seen him cry. But he didn't have time to cry. Today was a crescendo of a day."[50] Johnson had breakfast before going to Mass with Luci and Pat Nugent at St. Dominic's, a "somber, gray Victorian-Gothic structure, with twin spires."[51] It was a simple but busy parish, popular with both white and Black Washingtonians.[52] At several critical moments in his presidency, such as in 1966 when he ordered the bombing of Haiphong harbor, Johnson asked U.S. Secret Service agents to take him there for prayer and a late-night conversation with one of the priests or friars.[53] The press never knew of these visits.[54]

"After Mass was over and we were back in the car," Johnson wrote in his memoirs, "I closed the glass partition to the front seat and told Luci and Pat that I had something to read to them and that I wanted them to listen carefully. Looking at both of them, I experienced emotions too overwhelming to express."[55] The motorcade proceeded to Hubert Humphrey's apartment in Southwest Washington. "In a separate area of their living room I met alone with the Vice President and told him of my plans," Johnson wrote. "He had already been informed, in effect, more than a year before."[56] Jim Jones, the future Oklahoma congressman, was there and remembered Humphrey's reaction. "He was just defeated from the start," Jones said.[57] "His face flushed, and tears ran from his eyes. 'You can't do this. You can't resign from office. You're going to be reelected,'" Jones recalled Humphrey telling Johnson. "There's no way I can compete against the Kennedy machine."[58]

Johnson arrived in the Oval Office shortly before nine o'clock on the evening of March 31. He asked Marvin Watson to call Cabinet members and others who should not be caught off guard.[59] It must have been a moment in which Johnson could feel what was left of his political power drain from his body. "I was under no illusion that I had as much power in 1968 as I had had in 1964," he reflected later.[60] Lady Bird was radiant and happy, but daughters Lynda and Luci were not. "I went to him and said quietly, 'Remember—pacing and drama,'" Lady Bird wrote in her diary. "It was a great speech and I wanted him to get the greatest out of it—and I did not know what the end would be."[61] The press received a transcript of the speech in advance, but syndicated columnist Drew Pearson did not see anything unexpected in it.[62] The advance copy did not include the surprise ending.

The speech, to an audience estimated at 75 million, began with the announcement that the bombing north of the twentieth parallel would be halted. "Tonight I want to speak to you of peace in Vietnam and Southeast Asia. No other question so preoccupies our people." Johnson then tiptoed into the reasoning behind the latest bombing halt.[63] Despite several previous failed peace efforts, he still held out hope that extending an olive branch could lead to negotiations. A bit more than half an hour later came the stunning ending. "With America's sons in the fields far away, with America's future under challenge right here at home, with our hopes and the world's hopes for peace in the balance every day, I do not believe that I should devote an hour or a day of my time to any personal partisan causes or to any duties other than the awesome duties of this office—the Presidency of your country," Johnson said, building toward the peroration. "Accordingly, I shall not seek, and I will not accept, the nomination of my party for another term as your President."[64]

"The speech was magnificently delivered," Lady Bird wrote in her diary.[65] It brought the most positive outpouring of support since Johnson's landslide victory in 1964.[66] "If I had it to do over again, I'd put my whole stack in again," he said later. "I could have either announced a bombing pause or that I wasn't going to run. But I thought it would have more impact if I announced them both together. And I think it did. I think it was the thing to do."[67] His presidency, and his political career, would be over within months. "In forty-five minutes, I had finished. It was all over and I felt better. The weight of the day and the weeks and the months had lifted," he wrote in his memoirs.[68] He had been determined for some time to end his presidency; the "problem was how to get the right word and phrase to say exactly what I meant," Tom Johnson recorded in his notes.[69] Yet it was a shock to the nation, and even to the aides who knew of the announcement written into the State of the Union Address but left unread.[70] Some called it Johnson's abdication speech. He did not intend it to be interpreted that way, but it did to some degree mark an abdication in Vietnam. It signaled the beginning of the end of the deep American involvement in Indochina.[71]

The March 31 speech was not delivered as it was conceived. "We thought we were drafting a speech for an embattled candidate," Secretary of Defense Clark Clifford wrote in his memoirs, "not a man ready to sacrifice his career, in his own eyes, in pursuit of peace."[72] The members of the press corps immediately seized on what the speech meant for the continuation of the war, and for the approaching political season. Johnson's announcement threw the race wide open, but the speech's timing, in the wake of the Tet Offensive and the New Hampshire primary, also caused it to be misunderstood.

The weeks-long Tet Offensive, which began on January 30 with a communist assault on American and South Vietnamese troops, weakened American public support for the war. Tens of thousands of North Vietnamese and Vietcong soldiers launched simultaneous, coordinated attacks on much of South Vietnam, surprising Americans at home, who had been led to believe the enemy was weaker and the war was going better. Johnson's lack of retaliatory measures, combined with the timing of his announcement, made it seem as though he was reacting to the situation in Vietnam, and to Tet specifically. The media interpreted it as such, and that myth has remained largely part of the conventional wisdom. Only years later, with the declassification of the documentary record, did a fuller picture emerge.

Chairman of the Joint Chiefs of Staff Earle Wheeler's request following Tet for 205,179 additional troops triggered the first fundamental debate within the administration about Vietnam since the build-up in 1965.[73] "Under the circumstances, the President had asked General Wheeler to tell me making a major call-up of Reserves and contesting the enemy geographical widening of the war was politically infeasible," General William Westmoreland wrote in his memoirs.[74] Johnson denied the request for more troops, a turning point in the war at a moment when the United States had the opportunity to capitalize on communist weakness. He was unwilling to risk widening the war.[75] The decision meant that military victory would no longer be possible during Johnson's tenure in office.[76] "It seems now more certain than ever that the bloody experience of Vietnam is to end in stalemate," Walter Cronkite reported on February 27.[77] Some reporters compared the situation to the French defeat in 1954 at Dien Bien Phu, which was preposterous.[78] Johnson, influenced by the media, was indeed concerned about a catastrophic military defeat on that scale.[79] Members of the media were overwhelmed in their efforts to quickly cover a distant, complex, fast-moving story.[80] When the Vietcong tried to seize the U.S. Embassy in Saigon on January 31—and did penetrate the perimeter and the compound but did not get into the building—the media initially reported that Vietcong snipers had penetrated the embassy building and fired down on rescuers from its rooftop.[81]

The speech was also misinterpreted as a response to the presidential campaigns of Senators Eugene McCarthy and Robert Kennedy. The timing was coincidental, but it did not seem so to those who were unaware of Johnson's long process of soul-searching over whether to seek another term. Much of the coverage of Johnson's challengers was written by admirers who produced something closer to hagiography than rigorous history.[82] Neither campaign received the scrutiny that Humphrey, Nixon, and Wallace—and Johnson himself—later did. It seems forgotten that Johnson won the New Hampshire primary as a write-in, defeating all challengers despite having no campaign organization and no line on the ballot. McCarthy was the only candidate listed on the ballot, yet he did not muster a majority.[83] The *New York Times* estimated that Johnson was likely to win at least 65 percent of the delegates at the coming convention in Chicago.[84] "I was not expecting a landslide," he wrote in his memoirs. "I had not spent a single day campaigning in New Hampshire."[85]

Johnson predicted McCarthy would get "at least 40 percent" because of dissatisfaction over Vietnam and the overall national mood. Even Nixon won almost 5 percent of the Democratic vote—more than Robert Kennedy.[86] McCarthy outspent pro-Johnson forces by a factor of six to one.[87] "Every son-of-a-bitch in New Hampshire who's mad at his wife or the postman or anybody is going to vote for Gene McCarthy," Johnson griped, but he still won 49 percent of the vote, and 20 delegates, while his challenger won 42 percent and four delegates. Many did not know McCarthy's views. Less than six months before, few had even heard his name, and some thought he was Republican Senator Joseph McCarthy of Wisconsin, who had died in 1957. Sixty percent of Gene McCarthy's supporters believed Johnson's error on Vietnam was that he was not hawkish enough.[88]

McCarthy was a genuinely talented politician, but the national media created expectations for his campaign that no one could fulfill.[89] The former Democratic chairman of Ramsey County, Minnesota, he was an orator, a writer, a poet, and a scholar who was well versed in history, philosophy, and theology.[90] His political rhetoric was sprinkled with phrases from the progressive encyclicals of Pope John XXIII.[91] "In one sense our task was easy, made easy by the four years of Lyndon Johnson's administration," McCarthy aide Curtis Gans reflected. "We had, at the very beginning, all the arguments that might appeal to mainstream America."[92] McCarthy's brigades of young volunteers declared themselves "clean for Gene" by shedding their long hair and beards.[93] They knew nothing about the candidate's past and did not want to. They wanted to know what he was saying *today*. His bread-and-butter campaign stop was a small, religiously affiliated college where he could speak to a small group about why the Vietnam War was wrong.[94] His campaign was at least as much about standing up to the military-industrial complex and its influence on policy making as it was about challenging Johnson.

McCarthy was hardly a backslapper. His Senate colleagues did not consider him especially likeable or hardworking, and he probably would not be remembered even to the extent that he is if he had not come out in opposition to Vietnam—the first who not only directly opposed Johnson from within the ranks of his own party but challenged him for the presidency. With small groups of supporters, according to one of his speechwriters, he was "chillingly impersonal, and with non-white or noncollege people the presentation simply didn't take."[95] McCarthy declared his candidacy on November 30, 1967, in response to political activist Allard Lowenstein's long effort to recruit a challenger to bring the president down. He was the only one who rose to the challenge. "I'm twice as liberal as Humphrey," McCarthy liked to say, "twice as Catholic as [Robert] Kennedy, and twice as smart as [Stuart] Symington."[96] He never bought into the mystique of the Kennedys, seeing them as idolized and insincere.[97] He took full advantage of the spotlight that found him, damaging longtime relationships and never making up with friends like fellow Minnesotan Hubert Humphrey.[98]

McCarthy had a particular motivation for running against Johnson after being rejected as his vice-presidential running mate in 1964—when he was so confident of being chosen that his family flew down from Minnesota to Atlantic City to the Democratic Convention. Johnson strung him along until the last moment before choosing Humphrey.[99] "I vowed

I would get that son of a bitch," McCarthy told Humphrey biographer Edgar Berman, "and I did."[100] He never wanted the presidency, and his campaign was arguably not for it but against it. He was quirky; you could never quite tell whether his motivation was political or personal.[101] Even his allies saw him as an unrealistic revolutionary.[102] His habitual use of "we" and "our" made him sound like he was leading a movement.[103] He openly wondered whether democracy was up to the test of the 1960s.[104] His campaign was a risk; if he failed, it could actually strengthen Johnson. While the polls showed LBJ's weakness, they did not indicate that his rivals had any strength.[105] McCarthy barely spoke to donors and did not thank them, his national campaign infrastructure was basically nonexistent, and he had no polling operation, no advertising, and no campaign materials. *Newsweek* called the campaign "hardly even an embarrassment."[106] No seasoned political observer took it seriously, but it got a lot of attention because of what it symbolized.

Bobby Kennedy, who had hesitated to join the race, did so as soon as he saw McCarthy's finish in New Hampshire, siphoning off some of McCarthy's supporters.[107] Some liberals resented Kennedy for making a late decision after leaving McCarthy the difficult task of being the first to challenge Johnson openly.[108] McCarthy said he would give Kennedy a job licking postage stamps for his campaign, provided Bobby cut his hair. He took delight in a sign at a campaign rally at Brooklyn College that said, "Bobby, you support the wrong McCarthy," referring to the close friendship between the Kennedys and Joe McCarthy.[109]

The younger brother of John F. Kennedy had his own turbulent relationship with Johnson, which the national press built up whenever possible.[110] Robert Francis Kennedy was arguably the most intense of the Kennedy sons, more like his father than his siblings.[111] His politics had moved from conservative to reluctant liberal to increasingly radical.[112] Most political observers, even his close advisors, thought his best shot at the presidency would be in 1972—assuming Johnson would run and win in 1968.[113] As a first-term senator, Kennedy did not have the track record of a serious contender, but he had tremendous emotional pull with Americans—the kind that would make any competitor jealous, including Johnson.[114] "Here is a young man who looks younger than he is and whose only real asset is the fact that he's the brother of a dead president yet who is determined to become president," columnist Drew Pearson wrote in his diary.[115] Robert Kennedy, born in 1925 and thus still young, needed only to wait out his enemies. He had run for office just once, for the Senate in 1964.[116] "Many in the Nixon camp, with memories of 1960, were fearful of Kennedy, the name, and the magic. I never was," Pat Buchanan recalled. "I preferred him as the Democratic nominee, but doubted he would be the man. To me Bobby was nothing like his charismatic brother, nor had he any of JFK's conservative and centrist appeal."[117]

Robert Kennedy said that he would not "under any conceivable circumstances" challenge Johnson.[118] But he sent mixed signals; he seemed out of the race but left feelers that suggested he might be in. During appearances for other candidates in 1966, it seemed that he was the one running.[119] When his brother Edward "Ted" Kennedy asked whether he should go to New Hampshire to see if he could start a write-in movement, Bobby responded, "Mind your own business. . . . Robert Kennedy, spelled R-O-B-E-R-T-K-E-N-N-E-D-Y is not a write-in candidate."[120] Once he did throw his hat into the ring, it was a throwback to Camelot: he drew fawning press attention, escaped the scrutiny that other presidential candidates received, and ignored political polls that showed twice as many people had an "intense dislike" for the "cold, cynical, arrogant, ruthless" Kennedy as for Johnson. Kennedy was a redeemer who could rewind the clock to an era before Vietnam, civil unrest, and his brother's murder.[121] As for how he would heal the nation's great divisions, Ted Sorensen said "he would have brought black and white together," resulting in a "different country."[122] Drew Pearson did not buy it. "If Bobby were nominated, I might well vote for Nixon," he wrote in his diary.[123]

Kennedy seemed immune to the legendary Johnson treatment. He had never wanted Johnson as his brother's running mate in 1960, and he wanted Johnson even less in his brother's White House.[124] Unlike others who had been close to John F. Kennedy, Bobby never changed how he treated Johnson after he became president.[125] "During the four and a half years of my Presidency," Johnson wrote in his memoirs, "I had never been able to establish a close relationship with Bobby Kennedy." Despite the conventional wisdom that Johnson could only be brash and crude, he also could be extremely warm and charming. But Robert Kennedy, once he emerged as a direct competitor, was not likely to see that side. "Perhaps his political ambitions were part of the problem. Maybe it was just a matter of chemistry," Johnson recalled.[126] Kennedy was set up well to run against Johnson, but he could not really attack Humphrey except by attaching him to the Administration.[127]

When Johnson said he would withdraw from the presidential race, it did not mean he was withdrawing from public life, including saying and doing things that could influence the campaign. Staffers like Fred Panzer continued to churn out the voluminous political reports that Johnson craved.[128] From Alabama to Washington, Johnson continued to monitor the situation closely.[129] When his focus shifted from the ballot to his legacy, every ounce of his energy was channeled to his planned key legislative and diplomatic achievements, including Vietnam and bilateral negotiations, and to influencing the selection of his successor. He would become a post-president on their watch, he would lead the transition to the new administration, and the new president could do a great deal to help or hurt Johnson's image and legacy.[130]

There was also the growing pull of the Ranch, with its twelve thousand acres and thirteen thousand head of cattle. The Ranch gave him an identity and an anchor in an increasingly volatile world.[131] As a past president, Johnson could also pour his energies into teaching at the University of Texas at Austin, where his presidential library would be built, along with the Johnson School of Public Service. The Hill Country was not far from San Marcos, either, where his alma mater, now Texas State University, was located.[132] All of these were waiting for him at the other end. Until then, he would be busy making the most of the remaining time, closing loose ends, and planning his legacy. The biggest loose end, and the least secure part of his legacy, was the war in Vietnam. His March 31 speech was a step toward settling that issue, with its call for a bombing halt and peace negotiations, but he needed help from North Vietnam. "Just before I drifted off to sleep that night," he wrote, "I prayed that Hanoi had listened and would respond."[133]

In the brief honeymoon period following Johnson's announcement, public opinion rebranded him as a selfless elder statesman interested in peace. His advisors decided the best strategy was to stick with the public proposal he had made on September 29, 1967: "The heart of the matter is this: the United States is willing to stop all aerial and naval bombardment of North Vietnam when this will lead promptly to productive discussions. We, of course, assume that while discussions proceed, North Vietnam would not take advantage of this bombing cessation or limitation."[134] That September speech was mentioned so often in internal White House deliberations that the proposal became known as the San Antonio Formula, after the South Texas city where the speech was delivered.[135] Under the code name Operation Pennsylvania, the proposal was sent secretly to the North Vietnamese by Harvard Professor Henry Kissinger, who served as a national security consultant in the Kennedy and Johnson administrations.[136] The San Antonio Formula was kept vague so as to prompt a response but not commit the administration to specifics.[137] It allowed Johnson to accept or reject any given peace offer based on his interpretation of it.[138] That formula was also the basis for the peace proposal announced in his March 31 address.[139]

Johnson did not wait long for a response from North Vietnam. "On April 1," he wrote in his memoir, "a few of our planes attacked military targets in and near the town of Thanh Hoa, just south of the twentieth parallel. This was a major transfer point for men and supplies moving toward South Vietnam—either down south toward the demilitarized zone or westward into the infiltration routes through Laos."[140] On the 2nd, however, he ordered that a strike be canceled as a gesture of goodwill consistent with his March 31 announcement. Hanoi responded the next day, leading LBJ to order the military to avoid any actions inconsistent with the spirit of the bombing halt.[141] While the bulk of Hanoi's response was its usual anti-American diatribe, it was "further perhaps than Hanoi has ever gone before" toward peace, Johnson wrote in his memoirs. "It is the first time that they have shown any willingness to have their representatives get in touch with ours."[142] Johnson announced only a partial bombing halt rather than the total pause that Hanoi demanded. Half of North Vietnam was still in the bombing zone. Nonetheless, on April 3, Hanoi said it was "prepared to send its representatives to meet and to determine with the U.S. representative the unconditional cessation of the bombing and all other acts of war against the DRV, so as to start the talks."[143]

Johnson and his inner circle debated this apparent change of heart after more than two years in which Hanoi had refused to come to the negotiating table.[144] The reason was Tet. While many in the media wrote it up as a failure for the United States, American and South Vietnamese forces had actually scored a decisive military victory.[145] In engagement after engagement, the Vietcong and North Vietnamese army had suffered terrible losses.[146] The communists lost an estimated fifty-eight thousand men in three weeks, or as many as the U.S. lost during the entire Vietnam War.[147] Contrary to the communist myth that Tet was a spontaneous popular uprising against the corrupt government in Saigon, the South Vietnamese saw it as a major defeat for the communists.[148]

Johnson's personal approval ratings soared in the wake of his March 31 announcement and the swift response from Hanoi.[149] In an instant, he had erased his rivals' two main issues, the war's unpopularity and his own.[150] Gallup showed on April 3 that Americans were still hawkish and opposed to a wider bombing halt, 51 to 40.[151] Johnson's announcement was a compromise as well as an act of self-sacrifice. "At first there were those four or five days of almost euphoric relief, with thousands of letters pouring in from all over the nation—mostly admiring, grateful, understanding, and some urging him to reconsider," Lady Bird confided to her diary. The optimism was short lived. "Then the whole nation had been convulsed by the hideous assassination of Martin Luther King and the ensuing riotings and killings in the cities."[152]

On April 4, 1968, at 6:01 P.M., forty-one-year-old James Earl Ray fired a Remington 30-06 Gamemaster slide-action rifle in the direction of the balcony of the Lorraine Motel in Memphis, Tennessee, just outside room 306. A metal-jacketed bullet pierced the right cheek of civil rights leader Dr. Martin Luther King Jr. while he was having a casual conversation. It severed numerous vital arteries, fractured his shoulder, and came to rest on the left side of his back. An hour later, he died in St. Joseph's Hospital.[153] An estimated 120 million people watched King's funeral, the biggest audience since John F. Kennedy's.[154] Johnson was thunderstruck at the assassination, after all he had done to help race relations.

Few people had been paying attention to the Memphis sanitation workers' strike, which King was in town to support. In recent years, as many African Americans became frustrated with the slow pace of change, he had started to drift away from strict nonviolence to supporting more direct action.[155] He also tied American military involvement in Vietnam to racial oppression at home.[156] This evolution can be seen in his testimony before the Kerner Commission in October 1967.[157] "All of America's wealth today could not adequately compensate its Negroes for his centuries of exploitation and humiliation," King said.[158] While King believed that the worst brutalities were over for Blacks, he thought the nation had never truly committed to helping them out of poverty, exploitation, and all forms of discrimination. "The limited reforms," he wrote shortly before his death, "have been obtained at bargain rates."[159]

It took less than two hours after the assassination for the tinkle of broken glass to be heard in a hundred cities across the nation, followed by looting. Riots broke out across the country, and in Washington, the

Capitol dome was illuminated by flames from downtown. "I remember the sick feeling that came over me the next day as I saw the black smoke from burning buildings fill the sky over Washington," Johnson wrote in his memoirs, "and as I watched armed troops patrolling the streets of the nation's capital for the first time since the Civil War."[160] More than fifty thousand federal and National Guard troops were called in to restore order, in one of the largest peacetime deployments on American soil in history. The Capitol was defended by soldiers in full battle gear, and the bloodshed and violence continued in Washington for a week.[161] Johnson took a secret helicopter ride on April 7 to survey the damage, and he was rendered nearly speechless by the extent of the devastation.[162] Remembering the experience of 1932, when General Douglas MacArthur used tanks and cavalry to remove twenty thousand World War I veterans from Washington, Drew Pearson said "the threat of the Bonus Army was peanuts compared with what happened when the students of Howard University and a lot of other young Negroes started burning and looting today."[163] King's death also pushed back Johnson's plans to meet South Vietnamese President Nguyen Van Thieu prior to the start of the Paris peace talks. Thieu did not hide his outrage at the bombing halt announced in Johnson's March 31 address, and he was eager to discuss other issues, including North Vietnamese infiltration.[164] Hosting him in Washington, however, was not an option with the town looking like a war zone, even within blocks of the White House.

Johnson had used his brief surge in popularity to persuade Congress to pass the Fair Housing Act—also known as the 1968 Civil Rights Act—and a gun control bill. But King's death abruptly stopped any further progress Johnson hoped to make on civil rights during the remainder of his term. With Vietnam on a path toward resolution, even if a long-term path, the nation's attention became focused on domestic issues, especially law and order.[165] Johnson felt powerless to make any bold moves to address his unfulfilled agenda. He did not understand why so many former friends on the Hill, fellow Democrats, denied him the chance to engage in the one thing he always enjoyed—legislating.[166] And a public weary of racial issues was unlikely to support further major pieces of civil rights legislation.[167]

Martin Luther King Jr. had planned to lead the Poor People's Campaign in early May 1968, and it went on in his absence.[168] Demonstrators carried out sit-ins and civil disobedience in the Capitol and in Cabinet departments in Washington, and lived in a Poor People's Camp, also known

as Resurrection City, built from makeshift prefabricated housing on fifteen acres on the east side of the Lincoln Memorial. Ralph Abernathy
led the initiative in King's memory, but the press coverage was largely
negative. Perhaps some of the negativity was unfairly earned after recent
protests and sit-ins at Columbia University, which prompted the FBI to
scrutinize organized protests more closely.[169] Columbia was a bellwether
for what can happen when activism becomes separated from a base of
political support.[170]

Lacking King's unifying leadership, the Poor People's Campaign
earned its bad press. Women were assaulted in Resurrection City, where
conditions were so squalid that Abernathy was rumored to have checked
into a nearby hotel. Curious tourists were relieved of their wallets, cameras,
and other valuables.[171] Torrential spring rains turned the site into a muddy
mess. "It has been described as a jungle and there have been numerous
instances of immoral activity," Jim Jones advised Johnson, according to
FBI sources. "On the evening of June 19 there were reportedly 18 different assaults in Resurrection City."[172] That was the day of the "Solidarity
Day Rally for Jobs, Peace, and Freedom," attended by some fifty thousand
participants.[173] During the rally, Abernathy declared that "the promise of
a Great Society was burned to ashes by the napalm of Vietnam, and we
watched the Johnson administration perform as the unwitting midwife at
the birth of a sick society." He pledged that his followers would remain
"until justice rolls out of the halls of Congress."[174] Resurrection City's permit expired on June 23, and the government moved in the next day to
dismantle the housing and arrest those who remained.

It was no more peaceful on the other side of the world. On April 30,
Earle Wheeler warned Johnson that the North Vietnamese were rapidly
moving men and equipment southward, violating the terms of the bombing halt. Johnson was eager to get negotiations started. Hanoi rejected
every proposed site for the talks, but on May 3, a representative called
the U.S. embassy in Vientiane and officially suggested Paris. The United
States quickly agreed, even though Franco-U.S. relations were strained
and the French did not support U.S. policy in Vietnam. Talks would begin
on May 10 or soon after.[175] South Vietnam was not permitted to participate, a problem that would become a major stumbling block, but American diplomats in Saigon agreed to keep Thieu informed.[176]

Johnson did not have high hopes for peace in Vietnam, believing
that North Vietnam simply wanted a bombing halt, but he still had much

he wanted to accomplish. "He has accelerated his activity if anything," Lady Bird wrote. "No backward look, but a determination to push with every power he has toward peace abroad and toward furthering his programs here at home . . . the most philosophic and detached I've ever seen him."[177] He did not consider himself a "crippled waterfowl," and unlike most outgoing presidents, he did not become one overnight.[178] His long wish list included addressing the nation's $20 billion fiscal deficit with a 10 percent tax surcharge, a farm bill, occupational safety and health, securing the USS *Pueblo* crew's release from North Korea, pension reform, the nonproliferation treaty, the beginning of arms negotiations with the Soviets, an independent postal service, seeing the astronauts off on their journey to the moon, and peace in the Middle East.[179] In the end, the only agenda items Johnson could not ram through Congress were a repeal of the Taft-Hartley Act's right-to-work provision and home rule for the District of Columbia.[180] "He wanted to leave the office of the Presidency in proper shape for his successor and the state of the union as strong as he could make it in the limited time left to him," White House Press Secretary George Christian recalled.[181]

Johnson told his Cabinet that they were free to support whomever they liked in the upcoming election, which Humphrey must have taken as an insult. But after Secretary of the Interior Stewart Udall and Attorney General Ramsey Clark came out for Kennedy, Johnson changed his mind and demanded neutrality.[182] He had met with Kennedy at the White House on April 3 and come away convinced that Bobby was a serious candidate.[183] The next day he tried to persuade Nelson Rockefeller to enter the race. Only someone with the political brand name and financial resources of a Rockefeller, he thought, could defeat a Kennedy. He lobbied Rockefeller again on April 23.[184] Johnson had always gotten along best with those from the Republican Party's moderate to liberal wing, and if it was to be a Republican year, Rockefeller seemed like the most congenial successor. Ideologically and politically, their positions were similar and neither man was a threat to the other. Rockefeller's use of Henry Kissinger as his in-house national security expert ensured that his positions on Vietnam did not stray far from Johnson's.[185] On May 18, Johnson paid Rockefeller a visit in Sleepy Hollow, New York, to make one more effort to convince him.[186] While Rockefeller had made a campaign debut on May 1, it was a half-baked operation and he had been surprisingly critical of Johnson's Vietnam policy.[187] There would be no alliance with

Rockefeller; Johnson had to think of another plan. Kennedy might not be as successful in the upcoming Oregon primary because Democrats there were not Catholic, blue-collar, or urban—but California was a different story.[188] Kennedy had to be stopped before then, before he could run away with the nomination.[189]

Four days before the Oregon primary, on May 24, a bombshell *Washington Merry-Go-Round* story by Drew Pearson and Jack Anderson reported that as attorney general, Robert Kennedy had authorized the wiretapping of Martin Luther King Jr.[190] Worse, Kennedy had not only approved the wiretap, he requested it.[191] After the FBI objected to the order, Pearson and Anderson reported, "the Attorney General remarked that he was not interested in repercussions in the least."[192] Pearson wrote in his diary that "Bobby had telephoned me some months ago claiming he had nothing to do with wiretapping and putting the blame on Hoover. . . . These documents show quite the contrary."[193] James Reston had reported the wiretaps in the *Times* in December 1966, just weeks after Kennedy's election to the Senate, but at the time people accepted Kennedy's denial. They did so even though the memo authorizing the wiretaps, signed by Kennedy on August 17, 1961, had been declassified on the eve of the 1966 election.[194] (Perhaps because of internal misgivings, the FBI did not begin tapping King's phone until July 1963.) Now this new story, with even more proof, was a tremendous blow for a candidate trying to rally the Adlai Stevenson liberals—but that was what Pearson and Anderson intended: "a death blow prior to the Oregon primary."[195] A leak like that could only have been authorized by the White House. "Drew got it from Lyndon," Anderson said later. "Of course it was timed."[196]

In the Oregon primary, McCarthy delivered the first electoral defeat that any Kennedy had ever suffered, 44.7 percent to 38.8.[197] Before that, the Kennedy streak was twenty-four straight wins in general and primary elections.[198] The result seemed to support McCarthy's view that if he and RFK divided the liberal wing of the Democrats, neither could win.[199] After the primary, the two agreed to have the first presidential debate since 1960. Broadcast nationwide by ABC, the debate in San Francisco reached an estimated audience of 32 million. They agreed more than they disagreed, but Kennedy surprisingly shifted to the right of McCarthy on some issues, much as his brother had done during debates with Henry Cabot Lodge Jr. in 1952 and Richard Nixon in 1960. Bobby argued that McCarthy would negotiate with communists, move Blacks from Watts to Orange County, and give jets to Israel that they had not requested.[200] McCarthy called Kennedy's attacks "the most disappointing part of the entire campaign." In McCarthy's defense, the *New York Times* noted that Kennedy's charges distorted and even falsified McCarthy's record, which had been close to John F. Kennedy's.[201]

On June 4, Kennedy won the California Democratic primary, 1,445,880 votes to McCarthy's 1,305,728, and claimed it was the decisive victory he needed in order to build momentum before the convention. McCarthy refused to concede and said he would not support Kennedy. "It is his intention to maintain his campaign on at least as high a level as it has been," Bill Connell, Humphrey's chief of staff, reported to his boss. "He will not welcome a 'personal' confrontation but it is his feeling that if you or the President 'lower' yourselves to 'personally attack' him, it will be the greatest bonanza that his campaign could come across."[202] The odds for a Kennedy nomination still seemed long.[203] He had won fewer primaries than McCarthy, and Humphrey controlled most of the delegates.[204] None of his primary wins were landslides.[205] Yet his presence in the race was powerful fulfillment for millions of Americans who yearned to see another Kennedy in the White House.

That night, after he gave a victory speech at the Ambassador Hotel in Los Angeles, Kennedy was shot by Sirhan Sirhan and critically wounded. Once word reached Johnson in the White House, in the early morning hours of June 5, he went to work immediately. "Lyndon was using the telephone almost from the first moment I went in, giving instructions about putting Secret Service on all the candidates," Lady Bird wrote in her diary.[206] By the following day, a second Kennedy had died from an assassin's bullet. "Senator Robert Francis Kennedy died at 1:44 A.M. today, June 6, 1968," said campaign press secretary Frank Mankiewicz.[207] That evening at 10:07 P.M., having had just two hours' sleep since he learned of the shooting, Johnson went on live television to comfort the nation. It was less than five years after he had performed a similar duty for another Kennedy. This time, no riots broke out; instead, an eerie calm descended.[208] The death of one Kennedy was tragic, but after a second, it was as though the nation's political class lost its bearings. "Camelot is ended," Kennedy operative Richard "Dick" Tuck said. "It began with John Kennedy's death, not before, and it ended with Bob Kennedy's assassination."[209] Johnson immediately provided additional protection for the remaining candidates. About half of the White House Secret Service detail was reassigned to the candidates.[210]

Kennedy was not mourned like a mere presidential aspirant. So much about him was conditional—what he would have been, what he would have done, and what it would have meant for the country—yet with his passing, the nation, in need of a hero in a dystopian year, gave him full advance credit for the promised transformation. He had been hated by Southern Democrats, distrusted by many liberals, opposed by organized labor, and resented by many of his party's rank-and-file for the divisions he had caused.[211] None of it mattered. JFK's circle had created the myth of Camelot, but the nation created the myth of Robert F. Kennedy.[212] When the Johnsons arrived at St. Patrick's Cathedral in Manhattan for his funeral, thirty-three hundred people were on hand, including most of the Cabinet, roughly a quorum of the Senate, many members of the House, and state and city officials including Governor Rockefeller and Mayor John Lindsay. "The ceremony was one of staggering drama and beauty," Lady Bird wrote in her diary.[213] Perhaps a million people watched his funeral train carry him on his final journey from New York to Washington, DC, while the train's bell tolled throughout the eight-hour procession, as it had for the last train ride of Abraham Lincoln a century earlier.[214] Bobby was buried near his brother, downslope from the eternal flame in Arlington National Cemetery.[215] Many considered it the most beautiful place in Washington, overlooking the city on the grounds of Arlington House, the former estate of Robert E. Lee.

The assassinations of King and Kennedy brought a period of national soul-searching. With the Vietnam peace talks stalled and Johnson's mission to influence the choice of his successor aborted after Nelson Rockefeller proved uncooperative, the president toyed with the idea of reentering the race. The chaos did not undermine him; Americans in search of stability rallied behind him. Johnson invited his close friend the Rev. Billy Graham to the White House the weekend after Kennedy's funeral. Graham was asked to provide friendship, spiritual counseling, and a private service for the first family.[216] It has been overlooked the extent to which Johnson was increasingly comforted by his Christian faith, especially during his final year in office. In her diary, Lady Bird described the year 1968 as nerve wracking for Johnson physically, mentally, and spiritually.[217] LBJ had a kind of frontier faith but was not seriously committed to a denomination. Attending several different kinds of churches, even sometimes on the same Sunday, was also good politics: it allowed him to see and be seen by supporters. He was also the first sitting president to meet a pope, visiting Paul VI in New York City on October 6, 1965. Johnson began attending Mass more regularly after Luci's conversion to Catholicism when she married Patrick Nugent in 1966—something Lady Bird found harder to accept.[218] Unlike Johnson, she was the genuine Southerner who hailed from Baptist country in the heart of the former Confederacy.

Graham flew to Washington immediately after Kennedy's funeral, on a plane filled with former Kennedy staffers. "I have never seen a more despondent and grief-stricken group of young men," he wrote in his diary.[219] On his arrival at the White House, he went right to room 303 on the top floor, his regular room when he visited. Johnson often consulted him during challenging times. "A number of times I had prayer with him in his bedroom at the White House, usually early in the morning," Graham recalled. "He would get out of bed and get on his knees, while I prayed. I never had very many people do that."[220] The two had first met in 1949 through their mutual friend Sid Richardson.[221] Graham symbolized millions of moderate white Southerners who traditionally voted Democratic but had supported Eisenhower before switching back to Johnson.[222] "He had a tremendous interest, as you know, in religion and in Christian things, and he could quite easily talk about it," Graham recalled.[223] Of all the presidents he had known, Graham had the most in common with Johnson—a Democratic populist and moderate Southerner who took risks for civil rights. At their core, they were two farm boys who had risen to the pinnacle of their professions through talent, ambition, and relentless energy.[224] "Although many have commented on his complex character, perhaps I saw a side of that complexity that others did not see," Graham reflected, "for LBJ had a sincere and deeply felt, if simple, spiritual dimension."[225] With Graham's help, Johnson sought a peace that he badly needed even though his restless side resisted.[226] "He was always a little scared of death," Graham recalled.[227] Johnson preferred to have a preacher nearby. His great-grandfather had been a frontier evangelist, and his grandfather was a professor of Bible at Baylor University. Johnson was the first sitting president to attend a crusade, one of Graham's, in Houston in November 1965. "I knew he was not a saint," Graham wrote in his memoirs. "Did he intimidate me? Maybe just the opposite. I think I intimidated him a little."[228]

As usual, Graham pledged neutrality in the 1968 campaign, but that pledge is as much misunderstood as Johnson's promise to stay out of politics. It did not mean he had no preference or might not suggest publicly what his preference was, but he was not a partisan and did not make formal endorsements. A syndicated columnist called Graham the "X-Factor" in the 1968 campaign, since he knew all the major candidates personally and was reaching the peak of his own career just as the South was politically up for grabs.[229] "I do not envy the man who is elected President," he wrote to Humphrey. "He will have to face the greatest problem that any President has faced since Lincoln."[230]

Graham and Johnson discussed Nixon. They agreed he had the most responsible position on law and order, which had emerged as the key political issue following the deaths of King and Kennedy.[231] All of the major candidates agreed on the need to disengage in Vietnam, so the war increasingly took second place to crime and violence in the public's concerns.[232] "For reasons more emotional than rational, it seems to me, this whole tragedy turns the nation toward the Republican Party," Lady Bird confided to her diary.[233] Johnson was convinced Nixon would be a better successor than Humphrey on the war, as he was not tied to Vietnam or the chaos of the decade. If Nixon maintained liberal enough domestic policies to win praise from Eastern Establishment Republicans, Johnson could not ask for more. Both he and Graham saw a political shift on the horizon.[234] Johnson, wrote Graham, "said that he thought Richard Nixon was going to be elected the next President of the United States. He said Nixon is probably the best qualified man in America to be President. He said, 'I don't always agree with him but I respect him for his tremendous ability.' I told him that if he gave me freedom to tell Mr. Nixon just what he had said that it would be of great encouragement to Mr. Nixon. He said, 'By all means tell him.'"[235]

Nixon had been a steady presence in American politics since the 1940s, and that made him desirable. Johnson could be helpful to Nixon, and Nixon could give Johnson the respect he craved as a former president. As a close friend to both, Graham understood that each could be good for the other. "One of my objectives during the past few years has been to say nice things about Johnson in the presence of Nixon and nice things about Nixon in the presence of Johnson," Graham wrote in his diary. "I could not help but feel in my heart that Nixon was going to be the next President and I felt that there would come a day when they would need each other just as Johnson felt the need of Eisenhower."[236] Public opinion polls throughout 1968 consistently showed a Nixon victory as the most likely outcome. Graham believed that "a big segment of the population," "a great unheard-from group," was likely "to be heard from loudly at the polls" in the fall.[237] When James Rowe, political confidant to both LBJ and Humphrey, wrote Johnson to complain that Graham favored Nixon, Johnson responded with a handwritten note: "I can't control him."[238] Rowe was one of the few who understood the significance of Graham's "getting ready to come out for Nixon."[239] When he saw Nixon in New York on June 10, Graham wrote in his diary, "I was very careful not to quote the President except where the President had given me permission."[240]

In a final surprise in the month of June, Supreme Court Chief Justice Earl Warren announced his retirement at the age of 77. Johnson wanted to elevate Abe Fortas, already an Associate Justice, to Chief Justice. Fortas had remained an advisor to Johnson even after he was confirmed to the court; the two had had 145 in-person meetings in addition to many telephone conversations.[241] While there was nothing illegal about their continuing their relationship, a promotion would look like a conflict of interest. Politicians of both parties had grown increasingly wary since President Kennedy had appointed his brother to the position of attorney general. Johnson also said he wanted to nominate Homer Thornberry, another longtime friend, to fill Fortas's vacant seat. Privately, Clark Clifford did not think Thornberry was Supreme Court material, but said, "Mr. President, it is a splendid idea, but I am concerned that it may not survive in this form. I regret to say this, but I do not think you can sell this package to the Congress." Johnson did not understand Clifford's objection. "They would probably accept Abe on his own," Clifford added. "But if his nomination is tied up with Homer Thornberry's, I am afraid that they will find some way to sidetrack it."[242]

Clifford's advice was on the mark. Both nominations were defeated by Congress after questions arose regarding the men's relationships with Johnson.[243] Fortas's nomination was struck down with bipartisan support including a filibuster by Senator Richard Russell of Georgia.[244] Warren ultimately decided to delay his retirement until 1969, so Johnson never got to name his successor. This sloppy series of events would not have occurred earlier in Johnson's career, when his grip on political power was more firm. It was a sign of things to come.

CHAPTER TWO

Humphrey

THE LAST SCHEDULED SPEAKER on the last day of the 1948 Democratic National Convention was a thirty-seven-year-old mayor from Minneapolis named Hubert Horatio Humphrey. Few of the delegates in the Philadelphia Convention Hall knew who he was. They stuck around to hear him only because President Harry Truman would arrive soon to accept the party's nomination for president. The temperature soared inside the hall after the Secret Service closed all the doors as a precaution. Humphrey walked up to the speaker's platform and waited nervously for his name to be called.

The night before, an expansive civil rights resolution pressed by a coalition of Northern liberals, including Humphrey, had been firmly defeated by the Platform Committee. It was a great disappointment, especially since the Republican Convention, held a few weeks earlier, had passed a progressive civil rights plank written by Senator Henry Cabot Lodge Jr.[1] Humphrey had repeatedly called for the Truman administration to move more aggressively on civil rights. He had seen the Jim Crow system up close as a graduate student in segregated Louisiana in the late 1930s, and the experience had given him a fervent commitment to the issue of race relations.[2]

Humphrey loved the rituals and fanfare of politics, especially the small-town version, which always stayed with him even when he rose to the national political stage. He believed in the power of Government, with a capital *G*, to improve people's lives. He was born on May 27, 1911, above the family drugstore in Wallace, South Dakota, the state having been carved during his parents' lifetimes from Dakota territory, which itself had been carved from Minnesota territory during his grandparents' lifetimes.[3] Doland, South Dakota, population five hundred, where he grew up, was not a model of diversity. It was home to one Jewish family and zero African Americans. His father, Hubert Horatio Humphrey Sr., was mayor, state legislator, and a Democratic delegate to the 1928 convention, where he cast his vote for Al Smith, the original happy warrior.[4]

Minnesota's history is a bit like that of Texas, but not nearly so prominent in the popular imagination. It was a vast state with just one major population center and a Western spirit of rugged individualism. Its harsh winters and dust bowl summers taught young Hubert not to be ambitious, and to appreciate humanity.[5] Combine that climate with FDR's New Deal and the region's unique patterns of settlement and immigration, and the result was a distrust of bankers and Republicans that lasted for generations. Humphrey's family had to move five times to pay debts and taxes. As a teenager with the nickname "Pinky," he worked as a soda jerk in his father's store, which was both a local meeting spot for political talk and the place where the future vice president received his first lessons about people. After a trip to Washington, DC, in 1935, he was bitten by the political bug. "Bucky," he wrote to his new girlfriend, Muriel Fay Buck, "I can see how someday . . . we can live here in Washington. . . . I'm going to try, but must prepare myself by always thinking as a liberal."[6]

Before *liberal* became a dirty word, it defined a generation of Americans who lived through the Depression and believed that without timely government intervention, the suffering of millions would have been incalculably worse. A certain prairie populism developed in Minnesota with Humphrey emerging eventually as its face. He began by following in his father's footsteps, earning a degree from the Denver College of Pharmacy in 1933 after his plans to attend the University of Minnesota were cut short by the Depression. He married Muriel in 1936, went back to the University of Minnesota, graduating in 1939, and then earned an MA in political science at Louisiana State University in 1940. Baton Rouge, where he arrived just four years after Huey Long's assassination, gave him his first real experience with the Deep South and segregation. Even on the all-white campus there were white and Black segregated drinking fountains.[7] And once he saw how racial attitudes permeated both Black and white people's lives, he was forced to reconsider his belief that Blacks had it any better in the North.[8]

As a New Deal administrator, Humphrey managed a Works Progress Administration (WPA) program that focused on adult education.[9] He also taught at Macalaster College, in St. Paul, Minnesota, and did radio news commentary. Denied wartime service for health reasons, he made up for it by being especially tough on communists at home.[10] Increasingly, however, he saw public office as his future. He ran for mayor of Minneapolis in 1943 and lost, but was not at all discouraged.

Humphrey's greatest contribution to state politics was healing the long-festering rift between the Minnesota Democratic Party and the progressive, occasionally communist-influenced Farmer-Labor Party.[11] At just thirty-two, in 1944, he founded the Minnesota Democratic-Farmer-Labor Party (DFL), a merger of the two entities that would become a dominant force in state politics for more than a generation. It produced passionate liberal statesmen—not just Humphrey but also Eugene McCarthy and Walter Mondale—and still produces politicians with philosophical ties to the progressive strain of agrarian populism.[12] With his stature enhanced by the merger, Humphrey ran again for mayor of Minneapolis in 1945 and won. During his tenure, he made an estimated four thousand speeches— roughly three per day.[13] His progressive record included the first city-wide Equal Employment Opportunity Commission.[14]

Humphrey's speech at the 1948 Democratic National Convention lasted just eight minutes. Calling civil rights the next great national challenge, he proclaimed that the Democratic Party had to "get out of the shadow of states' rights and walk forthrightly into the bright sunshine of human rights." He condemned half-measures as "a bunch of generalities" and "a sellout to states' rights," and pleaded with his fellow delegates not to yield the issue of civil rights, which Franklin D. Roosevelt had worked so hard to win, to the liberal wing of the Republican Party. "There are those who say to you—we are rushing this issue of civil rights," he said. "I say we are a hundred and seventy-two years late."[15]

A combined radio and television audience of 70 million listened as Humphrey unleashed pandemonium in the convention hall. He called for an end to lynching, a commission to curb employment discrimination, ensuring African Americans the right to vote in the South, and open military service for all Americans. For the first time since Reconstruction, the status of African Americans became a national issue. Humphrey's speech prompted a revolt by liberals in the convention hall; someone put forward a motion to overturn the previous night's action and throw out the Truman administration's compromise civil rights plank in favor of the stronger liberal plank, and the motion passed on a vote of 651 ½ to 582 ½.

Some then followed Humphrey's urging to "walk forthrightly."[16] The vote on the civil rights plank prompted a walkout of Southern delegates. Alabama's George Wallace, then a moderate, ran after his delegation, took the state banner out of Bull Connor's hands, and restored it to its place on the floor.[17] He did not join the splinter group that adopted the States' Rights platform on July 17, 1948, formed the States' Rights Democratic Party, and held a rump convention in Birmingham, Alabama, that nominated J. Strom Thurmond as its presidential candidate.[18]

Humphrey became an instant national figure. Democratic regulars, alarmed by the split in the party, told him that he might have cost Truman the election. The president had earlier released a report, "We Hold These Truths," that called for broad new civil rights legislation, but liberals criticized that there had been little follow-up.[19] Humphrey emerged as a household name among liberal Democrats who saw him as far ahead of party leaders. Having gambled everything with such a bold proclamation, the mayor of Minneapolis further pressed his luck by running for a seat in the Senate that fall against the incumbent Republican, Joseph H. Ball. When he arrived in Washington as the first Democratic senator from Minnesota in ninety years, the accomplishment earned him the cover of *Time* magazine.[20]

As the only Democratic senator from the upper Midwest, Humphrey maintained one of the busiest Senate offices, introducing about fifteen hundred bills and resolutions over two-plus terms from 1949 to 1965.[21] "This job is getting almost too much for a fellow," he wrote to George Ball, then known as a former aide to Adlai Stevenson, in 1958.[22] Lyndon Johnson, who quickly ascended from Senate majority whip in 1951, to minority leader in 1953, and finally to majority leader in 1955, placed Humphrey on the Senate Foreign Relations Committee in 1953, giving him his first international exposure.[23] In 1958, he had an eight-hour late-night meeting in the Kremlin with Nikita Khrushchev that helped him with Soviet support in future runs for the presidency.[24] Later Soviet support even included an offer of badly needed campaign cash.[25] Johnson also supported Humphrey's election as majority whip in 1961, after Johnson ascended to the vice presidency. He was loyal, worked hard, was well liked, and delivered results, which was exactly what Johnson needed to keep the party's left flank in Congress in line—a primary duty of his during the Kennedy administration.[26]

Humphrey also survived an unsuccessful run for the presidency in 1960. While no candidate could match his energy or enthusiasm, he could not compete with John F. Kennedy's money and campaign organization, and suffered a brutal defeat in the Democratic primary in West Virginia. He withdrew but did not endorse Kennedy, ultimately supporting Adlai Stevenson even after it was clear that the nomination would go to Kennedy.[27]

Humphrey was at his best when he was out in front, leading the liberal agenda, which was why Lyndon Johnson chose him as his vice-presidential running mate in 1964. Humphrey believed that the most direct route to being president was by being loyal to Johnson—and he always was, even when some said otherwise.[28] "I want to be loyal, and my guts, my heart, won't let me do it any other way," he recalled.[29] Johnson, he wrote in his memoir, had "made possible my being Senate majority whip and vice president of the United States. No one played a more important role in my receiving the nomination for the presidency."[30]

As vice president, Humphrey was the right man at the right time to help Johnson pass his Great Society programs through Congress. While Kennedy or Johnson got the credit, it was Humphrey who was the driving force behind such policies as the Peace Corps, Medicaid, and the Civil Rights Act of 1964—perhaps the most significant piece of domestic legislation affecting race relations since the Kansas-Nebraska Act of 1854. He was successful because he knew how to connect with people. "When it comes to getting the necessary vote from a senator," he once said, "a mouthful of logic can't match that little heart-to-heart talk in the Oval Office, that late-night 'philosophical' discussion over a beer, or a two-minute phone call to his home. You don't know what it means to a senator's wife or his kids to hear, 'the president's on the line.'"[31]

Working for someone involved in so many key initiatives meant long hours, and Humphrey's extreme thrift meant that his staff was among the lowest paid on Capitol Hill. He had an open-door policy, even though his staff—who adored him—generally understood when he could or could not be disturbed.[32] Despite his preference for New Deal–sized spending bills, he never shook his parents' fear of owing money, especially to bankers. The fringe benefits for his staff often included a drink with the boss for those still in the office at the wee hours, along with a late-night snack of cheese or peanuts. Humphrey preferred Canadian Club and soda, and he liked his steaks drowned in ketchup. His personal physician recalled

that Humphrey "bordered on being a junk food addict." He once sent an
assistant to find a McDonald's in Rome and asked for a cheeseburger to be
waiting for him after a seventeen-course dinner in Taiwan.[33]

In Humphrey's eyes, being vice president redeemed his 1960 loss
to John F. Kennedy. He liked Kennedy but not his entourage. He liked
Bobby Kennedy, too. By 1968 they belonged to the same wing of the party
and went out of their way to talk regularly. There was some speculation
that Kennedy might be Humphrey's running mate that year; Humphrey
was interested in the idea, but it was not clear whether Kennedy would
accept. But Humphrey did not care for the larger Kennedy clan or the
fawning press attention Bobby received.[34] During a campaign stop while
visiting his mother in Huron, South Dakota, he got just forty seconds of
television time; Kennedy, visiting the old Humphrey drug store the same
day, got about three minutes of coverage.[35]

Humphrey resembled William Jennings Bryan in both his moral commitment and his long-windedness.[36] "In Minnesota, people don't drive for
two hours to hear a twenty-minute speech," he said.[37] His speeches were
riveting. "A good speech," he once said, "is like a good nap; you come
away physically refreshed."[38] His campaigning style was warm and personal, and he did not hold grudges. He rarely arrived at an engagement
on time, often having been delayed by the opportunity to do a favor for
someone.

Humphrey treated people better than he was treated, and he never
seemed to take setbacks or rejection personally. Former Minnesota Governor Elmer Benson once criticized him harshly in public, but "after
the meeting [Humphrey] came over and shook hands with me and said,
'Elmer, I want to thank you very much for calling my attention to it.'"[39]

Whatever the government does during any administration, the president gets most of the credit or blame. In the case of the Civil Rights Act of
1964, we generally remember the significance of the event without even a
footnote for Humphrey, who was the lead official on the bill. Humphrey
had been a national champion of civil rights since 1948, whereas Johnson
had his own consistent record on the subject—as an opponent. He started
to shift on the issue only in 1955, when he became Democratic leader in
the Senate and was forced to retain the support of both the Northern liberals and the Southern conservatives in his caucus. Sometimes, however,
the resulting compromises went against civil rights, as when he helped to
significantly weaken the Civil Rights Act of 1957. By allying with Johnson,

Humphrey caused his old liberal friends to abandon him over time—but this loyalty earned him little credit from Johnson.[40]

The Civil Rights Act of 1964 had been proposed by Kennedy in a national speech on June 11, 1963, but it became bogged down in opposition by Southern Democrats, including the longest Senate filibuster in history. Senate Majority Leader Mike Mansfield, who had been elevated to that role when Johnson became vice president, asked Majority Whip Humphrey to act as the bill's floor manager, and Humphrey cheerfully took the assignment. His whole career had prepared him for it: he had previously proposed thirteen civil rights bills and had repeatedly lobbied Kennedy to take action, especially in addressing discrimination—in hotels, restaurants, and public facilities, for example.[41] Now, given Johnson's understanding of Congress and desire to complete the unfinished Kennedy legacy, Humphrey thought the task was difficult but, at long last, not impossible. "I had to make up my mind as to my mental attitude and how I would conduct myself," he said later. "I can recall literally talking to myself, conditioning myself to the long ordeal. I truly did think through what I wanted to do and how I wanted to act."[42]

The House of Representatives finally passed its version in February 1964. Arm twisting and favor trading do not begin to explain the extraordinary effort involved in studying every potential moderate-to-liberal vote, many of which came from Republicans. Humphrey had to get the bill through the Southern Democrats without making any substantial compromises. Over the next five months the bill overcame a series of hurdles, including procedural delays, a succession of debilitating amendments, and the filibuster. After all that, the Senate passed the bill on June 19, 1964, by a margin of 73–27.[43] The House then accepted the Senate version—avoiding a conference committee that could have gutted it—and Johnson signed it on July 2. Humphrey's dubious reward was the vice presidency.

Humphrey and Johnson were oil and water in the sense that each functioned best with a minimum of the other. Johnson never trusted Humphrey, whom he saw as lacking the killer instinct a president needed.[44] Humphrey was not an ordinary politician; no matter how high he rose in his career, he maintained an innocence about how politics actually worked.[45] While he thought he would have another shot at the presidency, he never thought he would get it by opposing the president he served. And he could not have expected the Democratic Party to become known as the war party during his time as vice president.[46]

Less than a month after he was sworn in, at a National Security Council meeting on February 13, 1965, Humphrey expressed his concerns about the escalation of forces in Vietnam.[47] A few days later, on February 17, Humphrey wrote to Johnson: "I intend to support the Administration whatever the president's decision."[48] Johnson had kept his mouth shut as vice president when he thought Kennedy was making mistakes, and Humphrey said he would do the same for Johnson.[49] Humphrey's criticism of Johnson, as gentle as it was, marked the first time Johnson wondered about his vice president's loyalty. Their relationship abruptly cooled until Humphrey reemerged to publicly defend the administration's Vietnam policy.

While Humphrey remained a statutory member of the National Security Council, Johnson resorted more and more to informal Tuesday lunches with a small group of close advisors as the primary forum where key decisions were made.[50] If Johnson had endured continual slights and humiliations when the Kennedys were in charge, and had been excluded from the most important meetings, the conditions he now imposed on his own vice president were even worse. Humphrey had to ask for Johnson's permission to use an official plane; he was barred from the routine practice of hiding staff on the payroll of government departments; he never got to use the presidential yacht *Sequoia* or Camp David even when they were sitting idle; and his role became reduced to championing Johnson's policies in speeches that were vetted closely by White House staffers. "When I was frozen out," he wrote in his memoirs, "the symptoms were everywhere. The staff took their cues from the boss."[51] He felt partially vindicated that many of his predictions about Vietnam came true.[52] He was at his best when he led, but he was not leading under Johnson. His former liberal following called him "obscene," "truthless," "swine," and "totally dishonest." "I've changed," Humphrey admitted. "I've become more prudent. I've been more tolerant, too. When you come up the hard way, as I did, you become a bit brittle. Then, when life has been good to you, you become more tolerant."[53]

While he increasingly struggled with the issue of Vietnam, he defended White House policy and kept his opinions to himself.[54] A rare exception was the fall of 1967, when he was chosen to head the U.S. delegation to South Vietnamese President Nguyen Van Thieu's inauguration in Saigon.[55] The visit was part of a tour of anticommunist allied nations in Southeast Asia to meet with top political and military leaders.[56] Humphrey hoped to use the stop in Saigon to "really lay it on the line in terms of reforming the Vietnamese Armed Forces."[57] He also planned to urge that the National Liberation Front—a vehicle for popular resistance against the Saigon government—be allowed more involvement in the government.[58]

Humphrey had a private discussion with Thieu in his ceremonial office, with only his assistant Ted Van Dyk and Ambassador Ellsworth Bunker in attendance.[59] Bunker warned that the meeting was not the right occasion to be tough on Thieu, who was facing rising anti-American sentiment.[60] Humphrey was undeterred. "You need to know the political picture in America," he said to Thieu; "time is running out and a transition is needed to greater Vietnamese self-help."[61] "Yes, we understand," Thieu replied, "but we also understand it will be necessary for you to remain here at the present levels." Humphrey could not hide his disapproval. "Several years more at the same levels, militarily and economically, are not in the cards," he said.[62] Thieu listened politely, without interrupting, and then ended the meeting. It is not clear if Humphrey understood how unfavorably Thieu and his vice president, Nguyen Cao Ky, viewed the interaction.[63] Humphrey had broken the cardinal rule against lecturing a Vietnamese. Later he wondered if he had been too tough.[64] "Until Thieu and Ky are in a position to give orders and make them stick both to the Vietnamese armed forces and to the Province and District Chiefs, we cannot expect the armed forces to fight better, nor the widespread graft and corruption in the countryside to be overcome," he wrote in his official report of the trip.[65]

In a talk to Saigon embassy personnel, Humphrey compared the American resolve to those who persevered at Valley Forge.[66] "Steady progress" had been made, he asserted; "I believe that Vietnam will be marked as the place where the family of men has gained the time it needed to finally break through to a new era of hope and human development and justice.[67] This is the chance we have. This is our great adventure, and what a wonderful one it is!"[68] Afterward, he cabled the former ambassador to South Vietnam, Henry Cabot Lodge Jr., to tell him how reassured he was to see such progress in Vietnam since his last trip in 1966, and gave overwhelmingly positive reports to LBJ, his top aides, congressional leaders, and the National Security Council.[69] "A military victory by the Viet Cong or North Vietnamese is no longer a realistic possibility," he concluded.[70] After the visit, he continued to defend Johnson's policy even after foreign policy advisors George Ball, Robert McNamara, and the other "Nervous Nellies," as Johnson called them, had broken rank.[71]

Humphrey's public remarks would have served him well as Johnson's running mate in 1968, but they were less suitable for a presidential candidate. While he kept himself composed in public, in private he lashed out. "We've got to start withdrawing troops. I'd do that quickly," he wrote in his memoir.[72] He called the Thieu government "little bastards" who "wouldn't be alive if it weren't for us."[73] Privately, Humphrey told others that in supporting Thieu, the United States was "throwing lives and money down a corrupt rat hole."[74] He left Saigon publicly supportive of Johnson's Vietnam policy, but his private doubts had grown exponentially. "I'm damn sure we're not doing the Vietnamese or ourselves any good," he said privately to his physician, Edgar Berman. "We're murdering civilians by the thousands and our boys are dying in rotten jungles—for what? A corrupt, selfish government that has no feeling—no morality. I'm going to tell Johnson exactly what I think, and I just hope and pray he'll take it like I give it."[75] Often, after his meetings with Johnson, Humphrey returned to his office upset and slammed the door; his secretary at the time, Patricia Gray, said she and the other staffers could hear him crying.[76] Johnson affected Humphrey in a way that no one else could.[77]

As divided as they were on Vietnam, the Democrats were also split on domestic policy. Liberals like Daniel Patrick Moynihan, the former assistant secretary of labor who wrote the infamous "The Negro Family: The Case for National Action" (commonly known as "The Moynihan Report"), criticized other liberals over the deteriorating social and economic situation in the country, especially for African Americans.[78] He said the nature of poverty had changed but policy making had not adapted, noting that for the first time, a majority of poor Black children lived in female-headed households.[79] Moynihan predicted Democrats would be blamed. The report, completed in March 1965, was leaked to journalists Rowland Evans and Robert Novak, who featured it in their August 18 syndicated column, "Inside Report."[80] It catalyzed a profound change in thinking: for the first time since the New Deal, Americans asked out loud whether federal antipoverty programs were doing more harm than good, and whether more of those programs' power and resources should be distributed to states and local communities.[81] Critics used the report to argue that Blacks could never be elevated to white levels of wealth, education and social acceptability, and the government knew its social experiments were failing.[82] Moynihan's diagnosis, rejected by liberals and resented by African Americans, divided the civil rights community.[83] He defended himself by saying that the critics had not read his report.[84] "The presumption of superior empathy with the problems of the outcast is surely a characteristic, and a failing, of this liberal mindset," he wrote later.[85] The leak of the report marked the beginning of the end of the Great Society.

As the 1968 New Hampshire primary approached, Humphrey encouraged Johnson to use the Tet Offensive to press Thieu for reforms. He suggested a UN-supervised ceasefire, the withdrawal of foreign troops from South Vietnam, and new elections there in which all parties could take part. One can only wonder what Johnson thought about Humphrey's proposal to effectively liquidate an American ally—but he did not let the suggestions stop him from using Humphrey to defend the administration's war record. Speaking in California to a thousand delegates at the Central Democratic Committee conference, the vice president said the United States was in Vietnam "not to make war but to maintain peace" and to "build a nation." Even as the war grew more unpopular, Humphrey said, "when the chips are down" the American people would stick with the administration.[86]

The Humphreys were leaving for Mexico City, preparing to lead a delegation for the signing of a treaty to ban nuclear weapons from Latin America and the Caribbean, when Johnson paid them a surprise visit on March 31.[87] Swearing Humphrey to secrecy, Johnson said that he might announce that evening that he would not run for reelection. For the rest of the day, Humphrey could think about nothing else. Johnson had mentioned earlier that he might not run, but Humphrey never thought he would go through with it. "I felt so sorry for him," he told Edgar Berman. "He said the saddest thing. He said, 'As much as I've tried to do for the Negro and the poor, even they're against me. . . . Maybe the people just don't like my face.' Then I thought he'd break down. He was almost crying."[88]

Air Force Two sat at Andrews Air Force Base waiting to take Humphrey to Mexico City. When he arrived, rather than greeting everyone, chatting, and joking around until takeoff, he went right to his office and stayed there. Others noticed. "You know, Johnson's a strange man. He takes delight in keeping people dangling," Humphrey said later.[89] That evening, he watched the clock in his room at the Maria Isabel Hotel as the time of Johnson's speech approached. At 7:45 P.M., a buffet dinner was served at the embassy residence of U.S. Ambassador Fulton Freeman with Mexican President Gustavo Diaz Ordaz. A radio was found so Humphrey and his party could listen to the speech on Armed Forces Radio at 8:00 P.M., one time zone behind Washington.[90] In the middle of the speech, LBJ aide Marvin Watson called Humphrey to confirm that Johnson would use the alternate ending.[91] When Johnson read the key line, the feeling among Humphrey's party was that Johnson was giving the nomination to Kennedy. Senator Wayne Morse, sitting with Humphrey, told him, "You must announce right away."[92]

The phone started ringing almost immediately as well-wishers encouraged him to run.[93] The first call was from Margaret Truman Daniel, daughter of the former president. Humphrey suddenly went from being a nonentity in the Johnson administration to the man of the hour. "It doesn't take much to bring your respect quotient up to presidential levels," he said.[94] The instant analysis was that Johnson's withdrawal gave Humphrey an advantage, because his announcement took the war issue away from McCarthy and Kennedy. Vietnam was the toughest subject for Humphrey politically, but once the administration's policy shifted to ending American involvement through a negotiated settlement, he had more room to maneuver. Humphrey asked his staff to say nothing in response to inquiries. "Just cool it and we'll talk about it a little later," he said. "I'll meet the press for a few minutes as I go out. But before we go, no rumors, no threats, no slurs against Bobby or Gene."[95]

One person who did not call Humphrey was the president. When Humphrey awoke the next morning in Mexico, he half expected to receive word that Johnson had reconsidered. But there was nothing: no invitation to run in his place, no endorsement, not even a private pledge of support. "If I run," he told Edgar Berman, "Johnson's not going to make it easy."[96] Johnson had no choice but to remain neutral until the convention, but Humphrey assumed he did not want a Kennedy to succeed him. Humphrey went through with the treaty signing and returned to Washington.[97]

He had some distinct advantages. Registered Democrats outnumbered Republicans by almost two to one.[98] The core of Humphrey's support would be the old Democrats from the union-heavy industrial Midwest, along with Democratic governors and city mayors. His chief of staff, Bill Connell, had an eight-foot bookshelf of black binders breaking down Democratic voting habits by region, city, county, and precinct—a Democratic political encyclopedia.[99] Humphrey had racked up countless favors over the preceding four years, traveling a quarter million miles to six hundred cities and towns in all fifty states.[100] That gave him greater strength than even he knew. And none of these strengths required entering any primaries or engaging in debates with his challengers. He could sit back and let McCarthy and Kennedy fight each other.[101]

But history was not on his side. The last sitting vice president to win a presidential election had been Martin Van Buren, in 1836. Before Van Buren, only John Adams (1796) and Thomas Jefferson (1800) had pulled it off. Before Humphrey's run for the presidency in 1968, the last to attempt it was Richard Nixon in 1960. Nixon knew firsthand how difficult it was. Elections without incumbents are usually won by the party out of power.[102] A sitting vice president has the awkward task of defending the president's agenda; otherwise they will likely lose the president's support and be criticized for accepting policies they did not believe in. Yet the same candidate must also argue the president's agenda was incomplete. It is difficult in such a campaign to organize around a meaningful theme.[103] The opening months of the year had shown how eager the American people were for new leadership and a change of direction.[104]

Humphrey was set up to run not as the liberal firebrand of 1948 but as a surrogate for and chief defender of Johnson.[105] That had been his posture during his entire four years as vice president. But while he was saddled with Johnson's liabilities, he did not have Johnson's assets and had never commanded broad support from Democrats. He could not yield too much to Northern liberals without losing some moderates and conservatives, especially in the South.[106]

Humphrey's immediate challenge was launching a campaign. He planned to begin the first week of April, but on April 4, while he was at a Democratic fundraiser at the Shoreham Hotel in Washington, DC, the master of ceremonies interrupted the dinner to tell attendees that Martin Luther King had been shot in Memphis. Senator Walter Mondale said of Humphrey's reaction: "He stood up, politely stopped the proceedings, and asked for the microphone. He said the country had just lost a magnificent American, that this was a sad moment in American history, and that it would be a good idea if we stopped right there, said a prayer, and went home. And that's what we did."[107]

After a series of starts and stalls, Humphrey finally made his announcement on April 27.[108] "Here we are the way politics ought to be in America, the politics of happiness, politics of purpose, politics of joy, and that's the way it's going to be," he said, throwing his hat in to the ring.[109] In a year that had seen King's assassination, the war in Vietnam, and riots in more than six hundred cities, the happy warrior was back.[110] Like Nixon, Humphrey had matured since his run for the presidency in 1960. "I am a little older and I hope not quite as intense as I have been," he said.[111] He chose two campaign co-chairmen who were young, energetic, and liberal, and could help him appeal to young voters swayed by McCarthy and Kennedy. The first was Mondale, who held Humphrey's old Senate seat; the second was Oklahoma Senator Fred Harris, a former Kennedy man who could reach ethnic voters due to his service on the Kerner Commission.[112] Humphrey asked Harris to lead the hunt for delegates, and put Mondale in charge of convention planning.[113]

Other key staff included chief of staff Bill Connell, executive assistant Ted Van Dyk, and press secretary Norman Sherman. John Rielly covered foreign affairs and John Stewart handled domestic policy, while Bill Welsh served as Humphrey's chief Capitol Hill operative.[114] Rufus Phillips was an unofficial advisor on Vietnam.[115] According to Ted Van Dyk, they squabbled constantly, a problem that Humphrey's eighteen-hour-a-day schedule as vice president gave him an excuse not to tackle.[116] Max Kampelman was briefly chief of staff before he quit and threatened to sue, for reasons I have been unable to discover. Van Dyk thought he deserved Connell's job, and it seems almost everyone disliked Van Dyk for his abrasive style and for inflating his role during the campaign.[117] Also traveling with Humphrey was his physician, Dr. Edgar Berman, who began in that role, always without pay, in 1964. Berman did more than supply tranquilizers; he offered counsel and friendship, and his constant proximity to the boss made him a force to reckon with. A *Time* magazine profile described him as Humphrey's "Colonel House, a Harry Hopkins—or even a Svengali."[118]

On the campaign trail, Humphrey emphasized the Johnson-Humphrey team even though Johnson did not. He saw an association with Johnson as prestigious, at least until it became a liability. At first, campaign contributions came in steadily, presumably to help Humphrey win the nomination over Kennedy.[119] Humphrey believed Johnson's overt endorsement could put him over the top, but that support came with risks. "Remember," he said to his staff early in the campaign, "having the president behind me is a pure pot of gold—but don't forget, it can turn into a casket of lead at any moment."[120] Reporters wondered whether Humphrey could become his own man, then whether he would debate; finally they decided that Humphrey was the status quo, the old politics.[121]

Nixon knew how difficult Humphrey had it. He had to defend the
Democratic record of the 1960s: the war, crime, and spending. Nixon and
Humphrey had been cordial during the Eisenhower administration. "I am
most grateful to you for the friendly manner in which you have treated
me," Humphrey wrote in 1955.[122] "We, of course, have some differences
on the issues which come before us," Nixon responded, "but the test of
democracy in action is our ability not to allow those differences to destroy friendly relations between members of the two parties."[123] He chose
Humphrey, rather than a fellow Republican, for honors such as the reading of George Washington's farewell address for the Senate commemo-
ration of the first president on February 22, 1956.[124] When Humphrey's
son scheduled a lunch visit to the Senate for his junior high school class,
it was Nixon, not a fellow Democrat, whom Humphrey invited to visit
with them.[125]

As Nixon had done in 1960, Humphrey planned to campaign on a
promise of continuing the Johnson legacy and the unfinished work of the
Great Society while winding down the Vietnam War as quickly as possible. But he was seen as Johnson's willing accomplice in Vietnam. "I was
to fall heir to virtually all the animosity directed toward the Johnson administration and be beneficiary of practically none of the goodwill due an
administration whose domestic accomplishments were historic," he wrote
in his memoirs.[126] He tried to change his reputation, Berman recalled later,
but encountered "problem after problem."[127] Yet since he didn't have to
run in a primary—he dismissed them as "nothing more than popularity
contests" since they had no binding effect on delegates—he could focus
immediately on the general election and assume he would face Nixon.[128]
The national media criticized him for avoiding the primaries, but he
pointed out that the same national media called these contests "ridiculous,
wasteful and unrepresentative" when John F. Kennedy ran.[129]

What McCarthy and Kennedy did not seem to understand was that
the 20 percent of voters who were antiwar already supported them. They
did not successfully bridge to a broader anti-Johnson effort or offer other
substantive proposals to expand their support.[130] Humphrey inherited the
traditional advantage that Democrats held over Republicans, including
a party registration edge of around 38 to 22 percent, with 40 percent
claiming to be independent, according to Gallup. This made his path to
the White House wider than Nixon's.[131] But avoiding the primaries left
Humphrey open to charges that he could not win the nomination in an

open contest and had to rely on back-room deals with Democratic power brokers.[132]

As the establishment candidate, Humphrey inherited Johnson's overwhelming delegate strength. Of the 1,312 delegates needed for nomination, he had an estimated 1,200 without lifting a finger. A poll of Democratic county chairmen, many of whom would be delegates, showed that 70 percent preferred Humphrey, with Kennedy at 16 percent and McCarthy at 6 percent. While much has been written about whether McCarthy or Kennedy could have been nominated—and they certainly excited the Democratic Party's liberal wing—it is not clear how that could have happened. Humphrey had a much easier path. Five days after he joined the race, he was ahead of his competitors in the polls by double digits. By the last week of May, he had virtually clinched the nomination with primary wins in Missouri, Maryland, New Jersey, and Alaska without appearing on any of those states' ballots.[133] On the other hand, because he did not need to work hard to earn the nomination, he was not battle-tested to win the general election that fall.[134]

In his first full month of campaigning, Humphrey picked up endorsements from AFL-CIO leaders George Meany and Al Barken, I. W. Abel of the steelworkers' union, Joe Beirne of the Communications Workers of America, and several Jewish leaders.[135] They despised Kennedy for going after Jimmy Hoffa, but the union backing meant Humphrey risked losing support from the Black community, whose leaders tolerated him mainly because they detested McCarthy. McCarthy and Kennedy, seeing Humphrey in the lead, began attacking him. He refused to return the punches. "Don't hurt Bobby," he told his staff. "He's a good liberal senator and we'll need him later. Let the press find out how Bobby works, not through us."[136]

On June 4, 1968, Humphrey was in Colorado to give a commencement address the next day at the Air Force Academy. When an aide awakened him that night with the news that Kennedy had been shot, he offered his full cooperation to the family.[137] Kennedy's press secretary, Pierre Salinger, asked for a government aircraft to fly a neurosurgeon, Dr. James Poppen, from Boston to Los Angeles.[138] Humphrey called U.S. Air Force chief of staff General John McConnell to request the plane, and a second one to fly the Kennedy children from Washington, DC, to California. When McConnell asked him on what authority the request was made, he said, "Just order it in the name of the Vice Commander in Chief!"[139] But in Johnson's White House, Humphrey had no such authority. The White House canceled the request. Aircraft assignments were approved by Johnson, who wanted to know why he was not called before Humphrey made the request. "For God's sake," Humphrey burst out, according to Berman, "how much can one family stand? Put in a call to Ethel—to Teddy. Jesus, what about all those kids? What in God's name is happening in the country?"[140] The flights took place.

Humphrey and Berman flew to New York two days later, on the eve of the funeral at St. Patrick's Cathedral. Humphrey was not himself.[141] That night, agitated and unable to sleep, he asked Berman to take a walk, so they left the Waldorf-Astoria and began walking up Park Avenue.[142] They crossed over two short blocks, turned right at 5th Avenue, and kept going north. They walked almost the entire eastern edge of Central Park, turning around at 100th Street, a distance of about fifty blocks. When they got back, about two o'clock in the morning, Humphrey still was not interested in sleeping. They dropped into an all-night coffee shop. People who recognized him kept their distance since he seemed so disturbed. Humphrey told Berman that he was still haunted by the drums at JFK's funeral.[143]

Following the assassination of Kennedy, coming so soon after that of King, all candidates suspended their campaigns. Humphrey arguably never returned at full strength. With the slate of serious primary challengers wiped clean, he could afford to take a break—more, in fact, than he could afford to campaign.[144] He needed to save his resources for the general election, as the flow of donations had dried up after Kennedy was killed.[145] He was ahead in the delegate count, but little in the primary phase of the campaign helped prepare him for a Republican challenger; he was better positioned to run against McCarthy or Kennedy.[146] With no opponent against whom to frame his message of moderation in turbulent times, his offerings were opaque. He was not only personally shaken up by Kennedy's death but also professionally. Humphrey's entire campaign strategy had to be reformulated, and after the tragedy he lacked the necessary energy.[147] Johnson reassured him that he would get the nomination, and that he backed him "one million percent." But that made Humphrey concerned that Johnson would try to choose his running mate, someone like Texas Governor John Connally.[148]

Humphrey all but refused to engage in fundraising. "I'll be out in front to give them a talk that will warm the cockles of their hearts and grease the skids of their pocket books," he told his staff. "But you ask for the money."[149] No matter how desperate or late in the campaign, it was a part of the job he never warmed to. "Whenever we have a big meeting we ought to have someone to put on a pitch for raising money," he instructed, "particularly when we are so desperate for funds."[150] It was difficult to raise money with the Democrats so divided, especially over Vietnam. United Democrats for Humphrey got off to a flying start, spending $40,000 to $75,000 a month, but Humphrey constantly quibbled over campaign spending and questioned its impact. Johnson was tapping some of the same donors to raise money for his presidential library and school of public service to be built at the University of Texas at Austin.[151] Humphrey dared not find another reason to upset Johnson, who threatened to personally ensure he lost Texas and dry up every Democratic dollar from Maine to California. "That no-good son-of-a-bitch. The way I've treated him—I must be a goddamned fool," Humphrey said.[152] To minimize his travel expenses, he politicked as much as he could on the margins of official duties. His staff was minimal; there was little money for supplies and almost nothing for advertising. Humphrey, who would have been happy to have been Johnson's running mate again, was as financially unprepared to make a run for the presidency as he was organizationally and psychologically.[153]

With Kennedy out of the race, Johnson felt freer than ever to harass his vice president and withhold support from him. When Kennedy was in, any Democrat was better. Now Johnson, who had once said that Humphrey's "broad range of knowledge" made him "the best man in America" to be vice president, called him "disloyal" and lacking the "balls" and "ability to be President."[154] *New York Times* columnist James Reston did not think Humphrey had a chance of being elected unless he mended fences with Johnson, especially over Vietnam. With Johnson carefully enforcing discipline on both Humphrey's policy positions and the party as a whole, it seemed impossible to establish an independent campaign.[155] Humphrey tried to make peace with McCarthy in the wake of Kennedy's death but was unsuccessful.[156] While admitting Humphrey's nomination was inevitable, McCarthy would not support him unless he changed his position on the war.[157] Each denied the other a victory.[158] McCarthy failed as a presidential candidate, but he showed that an insurgency could make a difference.[159] Humphrey's campaign crowds were small and often included hecklers— young people drawn to McCarthy because of Humphrey's stance on the war or African Americans drawn to Kennedy for his commitment to the issues of race and poverty.

Together, McCarthy and Kennedy painted Humphrey as old and out-of-date. "Hubert's face on television comes off as if he were an old-fashioned politician," Pearson wrote in his diary.[160] Even in death, Kennedy continued to hurt Humphrey. "Daddy, the shot that killed Bobby has wounded you," Muriel Humphrey warned her husband. Fairly or unfairly, Democrats would be blamed for what was wrong with the country. "It's just going to be impossible to do anything," she said. The two political murders took a great psychological toll—on Humphrey, his family, friends, and supporters. Many of his would-be voters saw him as the representative of the establishment. "The results of the political events of the past few months," Bill Moyers wrote, "from New Hampshire through all the primaries, the President's withdrawal, and the other developments which we have all watched—add up to one certain conclusion: the country wants a change."[161] Humphrey warned at Kennedy's funeral of the "poison" and "irrational hate among us." But on the campaign trail he was going through the motions. There was no more joy in politics for the happy warrior.[162]

CHAPTER THREE

Nixon

ICHARD NIXON HAD ONE of the most linear rises to the White
House in American history, even taking into account his spending much of the 1960s in the "wilderness." The first since Andrew
Johnson to serve in the House, the Senate, and the vice presidency, Nixon represented moderate views, middle-class values, and the
center lane of the Republican Party. He understood the importance of
taking popular positions on popular issues, and he was not tied to the
Vietnam War or the upheaval of the decade. While Lyndon Johnson was
the first true Western president, Nixon also benefited from being from
a fast-growing part of the country. But his rise, especially the political
comeback that positioned him for a second run at the presidency, was
anything but easy. A pragmatist by instinct, he had to reinvent himself
more than once.

Richard Milhous Nixon was born on January 9, 1913, to Frank and
Hannah Milhous Nixon in Yorba Linda, California, in a seven-hundred-
square-foot bungalow that his father built, originally with no indoor
plumbing or electricity.[1] Yorba Linda, a hamlet founded by Quakers in
1887, was then an outpost of two hundred people in undeveloped southern
California.[2] His mother's family, the Milhouses, were Quakers who emi-
grated to the United States before the American Revolution. They were
somewhat more evangelical than their eastern counterparts, and Richard
himself had a kind of born-again experience in 1926 while attending a
religious revival.[3] His father took him and brother Don to a tent meeting in Los Angeles, hosted by evangelist Paul Rader. "He is a Quaker,"

47

Billy Graham said, "and Quakers don't believe in expressing their religion much, but he would to me privately. There is a very deep religious side to Richard Nixon that never came out."[4]

It was his Grandmother Milhous who spurred his interest in a wider world. She always kept a copy of the newspaper, with its intriguing news of the world, waiting for him when he visited. Nixon devoured information.[5] When he stayed up too late reading, his punishment was a battery of chores to help him contemplate the virtue of hard work and order.[6] Offered a scholarship at Harvard but unable to afford the balance of the cost, he enrolled at local Whittier College instead. The knowledge that he was good enough to go to Harvard yet could not overcome barriers to go there contributed to his early resentment of East Coast elites. It was his time at Duke Law School that transformed Nixon into a kind of liberal on racial issues, like Humphrey. He saw segregation and Jim Crow up close and was appalled.[7] In addition to many hours studying, Nixon also pursued Thelma Patricia "Pat" Ryan for two years. She had grown up in Artesia, about eight miles from Whittier, and both of her parents had died before she turned seventeen. In March 1940, she finally accepted his proposal, and they married on June 21 amid the growing drumbeat of World War II.

Nixon's naval wartime service in places like New Caledonia, the Solomon Islands, and Green Island exposed him to a vast unknown Pacific world. When he returned from the war, he was encouraged to run for Congress. Among his earliest backers were the *Los Angeles Times* and its publisher, Norman Chandler.[8] He defeated incumbent Jerry Voorhis and rose to become the most famous freshman congressman in the country, elected in 1946 to the same Eightieth Congress as John F. Kennedy and John Davis Lodge, both from families that would help shape his career. Nixon was an original member of the Chowder and Marching Club, a caucus of some fifteen young Republicans that included Kenneth Keating, Thruston Morton, and Gerald Ford. He considered himself a liberal but not a radical. He denounced the John Birch Society, and his heroes at Duke Law School were Louis Brandeis, Benjamin Cardozo, and Charles Evans Hughes.

Nixon quickly made a name for himself by helping to expose former State Department official Alger Hiss, an icon of the liberal establishment who was accused of spying for the Soviet Union.[9] Nixon's pursuit of Hiss as a member of the House Un-American Activities Committee introduced him to the media, leaks, cover-ups, and Washington scandal—and gave him a level of scrutiny he was not prepared to handle. He was right about Hiss's perjury—it was confirmed decades later by Soviet intelligence sources—but he paid a heavy price.[10] "You signed your political death warrant with the Alger Hiss-Whittaker Chambers case," Ruth Graham, Billy's wife, wrote to him in 1979.[11] The experience permanently defined many of Nixon's political assets and liabilities.

Nixon was no conservative in the mold of Robert Taft, known as "Mr. Republican."[12] He joined with the party's moderate-to-liberal wing on many of the initiatives of the day, including the Marshall Plan, aid to Greece and Turkey, NATO, and support of New York Governor Thomas Dewey. In his run for the Senate in 1950, against Helen Gahagan Douglas, a campaign partly funded by the Kennedy family, Nixon won more votes than any candidate in California history. But he was tarnished by accusations of running a dirty campaign against Douglas—and against Voorhis four years earlier—because he attacked his opponents as soft on communism.

Nixon was selected as General Dwight Eisenhower's vice-presidential running mate in 1952, when the party was divided between isolationist conservatives, who supported Taft, and internationalist moderates and liberals, who supported Eisenhower. As a compromise candidate, Nixon was not the first choice of either side, but he could win the support of both. During the campaign, he was accused of improperly receiving an $18,000 "Secret Fund." He presented his defense that it was all a misunderstanding—the money legally covered his Senate office expenses—in a televised appearance on September 23, 1952, that became known as the "Checkers" speech, after the Nixon family cocker spaniel which got an emotional mention during the address. Nixon claimed it was common practice to have legitimate expenses covered. Adlai Stevenson later admitted that his campaign fund was four times the size of Nixon's and also covered such personal expenses as paying for the orchestra at a dance for Stevenson's son.[13] As far as Eisenhower was concerned, Nixon had cleared his name and deserved to stay on the ballot. The scandal marked the beginning of aggressive investigations into Nixon's past.[14] No hard evidence of impropriety ever emerged.[15]

Nixon's rise occurred long before that of the New Right, when government was still considered the solution and not the enemy.[16] On January 20, 1953, only six years into his political career, the forty-year-old

Nixon was inaugurated as the second-youngest vice president in U.S. history. Part of the New Deal generation, he carried forward many of its ideas and ultimately was among the last who harked back to such a time. He served eight years as vice president under Eisenhower and in 1960 was the obvious choice to carry moderate Republican values into the next decade. By then he had replaced Taft as Mr. Republican, survived a mob in Caracas, stood up to Khrushchev in Moscow, and become a household name. As the party's presidential nominee in 1960, he and running mate Henry Cabot Lodge Jr. were outmatched by Democratic rivals John F. Kennedy and Lyndon Johnson. Nixon was called "Tricky Dick" and depicted with a shifty look over the caption "Would You Buy a Used Car from This Man?"[17] The labels affirmed the popular view of Nixon, at least among liberals and the media, but he was no trickier than Kennedy or Johnson.[18] To appoint one's barely qualified brother as attorney general was an outrageous move that even Robert Kennedy said required "the guts of a burglar."[19] Yet Nixon struggled to shake off the "tricky" label for the rest of his life. The popularity of this image of Nixon within intellectual circles revealed liberals' own prejudices. While researching his book *The Making of the President, 1960,* journalist Theodore White wore a "Kennedy for President" button to meetings with the Nixon campaign.[20] In demonizing Nixon for his outreach to the middle class, some liberals showed how increasingly out of touch they were with average Americans.[21]

Nixon discovered that year how difficult it is for a vice president to run for president. Such a candidate is always caught between defending the administration and arguing that its record remains incomplete. Kennedy looked personable and self-assured, whereas Nixon looked worn and tired. By the time of their first televised debate in Chicago, Nixon had lost ten pounds after a two-week hospitalization for a knee infection. It was difficult to get people excited about a campaign that offered competence against Kennedy's youthful energy. By putting Johnson on the ticket, Kennedy also held areas of the Democratic South that Eisenhower and Nixon had begun to infiltrate. Nixon never led a Gallup poll after mid-September. Joe Kennedy's money, Jack's Harvard background and dramatic war record, and the glamorous Kennedy family proved decisive against Nixon and Lodge.[22] They ultimately lost in one of the closest elections in American history, by an average of less than one vote per precinct, although the electoral college outcome was more decisive, 303–219, with 15 for Senator Harry Byrd.[23]

Not sure what to do next, and against the advice of many, Nixon decided to run for the governorship of California in 1962. He needed a political base independent of Eisenhower, and California was not only his home but had also recently passed New York as the nation's most populous state. Nixon had won the state against Kennedy in 1960; in fact, he had never lost there, going back to his first congressional race in 1946. But he underestimated conservative ambivalence about him. The so-called Compact of Fifth Avenue, a political deal struck on the eve of the 1960 convention in which Nelson Rockefeller agreed to support Nixon as long as Nixon incorporated his agenda into his campaign and presidency, was something conservatives never got over. Some also found it hard to believe he truly wanted to be governor and was not simply looking for a good base from which to run again for the presidency. His rival, Pat Brown, claimed Nixon only wanted to "double park in Sacramento" before trying once more for the White House.[24] The most memorable part of the campaign came after Nixon's loss, when he scolded the press for their unfair coverage of his campaign. "You don't have Nixon to kick around anymore, because, gentlemen, this is my last press conference," he said. His career was so universally agreed to be over that ABC anchor Howard K. Smith chaired an hour-long program, "The Political Obituary of Richard M. Nixon." The program's inclusion of former Nixon enemies like Jerry Voorhis and Alger Hiss seemed to confirm what Nixon said about past media coverage.[25] "Barring a miracle," *Time* magazine concluded, "his political career ended last week."[26]

Even his friends wondered if he was beyond redemption.[27] "I thought at that point that my political career was certainly over, or certainly I had no aspirations or no hopes I thought, or reasonable hopes for a political career in the future," Nixon reflected.[28] He had accomplished nothing at the ballot box in his own name since 1950. Bookies put the odds on his comeback at 1,000 to 1.[29] Nixon opted for a fresh start, relocating to New York in May 1963. Elmer Bobst, chairman of the board at Warner-Lambert, urged Robert Guthrie, senior partner at Mudge, Stern, Baldwin, and Todd, to recruit Nixon to the firm.[30] Bobst had been a friend of Nixon's since 1960 and was an important client of the law firm.[31] Nixon could practice law, earn a good living for the first time, and reenter the political arena if the opportunity arose.[32]

The Nixons moved into a twelve-room apartment on the thirty-ninth floor of the Hotel Pierre on 5th Avenue, paying $100,000 a year in rent, and Dick began work at the newly renamed law firm Nixon, Mudge, Rose, Guthrie, and Alexander at 20 Broad Street, next door to the New York Stock Exchange.[33] The firm was founded in 1869 and had long been a fixture of the city's legal establishment.[34] During Nixon's tenure, it became one of the ten largest firms in the nation.[35] Major clients included Warner-Lambert, PepsiCo, General Cigar, Stone and Webster Engineering Corporation, Studebaker-Worthington, Continental Baking, and El Paso Natural Gas.[36] Outside Nixon's inner office sat Rose Mary Woods, who had been his personal secretary since 1951; Pat Buchanan, his first new staff hire; and "Miss Ryan"—code name for Pat Nixon, who went by her maiden name in order to avoid identification.[37]

Nixon couldn't stay away from politics. He made a tentative run for the Republican presidential nomination in 1964, but it never got off the ground. At the Republican National Convention at the Cow Palace in San Francisco, he introduced that year's nominee, Arizona Senator Barry Goldwater. "Before the convention," he told the crowd, "we were Goldwater Republicans, Rockefeller Republicans, Scranton Republicans, Lodge Republicans, but now that this convention had met and made its decision, we are Republicans, period, working for Barry Goldwater."[38] Rockefeller, offered a Goldwater button for his lapel, refused to wear it. Many moderate to liberal Republicans felt similarly. Nixon sat on his hands when Goldwater, in his acceptance speech, declared that "extremism in the defense of liberty is no vice," but that fall he put aside the rancor of the convention and focused on the party's ability to challenge Johnson while building a bridge to moderates.[39] He was viewed as a uniter at a time when no one else would take the role, much as he had done in 1952 with Eisenhower. While other moderates declined to be associated with Goldwater, Nixon made over 150 appearances in thirty-six states during the campaign.[40] He was virtually the only party luminary who thought the conservative wing of the Republicans deserved a prominent voice.[41] His support for Goldwater would be key to his winning the early endorsement of conservatives in 1968, including that of Goldwater, who said that Nixon "worked harder than any one person for the ticket" in 1964.[42] Even though Republicans lost in one of the great landslides of the twentieth century, Nixon praised the defeated nominee. "I complimented Goldwater, saying that he had fought courageously against great odds," Nixon wrote later. "I said that those who had divided the party in the past could not now expect to unite it in the future."[43] That remark was a direct shot at Nelson Rockefeller and others who sat out the race. Nixon eagerly went over the cliff with Gold-water and said so. He regained conservatives' goodwill but was not per-sonally close enough to Goldwater to be blamed for his shortcomings.[44] "It's even worse than I expected," Nixon said later of the senator's political ideas. "Hell, Barry was against Social Security, price supports, the UN, and all the rest."[45] Republicans were at their lowest point since the 1930s, out-numbered 68–32 in the Senate, 295–140 in the House, and 33–17 in state governors. They controlled both chambers of the legislature in only six states.[46] Yet conservatives saw 1964 as a victory. They had lost the country but won the Republican Party, and in the coming decades they would use their control of the party to gain control of the country.[47]

Nixon effectively launched his 1968 campaign two days after the 1964 election. "I began making lists of the odds for and against my nomination in 1968," he reflected later. "After 1960 and 1962, I had what every poli-tician dreads most, a loser image. In fact, after the 'last press conference,' I had a *sore* loser image."[48] Only once since William Jennings Bryan in 1908 had a major party renominated a defeated former candidate—and that second-time nominee, Adlai Stevenson in 1956, had lost decisively.[49] Nixon also had no clear constituency. He had given up his West Coast base but was not considered by New York Republicans to be one of them. Still, by bridging the two wings of the party, he was not repugnant to either.[50] He had a good grasp of the issues facing the nation in the 1960s, especially with regard to foreign policy. He believed that LBJ had promised far more than he could deliver, and that created an opening for Republicans.[51] "The philosophical distinction between the Republican and Democratic parties was never clearer than in the middle 1960s," Nixon wrote later. "It was therefore the perfect time for Republicans to lead an active opposition."[52]

While out of office, Nixon spoke in support of the Civil Rights Act of 1964 and Voting Rights Act of 1965. "Nixon was sympathetic to the Negro cause but was no Great Society liberal," Pat Buchanan recalled. "He shared a conservative skepticism on the wisdom of programs piled one on top of the other to bring about social progress in the inner city."[53] After the right's flirtation with extremism in 1964, Nixon made conser-vatism respectable again while rebuilding his reputation as a centrist Re-publican.[54] He believed racists should be expelled from Republican ranks, and he also demanded that Johnson purge the demagogues from his own party. "I made it clear that contrary to what some conservatives might have thought, George Wallace did not belong in the Republican Party," he wrote later.[55] He and Buchanan played around with the theme of "the forgotten man at the bottom of the economic pyramid," later shortened to "the forgotten man," "the silent center," and finally "the silent majority."[56] They did not invent the concept, but Nixon was the first Republican to use it effectively.[57] He spoke of "the millions of people in the middle of the American political spectrum who do not demonstrate, who do not picket or protest loudly."[58] The experience of the 1960s, he thought, had transformed them from a minority to the majority.

With midterm elections approaching in 1966, Nixon emerged as an important face of the party. Since the end of 1964, he had traveled more than 127,000 miles, raising more than $4 million in forty states while speaking in front of more than four hundred audiences.[59] By the mid-1960s, the party had significantly receded. "From the first time I spoke to Nixon, he would harp on this shrunken base, in House and Senate seats, and state legislatures, as a near-fatal weakness," Pat Buchanan recalled later. "Before we can even think about 1968, he told me many times, we must restore the party base."[60] Nixon needed success in 1966 in order to have his shot at redemption in 1968; without some gains, the Republicans would almost certainly want a fresh face for their next presidential candidate. He brought the growing conservative movement into the party's mainstream.[61] Even if Wallace did not belong, Nixon was glad to borrow his more popular ideas. For example, in his essay "If Mob Rule Takes Hold in the U.S.," published in *U.S. News and World Report*, he expressed a concern about growing disrespect for law enforcement that would eventually become his law-and-order platform.[62]

President Johnson asked Nixon to stop by the White House on March 13, 1966, the morning after they both attended Washington's annual Gridiron Dinner. They met in Johnson's private bedroom, a place more suited to gatherings with confidants than political rivals.[63] "I am receiving the benefit from the support I gave you and Ike in the foreign policy field in the eight years you were here," Johnson told him.[64] Nixon liked Johnson and thought he had "moderately conservative instincts."[65] Each had led the opposition when the other was in power. They went back more than fifteen years, when they were recovering at Washington Naval Hospital after slips on the ice. With rooms across from each other, they had time to talk about their service in the House of Representatives as they enjoyed Texas-style chili from a place in Rockville, Maryland, that reminded Johnson of home.[66] Not only did Nixon believe Johnson was "the most effective legislative leader of the century," but he was well-dressed as well: "The rest of us wore just sort of store clothes," but Johnson wore "well-tailored suits" with cufflinks and was "a very impressive fellow."[67]

Johnson believed Nixon had been much fairer to him and other Democrats than previous Democratic vice presidents had been to Republicans. Vice President Nixon usually opened Senate sessions and then turned the gavel over to Robert "Bobby" Baker, an LBJ aide. Johnson had headed the homecoming reception for Nixon in 1958 when he returned from his infamous tour of Latin America, where his limousine had been stoned in Caracas by an anti-American mob. Johnson also found creative ways for Nixon to visit him at his ranch so Nixon would not have to endorse Texas Republicans or raise money for them when he visited the state. "A Democrat would never have turned down a good friend for a few lousy shillings," Johnson wrote in 1954. "I'll get a comment from all Texas Republicans that they are sufficiently well-heeled to permit you to relax with an old friend for a few hours."[68] When Nixon traveled internationally while out of office in the 1960s, he vigorously defended American policy abroad even though it was Democratic policy—to the delight of Johnson's foreign service officials but not of Nixon's fellow Republicans.[69] Despite being very different politically, personally and professionally, they admired each other.[70] Nixon inscribed a photo for Johnson's study that read, "To Lyndon Johnson, with deep appreciation for the wise counsel and friendship of a fine Senator and a great American."[71]

It was a different time. "Johnson's attitude was unrelated to any personal rivalry," John Connally wrote in his memoirs. "He thought Nixon was an unscrupulous campaigner—ironic, considering that the same had been said of Johnson—and held him responsible for the ruined careers of several Democrats who were painted as soft on communism."[72] Political leaders of all stripes rallied around what was best for the country, especially in foreign policy. Disagreements were expressed and worked out privately, on the basis of long-standing relationships—even friendships. Johnson and Nixon were not personal friends, but they were friendly, as long as they were not facing each other on a ballot. More importantly, they had common enemies. Both came from modest means, had not attended the best schools, were centrists who sided with the populists in their parties and not the elites, and felt the scorn of the media and Eastern Establishment.[73] "Between Lyndon and myself that bond had an added dimension," Nixon wrote later. "It is a respect that will be part of me always together with the memories it evokes."[74]

When they met that March, they agreed on rules of engagement for the upcoming midterms.[75] "I know you will understand and not take any criticism I make on issues as being directed personally at you," Nixon said. "I know, Dick," Johnson responded. "We politicians are just like lawyers who get together for a drink after fighting each other like hell in the courtroom."[76] Shortly after their meeting, Nixon had a taste of that courtroom. On April 27, 1966, he led the oral argument before the Supreme Court in *Time, Inc. v. Hill*. Leonard Garment, his law colleague, said Nixon made the best argument he had ever heard regarding the first amendment right of the press, which included a lengthy exchange with Hugo Black.[77] Nixon represented the Hill family, which claimed damages as a result of allegedly false information published by Time, Inc. The case established Nixon's credentials as a distinguished appellate lawyer.[78] He ended up losing by a 5–4 margin after the Court found that unless Time, Inc. had knowingly published false statements, it was not at fault. But the *Washington Post* called his appearance "one of the best oral arguments of the year."[79] The case was important to Nixon's comeback because it showed that he was the mental equal of the high-powered figures he dealt with in New York.[80]

Nixon and Johnson soon had the chance to test their understanding as the fall midterm elections approached. Over his career, Johnson had become a master of the "October surprise," a last-minute electoral gambit on the eve of Election Day. At the end of September, he unexpectedly announced that he would meet with South Vietnam President Nguyen Van Thieu and other allied leaders in Manila in late October, about two weeks before the elections. Until that point, Nixon's strength in foreign policy had been neutralized because he had no hooks for an attack.[81] He sensed the Manila Conference might be Johnson's October surprise, meant to show allied solidarity and restore public confidence in the president's handling of the Vietnam War right before the election. Following the Manila summit, Nixon attacked Johnson for suggesting that the United States could reduce the number of troops deployed in Vietnam. "Is this a quest for peace or a quest for votes?" he asked. "There have been many firsts in the Johnson Administration, but this is the first time a President may have figured the best way to help his party is to leave the country."[82] Nixon wrote an extended written critique of the summit that the *New York Times* printed in full, accompanied by a front-page story. That itself was astonishing, since the *Times* had run very little of what Nixon had said as vice president and nothing since he had come to New York in 1963.[83] It was the critical day in the critical year of Nixon's comeback. Johnson, who Bill Moyers had said would barnstorm the country in the final week of the campaign, instead retreated to the Ranch.

When asked to comment, Johnson gave some uncharacteristically rambling remarks that turned into a two-minute tirade against Nixon. He slipped out of gear almost as badly as Nixon in 1962. "I do not want to get into a debate on a foreign policy meeting in Manila with a chronic campaigner like Mr. Nixon," he said. "Mr. Nixon doesn't serve his country well by trying to leave that kind of impression in the hope that he can pick up a precinct or two or a ward or two."[84] Johnson immediately grasped his error: by calling Nixon out by name, he had raised the former vice president's status. "It was a stupid mistake," he admitted later. "I probably nominated him."[85] Nixon wrote that "with a few days before the election, I suddenly found myself the center of national attention."[86] "I sat stunned," Pat Buchanan recalled. "Not only had Nixon drawn blood, the President had lost it, confirmed by his defensiveness and unbuttoned anger."[87] It was the biggest coup of Nixon's political career since the Checkers speech.

Johnson's remarks produced eight-column headlines in the *Washington Post* and *Washington Star.* "In the span of a single autumn day, the 1,000 day reign of Lyndon came to an end," *Newsweek* said.[88] *Time* called it a "savage swipe." It was the most direct attack by a president on an opposition leader in living memory, and it reshaped the 1966 election into a match between Johnson and Nixon. The Republican National Committee bought Nixon a half hour of airtime on NBC on Sunday, November 6, to respond to Johnson. "For fourteen years I had the privilege of serving with you in Washington," Nixon said, addressing the president directly. "I respect you for the great energies you devote to that office, and my respect has not changed because of the personal attack you made on me."[89] He described Johnson as "probably the hardest-working president in this century," and urged that they debate "like gentlemen."[90] That he took Nixon's Manila criticism so personally showed that Johnson either had not decided whether to run in 1968 or wanted to see what the 1966 midterms would do for his political fortunes.

Republicans reversed the losses incurred in 1964 and even came out a little ahead. Nixon predicted that his party would win 40 seats in the House, 3 in the Senate, 6 governorships, and 700 state legislative seats.

The final numbers were 47, 3, 8, and 540 in an election in which a record 56.7 million Americans voted.[91] Prospects for a future Republican takeover of both the White House and Congress had not been so good since 1932.[92] Nixon worked harder than any other Republican, racking up hundreds of favors to cash in later. He even campaigned in upstate New York for Nelson Rockefeller, whose race was close because a conservative third-party candidate was dividing the Republican vote.[93] Nixon put everything on the line for the party's success, raising $6.5 million for Republican coffers even though he was not on the ballot. On average, a candidate for whom Nixon campaigned stood a 67 percent chance of winning, while candidates he did not campaign for had only a 45 percent chance.[94] "It was gratifying to know that I had played a major part in this Republican victory—a prerequisite for my own comeback," he reflected later.[95] He campaigned in every state and congressional district to which he was invited, including the Deep South, incurring IOUs from scores of new congressmen and even losing candidates who were thankful he had made the trip. He emerged as the undisputed leader of the opposition and the clear choice of both party regulars and Goldwater supporters for the 1968 nomination.[96] "I'm right in there with you," Goldwater wrote him in 1967.[97]

The day after the election, Nixon called a press conference to announce that he was taking six months off from politics in order to study. The break gave him time to reflect. "He had not, in fact, been far off," he later wrote of the Johnson diatribe that had propelled him back to center stage. "I *was* something of a chronic campaigner, always out on the stump raising partisan hell. But my years in the 'wilderness' and the simple process of growing older had probably rounded off some of the hard edges of the younger Nixon."[98] He wanted to run for president again in 1968 but did not want to commit too early in case he changed his mind. He scheduled four trips—Europe and the Soviet Union in March, Asia in April, Latin America in May, and Africa and the Middle East in June— to become better acquainted with the international issues that would be important in the campaign. "I met the leaders, met the people, and saw at first hand the problems, opportunities, and dangers confronting the United States," he recalled. "The result was to reinforce some views I already strongly held and to modify others."[99] Nixon first codified some of these views in a speech at Bohemian Grove on July 29, 1967, and then in an article entitled "Asia after Vietnam" in the October 1967 issue of *Foreign Affairs*.[100] "It was a new view of the Nixon personality," Theodore

White wrote, "in which the trait uppermost was a voracious, almost insatiable curiosity of the mind, a hunger to know, to learn, to find out how things work, to understand and explain detail."[101]

Many Republicans remained uncommitted to a candidate. Moderates and liberals were slow to embrace Nixon, but he was finally invited to his first New York City Republican event, a reception for Jacob Javits, in November 1967. Nixon was seen smiling and laughing with Javits and Rockefeller.[102] "Nixon had taken liberal enough public positions to make it comfortable for the eastern liberal Republican wing," Humphrey wrote in his memoirs.[103] On Vietnam, even Eugene McCarthy said Nixon "was restrained, almost antiwar."[104] Conservative Republicans, meanwhile, had nowhere else to go. Nixon knew that many of them preferred California Governor Ronald Reagan, but after Goldwater's devastating loss in 1964 they were feeling more pragmatic about selecting someone who could unite the party and win.[105] "No matter how well qualified I think a man might be, he still had to get elected," Eisenhower told the *New York Times* that December. "And I would like to see the convention pick a man who can win over Johnson in November."[106] His remarks reflected the growing consensus of Republicans.

If Nixon was acceptable to Javits, the party's foremost liberal, and Goldwater, the party's foremost conservative, that meant he could unite Republicans across the entire spectrum.[107] He had identified the center of the party and rode that lane the remainder of the year.[108] Even his geographical roots suggested compromise: he had come of age in California, attended law school in North Carolina, and was now running from New York.[109] Richard Whalen wrote that "the pathological Nixon-haters in the press, by denying his humanity, ironically gave him an advantage in personal encounters."[110] "There was no new Nixon, he insisted—it was only that in the past years, while Rockefeller and Johnson had been so busy, he had had time to read," Theodore White wrote. "All his eight years as Vice-President he hadn't had time to read a thing."[111] Yet Nixon was far from decided about running again. His daughters were enthusiastic, but Pat was not. They were living comfortably for the first time, and she remembered how difficult the 1960 campaign had been. After losing by such a close margin then, and decisively in 1962, to come all the way back and lose again in 1968 would be devastating—and virtually unprecedented in American history. But he was considering it. "My first impression," Pat Buchanan recalled, "was that Nixon was bored to death with corporate law. He would bring me into his office for two-, three-, four-hour sessions to talk foreign policy, politics, personalities, and he began to confide in me."[112] "The chances for a Republican to be elected President in 1968 looked better all the time," Nixon wrote in his memoir, as the nation saw its first large-scale antiwar demonstration at the Pentagon in October 1967.[113] "By the end of 1967 I knew that I had to make a final decision about running."[114]

Billy Graham often encouraged him. Graham had come to Nixon's home in Washington after the close defeat in 1960. They drank coffee, ate peanuts, and talked until late in the night, while Graham tried to convince him that he would have an opportunity to reenter politics. Nixon called it ridiculous.[115] After his humiliating defeat in 1962, Graham encouraged him to remain a relevant figure: "Dick, I believe you'll have another chance at the presidency. You have the ability and the training to be president of the United States. Don't give up," he told him, even though Nixon no longer believed in himself.[116] "Never," Nixon responded, refusing to believe he would have another chance.[117]

Even before the Los Angeles crusade in 1949 that first made him a national figure, Graham had been close to the Nixons. He had spoken at a Youth for Christ meeting in Whittier, where he met Frank and Hannah Nixon. "I was told that whenever a religious meeting was held within driving distance in Southern California, the Nixons were always there," Graham said later. "I was also told that their son was a rising political figure in Southern California."[118] Hannah was "the great spiritual force in our family," Julie Nixon Eisenhower recalled later, and it was she who brought the Grahams and Nixons together.[119] North Carolina Senator Clyde Hoey introduced Graham to Nixon in the Senate dining room in 1951, noting that Nixon went to law school in his home state. They discussed how Graham already knew Nixon's mother.[120] "That was the beginning of one of the most cherished friendships that I have ever had with anyone," Graham said later. "We become personal friends from the very beginning."[121] The long association did not mean they always agreed. During Nixon's 1960 campaign for the presidency, Graham urged him to consider Walter Judd as his running mate. "He gave me his reasons for not taking my suggestion," Graham wrote in his memoir. "I did not think they were valid."[122] Even though Nixon ignored his advice, Graham privately supported the Republican ticket of Nixon and Lodge over Kennedy and Johnson. He refused to make any public endorsement, and he resisted pressure to make an issue out of Kennedy's Catholicism. "Had I been foolish enough to declare myself, it would have been for Mr. Nixon," Graham wrote in his memoirs. "Frankly, I thought Nixon's eight years in the Eisenhower administration qualified him better."[123]

By December 1967, after many conversations about whether he should run again, Nixon was still deadlocked. He saw his nomination and election as possible but not probable.[124] "I was not sure whether I still had the heart," he wrote in his memoir, "whether I had not reached the time in life when I lacked the zeal to continue a political career."[125] He faced an imminent deadline for making the decision, and the *Times* interview with Eisenhower, which quoted the general as saying he did not plan to endorse any Republican before the convention, almost persuaded him not to run.[126] The stars were not aligning for him. He asked Graham to join him in Key Biscayne at the very end of December. Graham was battling viral pneumonia, which doctors said would take four to six weeks to overcome. He had canceled many appearances and rearranged his schedule for more rest, but he agreed to see Nixon. "There are times," he said, "when some things are more important than health."[127] Worried he was too ill to travel by commercial jet, Nixon reimbursed him for the cost of a private plane.[128] The two spent three days walking on the beach, talking, praying, and reading from Scripture. "I told him that I was genuinely torn on the question of whether to run," Nixon recalled. "One part of me wanted to more than anything else, but another part of me rebelled at the thought of all it would entail. . . . Ten months of campaigning would mean great stress and strain on me and on my family, especially Pat."[129] It was the most important decision of his career. He would rather not run than lose again, but without politics, it was not clear what he would do for the rest of his life. At the same time, "losing again could be an emotional disaster for my family."[130]

"I was somewhat surprised to learn that he really had not yet definitely decided to run," Graham wrote in his diary.[131] Without telling Nixon what to do, he used the arguments he thought would persuade him to run. During a long walk on the beach to the lighthouse, they discussed each family member's opinion. An encouraging letter from David Eisenhower made a tremendous impression.[132] Graham told Nixon that he believed presidents were divinely chosen, and each was called to serve. He said Hannah Nixon, who had died that September, would have wanted him to do it. He reminded Nixon of his mother's admonition on her deathbed:

"Dick, don't quit." Moreover, Graham did not think Johnson would seek reelection.[133] "I made it a point never to quote President Johnson to him," he wrote in his diary, "but I had gathered from private conversations with the President by putting two and two together that there was a possibility he might not run."[134] Nixon doubted that. Graham also said, "If you don't run, you will always wonder if you should have."[135] They left the matter unsettled, but it came up again on New Year's Day as Graham was getting ready to leave.[136] "Well, what is your conclusion?" Nixon asked. "Dick, I think you should run," Graham told him. "You are the best prepared man in the United States to be President. . . . I think it is your destiny to be President."[137] He added, "I think you owe it to yourself and to your country to run for it. The country is in serious condition and it needs you."[138] Julie Nixon Eisenhower wrote that Graham "was a crucial factor in the decision to make the race."[139]

Nixon referred to his conversations with Graham as the "decisive factor in his decision."[140] "By January 9, my fifty-fifth birthday, I was back in New York. My mind was made up."[141] Those around him believed he was destined be president, and he wanted to fulfill his mother's dream that he "leave footprints in the sands of time."[142] Nixon was more confident, self-assured, and mature after the losses of 1960 and 1962. The break from politics gave him the opportunity to find a new voice and a new place within the Republican Party. He was no longer a man in search of Alger Hiss.[143] Before he could win an election, however, he had to unite his own party. While he focused on the moderates and liberals, Buchanan worked to bring the New Right "into alliance with the Nixonian center of the GOP, and deny any challenger the big divisions necessary to block a Nixon nomination."[144] The strategy was simple, but difficult in execution: Nixon needed to be a combination of Dwight Eisenhower and Barry Goldwater, and he needed to bring the New Right along without looking as though he had capitulated to them.

On February 1, 1968, Nixon flew to Boston under cover of darkness, drove to Nashua, New Hampshire, and checked into a motel under the name "Benjamin Chapman." The day before, local Nixon booster Dave Sterling had walked into the office of Secretary of State Robert Stark in Concord, three hours before the filing deadline, and presented 808 signatures to register Nixon's candidacy in the New Hampshire primary.[145] "We could not have cut it closer," Buchanan recalled.[146] Nixon tried to keep expectations low for as long as possible. He was seen as a loser, but he hoped the New Hampshire primary would redeem him.[147] The next day, 150,000 New Hampshire residents, 85 percent of eligible voters, found a letter from Richard Nixon in their mailboxes. "During the past eight years I have had a chance to reflect on the lessons of public office, to measure the nation's tasks and its problems from a fresh perspective," he wrote.[148] It was a staggering direct-mail effort for the time, done in complete secrecy. "I began my second campaign for the presidency with a press conference on the afternoon of February 2, 1968," he wrote in his memoir. "I came to the microphones and announced, 'Gentlemen, this is *not* my last press conference.'"[149] From that moment, the pressure was on Michigan Governor George Romney. Romney had started his campaign as the front-runner. He looked like a president and had won the governorship three times after a private-sector career transforming American Motors.[150] But his campaign had started to unravel in August 1967, when he said, "Well, you know when I came back from Vietnam [in November 1965], I just had the greatest brainwashing that anybody can get when you go over to Vietnam. Not only by the generals, but also the diplomatic corps over there, and they do a very thorough job. I no longer believe that it was necessary for us to get involved in South Vietnam to stop aggression."[151] These remarks were widely criticized, and the White House aggressively defended its military and diplomatic personnel. Republicans thought Romney sounded wishy-washy. The media seized on "brainwashing," editorial pages mocked him, and the *Detroit News* urged him to drop out and support Nelson Rockefeller.[152] Buchanan took one look at that and thought "we simply needed to avoid mistakes and run out the clock."[153]

The major issue in New Hampshire, with the primary coming so soon after the Tet Offensive, was the war. At the American Legion Hall in Hampton on March 5, Nixon described the goal in Vietnam as an "honorable peace" and no longer called for military victory.[154] "I felt that there were a number of unexplored avenues to probe in finding a way to end the war," he wrote later. "As a candidate it would have been foolhardy, and as a prospective President, improper, for me to outline specific plans in detail."[155] Garry Wills recalled Nixon saying, with surprisingly unguarded emotion, "It is a time when a man who knows the world will be able to forge a whole new set of alliances, with America taking the lead in solving the big problems."[156] Nixon spoke of ending the draft as a way to appeal to disenchanted youth and unite liberals and conservatives who had long been opposed to it.[157] He refrained from saying much about Vietnam because he did not want to appear to be in opposition to Johnson, especially if Billy Graham turned out to be right that Johnson would not run for reelection. Nixon instead pivoted to domestic issues, a traditional Democratic strength. During an NBC radio address on March 7, Nixon called "the problem of order . . . the number one issue in the United States—and the number one issue in the world."[158]

Nixon won the New Hampshire primary on March 12 with 78 percent of the vote. Rockefeller finished with 11 percent, and Reagan with less than 1 percent. Romney withdrew on the eve of the primary, before the first vote was cast.[159] He'd been unprepared for the scrutiny he would receive as the frontrunner.[160] The day after the primary, Eisenhower unofficially endorsed Nixon by saying he was "all for Dick."[161] According to one account, the Republican result in New Hampshire concerned Johnson more than McCarthy did. He was not sure he could defeat Nixon, who had won New Hampshire with 80,606 votes, versus fewer than 30,000 for McCarthy or Johnson.[162] But Nixon had a long way to go. His campaign did not have enough cash on hand to meet the March 31 payroll. His top fundraiser, Maurice Stans, personally lent the campaign $25,000 to keep it afloat. W. Clement Stone of Chicago said he would match all contributions over the next sixty days, up to $1 million, and provided the first $200,000 as an advance. "That was the turning point," Stans wrote in his memoirs. Even though Nixon spent $9 million during the primaries, the campaign was able to run a surplus that rolled over into the general election.[163]

Nixon was back. He had learned from his defeats in 1960 and 1962 and had six years to plan before declaring his candidacy in 1968 around the theme "Bring Us Together."[164] The campaign's headquarters, in a nondescript building at the corner of 5th Avenue and 43rd Street in Manhattan, were not mentioned in the building directory in the lobby. Nixon's advance men were as good as JFK's were in 1960.[165] His campaign was active for the entire four-month period from New Hampshire through Oregon, getting them in shape for the fall. He bolstered his staff, adding figures like Ray Price, who, while at the *New York Herald Tribune*, had written the editorial endorsing Johnson in 1964—the only time the newspaper endorsed a Democrat. Alan Greenspan, Martin Anderson, Bill Safire, Richard Allen, Robert Ellsworth, Leonard Garment, and Herb Stein were also part of the campaign. Most were moderate to liberal, and many were Jewish.[166] Nixon later brought in Pat Moynihan, Henry Kissinger, and John Connally, showing he was no ideologue.[167] He admired "scrappers," meaning people who fought to make their own way, and he wanted the best he could find.[168] "He had instincts one could call conservative," Buchanan recalled, "but reflexive reactions that were liberal."[169]

Nelson Rockefeller led the charge on behalf of those who thought Nixon's loser image would doom the party again. He claimed to have the support of eighteen Republican governors but was hesitant to challenge Nixon at the ballot box.[170] "If Nixon is such a loser, we said, why don't they come out into the primaries and prove it?" Buchanan wrote.[171] Even the *New York Times* commented it was "difficult to continue describing as a loser a man who is so overwhelmingly powerful that no challenger will even take him on."[172] But in New York, Rockefeller was beholden to no one.[173] "Your position of noncandidacy has put you where you are today," advisor George Hinman wrote. "It has put you at the top of public esteem."[174] After Robert Kennedy entered the race on March 16, Rockefeller announced that he would hold a press conference. It was a front-page story for two days in the *New York Times*, with nothing but conjecture about its content. At the event, on March 21, instead of announcing a challenge to Nixon, Rockefeller told the packed Hilton Midtown ballroom that he would not actively seek the nomination. While he would not campaign, however, he was open to a draft. He had obstacles to overcome: an image of vacillation, no campaign organization, and an uninterested press. Upstate New York Republicans depended on his generosity as governor but otherwise resented him.[175] Rumors of womanizing always chased him, and he was damaged by his divorce from Mary Clark, the mother of his five children, and his remarriage to Margarita "Happy" Murphy.[176]

Ronald Reagan was the conservative dream candidate. "Ronald Reagan could pull the conservatives away from Nixon," Buchanan recalled.[177] No one had benefited more from liberal missteps in domestic and foreign policy during the 1960s.[178] Reagan had made himself a national political figure in 1964 with his "A Time for Choosing" speech, in which he endorsed Arizona Senator Barry Goldwater's run for the presidency.[179] He was effectively Goldwater lite, without the senator's abrasive temperament or severity.[180] In 1966, after beating Pat Brown, who had defeated Nixon in 1962, to become governor of California, Reagan had quickly emerged as the leader of the right wing of the party. During his 1966 campaign, he promised not to seek the presidency in 1968—a pledge he found difficult to keep.[181] As governor, Reagan was no ideologue. He opposed the

Civil Rights Act of 1964 but submitted the largest budget increase in state history and did not reverse open-housing policies. He was not thrilled by Nixon's rise but preferred him to Rockefeller.[182] As 1968 approached, Reagan was cautious. He represented what conservatives wanted: the un-fulfilled promise of the Goldwater revolution. Reagan's magnetic person-ality radiated optimism and hope—the ideal message in a revolutionary decade.[183] But he was not battle tested, pragmatic party leaders needed a win, and it was not clear that Reagan would be any better than Goldwater for uniting the party.[184] In an exchange of letters with Nixon in April 1967, Reagan agreed that Nixon, if he ran, would have the first shot at success in the primaries. If he did not vanquish Romney by Wisconsin, Reagan was free to move in.[185]

A year later, with Romney gone and the challenges by Rockefeller and Reagan contingent at best, Nixon was the last man standing. He thrilled no one but did not offend anyone either. His campaign published two volumes on his views, the most extensive campaign resource ever pro-duced. On the Equal Rights Amendment, for example, there was a record of Nixon's statements in support since 1951.[186] Never had a campaign made so much information available, and never before had a candidate taken such an organized approach. To keep Nixon fresh and on message, the campaign changed the way they scheduled him based on the lessons learned in 1960. For example, he would fly to New Hampshire for two or three days of hard campaigning, then let ads and surrogates carry the campaign. He would move on to the next primary state to initiate his pres-ence there, then to Key Biscayne for rest and planning.[187] That became his pattern for the rest of the campaign.[188] "It became plausible," Richard Whalen reflected, "to imagine the impossible—that Nixon could continue indefinitely to pursue the presidency at an unhurried walk."[189]

Nixon purchased airtime for a nationwide radio address on the eve-ning of Sunday, March 31, in advance of the April 2 Wisconsin primary, specifically to outline his views on Vietnam. It was meant to be the first in a series of speeches on the subject.[190] "Unless a start is made soon in a new direction, the United States will confront a grim choice between the massive risks of a larger war and more brutal war, and the disastrous consequences of defeat," Nixon planned to say.[191] He wrote later that "I intended to propose that America vigorously try to convince the Soviet Union to reduce its military support for North Vietnam. I also planned to deliver a sharp criticism of the Johnson policy of gradualism on the military front."[192] But upon learning that Johnson reserved national television airtime that same evening, he canceled his own address. "Dammit," he said. "We've got to cancel. That's all we can do."[193] He expected a dramatic turnaround in Johnson's Vietnam policy, and possibly a limited bombing halt, but he seemed genuinely caught off guard by the surprise ending.[194] "I hope the President's initiative succeeds," Nixon said publicly about Johnson's shift toward negotiations to end the war.[195]

Shocked that Billy Graham's prediction had been correct and momentarily forgetting that he himself was the greatest beneficiary of Johnson's withdrawal, Nixon publicly referred to the president as a "drop out"—a comparison to Romney and Rockefeller. "I was justifiably criticized for thus characterizing Johnson's action," he wrote in his memoirs.[196] It was the last time in the campaign that he directed a personal criticism at Johnson. "He announced that he would observe a personal 'moratorium' on Vietnam and would say nothing about the war or the peace-seeking initiative until he could judge the effects of the bombing halt and North Vietnam's response," Whalen wrote.[197] Withholding criticism and expressing sympathy for Johnson could pay important dividends. By leaving the race, Johnson laid the foundation for the nonaggression pact between the two—an expanded version of the understanding they had reached in 1966. "I'd compare the President and Dick Nixon to a couple of fighting roosters, circling each other, with knives attached to the spurs," Bryce Harlow later said. "Nothing will happen, mind you, unless one makes the first move."[198]

All candidates suspended their campaigns after the assassination of Martin Luther King Jr. Nixon flew to Atlanta on April 7 to pay his respects to the family. "I went to their home and met his four children, still dazed over their father's murder," he wrote later. "I saw Mrs. King in her room, where she was resting; I was moved by her poise and serenity. His death left Black America without a nationally recognized leader who combined responsibility with charisma."[199] He returned to march in King's funeral procession, but he also condemned the riots and violent protests. Later, he told Pat Buchanan that being captured in photographs at the funeral cost him heavily in the South, but he did it anyway—just as he supported the open-housing bill that quickly moved through Congress the week following King's death.[200] After a period of reflection and study, he returned to the campaign trail with a major address on civil rights and social policy. His "Bridges to Human Dignity" speech, broadcast on CBS national radio

on April 25, introduced a proposal for Black capitalism, greater private
investment in cities, and federal loan guarantees for urban areas.[201] "America has got to make the black man a capitalist, and do it damn quick," civil
rights leader Floyd McKissick said.[202] "Handouts are demeaning. They do
violence to a man, strip him of dignity, and breed in him a hatred of the
system."[203] In his own way, Nixon gave the civil rights movement new life
by balancing political expediency, practicality, and principle. "It's time,"
he said, "to move past the old civil rights, and to bridge the gap between
freedom and dignity, between promise and fulfillment."[204] The proposal
offered Blacks "a share of the wealth and a piece of the action" and was a
high point of the campaign.[205] It included assistance to Black-owned businesses, job training, federal mortgage assistance to boost Black home own-
ership, and programs to connect Black entrepreneurs with white-owned
banks. Nixon believed it would bring increased Black pride and dignity.[206]
He genuinely questioned whether giving minorities an "equal chance"
was enough, which suggests he was not opposed to applying the invisible
hand of government to social policy.[207] "That strategy actually looks quite
progressive today," Walter Mondale wrote in his memoirs about Nixon's
proposals.[208] While some Republicans cringed at his willingness to engage
the subject of race, the speech showed that Republican ideology and Black
aspirations need not be mutually exclusive.[209]

In his September 27 speech in Omaha, "A Better Day for the American Indian," Nixon proposed new economic opportunities and greater
sovereignty for Native Americans.[210] He described past policy as "unfair,"
"demeaning," and "tragic," and vowed to do "all I can" to improve "Indian
life and education."[211] Discussing racial issues in economic terms allowed
him to walk a careful line during the campaign.[212] "On the race issue I'm
a liberal," he said. "On economics I'm a conservative. Domestically, you
could say I'm a centrist."[213] Despite his campaigning on a modified Great
Society with Republican shading, Nixon later wrote that in their many
conversations, Johnson never asked Nixon to preserve his centerpiece domestic initiative.[214] Perhaps Johnson did not feel the need, since Nixon did
not oppose its goals—only the reliance on big spending programs for its
implementation.

Nixon praised peaceful protesters while condemning the disruptive
student protests at Columbia University. He gave anticrime statements
and condemned the findings of the Kerner Commission, which blamed
white racism for nationwide violence. "The old way, the government way,

will no longer do," he said in a nationwide address on May 2. "The old way is still the conditioned reflex of those whose policy approaches are rooted in the '30s—the old way of massive spending piled on massive spending, and of looking to Washington to solve the problem of Watts."[215] None of Nixon's positions were controversial.[216] In a speech on May 16, "A New Alignment for American Unity," he appealed to the "new majority" and "new South."[217] It was a play for moderate Southerners who might otherwise be wooed by former Alabama Governor George Wallace.

The more conservative Nixon was, the more Wallace could hurt Republicans. On the other hand, the more Nixon floated to the left, the more Wallace could hurt Democrats.[218] "While R.N. was positioned as tough on law and order," Buchanan recalled, "he did not try to rival George Wallace, and Nixon's campaign thrust was really 'peace with honor' in Vietnam and 'new leadership' which could unite the country. In those years, Governor Reagan was more passionate and tougher on the law-and-order issue than R.N., who I think it is fair to say did what he had to do, but it was not why he was running for president."[219] Public opinion polls consistently showed that crime was Americans' chief domestic concern, especially among women.[220] Nixon's position on law and order was a response to fear, but he did not create that fear.[221]

At the end of April, Nixon recalled, "Rockefeller convened a press conference in Albany and announced a complete turnaround."[222] He would run after all, although he joined the race too late to appear on any primary ballot. Rockefeller said the dramatic events in recent weeks, referring to Johnson's withdrawal and national unrest in the wake of King's death, had compelled his change of mind. "The true memorial to Martin Luther King cannot be made of stone," he said. "It must be made of action."[223] He hoped to forge an alliance with Reagan to block Nixon from winning on the first ballot. It is not clear that Reagan really wanted a political marriage with Rockefeller, but there was enough interest that he received Rockefeller's chief surrogate, Emmet Hughes, at his Palisades Park home in Los Angeles.[224] Rockefeller's campaign began even later than Humphrey's. He had to work hard to catch up. Having missed filing deadlines for the primaries in Indiana, Nebraska, and Oregon, Rockefeller competed as a write-in using massive ad buys, spending $5 million in the nation's top forty-one newspapers.[225]

Nixon did not feel threatened by Rockefeller or Reagan, but Rockefeller *and* Reagan could nibble away from both left and right. The media referred to a Rockefeller–Reagan dream team, an idea tested during an unusually competitive Nebraska primary in which Rockefeller's supporters bought 247 television spots and 564 newspaper ads in a full-court-press write-in effort. He was the first to wage political war, not through direct competition but through mass media advertising.[226] Reagan disavowed any efforts on his behalf, which included several prime-time showings of a very effective half-hour television documentary about him. A Rockefeller–Reagan ticket might really have been a dream team but for one problem: each side's supporters detested the other side. That allowed Nixon to cruise to victory, 70 percent to Reagan's 22 percent, with Rockefeller capturing only 5 percent.[227] "In 1960 they say I dropped out too soon," Rockefeller commented. "In 1964 they said I stayed in too long. Well, this year I've done both."[228]

The last competitive primary was expected to be Oregon, since Nixon did not plan to compete head-to-head against Reagan in California. "I had decided not to risk dividing the party by challenging his favorite son status," he wrote in his memoirs. Victory in Oregon was hardly guaranteed. "I was worried about Oregon because Reagan's people were spending heavily in an attempt to make a last-minute sweep."[229] As in Nebraska, Rockefeller and Reagan forces each spent several hundred thousand dollars in Oregon trying to compete virtually, with Reagan again relying on strategic airings of his half-hour documentary and Rockefeller on hundreds of paid advertisements.[230] "I doubled my efforts in Oregon," Nixon recalled, "and, unlike Reagan and Rockefeller, I went to the state to campaign." He cruised again to the finish line, capturing 73 percent of the vote against Reagan with 23 percent and Rockefeller with 4 percent. "It was far from over, but things were falling into place," he wrote.[231] After Oregon, the press following the Nixon campaign began to grow, since he was considered the odds-on favorite for the nomination.[232]

With no chance of competing against Wallace in the Deep South, Nixon concentrated on border states. Had Humphrey been his only opponent, he might have taken a more forceful approach to the South and probably would have been successful.[233] But in a three-way race, he was happy to let Wallace make the most extreme appeals to Southerners. Wallace was no Democratic aberration. He dominated the eleven states of the Confederacy that Woodrow Wilson and FDR had won all six times they ran between 1912 and 1944. Nixon did not attack Wallace or his supporters, but he emphasized that a vote for Wallace was effectively a vote for

Humphrey, since Wallace had no chance to win.[234] He was criticized for not condemning Wallace, but he reintroduced genuine two-party competition in the South, increasing the region's national political importance.[235] He did this while proposing civil rights policies that, for a Republican, were fairly radical.[236] If anything, his public support of every civil rights initiative from 1957 onward delayed his party's later dominance in the South. Nixon had been careful to avoid appearances there with Goldwater after 1964, and he blasted Democrats for continuing to nominate segregationist candidates in several states. Republicans, he warned, must "not climb aboard the sinking ship of racial injustice."[237] He ultimately won the South's early support by providing assurances regarding national defense—not civil rights, future Supreme Court picks, or his running mate.[238]

Nixon was never very concerned about a challenge from the left, from either Romney or Rockefeller. Romney seemed to get in trouble every time he spoke to the press, and Rockefeller's shift to the left on Vietnam, presumably to attract Kennedy's supporters, made it difficult to see how he could win over enough conservatives to get the nomination.[239] To his right, however, Nixon was consistently concerned about the enthusiasm for Reagan and Wallace. Winning the early endorsement of Goldwater, still considered a betrayed martyr, was invaluable.[240] "Until I had the nomination," he wrote in his memoirs, "I had to pay careful attention to the dangers of a sudden resurgence on the right."[241] To head off such a challenge, he flew to Atlanta on May 31 to speak at a two-day gathering of Republican state chairmen representing thirteen states from the South and border areas.[242] The occasion also allowed him to meet privately with those he was seriously courting for support, and there was no bigger prize than South Carolina's Strom Thurmond. Other movers and shakers included John Tower of Texas and Howard Baker of Tennessee.[243] "I had been consulting privately with Thurmond for several months," Nixon wrote, "and I was convinced that he would join my campaign if he were satisfied on the two issues of paramount concern to him."[244] Neither concern centered on race or civil rights.[245] "On civil rights, Thurmond knew my position was very different from his," Nixon recalled. "He knew that I would enforce the law, but that I would not make the South the whipping boy."[246] Nixon did not need to say much about race because for a Southern conservative like Thurmond, it was understood he would be preferable to Humphrey. Thurmond's main stated concerns were national defense and enacting tariffs against textile imports to protect South Carolina manufacturers.[247] Nixon emerged from his meetings in Atlanta feeling good about his chances of holding Republican support in the South, but there were weak spots. For example, North Carolina Congressman Jim Gardner, the head of his state's delegation to the coming convention in Miami Beach, threatened to rebel. Whether it was a genuine consideration or not, he controlled a bloc of delegates from an important swing state. Nixon needed an intermediary to work on him, and he had one: fellow North Carolinian Billy Graham. "This was the first time he had ever asked me to do anything for him politically," Graham wrote in his diary. "I called Congressman Gardner and he said that he would give his all-out support to Nixon if Nixon would speak out on textiles, tobacco, and would make a trip to North Carolina early in the campaign. Nixon agreed to do all of these."[248]

What Nixon's critics never acknowledged is that he brought more of the South into the Republican column, not because of shared views on segregation or civil rights, but because he successfully exploited the increasingly unstable Democratic coalition.[249] It is well documented that from his time as a law student at Duke, Nixon did not share the South's traditional views on race. He was as shocked by what he saw there as Hubert Humphrey was when he moved to Louisiana to study political science. With the help of Billy Graham, who represented the kind of Southerner Nixon targeted, he could peel off moderates who were not obsessed by race or bound by the South's past, while conceding the rest to Humphrey and Wallace. "In 1968," Theodore White wrote, "Nixon conspicuously, conscientiously, calculatedly denied himself all racist votes, yielding them to Wallace."[250] The *Miami Herald* published a secret recording of Nixon making assurances to Southern delegates during his visit to Atlanta, and what he said in private was almost the same as what he said in public.[251] For those looking for evidence of a cynical "Southern Strategy" it was a great disappointment.[252] "On the face of it, the notion is preposterous," political analysts Richard Scammon and Ben Wattenberg wrote about the enduring myth of the Southern Strategy. "When examined closely, it remains preposterous."[253] "Forget the Goldwater South," Nixon told his aides.[254] The main goal was not to divide the party, and if Nixon made promises to Southern racists, it would cost him elsewhere in the nation. "I would estimate that between five and eight percent of his [Wallace's] support is hard-line racists," Safire advised Nixon. "We can't get these people and we should forget them." In the margins of Safire's memo, Nixon wrote "excellent analysis" and "very perceptive."[255] It was a tightrope walk, but he pulled it off in Atlanta. "The ball game for all intents and purposes is over," Nixon campaign manager John Mitchell said after the trip.[256] While in 1964 conservatives rallied to Goldwater, in 1968 they were more pragmatic. With the support of Southern leaders solidified, Nixon appeared to have locked up the nomination.

The candidates suspended their campaigns a second time after Senator Kennedy was assassinated. If King's death had shocked the nation, Kennedy's shook the political establishment. One death was tragic enough, but two prompted many to wonder if Democrats were somehow being punished for having presided over such a chaotic decade. It was hardly a fair assessment, but their control of virtually all levels of government at such a time made it harder for a Democrat to ask voters for another term in office. Kennedy's death symbolized the beginning of an era when the radicals and nihilists seemed to have taken over.[257] "Pat and I attended the funeral mass at St. Patrick's Cathedral in New York, and we were deeply moved by the eloquent eulogy delivered by his brother, Teddy," Nixon recalled.[258] "I believe that Hubert Humphrey had waited too long before declaring his candidacy, and I saw no way a Kennedy juggernaut could be stopped once it had acquired the momentum of a California victory."[259] Of his potential opponents, he considered Humphrey the weakest.[260]

"The Nixon campaign has been almost flawless," wrote the *Washington Post*'s Ward Just, one of the few members of the press who traveled with the campaign throughout the primaries. "He wins the presidential primaries in New Hampshire, Wisconsin, Indiana, and Nebraska by staggering majorities—in each case by more than 70 percent of the vote. He forces George Romney out of the race, then lures Nelson Rockefeller into an in-out-and-in-again performance so indecisive and amateurish Adlai Stevenson looks in retrospect like Napoleon."[261] Drew Pearson wrote in his diary that "Nixon appears to be going like a house afire. He has had conferences with various GOP leaders who were against him prior to Miami Beach. They appear to have patched up differences."[262] H. R. "Bob" Haldeman and John Ehrlichman began traveling with Nixon at the end of the primaries. They were UCLA classmates, fellow Christian Scientists and World War II veterans, and had worked on Nixon's campaigns in 1960 and 1962.[263] With Haldeman came a number of his advertising protégés from J. Walter Thompson, including Dwight Chapin, Larry Higby, Ronald Ziegler, and Kenneth Cole.[264] Campaign manager John Mitchell gradually tightened his grip on the Nixon operation, and the candidate was glad to see it.[265] Mitchell put his law firm relationship with Nixon to work with his coast-to-coast network of contacts.[266] "Wreathed in pipe smoke and an aura of imperturbable certainty, he gave reassurance," Richard Whalen wrote.[267] While he had never been involved in politics, his specialty as a municipal bond attorney meant he knew local and state officials all over the country. Unlike Nixon, Mitchell was comfortable around people like Nelson Rockefeller and had a talent for getting and keeping what he wanted. He was absolutely indifferent to the press and never gave a single news conference.[268]

What had been one of the more casual campaigns in terms of press relations—certainly more casual than Nixon's 1960 campaign—became restricted once Nixon solidified his front-runner status and his enhanced Secret Service detail limited access. Even for the handful of national reporters who had documented the campaign from its beginnings, covering Nixon offered little hard news after he vanquished his primary opponents. The press could no longer wander his plane and mingle. With little new to say, reporters fell back on preconceived ideas about Nixon from 1960 or 1962, and it was more difficult for voters to see how much he had matured in the intervening years. "The Nixon of 1968 was so different from the Nixon of 1960 that the whole personality required re-exploration," Theodore White wrote. "Something had transformed his thinking; it was important to try to read all over again the quality of his mind."[269]

CHAPTER FOUR

Wallace

MONG THE THREE MAJOR candidates in 1968, the presidential
campaign of former Alabama Governor George Wallace created
the most lasting movement. As the only four-term governor in
Alabama history, Wallace dominated the state for a quarter-
century and was one of the most recognizable governors in U.S. history. He ran for president four times.[1] With his vigilante, anti-elite, anti-
Establishment ethos, he was the incarnation of the "folks" he wooed.[2] He
single-handedly brought their views into the mainstream. By 1968, he had
become the living embodiment of resistance to social change, even though
he personally had undergone a transformation from a segregationist demagogue to a populist conservative for whom racial resentment, while not
abandoned as a source of his political appeal, was folded into a larger set of
grievances. The national media, which could never comprehend Wallace's
popularity outside Alabama, made him one of the most misunderstood
politicians in American history.[3]

George Corley Wallace Jr. was born on August 25, 1919, to George
Corley and Mozelle Wallace. His grandfather was a teetotaler physician
who delivered many of the babies in Barbour County, a hamlet that produced seven Alabama governors.[4] His father had two years of education at
Southern University but dropped out to become a farmer.[5] As a boy during the Great Depression in Clio, Alabama, he had nothing to suggest a
politician in the making except an extraordinary ability to remember people and their names.[6] Young George Jr. picked berries and pecans for ten
cents a gallon to help the family. When he was older, he chopped cotton,

plowed a mule, and drove an ox team.[7] He had a restless energy that suited his training as a boxer, and he was comfortable facing bigger opponents. "I thrived on the raw, face-to-face competition that boxing demands," he wrote later, entering his first bout in 1935 at 118 pounds.[8] In 1936, he won the statewide Golden Gloves bantamweight championship, did it again in 1937, and also quarterbacked the football team and served as president of his senior class.[9] The oldest of four children, he was thrust into an adult role when his father died at age forty in 1937.[10] After the family lost the farm to foreclosure following his death, Wallace traveled the country selling magazines to support the family while his mother worked as a sewing supervisor for young girls.[11] It was his first experience outside the South. He had a talent for talking to people of different backgrounds—and making the sale. Sometimes he was paid in chickens, eggs, and vegetables.

A former college classmate said George arrived at the University of Alabama in 1937 with nothing but a cardboard suitcase—plus "brains, grit and guts."[12] He was flat broke and had no connections. He sold coat hangers and then worked as a tool checker for a government aircraft school in Tuscaloosa. "I felt real lucky," Wallace said. "I got a pay increase of 20 cents an hour and worked inside to boot."[13] He earned his law degree in 1942, at the age of twenty-three, and immediately signed up for the Army Air Force cadet program to become a pilot. That fall he met a beautiful young woman while buying hair oil at Kresge's Five and Dime in Tuscaloosa. In 1943 he married sixteen-year-old Lurleen Burns—reserved and petite at 5'2" and 105 pounds—a Southern belle from the Tuscaloosa County city of Northport, who was quickly smitten by George's talk of one day becoming governor.[14]

Before completing pilot training, George developed spinal meningitis, which left him with partial hearing loss and permanent nerve damage. His dream of being a pilot dashed, he trained to be a flight engineer and went on to serve in General Curtis LeMay's Fifty-eighth Wing of the Twentieth Air Force.[15] Assigned to the B-29 *The Sentimental Journey* in the Marianna Islands, he was given duties that included stacking TNT at the Army Ordnance Plant, which provided critical resupply for the continuous bombing of the Japanese coastline near the end of the war. He was ultimately discharged on medical grounds and returned to Alabama as a veteran on December 8, 1945.

Wallace had gotten his first taste of politics in high school when he won a contest to serve as a page in the Alabama Senate. When he returned home from the war, he was appointed assistant attorney general by a fellow Barbour County native, Governor Chauncey Sparks. Less than a year into the job, he ran for the state legislature in 1946, at the age of twenty-seven, defeating two opponents and serving a total of six years. He styled himself as a populist in the mold of Jim Folsom, who served as governor from 1947 to 1951 and 1955 to 1959. When national Democrats adopted a pro–civil rights platform in 1948, Folsom and Wallace did not join those who bolted the party.[16] Wallace had the support of Black Alabamians, even though most did not vote.[17] He was a conservative New Deal Democrat in a de facto one-party state.[18] His personal political hero was Theodore Roosevelt, whose famous 1905 visit to Alabama at the invitation of Booker T. Washington, hardly a timid thing to have done at the time, was still remembered by some.[19] After the 1948 convention, while friends and colleagues established the States Rights Party, Wallace remained a New Deal Democrat, spoke out against the Ku Klux Klan, and was endorsed by the NAACP.[20] He served as a trustee of the all-Black Tuskegee Institute. In 1952, he was appointed as the youngest circuit judge in the United States.[21] It was an intentional move in his climb to become governor.[22] As a county judge in Alabama's Third Judicial District, he was well-liked by the Black attorneys who tried cases in his courtroom.[23] He called them "Mister" in his courtroom, an honorific some had never heard. There was nothing in his conduct to suggest the racist statements he expressed later.[24]

The turning point came in 1958, during his first race for governor, which he announced in front of the Clayton County courthouse less than three blocks from his home.[25] John Patterson, the handsome young attorney general from Phenix City, was the favorite candidate. He had been elected to that post after his father, Attorney General Albert Patterson, was gunned down in 1954 by gangsters after he shut down their illegal gambling parlors. John Patterson defeated Wallace for the governorship by successfully sticking Wallace with accurate labels: a big government, progressive New Dealer. Patterson ran as a hardline believer in segregation and was endorsed by the United Klans of America's founder, Imperial Wizard Bobby Shelton. He appealed to conservative whites by stoking fears that a Governor Wallace would support civil rights and integrate Alabama's schools in the aftermath of *Brown v. Board of Education* and Little Rock High School.[26]

The social structure of the South had been confirmed by the U.S. Supreme Court in *Plessy v. Ferguson* in 1898, and it remained that way until

1954, when *Brown v. Board of Education* began to overturn it. The *Plessy* ruling allowed generations of Southern politicians to claim they were not racist but segregationist, and that segregation was best for both races. "And yet, like so much in the South, it was complicated," Wallace's daughter reflected later.[27] In 1958, her father was unprepared to fight a campaign on the issue of race. He suffered his first political loss, by a margin of 64,902 votes, for being too liberal and too timid. There are different versions of how he reacted to that. The most famous version is more apocryphal than documented. "John Patterson out-niggered me," Wallace is supposed to have said. "And boys, I'm not goin' to be out-niggered again."[28] Another version is that Wallace said he would not be "out-segged."[29] Wallace denied both versions, later telling journalists that they were creations of those obsessed with the issue of race. Patterson, not Wallace, demonstrated that an obsession with race could bring political success. If Wallace wanted to be successful statewide, he needed to emulate Patterson.[30]

Wallace's loss guaranteed him temporary political oblivion, a hardship shared by his family. Frequent absences from home and growing accusations of drinking and womanizing continued for four years while he prepared to run for governor again. The family moved from Clayton to Montgomery so he could be near the action.[31] Wallace was an attentive father, but politics demanded more and more of his time.[32] The focus on political duties over family sent Lurleen to the brink, and they came close to divorce. When asked about it, however, she evaded a direct answer.[33] "He would have done whatever it took to be elected," his daughter Peggy recalled, and divorce would have ended his political career.[34] With Patterson barred by term limits from running in 1962, Wallace contacted all of Patterson's key supporters—"checking the pulse," he called it—to let them know that he would be their guy.[35] In Alabama, if you lost a race for governor you were the odds-on favorite to win next time due to the statewide name recognition.[36] Driven to redeem himself, Wallace used the issue of segregation to catapult himself into power. He made a Faustian bargain, promising the segregationists he would get on the right side of the issue.[37] It was a calculated shift as he watched the national response to forced desegregation and federal intervention.

Wallace raised $380,000 in a statewide effort that put him in a strong competitive position.[38] Fundraising was one of his strengths, not just accumulating a war chest but understanding how to make the ask with different kinds of donors. He railed against local representatives of big government like longtime federal Judge Frank Johnson, whom he called "a low-down, carpetbaggin', scalawaggin', race-mixin' liar."[39] Wallace electrified a packed Montgomery rally on March 10, 1962, with a promise, if elected, that he would personally "stand in the schoolhouse door" to block integration of the University of Alabama.[40] He wrote later that "the issue did not involve the color of the students" but whether local and state government could survive with "big government . . . rapidly destroying them by federal court orders."[41] Wallace naïvely thought that such a statement would not mortgage his political future. He emphasized race at campaign stops in all sixty-seven counties leading up to the May 1 primary election.[42] The same Klan members who supported Patterson in 1958 were much more enthusiastic about Wallace in 1962. He carried fifty-six of those counties.

Wallace was a New Deal–inspired Southern populist, a demagogue first and a segregationist second—a bit like former Louisiana Governor Huey Long.[43] There is no question that he made racist statements on the path to power, but it is more difficult to assign a simple label to his entire career. "I was a friend of Malcom [X]," journalist Mike Wallace said. "I was a friend of Dr. King. I'm a friend of Jesse [Jackson]'s. For me to say that George Wallace was not a racist . . . when you get a little older, and when you get a little perspective on things, I do believe that he was not."[44] While Governor Wallace reflected the views of the majority of his era, it was disappointing that he transformed himself not as a force for good during the civil rights era but against its aims. His decision to become a segregation hardliner was based on political pragmatism.[45] It was a path to getting ahead for which he paid a heavy price. He knew it was wrong, and he repented after his near-assassination in 1972, publicly asking for forgiveness at Martin Luther King Jr.'s Dexter Avenue Baptist Church in Montgomery and serving as a model for others in the South.[46] In the late 1970s he broke down during a meeting with John Lewis at Lewis's mother's house. "I've come to ask for your forgiveness," he said, while they held hands and prayed together.[47] But Wallace never retracted his earlier statements. He simply spoke less and less about race.[48] The chronic pain he lived with from the bullet wounds he received in 1972 forced him to empathize with those who suffered for civil rights.[49]

The Governor's Mansion at 1142 South Perry Street was open to the public for tours seven days a week.[50] Wallace was sworn in on the same steps as Jefferson Davis, just yards from the Senate chamber where legislators voted to secede in 1861.[51] In his inaugural address, he proclaimed "segregation today, segregation tomorrow, segregation forever."[52] The stance instantly made Wallace a conservative leader before Barry Goldwater or Ronald Reagan cast the mold of what a modern conservative was.[53] Whereas Reagan's soothing Hollywood style softened his message, Wallace was a truer reflection of the common man who struggled to earn a living, support his family, go to church, and pay his taxes.[54] "Daddy viewed not fighting back as a weakness," his daughter Peggy reflected.[55] He brought his instincts as a boxer into the political arena. Yet he always wondered whether acts of violence such as the bombing at the 16th Street Baptist Church in Birmingham on September 15, 1963, might have been triggered by something he said. The possibility deeply troubled him.[56]

President Kennedy nationalized the Alabama National Guard and ordered them to prepare to enforce racial integration at the University of Alabama on June 11, 1963, when Vivian Malone and James Hood were scheduled to register as its first two Black students. Wallace was well aware of what was to occur that day; the University of Alabama gave him regular updates, and he had attended at least one Board of Trustees meeting.[57] In an extraordinary recorded conversation with Attorney General Robert Kennedy, Wallace said he had supported John F. Kennedy for vice president in 1956, rallied the South to defeat Estes Kefauver in the Alabama delegation, and supported and raised money for Kennedy in 1960. But he had a warning for the president: "Both national parties should begin to consider the attitude of the people of our section of our country, and I feel that we have been kicked around by both parties, and especially our own national Democratic Party. If it were not for Southerners, you never could have organized, and even Southerners were responsible for the so-called New Deal program that Mr. Roosevelt and Mr. Kennedy, and of course you all support. We feel that in the days when states like Michigan and Ohio vote Republican, we vote solidly Democratic all the way through, and we haven't been paid too much attention to."[58]

Wallace and Kennedy agreed to settle integration at the University of Alabama without force. They would not use the media to stir up unrest and would try to keep integration a local issue. "I can assure you this, that I do not want you to use troops," Wallace said, "and I can assure you that there is not any effort on my part to make a show of resistance and to be overcome." "Well, I am glad to hear that," Kennedy responded. "I think it would be a mistake to try [to] create any controversy. Whatever I say, I want to make sure you approve of it."[59] Their plans were reviewed by Wallace and President Kennedy aboard the latter's helicopter a few weeks later.[60] Even the glass bottles had been removed from campus vending machines out of fear they could be thrown.[61] Fulfilling his campaign promise, Wallace stood in the schoolhouse door and made a brief statement against integration before moving aside during the largely scripted event.[62] He got what he wanted, and so did the Department of Justice. They had learned their lesson after the riots at the University of Mississippi in September 1962, when James Meredith was admitted.

Wallace made his first run for the presidency in 1964, after he saw how popular Goldwater was in Alabama.[63] His campaign was a limited effort, designed only to test the waters. He raised $360,000 and entered three carefully selected Democratic primaries: Wisconsin, Indiana, and Maryland.[64] The race ignited his passion and ambition for a national political movement.[65] Wisconsin Governor John Reynolds said that if Wallace won more than 100,000 votes, the state's image would be tarnished. Wallace received 266,984 votes and also won 29.8 percent of the vote in Indiana and fifteen of twenty-three counties in Maryland. He had proved he could win votes outside the South, and that the discontent with the Establishment that motivated figures like Strom Thurmond to campaign for Goldwater was a national phenomenon.[66] If race had been Wallace's only issue, the passage of the landmark 1964 Civil Rights Act and other legislation would have put him too far out of step with the times, and he could never have gained a national stage. He stood for something more.[67]

Governor Wallace spent more money than any previous Alabama leader while also promoting low taxes. He authorized the construction of four junior colleges and fifteen new trade schools.[68] He launched a $100 million public school construction program that included a free textbook policy, building upon his earlier work to establish George C. Wallace Community College in 1949 as a freshman state legislator. He approved the largest road-building project in state history, cleaned up waterways, and built nursing homes and medical clinics while gradually shifting his views on race to suit the tenor of the time.[69] While in office, he also tried unsuccessfully to change the clause in the state's 1901 constitution that prohibited him from running for a second four-year term.[70] He steamrolled the bill through the House, but it was held up by a filibuster in the Senate. Three Democratic state senators voted with the Republicans to sustain the filibuster; none of the three was reelected. They had sacrificed their state political careers to stop Wallace.[71] The idea of becoming a private citizen no longer in the center of the action depressed him. He had no hobbies, few vices, and zero interest in doing anything besides politics.[72] So he importuned his wife, Lurleen, to run for governor in 1966 in order to continue the political dynasty. She did and won, defeating nine male opponents as the first woman to run the state and only the third in U.S. history. What followed was surely one of the most unusual terms of office in modern American political history.[73]

Lurleen had the assets of the Wallace name but few of its liabilities. She had raised three children, held her sometimes volatile marriage together, and overcome cancer earlier in the decade. George remained close by as her "number one assistant" to ensure continuity and a public platform for his next run for national office.[74] While it was not her idea to run, once she won, she grew into the role.[75] Always well-dressed in public, in private she smoked, drank coffee and an occasional beer, and adored hunting and fishing. Lurleen had a great smile, and while she sacrificed so much for her husband's political career, she sacrificed even more to ensure his future after the state constitution was finally modified in 1968 to allow a governor to serve two consecutive terms.[76] She was a popular, authentic Alabamian who could relate to the hardships and simple pleasures that people faced in the Deep South.[77] As Peggy described it, "Mrs. George C. Wallace became Mrs. Lurleen Burns Wallace and finally just Miss Lurleen."[78]

Lurleen's husband remained the most powerful figure in Montgomery, and her election established him as the most self-confident Southern politician since Jefferson Davis.[79] Some of her rhetoric even resembled his, including her inaugural address, in which she criticized federal judges and "eggheads" in Washington who "proclaim to the world that 'God is dead.'"[80] She did initiate some programs, including mental health care reform and modernizing state parks.[81] But she had a secret. In June 1967, she told friend Catherine Steineker that she thought her stomach problems were evidence that her cancer had returned. She made a public announcement that she would seek treatment.[82] She kept smoking a pack of Benson & Hedges a day, even though it aggravated her condition. The next month, surgeons removed an egg-sized malignant growth from her colon. The Wallaces moved into a two-bedroom apartment across the street from M. D. Anderson Hospital in Houston.[83] She was able to relax and become her old fun-loving self in Houston, when she was away from the pressure of office and ceremony of duty at home. She loved seeing the Houston Astros play the Chicago Cubs at the new Astrodome, where she could not pass up a hot dog. Whether it was reckless or admirable, Lurleen hid her constant pain so the governor's office could continue to function and she could say she was fine. Her condition remained a secret, one that was easier to keep with her treatment taking place in Houston.

George Wallace first discussed running for president on a third-party ticket in 1966. He did not think either major party would nominate him.[84] His top aides, including Seymore Trammell, Cecil Jackson, Earl Morgan, and Bill Jones, all agreed. They believed Johnson would run for reelection, meaning much of Wallace's political support could come from Goldwater Republicans. From a checkerboard of state party organizations, some of which were already using the name, Wallace cobbled together the national American Independent Party (AIP) as a vehicle for his 1968 presidential campaign.[85] Running as a third-party candidate would allow him to criticize both major parties.[86] His central issues were big government, public education, busing, and crime—effectively, opposition to civil rights and most of Johnson's Great Society programs. Race was a common thread, although by 1968 it was more implicit than explicitly stated. That was an intentional move to maximize his popularity outside the South.

Wallace began to make his transition beyond his earlier fiery rhetoric. He was still a boxer. He was scrappy, took risks, weighed opponents' weaknesses, and knew when to conserve energy and when to become aggressive. He unofficially launched his campaign while appearing on *Meet the Press* on April 23, 1967, saying "there is more chance that I will run than I will not run."[87] Rather than focus on the primaries, he began trying to get on state ballots, especially in more restrictive states like California and Ohio.[88] A year before national convention season, he had 72 percent name recognition according to Gallup; Goldwater had 61 percent at a similar point in his 1964 campaign. Wallace made his candidacy official on February 8, 1968, during a press conference at the Sheraton Park Hotel in Washington, DC. "For over a year," he told reporters, "I have repeatedly stated that one of the existing political parties must offer the people of this country a real choice in 1968, or that I would lead a political effort which would in fact offer this choice."[89] Seymore Trammell came up with the idea of campaign pledges. A supporter would pledge a donation and then be billed for it in monthly installments. Shortly after he declared his intention to run, Wallace had more than 21,500 pledges signed up. Another key part of his fundraising apparatus was the traveling rally. A six o'clock dinner would be held for $25 a plate, followed by a show that was part county fair and part musical performance, while "Wallace girls," his brigade of young female volunteers, passed the yellow plastic buckets.[90]

Wallace ran on the conventional themes of faith, flag, and family. If it worked in Alabama, he thought, it could work outside the South.[91] His target voter was the "little man," the "ordinary American," who more often than not was white, blue-collar, and rural. Yet since his support came from pockets all over the country, his followers were difficult to stereotype. Wallace supporter and *Montgomery Advertiser* journalist Joe Azbell used space in the newspaper to highlight achievements by African Americans to counter the popular image that they dominated only coverage of criminal activity. Azbell, who was also a Wallace speechwriter, was credited by Martin Luther King Jr. with providing the critical coverage that made the Montgomery bus boycotts a success. He was the only journalist to initially cover the arrest of Rosa Parks for violating the floating color barrier on city buses.[92] Wallace shared Azbell's conviction that Black Alabamians deserved better.[93]

Early in his campaign, Wallace understood he had a chance to deny both major parties an outright victory, meaning he might be able to cut a deal with the candidate closest to his views.[94] He expressed his values in terms of rights, freedoms, and individualism.[95] By 1968 he was using something close to a class-based message that elites—which, for Wallace, included the national media, government bureaucrats, and academics—did not understand.[96] That was fine: he was not addressing them. His supporters were concerned about a rise in federal activism, only part of which had to do with race.[97] Wallace understood that times had changed, even in Alabama, and he was angling for the support of people like himself—a former taxi cab driver. His anti-elitist rhetoric did not propose to shrink the bureaucracy.[98]

As Wallace ramped up his campaign, Lurleen's health got worse. "I won't be here a year from now," she told Catherine Steineker.[99] The chemotherapy treatments she received had eased the pain caused by her tumor, but they made her ill. She made no public appearances after the January opening of her husband's campaign office in Houston and was determined that her declining health must not affect his speaking schedule. When he was not on the road, George stayed in their Houston apartment and communicated with his campaign staff almost exclusively by telephone.[100] By late April, Lurleen's cancer had spread to her lungs and liver, and she weighed less than eighty pounds. She began to plan her funeral service with the help of Rev. John Vickers, insisting on a closed casket despite the Southern tradition of viewing the deceased.[101] No longer able to exert her usual meticulous control over her appearance, she shut herself off and would see only her closest friends and family. On the campaign stump in the last week of April, Wallace insisted Lurleen was "upbeat and in good humor" and that her sickness was not cancer but the side effects of cancer treatment.[102]

On May 6, Lurleen pleaded with George to stay with her. "I feel like something's going to happen to me," she said. "George, I have faith there is an afterlife."[103] He was ill at ease in the hospital, pacing the floors and feeling useless. "I heard her say a little prayer," George wrote later, "'Oh, God, please let me live, because I want to live. But if I can't live, please help me face whatever I have to face.'"[104] At around ten-thirty in the evening, she fell into a coma, and he asked her to squeeze his hand if she heard him. She did. At around midnight, her grip loosened. She no longer squeezed his hand, and her breathing became deeper and more spaced out.[105] With her family by her side, Governor Lurleen Wallace drew her last breath at 12:34 A.M., after Alabama's television stations had signed off. Her husband sat on the edge of her bed and stroked her hair while tenderly whispering, "Oh, how much we love you. Goodbye, sweetheart."[106] She was forty-one and only the second person, after Jefferson Davis, to lie in state in Alabama's capitol rotunda.[107] Lieutenant Governor Albert Brewer was sworn in to replace her. "As a widow, I am acutely aware of the awesome burden thrust upon a surviving parent," Coretta Scott King wrote to Wallace. "It is as a Christian mother that I express my family's heartfelt sympathy to you and yours."[108]

Within seventy-two hours of her funeral, the couple's things were moved from the governor's mansion into a modest ranch-style house in the Montgomery suburbs that George and Lurleen had bought the previous year. He visited her gravesite daily and sent the children away to be cared for by friends and family. He wept openly. Lurleen had sacrificed everything for him, even comfort in her final months. Finally, after mourning for five weeks, he did the only thing that could get his mind off her: he announced a return to the campaign trail, hoping that the energy he drew from big crowds would return him to his old self.[109] Politics was the only thing he knew, and the only thing that could get him back in a routine.[110] He believed it's what she would have wanted him to do.[111] His daughter

Peggy remembered that "down-and-out white folks who had worked all their lives, gone to church on Sundays, never asked for a handout, and still took their hats off when the flag went by were furious. Daddy was no longer just another presidential candidate with the right ideas, he was part of the family."[112]

Wallace took a short break after Robert Kennedy's assassination, but on June 12 he was back campaigning, going from Tennessee through Virginia and the Carolinas, down to Florida, then back through the Deep South to Texas. He fidgeted, did not hide his sharp twang, and occasionally spit in his handkerchief during speeches. He carried plastic-tipped White Owl cigars in his breast pocket.[113] "'How you doin', pardner?' he said, singling out people in the crowd, one hand in his coat pocket," Peggy wrote. "He was cocky, snapping and strutting, a small, slight man with dynamic energy and tremendous charisma, the Confederacy's very own Napoleon."[114] A band would whip the crowd into a frenzy with a tune like "Are You from Dixie?" and then Wallace would give his classic speech about "briefcase toting bureaucrats who can't park a bicycle straight."[115]

At the end of the speech, the crowd would surge forward and try to reach up and touch him. His security people had to keep a grip on his belt to prevent the crowd from carrying him off. It was a style unique in presidential politics, and its authenticity attracted millions of voters while millions of others bristled at both his style and message.[116] The Wallace campaign was the biggest third-party challenge since Teddy Roosevelt's "Bull Moose" movement in 1912.[117] As his popularity rose, so did the backlash that labeled him a fascistic redneck racist from a backward state with backward ideas.[118] What he stood for, and how the media characterized him, was far more offensive than his actual speeches in 1968. Few of those with firm opinions about him ever heard him speak. The violence that occurred at his rallies—increasingly the norm at every appearance—was often instigated by anti-Wallace protesters, not Wallace supporters, a fact often overlooked by the media.[119] The former boxer was not intimidated. Rather than interrupt Wallace's script, the protesters became part of the spectacle by directing the crowd's wrath toward themselves.[120]

The Wallace team excelled at fundraising and had an eye for marketing. During one three-day stretch in Jackson, Mississippi, Wallace collected $450,000 in checks and cash. Over 80 percent of the donations were less than $50. The Wallace fundraising operation ran like a machine, each day holding an early-morning civil club breakfast and press conference, a small lunch with big donors and another press conference, a few private minutes with local leaders in his black Ford LTD en route to an afternoon event, then a large evening dinner and rally at a church hall, hotel, or Elks lodge. The cash intake was supplemented by the selling of bumper stickers, buttons, and campaign merchandise. Even the two-man bumper sticker team had their work down to a science. In only a few seconds, one wiped the bumper and the other applied the sticker before moving on to the next car. The average pledge worker collected $257 in an evening's work, and buckets passed by the Wallace girls could rake in as much as $35,000 in a night.[121] The campaign broke new ground in grassroots organization—seeing as many voters as possible up close.[122] While many in the media despised his views, they had to admit that his folksy style and accessibility to reporters made him a compelling political figure.[123]

It was particularly impressive that he did it all with a very small personal staff. "It was the most efficient and comprehensive political organization the state of Alabama had ever seen," his son George recalled.[124] Those who worked closely with Wallace were clean cut. He liked bright young attorneys, and he let them run things. He did not get involved in campaign nuts and bolts. "Do the best thing," he told them, "and don't get in trouble and don't break the law." They knew they were under constant observation. While the national press focused on Wallace's racism, his popularity outside the South came from a focus on issues like government overreach, excessive spending, declining morality, and the "forgotten man."[125] Many of Wallace's opponents heard a racial overtone in this message—and many of his supporters did too. But that was not the whole of Wallace's appeal. The concept of the forgotten man, often attributed to Nixon, made its political debut during the New Deal but had its origins in William Graham Sumner's eponymous 1883 essay.[126] "We pass him by because he is independent, self-supporting, and asks no favors," Sumner said.[127]

While many political campaigns run out of money or go deep in debt, the Wallace campaign methodically ran a surplus. He had the energy and stamina to make up to five major appearances in a single day, and he filled VFW, Sons of Italy, Knights of Columbus, and Moose Lodge halls from coast to coast—raising cash contributions at each stop. In Boston Common, some eighteen thousand came to see him.[128] The Alabama advertising company Luckie & Forney, Inc., produced a half-hour film, *The Wallace Story*, for $500,000. It was aired on CBS and NBC, and drew $600,000 in contributions.[129] Luckie & Forney did such a good job of promoting the Wallace brand that the national media became impatient at their lack of mistakes, resorting to debased characterizations of him and his supporters to explain his rising popularity. Reporters expected the typical Wallace speech to be a tirade filled with racist slurs, but those who attended came away disappointed. The managers of the state campaigns were another story, said campaign aide Tom Turnipseed, who called them "a motley group of segregationists, southern rednecks, northern ethnics, John Birchers, corporate executives, right-wing kooks and assorted bigots."[130]

Wallace courted people who were looked down upon in the South and beyond, even criticizing the National Press Club during an appearance for not admitting women members. His supporters represented the heart of his critique of big government, that the Great Society—including expanded civil rights—had gone too far too fast. Eighty-three percent believed that integration had been pushed too quickly. Some were outright bigots, but most were not. "Many of them are union members, white collar people, and the like," Nixon said of Wallace's supporters. "Good, honest, decent Americans, who are concerned about law and order, and concerned about the fact that our foreign policy has brought us a lack of respect around the world."[131] The national media found it particularly difficult to explain how the Wallace campaign engaged voters who had crossed over from other party affiliations as well as those who did not normally participate in politics. Wallace voters were more likely to call themselves FDR Democrats than anything else. Elvis Presley, returning to live concerts after a seven-year break, had a "Wallace for President" sign at Graceland.[132]

The Wallace campaign was anti-Establishment because the Establishment had let his people down. Wallace knew how to excite his supporters while keeping the subject of race in the background and instead focusing on local control over schools, protecting private property rights, and law and order.[133] It could be said that the call for "law and order" was thinly veiled racism. But rising crime was real and measurable. Every index of crime showed an increase, from property crime to violent crime. It was not Wallace who made law and order a political issue in 1968, it was the growth of seemingly random, brutal violence.[134] A poll showed that 53 percent of Americans felt "Wallace would handle law and order the way it ought to be handled."[135] Forty-seven percent of Americans believed the best way to handle looters was to shoot them; 82 percent of Wallace supporters wanted rioters and looters shot on sight.[136]

Wallace was confident he could beat Humphrey and Nixon in the states Goldwater won in 1964 and eat into their totals in other parts of the country. At his peak in 1968 he drew 23 percent in the polls, not just because he won Alabama but because he was popular in places like Anaheim, Milwaukee, and South Boston.[137] The antigovernment, anti-elitist favorite Wallace has been greatly misunderstood. He spoke for an America that felt its familiar world slipping out of its grasp. It was not only racial hierarchies that were in danger of disappearing; Wallace's supporters felt threatened by challenges to women's traditional roles as homemakers and to the place of Christianity in the public sphere, and by a condescending media that his constituents felt romanticized small-town life while encouraging contempt for it. All of these anxieties were of a piece. All were aspects of a country they felt was vanishing before their eyes. It is far easier to dismiss Wallace with labels like "racist" than to try to understand what he stood for, why he was popular, and why every conservative who has run for the presidency since 1968 has borrowed from his style and even his policies.[138]

PART II

Summer Heat

CHAPTER FIVE

Paris

AT THE BEGINNING OF the campaign, in the wake of the Tet Offensive, the war in Vietnam was the single biggest issue for Americans. More than any other subject, it defined whether one identified more with Democrats, Republicans, or the third-party challenge of George Wallace. It shaped how voters turned out in the New Hampshire primary, and it remained the focus following Johnson's withdrawal from the election on March 31. But since Johnson remained the commander-in-chief throughout the campaign, the major candidates were limited in what they could say about Vietnam without crossing him. He was desperate to make progress in the Vietnam peace talks before the end of his presidency; but as the prospect of a quick resolution receded, the negotiators' ambitions increasingly diverged from Johnson's. They came to view the talks largely as a vehicle to get Humphrey elected president, a goal the president came less and less to share.

Following his call for peace talks on March 31, President Johnson briefed his delegation twice, on May 6 and 8, before they left Washington. Despite the accommodating tone of his March 31 speech, he approached the negotiations with extreme skepticism about the chance of any enforceable deal with the communists.[1] His lead negotiator, Averell Harriman, privately expressed doubts about the chance for peace and wondered whether the murder and bloodshed now common in North Vietnam would spread to the South.[2] Much time would be spent arguing over very little. Most of all, Johnson had very little time left to make progress before his successor would determine the future of U.S. policy toward Vietnam.

French officials had helped to facilitate the establishment of the talks even though official French policy was opposed to U.S. involvement in the Vietnam War. The French officials' view was that Vietnam was a struggle for national liberation. If a communist takeover was inevitable, then the Saigon government was not a real government since it was ultimately dependent on the U.S., which would eventually withdraw.[3]

Harriman was among those willing to make concessions to the North Vietnamese in order to make a deal.[4] Nicknamed "the crocodile" for his snappy responses during presidential meetings, Harriman was short-tempered, parsimonious, and superstitious.[5] He had a long and distinguished record, but that is precisely what concerned the South Vietnamese, who knew him as the American negotiator who specialized in making concessions to communists. Heir to a fortune estimated at $70 million and the principal shareholder of the Union Pacific Railroad, Harriman had been close to the Russians since he was FDR's emissary to Moscow at the Yalta Conference in 1945, when Winston Churchill and an exhausted and dying Franklin Roosevelt effectively gave control of Eastern Europe to Stalin.[6] In 1961, with the Laotian government teetering near collapse, the Soviet Union and the United Kingdom called for fourteen-nation talks in Geneva to stabilize the country. Harriman was chosen to lead the American delegation, and he leaned on the Soviet Union against the American ally South Vietnam. The Laos talks were the prototype for what Harriman was to do at the Paris talks in 1968. "Harriman had more experience dealing with the communists than almost any man in government," Johnson wrote in his memoirs.[7] His appointment signaled an American assumption that the Soviets would play an important part in the talks.[8] Harriman shared this assumption with Anatoly Dobrynin, the Soviet Ambassador to the U.S. "I told him," he said, "that I believed the Russians would have to play a role, at least behind the scenes, in inducing Hanoi to be reasonable. I pointed out that they [the North Vietnamese] didn't live up to the Laos Agreement for a single day."[9]

Secretary of State Dean Rusk and U.S. Ambassador to Saigon Ellsworth Bunker both lobbied Johnson to limit Harriman's authority in Paris because they were unsure how closely he would follow orders.[10] Johnson had wanted Llewellyn Thompson to join Harriman in Paris to lead the talks, to serve as a moderating influence on Harriman, but he did not want to withdraw him as ambassador to Moscow at a time when the United States still hoped to make progress on bilateral relations during the remainder of the year. As a substitute, Johnson chose Cyrus Vance to join Harriman. Vance first came to Washington in 1957 as special counsel on Senate Majority Leader Johnson's Preparedness Investigating Subcommittee.[11] In addition to serving as general counsel of the Department of Defense, he had worked on several difficult problems, foreign and domestic, including the riots in Detroit, the Cyprus crisis, and the negotiations to return the crew of the *Pueblo*.[12] The Paris negotiators were backstopped by Ellsworth Bunker, whose duty it was to keep Thieu informed in Saigon. Initially, he urged that the peace talks be delayed five or six months, until South Vietnam was stronger, but Johnson resisted. A delay would assure that no progress would be made until after he left office.[13]

The original North Vietnamese delegation in Paris consisted of about seventy personnel: eighteen official members, plus staff.[14] Nguyen Thanh Le, a veteran of the 1962 Geneva Conference on Laos, was spokesman of the delegation, and the major figures included Xuan Thuy, Minister of State; Le Duc Tho, Special Adviser to the Minister; Ha Van Lau, Ambassador and Advisor to the Minister; and Mai Van Bo, Advisor to the Minister.

The South Vietnamese established a liaison mission in Paris but were otherwise on the sidelines and dependent for information on their American allies, who assured them that the talks would concern only military matters. The mission was originally headed by Ambassador to the United States Bui Diem, but when he could no longer manage both posts, Pham Dang Lam took over.[15] Part of the reason for assigning Bui Diem had been to minimize the appearance of differences between Saigon and Washington.[16] By taking the lead in negotiations in 1954, 1962, and 1968, the U.S. had allowed Saigon to be seen as a puppet government. Unilateral American escalation of war led to unilateral American escalation of peace.

The National Liberation Front (NLF) was not officially present at the start, either, but its representatives actively pressed to be admitted.[17] Its stated goals were "peace" and the "establishment of a coalition government."[18] Saigon predicted that Harriman would begin talks with the North, shutting South Vietnam out, just as he had done in Laos in 1961–62. He seemed more comfortable negotiating with North Vietnam, with the help of his old Russian friends, than he did negotiating with South Vietnam.

The preliminary talks, held at Paris's Majestic Hotel from May 13 to mid-June, were much more limited than those in later years. The participants established the format and range of subjects to be discussed later,

but they tackled only one major substantive issue: a unilateral U.S. bombing halt.[19] The United States offered to stop all attacks over the southern portion of North Vietnam in return for a "sign" that such a cessation
would not "immediately and directly endanger" the lives of American and
allied military personnel.[20] This was arguably the only thing the United
States had to offer; otherwise, it was at a disadvantage. "I'm under steady
pressure from people who say I'm causing loss of life by not bombing,"
Johnson told Drew Pearson.[21] Not only were the North Vietnamese not
in a hurry to end a war they had been fighting since the 1940s, the United
States did not even have formal negotiating points or a specific outcome in
mind. It is unclear whether the Johnson administration hoped to negotiate
a political settlement on the premise that a military victory was infeasible,
whether it hoped to buy time at the negotiating table to seek a military
victory, or even if it had a clear Vietnam policy at all. If this preliminary
round of talks was successful, it could lead to the beginning of more substantive negotiations.

    With over half a million troops in Vietnam, perhaps Johnson sought
to keep both options open for his successor while capturing some credit
for having started the process. The only guidelines Harriman and Vance
received were "to make arrangements with the North Vietnamese representative for prompt and serious substantive talks," which included, in
order of priority, a "cessation of the bombing," "prompt talks," "serious
talks," "to take account of the interests of the South Vietnamese Government," "the expectation that North Vietnam would not attempt to
improve its military position as a result of the U.S. cessation," and "to
continue certain reconnaissance flights."[22] But they would find they had
little room to maneuver: Johnson insisted on approving everything they
proposed and often used his veto power. "I would like to stress," Vance
later recommended to Henry Kissinger, in a not-so-veiled criticism of
Johnson-era policy, "that the negotiating instructions should be stated in
over-all objective terms and the maximum flexibility should be left to the
negotiators to operate within such broad guidelines. We should seek to
avoid a situation in which every move the negotiators wish to take must
be approved in Washington and Saigon."[23]

    These were not peace talks but exploratory talks to set the terms
for stopping U.S. bombing.[24] The Americans were willing to discuss it
but wanted something in return, which Hanoi rejected, insisting that
the United States put an "immediate and final end to bombing and all

other acts of war," including aerial surveillance—and to do so "unconditionally."[25] "Until some control mechanism could be agreed to by both
sides," Johnson wrote in his memoirs, "we would have to monitor North
Vietnamese performance ourselves. That meant continuing aerial reconnaissance of the North after the bombing ended."[26] Hanoi also sought an
end to the dropping of propaganda by air, to attacks on the coast of North
Vietnam, and to violations of North Vietnamese waters. Other issues that
the United States tried to bring up included restoring the Demilitarized
Zone, stopping the infiltration of the South by the North, a halt to the
shelling of cities in the South, and a withdrawal of non-South forces from
the South.[27]

Since the end of Tet, the communists had continued to harass cities, airfields, and various allied installations with rocket and mortar fire.[28]
During the first week of the talks, Saigon came under a fierce attack
from Chinese-made 122 mm. rockets that were so inaccurate that they
killed civilians indiscriminately.[29] The attacks, usually at night, continued throughout the Paris talks at random intervals of a few days to a few
weeks, using rockets transported along the Saigon River to the outskirts
of the city, where they were launched from portable tubes.[30] "Any move
we made that we had not made the week before would be regarded by our
critics as 'escalation,'" Johnson wrote in his memoirs. "But Hanoi could
send men by the thousands down the Ho Chi Minh Trail, could carry
out regimental attacks, and could hit Saigon, yet no one would mention
'escalation.'"[31] Johnson already had softened his position from calling for
an end of infiltration to simply reducing it, with no firm targets in mind.
While Americans did not see this as a substantial change, it was the type of
unilateral concession that irritated allies, especially the South Vietnamese.
The United States seemed so desperate for Hanoi to make any compromise at all that it even mistook regrouping and resupplying as a lull in
infiltration.[32] American POWs in Hoa La Prison, known as the "Hanoi
Hilton," started to wonder if the stopping and starting of bombing was
intentional, to allow North Vietnam to recover.[33]

Chalmers Roberts wrote in the *New York Times* that the United States
was willing to accept a coalition government in Saigon that included
members of the National Liberation Front. This drew a forceful denial
from Dean Rusk, leading Drew Pearson to think the idea must have been
circulating among Johnson's advisors. "I suspect Roberts jumped the gun
on something Averell [Harriman] was planning to spring later at the Paris

truce talks," he wrote in his diary.[34] Despite Johnson's insistence that he would seek "peace with honor," Saigon believed that negotiations had been forced too soon so Johnson could secure a hasty agreement before his term ended. But with Hanoi taking the opposite approach, serious observers thought there would be no final settlement for years.[35]

After making no progress at all with the North Vietnamese, the Americans began reaching out to Soviet diplomats in Paris to clarify what they were looking for in exchange for a bombing halt. This did not need to be a formal agreement; a "sign" would do.[36] Reaching out to the Soviets was a way to overcome the American lack of diplomatic representation in Hanoi.[37] Harriman had established himself as the U.S. liaison to the Soviet diplomatic corps, including Ambassador to France Valerian Zorin, Chargé d'Affaires Valentin Oberemko, and First Minister Sergei Bogomolov.[38] He believed a final settlement was probably not possible without their substantial participation.[39] The Soviets urged Harriman to study the NLF's proposals, which Harriman described as "generally acceptable" but "full of contradictions."[40] Zorin suggested that the Americans ask directly for private meetings to occur in parallel with the plenary sessions. Hanoi might reject the idea at first, but then change its mind.[41] When they did reject the proposal for private talks, Harriman became concerned that the plenary sessions could drift on without purpose.[42] This was confirmed when the American delegation indicated they would consider a willingness by the North Vietnamese to discuss DRV actions such as the "firing of artillery from and across the DMZ," ground attacks "launched from the DMZ area" and the "massive increase in infiltration" to South Vietnam as the "signs" the Americans asked for in return for a bombing halt.[43] But rather than discuss this proposal, the North Vietnamese claimed it was the United States that first violated the DMZ, and that if such violations ceased the DMZ would return to normal. Oberemko defended Hanoi's position, saying that the United States was a great power and had more freedom to negotiate.[44]

To Hanoi, the presence of American troops in Vietnam was a clear violation of the 1954 Geneva Accords, while the presence of North Vietnamese forces in South Vietnam was not.[45] Discussion of the American proposals could begin only after the United States made a firm commitment to stop the bombing over North Vietnam. A mere announcement was not enough; the United States had to "fully implement" a bombing halt in order for it to be considered "unconditional." That shift prompted the Americans to drop mentions of "reciprocity" and say they would accept a sign of "restraint" instead.[46] The North Vietnamese position varied from session to session, leaving it unclear whether a "determination" to stop the bombing was enough, or whether the bombing halt must take effect before serious negotiations could begin. Hanoi also added another dimension of confusion. In late May, Prime Minister Pham Van Dong told the National Assembly that all North Vietnamese have a right to fight everywhere in Vietnam, contradicting the regime's earlier assurances that there were no communists fighting in South Vietnam. Yet the North Vietnamese delegation adamantly refused to acknowledge that there were any North Vietnamese soldiers in the South.[47]

On May 30, North Vietnamese Politburo member Le Duc Tho arrived in Paris unannounced, as a senior counsellor to the delegation.[48] "Ducky," as Henry Kissinger later called him, did not modify the North Vietnamese negotiating position, but his presence was an upgrade in representation that clearly signaled something. It did not go unnoticed that Tho stopped in Moscow on the way to Paris or that his arrival in Paris coincided with increased Soviet influence over the talks.[49]

On June 5, Premier Alexei Kosygin sent a letter to Johnson that represented the Soviet government's first official effort to insert itself prominently into the subject of peace in Vietnam since February 1967, when it had tried to persuade British Prime Minister Harold Wilson to intercede with Johnson to call for a bombing halt.[50] Johnson wanted to keep the Soviets close to the negotiations in the hope of improving bilateral relations, leading to progress toward arms negotiations.[51] The letter from Kosygin revealed that the Soviets had "grounds" to believe that a bombing halt "could" contribute to a breakthrough in the negotiations and produce "prospects" for a peace agreement.[52] The Soviets would make every effort to assist the negotiations because they hoped to establish superiority in the region over communist rival China.[53] Harriman could not remember a time when they had been more direct.[54] Johnson asked for input from his top advisors and, he wrote in his memoirs, "each of us regarded the note from Moscow as significant."[55] For someone like Harriman, it was easier to negotiate with the Soviets, whom he had known since World War II, than with the North Vietnamese.[56]

Despite what he wrote in his memoirs, however, Johnson remained skeptical—as did Rusk, who "cut the ground" from under Clifford when he expressed support for Kosygin's letter. "The net effect of this was extremely hard line, turning Kosygin down," Harriman wrote, "and Clifford and I both thought we lost an opportunity to get the Soviet Government on the hook in a way that would be most valuable in future negotiations."[57] Moscow did not seem to have as much control over Hanoi as it sometimes implied. Johnson recalled that "I still remembered vividly Moscow's assurance late in 1965 that if we stopped bombing the North for twelve to twenty days, 'something good will happen.' On that basis we stopped bombing, not for twelve or twenty but for thirty-seven days—and nothing happened."[58] Nonetheless, he agreed to try again. In his response on June 11, he said that the United States would be willing to stop the bombing over North Vietnam if the Hanoi delegation would assure the Americans that there would be "no adverse military consequences to our own and the allied forces."[59]

It turned out that the Americans could arrange private talks, separate from the publicized plenary meetings, with someone directly connected to decision makers in Hanoi.[60] These organized private contacts emanated from two earlier efforts: brief visits outside the scheduled plenary sessions, and informal conversations during tea breaks. In each case, the Americans took the initiative after receiving encouragement from the French and the Soviets. The tea break conversations emanated from a "coffee break and refreshments, which the French government provided," during the sixth plenary meeting on May 31.[61] Both sides were more relaxed when talking informally. "Continue the fruitful public struggle," North Vietnamese Deputy Prime Minister Nguyen Duy Trinh instructed his delegation on June 3, "while preparing for starting, at a propitious moment, behind-the-scenes talks concurrently with public talks."[62]

By mid-June the tea breaks had grown to forty-five minutes and become a substantive forum of their own. When Harriman suggested formalizing these encounters into private side talks, Xuan Thuy immediately responded favorably, stating that it was customary to have both larger and private talks, and the North Vietnamese would consider the suggestion. "We stand for private contacts for probing purposes, not yet for bargaining," Hanoi instructed him on June 15.[63] The North Vietnamese also accepted American delegation member William Jorden's dinner invitation to his counterpart, Nguyen Than Le. Their dinner on June 18, though not a top-level meeting, provided the first progress of any kind in private talks.[64] Out of the public eye, the North Vietnamese were willing to discuss a range of topics. Le did not deny the presence of North Vietnamese troops in the South and even hinted at a willingness to discuss political issues in South Vietnam. Previously, the DRV had refused to discuss the Saigon government except to call it illegitimate and insist on its overthrow. Le asked Jorden what Harriman meant by "appropriate time and under the appropriate circumstances" for a bombing halt. Jorden explained the American position of mutual restraint and outlined specific steps that Hanoi could take to end the bombing over North Vietnam. This was the first time the DRV departed from flat denials and refusals to discuss American statements, and asked what the U.S. delegation meant.[65]

The dinner almost immediately bore fruit. During the tea break on June 19, Thuy and Tho said they were considering the American proposal for more regular private talks.[66] In the previous twelve days, rocket attacks in Saigon had killed more than a hundred civilians and injured more than four hundred, and Harriman and Vance reminded them of the need for North Vietnamese reciprocity in exchange for a bombing halt, to which the DRV riposted that it was the Americans who had escalated by intensifying the bombing.[67] Thuy suggested that what communist forces did in South Vietnam was beyond his control. Three days later, while Harriman was visiting Washington, the Soviets surfaced again, with Dobrynin telling him that the North Vietnamese were ready to begin private talks. Columnist Drew Pearson asked Johnson on June 22 whether Harriman was optimistic about a breakthrough. "He is not as optimistic as Clark Clifford, nor as pessimistic as I am," Johnson replied. "I don't think anything will come of it though Clark thinks we're making some progress." He had no idea the negotiations would become a major campaign issue that fall.

When Harriman returned to Paris, the second phase of the peace talks began. This phase, lasting until early October, saw the first private negotiations, in which both sides elaborated proposals that went beyond their public positions. The sessions at the Majestic continued, however, because they provided cover for the secret meetings, where the real substance was discussed. The press's lack of interest made it easier to manage potential leaks. Secret meetings had another advantage as well. The U.S. delegation assumed that any official venue provided by the French government was bugged. At one point, seeing workers hanging around in brand-new coveralls, Harriman ordered the French, "You get those damned goons away, and don't tell me they aren't security people."[68]

The second phase of talks also saw Saigon grow increasingly mistrustful of Harriman and his team. Ninety National Assembly deputies signed a petition seeking clarification of American intentions in Paris. "As usual," Bui Diem wrote in his memoirs, "we had not been consulted about these talks and were not to be formally included in them. We were hard pressed to explain why it was that the Americans were talking to the North Vietnamese."[69] He was upset at not being privy to points that would be raised in future negotiating sessions in Paris, even though the American negotiating team assured him the United States was telling him everything—which the Americans knew they weren't.[70] Ellsworth Bunker, the U.S. ambassador in Saigon, had been asked by Harriman not to brief Thieu on discussions related to a political settlement in South Vietnam.[71] In addition to his concern over that, Bunker was skeptical of the proposal to stop the bombing before beginning serious negotiations.[72] He thought Saigon would view that procedure as a backdoor to NLF participation in the peace negotiations, and that giving in on a point of such importance to the other side would make the United States look weak to Hanoi.[73] The NLF had insisted on independent approval of whatever agreement was concluded with Hanoi, while Xuan Thuy continued to demand recognition of the NLF, in addition to an unconditional bombing halt, as prerequisites for further talks.[74]

Cyrus Vance, at a tea break on June 26, offered an American concession: the United States would stop the bombing of the North on a "date certain" that would be communicated in advance, in exchange for the opening of private talks.[75] The North Vietnamese did not dismiss this proposal. They also showed new restraint in the fighting: starting about mid-June, U.S. combat deaths fell from 300 a week to around 175 a week. At the same time, however, U.S. military intelligence showed that infiltration had reached an all-time high. More NVA units were in the Saigon area than ever before, and the proportion of NVA soldiers assigned to Vietcong units had grown from 25 percent to 70 percent. These trends were partly in response to heavy communist losses in the fierce fighting that followed the Tet Offensive at the beginning of the year. Still, it was a shift, and each side tried to interpret such shifts whenever they occurred. The U.S. negotiators in Paris hoped to take advantage by proposing new peace terms.[76]

The North Vietnamese, however, wanted to more fully understand the conditions. Vance stated that the United States wanted to discuss such things as restoring the DMZ, reducing infiltration into the South, and ending attacks on the populations of southern cities.[77] While the North Vietnamese admitted that this new approach suggested some new flexibility in the American position, it still meant reciprocity. Vance emphasized that the United States was merely asking for an "understanding" and not reciprocity, meaning that Hanoi would agree to discuss certain subjects in private talks prior to the bombing halt. He said the United States was no longer insisting on conditions prior to a bombing halt, only on agreement of subjects to be discussed afterward.[78] The Soviets were uncertain whether the United States and the DRV could agree on this in advance.[79] Yet as evidence of the DRV's seriousness, Zorin said Hanoi would release three American POWs in response to an entreaty by Harriman, who was coming under increasing pressure to document the number and condition of American POWs in North Vietnam.[80] Creighton Abrams, newly promoted commander of the military assistance command, Vietnam (MACV), considered the release a direct appeal to the American people by North Vietnam.[81] The next day, Hanoi did indeed announce the release of three American pilots. It was obvious that Zorin had consulted with the North Vietnamese and was using the prisoner release to build up his own importance in the negotiations.[82]

The Soviets, who appeared to be well-informed about the Paris talks, pressed Johnson administration officials to get them moving. Ambassador Dobrynin met with Secretary of State Dean Rusk on July 8 and encouraged him to have faith in the word of the Soviet Union. Dobrynin reiterated that Kosygin's letter to Johnson in June was "extremely important" and that in his experience the Politburo never used phrases like "have grounds to believe," meaning the expectation of a North Vietnamese response, without good reason. Rusk said that the question was not his faith in the Soviets but the clarity of their message, and the United States would always give the Soviet perspective strong consideration.[83]

Two days later, during a tea break on July 10, the North Vietnamese argued that the recent pause in rocket attacks on Saigon was the indication of "good will" that Harriman had been seeking.[84] But when the U.S. delegation tried to clarify whether the lull would continue in exchange for some American de-escalatory measure, Xuan Thuy would not say.[85] The two sides agreed to have another private meeting on July 15, where they would discuss further de-escalatory measures such as ending all B-52 attacks.[86] That marked the beginning of what the United States termed Phase 1 / Phase 2, in which, while delicately avoiding any talk of reciprocity, each side discussed what could take place in Phase 1 in order to lead to more substantive talks in Phase 2.[87] The private meeting on July 15 also marked the first time the two sides raised the possibility of South Vietnamese government participation in the talks.[88]

Until then, the North had refused even to acknowledge the puppet government of Nguyen Van Thieu. The North's ally, the National Liberation Front, pejoratively known as the Vietcong, claimed it was the sole legitimate government in the South. The irony was that the NLF's actions caused suffering for the very people it claimed to be fighting for. Most of the victims of Vietcong attacks were innocent civilians killed by mines, rocket attacks, ambushes, or burning down houses and villages.[89] The NLF's Liberation News Agency was Hanoi's diplomatic and propaganda agent, even though some in the West bought into the claims of legitimacy.[90]

During the meeting, the United States proposed other de-escalatory actions it wanted to discuss during the second phase of the talks, which would follow a U.S. bombing halt.[91] These included restoration of the DMZ (including the cessation of shelling across the border as well as the movement of personnel and equipment); no increase in U.S. or DRV force levels following cessation (a significant modification because it allowed the DRV to replace personnel and equipment, just not an "increase"); the beginning of serious talks; the inclusion of Saigon in the talks as well as whoever else the DRV wanted (a way of including the NLF without mentioning them by name); no attacks on Southern cities; and American consideration of other actions the North might wish to raise.[92]

Lau pressed hard for a unilateral stop to all bombing and complained that the Americans had proposed nothing new. He expressed the North's concern that the American emphasis on the DMZ meant that the U.S. planned to make it a permanent border between North and South, thus securing the South's future. Matters regarding South Vietnam should be addressed to the National Liberation Front—as though this group had no relation to the North—an option that was totally unacceptable to the South. The idea that the NLF was an independent popular uprising against the fascist government in South Vietnam was simply propaganda.[93] Lau continued to emphasize the need for unilateral American action, with the hope, but no guarantee, that the North might reciprocate. But the North continued to reject any agreement based on reciprocity. Since the DRV considered the United States the aggressor, all acts of war from the American side must stop before any de-escalatory action by the North could even be discussed.[94]

But in the days that followed, the Northern delegation suggested several times that the American proposals were a starting point.[95] Ha Va Lau told a Canadian diplomat that the rocket attacks had stopped not only on Saigon but also on U.S. forces immediately south of the DMZ; he asked whether this was the type of signal the United States was looking for from the North. Xuan Thuy made similar points during an interview with journalist David Schoenbrun on July 16. A day later, the DRV foreign ministry hinted in a memorandum that its position on Saigon's participation in the peace talks might be changing. Rather than insist that the matter be addressed to the National Liberation Front, the DRV now said that any political settlement in South Vietnam should be based on a "right to self-determination."[96] But Hanoi, as the "injured party," backed by the Soviets, still insisted on a bombing halt before any progress could be made.[97]

In the midst of a busy week in Paris, Johnson set off for Honolulu to meet with Thieu, the final opportunity for a U.S.-Vietnamese huddle prior to the conventions and the formal start of the presidential campaign. Thieu had wanted a state visit to Washington but, informed it was out of the question, settled for an official meeting in Honolulu.[98] Visiting an American aircraft carrier in the Gulf of Tonkin a week earlier, he had told reporters he thought the United States might begin to withdraw some troops from South Vietnam in 1969.[99] But this statement could be misinterpreted as saying he thought the war could be wound down by then. He meant only that the South Vietnamese could take over a greater share of the fighting. In the spirit of those comments, he told Johnson in Honolulu that he was interested in developing his own private talks with Hanoi and the NLF. Johnson was eager to see him do so—especially if the result could be a step toward peace.[100] Thieu tried to get a commitment from the United States that it would not agree to a bombing halt until all North Vietnamese troops were withdrawn from South Vietnam.[101] That "would have constituted a major hardening of our position," Clifford wrote in his memoirs. "Yet the Paris talks seemed far away from Honolulu, and no one wanted to have a confrontation with Thieu over what amounted to a theoretical point."[102] Johnson assured Thieu that the United States would not accept a coalition government with the NLF in Saigon and the war would not be de-escalated.[103] Thieu left the conference believing he had a firm agreement that the United States would not undertake a unilateral bombing halt.

In the United States, reactions to the Honolulu summit were very favorable except among those seeking to separate themselves from Johnson on the issue of Vietnam.[104] Clark Clifford was less pleased; he believed the talks might have sunk Humphrey for good.[105] "We had gained nothing in return," he said, "not even a vague acceptance of the need for greater flexibility in Paris."[106] The communiqué following the conference affirmed that South Vietnam "should be a full participant playing a leading role in discussions concerning the substance of a final settlement."[107]

This harder language was met with harder language by the North. In an interview he gave to Murrey Marder of the *Washington Post* on August 1, Lau commented, "Recently the situation has shown that military action in South Vietnam has decreased since May. I wonder if Mr. Johnson is aware of this situation?"[108] Harriman and Vance had agreed to stop the bombing of North Vietnam on July 29 if Hanoi agreed to not take advantage. They thought their proposal that, following the bombing halt, substantive talks with the participation of both Saigon and "any South Vietnamese elements" the DRV wanted would satisfy Johnson's requirement for reciprocity, since Hanoi had shown military restraint during June and July.[109] But according to MACV intelligence, the restraint was an illusion: Hanoi had used those two months to move supplies and personnel and to regroup following earlier losses.

"It was the right proposal at the wrong time," Clifford wrote in his memoirs. "The President would have none of it. . . . 'The enemy is using my own people as dupes,' he said bitterly."[110] Johnson asked Rusk to hold a press conference to knock down the idea of making the U.S. negotiating position any more flexible. Harriman was furious. "I believe the failure of the President to stop all bombing of North Vietnam in late July or early August (as we recommended) is an historic tragedy of possibly wide consequences," he wrote in a private memorandum for his files.[111] "Later I found out that Hubert Humphrey had prepared a memorandum of his own position which included stopping the bombing."[112]

The *New York Times*, however, reported that Harriman and Vance knew the "lull" was not genuine; Humphrey and Clifford had used it as a ploy to convince Johnson, who called the Harriman-Vance proposal a "conspiracy" that "stank to high heaven."[113] Coming so soon after the Honolulu summit, the proposal also would undermine Thieu and demoralize South Vietnam. The other problem was that once the bombing stopped, it would be very difficult to advocate its resumption unless Hanoi committed a major provocation. Bunker argued that a bombing halt would signal weakness to Hanoi at a time when he considered "that our position is strong and becoming stronger by the day." He proposed continuing the private talks in Paris.[114]

The North Vietnamese had begun to wonder whether the American delegation in Paris still spoke for Johnson.[115] Harriman and Vance tried to reassure Soviet Ambassador Zorin that the Honolulu conference did not represent an American policy change, suggesting that the bombing halt proposal served to counter the appearance that Thieu had emerged with new American guarantees.[116] Still, they said, the United States needed some indication that North Vietnam would show restraint if the bombing were stopped. Zorin replied that the Americans were failing to take advantage of the restraint Hanoi had already shown. The U.S. position probably had not changed, but in the immediate aftermath of the Honolulu conference it appeared to have hardened, and Zorin, in trying to help, asked for things Johnson was not willing to give—at least not yet.

At the next private talk between the United States and the North Vietnamese, in Paris on August 4, the DRV representatives, for the first time, agreed to discuss having Saigon represented at the peace talks. Harriman and Vance proposed that the NLF be seated with the DRV and Saigon's representatives with the United States. Neither the NLF nor Saigon would have its own delegation. The DRV said the NLF could not "sit with the DRV," that the NLF must have the "determining" voice in any settlement of political issues in South Vietnam, and that the eventual settlement must be "in accordance" with the NLF's proposal. In effect, Hanoi was now insisting that the United States recognize the NLF and admit it to the talks. Hanoi continued to claim, as it did during the Laos Accords, that the NLF was composed primarily of Southerners, even though by 1968 its new recruits were between 50 percent and 75 percent Northerners.[117] In Paris, the North Vietnamese now insisted that the NLF must not only operate its own delegation, with its own independent voice, but that this was a requirement for any satisfactory settlement.[118] French officials supported this position, and even some prominent Americans, like Harrison Salisbury of the *New York Times*, did too—despite his having lived for years in Stalinist Russia, which presumably made him better able to judge the autonomy of liberation front groups.[119]

Harriman was increasingly desperate to break the deadlock, especially as former Vice President Richard Nixon had the Republican presidential nomination locked up. Denying Nixon the White House became an even more important goal for Harriman than reaching a peace agreement.

Rusk notified him on August 8 that the administration was considering letting Harriman publicly state the our side / your side approach, which would seat the North Vietnamese and NLF on one side and the United States and Saigon on the other.[120] If Johnson approved of that, it would help move the negotiations to more substantive issues.[121]

The issue exposed how fragile the talks were up to that point. While the North Vietnamese had not rejected the our side / your side approach in private meetings, proposing it publicly could ensure its rejection, since it would force Hanoi to take a position that might be difficult to abandon later. Thieu, who also would be forced to take a public position, could be swayed by how the North Vietnamese reacted—and the makeup of our side / your side might be open to misinterpretation, especially over NLF representation and participation, which South Vietnam had consistently opposed. Some in Saigon believed the primary purpose of the new American negotiating formula was simply to allow Hanoi to admit the NLF to the talks, which previously had been defined as being between North Vietnam and the United States.[122] Thieu had hardly told anyone he was considering our side / your side, for fear of facing a firestorm of criticism for even entertaining the possibility that the NLF might be at the table.[123] Compounding the problem, Harriman interpreted Thieu's silence as agreement with the American proposal.[124] It was too risky to unveil the new four-party arrangement publicly just yet, Harriman argued; doing so could cause a breach with Thieu that could be very difficult to overcome in the remaining months of the Johnson administration.[125]

Rusk was concerned that Thieu did not share the Americans' sense of urgency. Clifford bluntly explained to Bui Diem that Thieu and South Vietnamese Vice President Nguyen Cao Ky did not understand the domestic situation in the United States.[126] The Americans, he said, had no intention of yielding their lead role in the peace talks; they wanted only to find out Hanoi's true reaction to the proposed our side / your side formula. Thieu sent Ambassador Pham Dang Lam to Paris on August 24 to make contact with Hanoi and NLF representatives, but nothing came of the effort. On August 14, Le Duc Tho returned from Hanoi, and five days later, a new offensive opened in South Vietnam, arguably to signal to Saigon and Washington that North Vietnamese and NLF battlefield resolve remained, and to show the Americans why they should cooperate in Paris.[127]

On August 17, Rusk made another proposal to Harriman and Vance. Hanoi and the United States, he suggested, could focus only on subjects of mutual interest, including mutual withdrawal, restoration of the 1954 and 1962 Geneva Accords, and other bilateral issues, while Saigon's representatives could discuss the South's political future with any parties they saw fit, including the NLF and Hanoi. The point was to separate the military and political issues, as well as to define Saigon's role in the talks. Harriman and Vance called Rusk's suggestion "constructive," but the episode created another opportunity for misunderstanding between Saigon and Washington. Bunker warned that Thieu could see the proposal as an American attempt to limit Saigon's role in the talks and allow Hanoi to decide which events were discussed in which forum and by whom. Rusk's plan might also require Saigon representatives to negotiate with the NLF, which Thieu consistently and firmly refused to do. It could cause "the most profound suspicion and even disillusionment," Bunker warned. "It would be interpreted as an abandonment of the GVN and utilized by Thieu's and Huong's domestic enemies to destroy them."[128] It was yet another moment in which Americans in Washington showed their failure to appreciate Thieu's precarious political position in his own country, even as rumors swirled of a potential coup.[129]

Bunker was also concerned that the new proposal would signal weakness and hint at an American willingness, given the right circumstances, to push Saigon aside. He saw it as a reminder that the U.S. negotiating position had constraints the others did not: Johnson fervently hoped to achieve peace in the remaining months of his term, and many around him wanted to improve Humphrey's political fortunes as well. If not for the political timing, Bunker felt, the American military position was strong enough that no additional concessions were needed.[130]

On August 19, just as the chaos in Chicago was heating up in anticipation of the formal opening of the Democratic National Convention, Vance met secretly with Lau and clarified that the United States had no new negotiating position and did not even require Hanoi to recognize Saigon before serious talks could begin. The DRV need only include Saigon before discussing subjects related to the future of South Vietnam.[131] It was a further loosening of the American requirements in response to the political timetable at home. "The U.S. government does not demand that your government recognizes the RVN as a legitimate government," Vance said, "just as the U.S. delegation does not recognize the NLF but it agrees to the participation of these two parties."[132] He merely restated the U.S. position that Saigon be present for such talks after the bombing was stopped. Lau replied that Hanoi had already said all it was going to say on the subject, but he did not reject the idea of Saigon's participation. He reminded Vance that the United States must directly engage the NLF on the future of South Vietnam.[133]

Humphrey had been developing a less rigid policy on Vietnam. Johnson was prepared to stop the bombing in exchange for an understanding of what would occur as a result. On the eve of receiving his party's nomination for president, however, Humphrey was saying simply that the bombing should be stopped. He was desperately trying to differentiate his Vietnam policy from that of the Johnson White House, but not in a way that would cause open rebellion or accusations of disloyalty to the president. He needed to do this to unify the Democratic Party, especially the left wing that so vocally supported McCarthy, McGovern, and other candidates not bound by the same loyalty to Johnson that was required of him as vice president. "I am certain," Johnson wrote in his memoirs, that "the fact that 1968 was an election year influenced Hanoi and affected the attitude of numerous Americans concerning our dealings with the North Vietnamese and our search for peace. Some officials in Moscow, and perhaps in Hanoi, may have thought it would be easier to deal with Humphrey than with Nixon." Or with Johnson in his final months.[134]

The president made the situation worse for the American negotiators in Paris with his speech of August 19, in which he restated that he had no plans to stop the bombing unless there was "good reason to believe" that Hanoi would join the United States in "de-escalating" the war. The speech showed the challenge Johnson faced in framing different messages for different audiences. While Humphrey was eager to develop his own policy, Johnson was just as eager to rein in those who might try to deviate from his. His speech was probably timed to ensure that a more radical Vietnam plank was not adopted at the convention. But these tougher American statements, intended for a domestic audience, brought the peace talks to a standstill for the rest of the month.

CHAPTER SIX

Miami

N IXON, WHO HAD WON every primary he entered, faced a smooth path to the Republican nomination. Even Humphrey said he seemed presidential. Romney had dropped out before New Hampshire, Rockefeller declared he would not be a candidate, and the party hesitated to back Reagan out of fear of another Goldwater. The smoothness with which the campaign rolled up victories made them seem nonchalant and unexciting.[1] But that was exactly why there was no reason to change any part of Nixon's strategy. Emphasizing competence and efficiency, Nixon shrewdly borrowed from rivals' positions, sewing up commitments needed to win on the first ballot. His campaign was the most thorough in history, with files on every delegate, including name, contact information, philosophy, hobbies, friends, and enemies. It was also the most expensive campaign in history, with a $36.5 million war chest; whereas the total cost of Humphrey's campaign was in the range of $16 to 18 million.[2] After losing to Kennedy in 1960, Nixon was determined never to be outspent again.[3]

That did not mean that the path to the nomination was easy. Nixon's was the only campaign that operated full-time from New Hampshire to Election Day. He adopted a number of progressive positions.[4] If he won, he would not gut the Great Society—just as Eisenhower had kept most of the New Deal.[5] Nixon believed the government had a constructive role to play in people's lives. While out of office, he had watched Republicans repudiate the creation of Medicare and Medicaid, but his personal experience of losing two siblings to tuberculosis and seeing the high costs of

medical care, including its occasional unavailability, gave him a greater understanding than most Republicans.[6] He won the support of liberals like
Daniel Patrick Moynihan for publicly proclaiming that the key to greater
social stability, especially in the cities, was better jobs.[7] His nuanced view
balanced need, pride, self-sufficiency, and the paramount importance of
working.[8] By focusing on the need for "new leadership" to tackle America's problems, he also carefully avoided offending Johnson.[9]

Nixon had learned hard lessons about running a campaign from his
dramatic losses in 1960 and 1962—before that, he had known only victories. In 1968, he also learned how to use television.[10] Harry Truman had
used it in his 1948 reelection campaign, and Eisenhower did so more fully
in 1952, but by 1968, television had changed the way candidates campaigned. "In 1960," Nixon said of his new strategy, "I felt the big speech
was the most important and I had to be up for it. Meeting committees
and politicians was next, then press conferences, and then TV. Now, we've
reversed the order."[11] If television had helped defeat him in 1960, this time
he would use the medium for his benefit.[12] "In June 1967, Bob Haldeman
gave me a memorandum on the use of media in the modern presidential
campaign," he wrote in his memoirs. Haldeman brought a new emphasis on marketing to the Nixon campaign.[13] As Pat Buchanan wrote later,
"Haldeman argued that in a presidential campaign, from Labor Day to
Election Day, a candidate might be seen in person by 1,440,000 people—
if he did six speeches a day, six days a week, for eight weeks, and had a
spectacular advance team that produced an average of 5,000 people for
every speech. However, tens of millions would see the candidate on the
evening news on any given night or on Sunday interview shows."[14] This
became the model for the campaign.[15]

"One of the operative assumptions of the 1968 team," wrote Buchanan, "was that the 1960 campaign had been mismanaged and the candidate mishandled. Not only was Nixon's writing and media staff entirely
new in 1968, we were all versed in the mistakes of 1960."[16] Rather than
having him work to the point of exhaustion, as Nixon had done in 1960,
his events and appearances could be more thoughtfully planned.[17] Fewer
but better appearances would conserve the candidate's energy; the campaign would also bypass the press so as to exert greater control over the
message that went to voters. Most journalists, having never written anything positive about Nixon, would find it difficult to come to terms with a
more seasoned, mature candidate.[18] So Nixon went around them, remov-

ing as much of the filter between him and the voters as possible. For example, the regionally produced taped television program, *The Nixon Answer*, produced by Frank Shakespeare while on leave from CBS, showed Nixon relaxed and cheerful while addressing questions in a townhall format.[19]

Nixon made other enhancements to his campaign on the road to the convention. An expanded headquarters was opened at 450 Park Avenue, at the corner of 57th Street. Kevin Phillips, a young analyst from Rep. Paul Fino's office, was brought on staff as part of an effort to go after Catholic voters in crafting a new political coalition.[20] Nixon needed to chip away at Wallace's growing support, lest Wallace deny an outright victory to either major candidate. The Humphrey campaign was trying a version of the same strategy. "Wallace was a mortal threat to us and the last best hope of the Democratic Party to hold the White House," Pat Buchanan wrote later. "You go hunting where the ducks are." As a pool of potential new Nixon supporters, Catholics outnumbered Blacks by a ratio of five to two and Jews by eight to one.[21]

Nixon's core strategy throughout the primaries had been to unite the party, not to engage in negative campaigning or attack other Republicans, even when he was attacked.[22] Following Robert Kennedy's death in June, Rockefeller had released a statement demanding that Johnson sign the crime bill, and when Nixon did not do the same, Rockefeller criticized him as weak on gun control even though Nixon supported controls on mail-order firearms. It was a more aggressive tone for Rockefeller, and it got young people energized the way they had been for Kennedy. If Rockefeller could have convinced enough Republicans that he was one of them, he might have put together an exciting campaign that fall. Nixon brushed off the attack and focused on the use of guns in crime. During an address to Republican congressional candidates on June 23 in Washington, DC, Nixon labeled the city a "crime capital" because of the two months of violence since King's death. The speech received excellent coverage in both the *Washington Post* and *Washington Star*. "We could not have gotten better coverage if I had been sitting in Ben Bradlee's chair," Pat Buchanan wrote later.[23] With his message on law and order getting through, Nixon had no need to pay attention to Rockefeller's attacks.

On July 9, Rockefeller challenged Nixon to a "battle of the polls." Each side would agree to be bound by the result of polls, which would also play a role in choosing the party's nominee at the convention. "I had never heard of such a ridiculous way to determine a party's nominee,"

Nixon wrote later. "This was clearly a last-ditch effort, born of desperation."[24] It was also evidence that Rockefeller had not done enough to woo delegates.[25] On June 12, former Eisenhower administration official Bryce Harlow urged Ike to speak out for Nixon.[26] Harlow had been visiting Eisenhower regularly on Nixon's behalf. He drafted a long memorandum in which he strongly encouraged the former president to remove any possible doubt about his feelings toward Nixon by officially endorsing him prior to the convention.[27] Nixon, too, visited Eisenhower on June 15. Eisenhower's endorsement was the most important one, as he was not only still greatly admired but, with Herbert Hoover's death in 1964, was now the only living Republican former president. But because he thought Nixon had the nomination clinched, Eisenhower preferred not to become involved politically. He was also concerned he could be criticized for endorsing Nixon after he was nominated, since that would merely affirm the convention's choice, as he had done for Goldwater in 1964.[28] Nixon, who as Eisenhower's former vice president had a different relationship with him than any other candidate, hoped he could change Ike's mind.

He got what he wanted.[29] During their visit, Eisenhower, who had become increasingly concerned about Rockefeller's courting of antiwar forces, agreed to a preconvention endorsement on July 18 during a press conference at Walter Reed Hospital.[30] "I do this," Eisenhower said from his wheelchair in his hospital suite, "not only for my appreciation of his great service to the country during the years of my administration but rather and far more because of his personal qualities. He's a man of great reading, a man of great intelligence, and a man of great decisiveness."[31] "I am sure you know how deeply grateful I am for what you did in my behalf yesterday," Nixon wrote the former president. "Your endorsement will have a great effect—not only at the convention but more important among the millions of Democrats and Independents with whom you have always had great strength."[32] Within a week, a Gallup poll showed that Nixon, for the first time in two years, was running better than Rockefeller against any potential Democratic opponent.[33]

Nixon checked in with Johnson at the White House on July 26 when he received a briefing on the Vietnam peace negotiations in Paris; Humphrey and Wallace received these briefings as well.[34] The big question was whether there might soon be a breakthrough in the talks along with a long-expected bombing halt. "I have admired the way all of you have stood up through the great fire," Nixon told Johnson and his staff. "This is a hard time."[35] "He assured me that no halt was planned at that moment," Nixon wrote. "I said that I would continue to support our goals in Vietnam even though I would be critical of some of the tactics that had been used."[36] Nixon said that when he criticized the war effort, he would blame the "Humphrey-Johnson" administration.[37] "Look, I don't want to give LBJ this much," he told Bill Safire, holding up a finger and marking half of it with his thumb, "not this much reason to help Humphrey toward the end."[38] After the briefing, Nixon and Johnson had some time to talk alone. "When the briefing was over and the others had left, Johnson seemed almost to deflate before my eyes," Nixon recalled. "He looked old and terribly tired. His voice sounded hollow as he detailed at considerable length his decision not to run again. He gave many reasons and explained the many clues that he said he had been dropping since August 1967."[39] Now that they were no longer facing each other on the ballot, Johnson could ease up on their long rivalry. Their history of acrimonious public feuds made their truce in 1968 even more notable.

Miami Beach was hosting a major party's national convention for the first time in its history. A plastic paradise of palm trees and pastel art-deco boulevards, it was about as different a place as one could get from the snows of New Hampshire where Nixon had begun his uphill climb back to center stage. His team occupied the top four floors of the Hilton Plaza Hotel, a two-hundred-room spread.[40] His personal staff had rooms with signs over their doors bearing their names, while overflow staff were scattered among neighboring hotels. The site was a fortress that could be sealed off by closing a couple of causeways, and within the hotel the corridors and stairways were patrolled regularly by Wackenhut Corporation private security.[41] Every detail was arranged: the staffers' rooms were even provided with burn bags next to the desks. Each room had multiple telephones, some of which connected to a private Nixon switchboard on the eighteenth floor. Each delegate had been called at home the week before. The Nixon team knew each one's itinerary; the "Sunshine Squad" met them at the airport.[42] Outside the Hilton, a performer on stilts dressed as Uncle Sam entertained passers-by. A brass band played patriotic music, gaggles of Nixonettes pranced and cheered, and the inevitable baby elephant made appearances before fawning fans.[43] Even critics were awed, seeing these as tangible examples of a new Nixon.[44]

The eleventh-hour marriage of convenience between Rockefeller and Reagan was operating at full force. Rockefeller led Nixon only in the Northeast. In the West, even with Reagan dominant in California, Nixon was strong enough everywhere else to carry the region.[45] The primaries proved that neither Rockefeller nor Reagan alone could block him, but together they hoped to deadlock the convention and cause a stampede toward Reagan.[46] Rockefeller worked on delegates from the Northern and Midwestern states while Reagan tried to chip away at Nixon's strength in the South. Neither was interested in being the other's running mate.[47]

Nixon did not simply sit back and watch them work but sent his own forces out to counter the offensive. "Strom Thurmond and Senator John Tower of Texas went to work, visiting or telephoning each delegate personally," he wrote in his memoirs.[48] On August 7, Thurmond made a sixty-second speech in which he bowed out as the favorite son from South Carolina and threw his delegates to Nixon. That was the signal that the South would back him.[49] The commitments to Nixon held, and the campaign had no rancor toward rivals the way they did toward him. "No such passions animated Nixonians as had stirred the Goldwater crusaders of 1964," Theodore White wrote. "Indeed, passion was the very emotion they sought to avoid—passion had ruined the party in 1964, passion ravaged the nation in 1968." Even if Rockefeller or Reagan succeeded in destabilizing support for the former vice president, delegates looking for compromise and unity would still end up back with Nixon. When he landed at Miami International Airport at 6:24 P.M. on August 5, in an arrival perfectly timed for television stations looking for live news breaks, he looked ready to unite the party.[50] Pounced on by the media at a press conference on August 6, he avoided tipping his hand, did not criticize Johnson when given the chance, and dismissed the threats of Rockefeller, Reagan, and even Wallace without insulting any of their supporters.[51] His campaign was criticized as boring, but that was a calculated gamble meant to convey a message: Nixon alone could restore calm.[52]

Because Nixon wanted to avoid talking about Vietnam—possibly due to a tacit understanding with Johnson—Michigan Congressman Gerald Ford, the convention chairman, directed the agenda toward the increasingly popular issue of law and order.[53] The term included not just social issues but also growing concern over the disruption caused by Vietnam protesters.[54] For Nixon, the full scope of law and order included organized crime, loan sharks, racketeers, and drug dealers in addition to rising racial violence. When the issue came up, he almost always pointed out that it was Blacks who were most frequently the victims of crime.[55] The *New York Times* reported that law and order was "one of the most powerful issues running in his favor this year."[56] It was easy to understand yet it meant something a little different to each person, and seemingly everyone had an opinion about it. Vietnam and foreign policy were more nuanced, and the presumed nominees of both major parties had already pledged to end the war honorably, if in different ways.[57]

The roll call vote began at 1:20 A.M. on August 8.[58] The final count for the nomination gave Nixon 692 votes, 25 more than needed to win on the first ballot; the 30 delegates led by Wisconsin Governor Warren P. Knowles put him over the top. The crowd roared, the band played, and balloons fell from the ceiling.[59] In a gesture of unity, Reagan moved that the nomination be made unanimous by acclamation. Nixon had earned something rare in American politics, a second act, and would appear on the Republican national ballot for the fourth time in five election cycles. Then came the nomination for vice president. Maryland Governor Spiro Agnew had placed Nixon's name in nomination at the request of John Mitchell, who told him that if he did a good job, he would be among those considered for the second spot on the ticket.[60] Two weeks before the convention, Nixon wrote in his memoirs, "Mitchell and I had tentatively—and very privately concluded that the nod should go to Agnew. In talking to Agnew, I had been impressed by him as a man who seemed to have a great deal of inner strength."[61] A first-term governor, he had defeated segregationist Democrat George P. Mahoney in 1966. "He had a good record as a moderate, progressive, effective governor. He took a forward-looking stance on civil rights, but he had firmly opposed those who resorted to violence in promoting their cause," Nixon recalled. But after King's assassination in April, Governor Agnew had publicly criticized Black leaders, accusing them of tolerating an eruption of rioting in Baltimore and sitting idly by while the civil rights movement was taken over by messages of Black Power. These comments made him as many friends as well as enemies and turned him into a lightning rod during the campaign.[62] The centrist Ripon Society praised him, as Buchanan later put it, as "a progressive on civil rights who had enacted the first open-housing law south of the Mason-Dixon Line and championed gun control and a graduated income tax—in other words as a law-and-order liberal."[63] The choice of Agnew brought a little of Wallace's anti-establishment energy into an otherwise establishment campaign. The pick also may have reflected a degree of insecurity on Nixon's part, since Agnew could not outshine him the way Henry Cabot Lodge Jr. occasionally did during their 1960 campaign.

Agnew had arrived in Miami on August 2, three days before the start of the convention, so that the Nixon campaign could give him national exposure before he joined the ticket. As a sign of unity, New York Mayor John Lindsay seconded his nomination, and he won 1,128 votes to George Romney's 186. Coming from a border state, he straddled North and South as well as the party's liberal and conservative wings. Tower or Reagan might have helped Nixon to win Texas, but the Nixon campaign believed Agnew would help hold Ohio, Illinois, and possibly California.[64] "From a strictly political standpoint," Nixon wrote in his memoirs, "Agnew fit perfectly with the strategy we had devised for the November election."[65] He was moderate, populist, handsome, and not difficult to get along with, and he exuded toughness in a political year that required it.[66] Agnew's anti-elite message echoed Wallace's, but he came across as less extreme to working- and middle-class voters who anxiously sought a voice.[67]

Johnson believed Agnew was a shrewd choice. He understood that a presidential candidate did not want a running mate who could upstage him; even if Agnew was not as experienced or refined as other potential choices, he brought assets and no major liabilities. Johnson was so pleased at the selection that on the day of the nomination he called Nixon at the convention and invited him and Agnew to lunch at the Ranch. "This is going a bit beyond the call of bipartisanship," Drew Pearson wrote in his diary.[68] According to George Christian, Johnson had "affection" for Agnew and thought he had been treated unfairly.[69] For Nixon, however, the choice was a mixed bag. The vice-presidential candidate rarely makes a difference to a campaign, but Agnew's verbal gaffes were a distraction. They ranged from ethnic and racial slurs ("Polack," "Jap") to criticizing city slums to comparing Humphrey's position on law and order to "appeasement."[70]

Nixon paid particular attention to preparing his acceptance speech. "No other campaign speech would be as important," he wrote in his memoirs, "because none would have a larger or more attentive audience."[71] The final text was kept secret even from his speechwriters.[72] The forty-minute address focused on the "forgotten Americans" and concluded with a dramatic peroration:

I see another child tonight.

He heard the train go by at night and he dreams of far away places where he'd like to go.

It seems like an impossible dream.

But he is helped on his journey through life.

A father who had to go to work before he finished the sixth grade, sacrificed everything he had so that his sons could go to college.

A gentle, Quaker mother, with a passionate concern for peace, quietly wept when he went to war but she understood why he had to go.

A great teacher, a remarkable football coach, an inspirational minister encouraged him on his way.

A courageous wife and loyal children stood by him in victory and also defeat.

And in his chosen profession of politics, first there were scores, then hundreds, then thousands, and finally millions worked for his success.

And tonight he stands before you—nominated for President of the United States of America.

And what I ask you to do tonight is to help me make that dream come true for millions to whom it's an impossible dream today. The time has come for us to leave the valley of despair and climb the mountain so that we may see the glory of the dawn—a new day for America, and a new dawn for peace and freedom in the world.[73]

No speechwriter could have prepared such a personal statement. At the moment of his nomination, Nixon was reminding his listeners of his long journey from the house his father built in Yorba Linda, California, to a political career that had brought him early victory, then humiliation, and finally carried him back to center stage. "I had written the conclusion of the speech," he wrote later, "as a personal testimony to the political and social opportunity we have in the United States. It was intentionally dramatic, and it was completely true."[74] As the world went mad, it was Nixon who, by capturing the Republican nomination, hoped to come to its rescue.[75]

The speech was one of the greatest in his entire political career. *Washington Post* owner Katharine Graham ordered an editorial praising Nixon for "admirable understanding and restraint in his public approach to Vietnam" and for demonstrating "commendable comprehension of some aspects of the nation's social ills."[76] One Nixon biographer noted that while Humphrey was a "gasbag" and Wallace an abomination, it was Nixon, a reassuring centrist with foreign policy experience, who had the edge in responding to the nation's needs in 1968.[77] "Nixon looked presidential," Humphrey wrote in his memoirs. "His acceptance speech was superbly done. The substance of the speech made me think he had been reading carefully some of the stuff we'd been saying."[78] The closing prayer was given by Billy Graham.

Graham was active at the convention in other ways as well. He bent Nixon's ear over dinner about his choice of running mate, as he did in 1960, and persuaded Southern delegates inclined to support Reagan that they should side with Nixon. He was in the room when Nixon and his aides chose Agnew as running mate.[79] The night after Nixon's nomination, Graham dined with him at the Key Biscayne Hotel restaurant to discuss the campaign ahead.[80] All the while, he downplayed his closeness to Nixon. "I vote independently," he said, "and I usually split. I vote for the man and not the party."[81]

Johnson was thrilled to see that the Republican platform largely supported the administration's Vietnam policy.[82] That was not coincidental. Rather than risk antagonizing Johnson during the campaign, Nixon could simply refer to the party platform.[83] "The pursuit of peace is too important for politics-as-usual," he said. It was enough to simply say he supported phasing out the American presence in Vietnam without specifying what that meant. As long as the Johnson administration continued to pursue "an honorable settlement," he pledged to refrain from any "partisan interference."[84] Like Johnson, Nixon insisted that Hanoi had to recognize Saigon's right to exist, end its support of insurgency in the South, and withdraw its troops south of the DMZ.[85] His policy had something for everyone, whether hawk, dove, or moderate.[86] "I pledge to you that new leadership will end the war and win the peace in the Pacific," he said. From that the press created the myth that Nixon must have a "secret plan," which he refused to disclose.[87] "I never said that I had a 'plan,'" Nixon wrote in his memoirs, "much less a 'secret plan.'"[88]

Following the convention, Nixon took Johnson up on his invitation to the LBJ Ranch.[89] Johnson's "anger at Humphrey led him toward his old adversary, Richard Nixon," Clifford reflected. "'I want to sit down with

Mr. Nixon to see what kind of world he really wants,' he told Rusk, Rostow, and me on July 24." Johnson suggested that Nixon "may prove to
be more responsible than the Democrats."[90] On the day of the visit, Lady
Bird recalled in her diary, "about Noon Mr. Nixon arrived, cordial and
confident, with Spiro Agnew descending the plane behind him."[91] Johnson gave opening remarks and then turned the meeting over to Richard
Helms for a wide-ranging briefing whose subjects included Czechoslovakia, the Soviet Union, the Middle East, Vietnam, Cuba, the Dominican
Republic, and Haiti.[92] Cyrus Vance described recent developments at the
peace talks in Paris, including the private talks with North Vietnam.[93]

While there is no verbatim record of their twenty-minute conversation, one account says that Nixon promised he would not criticize Johnson's conduct of the war in the coming campaign, provided Johnson did
not dilute his negotiating position in Paris.[94] "Thus began a relationship
between Johnson and Nixon, in which Nixon skillfully promoted himself
as more sympathetic to the President's position in Vietnam than Humphrey," Clifford wrote in his memoirs. "The President told me that Nixon
had said that as long as the Administration did not 'soften' its position, he
would not criticize us. I was as appalled as the President was pleased."[95]
Johnson "sold" Nixon on the merits of a bombing halt, leading him to expect one prior to Election Day.[96] Nixon told Johnson that although some
of his advisors favored a bombing halt, he himself viewed bombing as the
only real leverage in the American arsenal, and he did not think it should
be stopped.[97] But he would support Johnson's advocacy of a halt.

"Johnson was expansive and cordial, and I could see that he was already enjoying his role as a noncandidate in this election year," Nixon
recalled, adding that at the end of the visit, they walked together to the he-
lipad.[98] "As I started to board the helicopter, Johnson's dog darted past my
legs into the cabin. There was a great deal of laughter, and I practically had
to pick the animal up and carry him down the steps. Johnson shouted in
mock anger, 'Dick, here you've got my helicopter, you're after my job, and
now you're gonna take my dog.'"[99] The meeting formalized the new relationship between Johnson and Nixon that been planted in the wake of the
assassinations of King and Kennedy, nurtured by members of Johnson's
own party, and fully blossomed once Nixon publicly embraced much of
Johnson's record. "Johnson is not playing Humphrey's game," Nixon told
Bill Safire. "I know it's awkward, but I do not want to force Johnson into
helping Humphrey."[100] Nixon and Johnson seemed so much in tandem

that Clifford wondered whether they had struck a formal "deal."[101] Driven together by circumstances and shared enemies, their past differences had all but disappeared, and both Johnson and Nixon clearly recognized that a new relationship could benefit both of them.[102]

Johnson told veteran diplomat Robert Murphy that if Eugene Mc-Carthy were nominated in Chicago, he planned to publicly support Nixon, and if Humphrey were nominated and did not stay strong on Vietnam, a win by Nixon would be better for the country.[103] While Humphrey sought to publicly separate himself from Johnson and his Vietnam policy, Nixon emerged as the compromise candidate who hovered over the center. His pledge to support Johnson's policies made Humphrey's goal of separation that much more difficult.[104] It was an ideal position for Nixon. According to the polls, the election result would be decided by seven states: California, Illinois, Michigan, New York, Ohio, Pennsylvania, and Texas. Of those, Nixon had won only California and Ohio in 1960; he would have to finish strong. While much has been written about Nixon's so-called Southern Strategy, in essence he did not have one during the general election, because he knew that a rerun of the Goldwater campaign in the South would be political suicide.[105] "The Deep South had to be virtually conceded to George Wallace," he wrote in his memoirs. "I could not match him there without compromising on the civil rights issue, which I would not do."[106] Before diving into the fall campaign, Nixon went to Mission Bay, California, for a staff retreat, to rest, and to stay out of the limelight while the Democrats gathered in Chicago.

CHAPTER SEVEN

Chicago

CHICAGO WAS NOT LIKE other big American cities. It had not experienced the deadly riots seen in Los Angeles, Detroit, Newark, or Washington, DC, even after the assassination of Martin Luther King Jr. Urban violence was largely absent. It had hosted twenty-three previous national political party conventions, more than any other city. There were few hippies or agitators, and the reason for the relative harmony was Mayor Richard Daley.[1] Daley had been reelected in 1967 with 73 percent of the vote, capturing all fifty of the city's wards, and had chaired the Illinois delegation to the Democratic Convention every year since 1956.[2] The party chose Chicago—or "Czechago," as Jerry Rubin later called it—as the site of its 1968 convention partly because of the strong security.[3] Daley had at his disposal twelve thousand police, seventy-five hundred Illinois National Guardsmen, seventy-five hundred U.S. Army troops, and one thousand federal agents from the FBI, U.S. Secret Service, and others.[4] The Democrats wanted to be prepared in case of a mass demonstration like the one that marched on the Pentagon in November 1967.[5] Even the manhole covers were tarred shut to prevent protesters from planting bombs.[6] Daley ordered his police to "shoot arsonists and looters—arsonists to kill and looters to maim and detain."[7] Wild rumors circulated about planned disruptions to the convention: radicals were going to add LSD to the city water supply, people impersonating chefs would drug delegates' food, fake taxis would take delegates to Wisconsin, and Humphrey's pants would be pulled down while he was speaking at the convention podium.[8] Abbie Hoffman threatened to send

230 "sexy" members of the Youth International Party to Chicago to se-
duce delegates' wives, daughters, and girlfriends. While some, including
Humphrey, suggested moving the convention to Miami Beach, Johnson
refused to embarrass Daley, who had chipped in $900,000 to subsidize the
convention cost.[9]

In 1967, when Johnson chose Chicago as the convention site, he still
thought he would be the nominee and had set the date unusually late—
almost a month after the Republican Convention in Miami Beach, to
limit the time he would need to campaign. He thought he would coast
to another easy reelection.[10] Even after announcing he wouldn't run, he
remained almost completely in control of convention planning and, according to one Humphrey confidant, "totally emasculated the Democratic
National Committee."[11] A big staff and fundraising operation were unnec-
essary if Johnson were the candidate, and he did not go out of his way to
change anything as Humphrey emerged as the likely nominee. Johnson
even insisted that Humphrey and McCarthy each have the same number of telephone lines in Chicago—ten—even though McCarthy had no
chance of being nominated.[12]

As the Republicans were gathering in Miami Beach, Humphrey
worked up the courage to confront Johnson about a Vietnam policy alter-
native.[13] He presented the fifth draft of a working paper entitled "Vietnam:
Toward a Political Settlement and Peace in Southeast Asia" to Johnson in
the Oval Office on the evening of July 25 for a meeting that lasted over an
hour.[14] The paper had been developed over two months by a task force of
staffers and academics to help Humphrey establish an independent position on the war without crossing Johnson.[15] Humphrey thought his team's
work had been undercut by Johnson's Honolulu speech, which reaffirmed
a hard line in Vietnam just as Humphrey was looking for ways to soften
the American position.[16] "He pulled the rug right out from under me,"
Humphrey said to Drew Pearson. "It gave me an awful wallop."[17] He felt
he had no choice but to run the text by Johnson, since it was a shift from
the current White House policy. While some were pressing him to boost
his campaign by making a clearer break with Johnson, Humphrey's loyalty
was too great. The only reason he had gotten close to the presidency at all
was because of Johnson.

The main feature Humphrey hoped to include in a major Vietnam
campaign speech was a proposal for a virtually unconditional bombing
halt, to show the United States was serious about jumpstarting the peace

talks. Chester Cooper had gone to Paris on Humphrey's behalf to clear the text with Cyrus Vance, further politicizing the work of the American negotiators. "Humphrey's public advocacy of a bombing cessation would be the kiss of death" for his campaign, Cooper said upon his return.[18] Humphrey had known he would pay a heavy price if he announced a different policy without first clearing it with Johnson; but he also paid a price for sharing it with him. Johnson said the statement would endanger peace prospects and the lives of his two sons-in-law serving in Vietnam. If Humphrey put it into a speech, he would have "blood on his hands," and Johnson would "destroy" his presidential chances.[19] When he returned to the office that night, Van Dyk asked how the discussion went.[20] Humphrey said he had not been able to raise the issue.[21] "You know," he added, "I've eaten so much of Johnson's shit in this job that I've grown to like the taste of it."[22]

A couple of weeks later, Humphrey had another chance to talk with Johnson about his position on the war. Johnson told him that Nixon and Agnew would be visiting the LBJ Ranch on August 10, so he suggested that Humphrey come see him the day before. Even though Nixon was the one Johnson really wanted to talk to, he would have been criticized for seeing the Republican candidate without receiving his own vice president, the likely Democratic presidential nominee. The meeting was more of a social gathering with spouses present, but Humphrey brought along what was now the eleventh draft of his Vietnam proposal. This draft contained revised language regarding the proposal for a bombing halt. "I for one am willing to take that step now if North Vietnam is willing to offer an appropriate act of reciprocity," the key line read. Humphrey was not aware that the North Vietnamese wanted nothing to do with any suggestion of reciprocity, let alone an explicit mention of it. Johnson advised him that the proposal might "get a headline" but that Humphrey was better off letting Johnson work for peace.[23] He persuaded Humphrey that the current peace talks, should they succeed, would help him more than any speech.[24] Given that Hanoi had rejected every single American proposal to break the deadlock in negotiations, he said, it was not the time for the vice president to go softer.[25] "I confess I'm concerned and disappointed that I don't get any help from the administration," Humphrey told Pearson on August 11. "Not one member of the Cabinet is speaking up."[26] He felt on his own to persuade Johnson.

By remaining in control, Johnson would not only get the credit for brokering peace but would minimize the risk of further ruptures in the

Democratic Party. He had been strong enough to restrain the party's liberal wing, he said, but Humphrey could not. Liberals had persuaded a majority of the country to turn against the war, but Americans resisted accusations that their nation was immoral or imperialistic.[27] "We then discussed, with happy frankness, our opinions of Senator George McGovern and Senator Eugene McCarthy," Lady Bird reflected, assessing that year's damage to the Democratic Party.[28] The meeting between the Johnsons and the Humphreys was not open to the press, unlike the meeting with Nixon and Agnew, which showed everyone beaming and gave the appearance of old friends gathering for a grand Texas barbeque. Being photographed with the Johnsons might have hurt Humphrey at that point in the campaign, when he was desperate to win the endorsement of McCarthy and Kennedy supporters.[29] He left the Ranch with his plan rejected again, but he felt better about his relationship with Johnson than he did after their previous meeting. Still, he was out of options for his Vietnam statement.[30]

Less than two weeks later, on August 20, Johnson received another great setback when Soviet Ambassador Anatoly Dobrynin informed him the USSR had invaded Czechoslovakia.[31] Johnson had planned to visit Moscow before the end of his presidency; the first real summit in seven years would have built on the previous year's Glassboro meetings. The summit would have celebrated the success of the Nuclear Non-Proliferation Treaty (NPT), signed by the United States, the Soviet Union, and fifty other nations on July 1.[32] The treaty recognized both the United States and USSR as nuclear powers that worked together to limit the spread of such weapons.[33] Soviet Premier Aleksei Kosygin had proposed a date for Johnson's visit that coincided with the Democratic Convention, a detail that did not go unnoticed, but Johnson was willing to accept. The chance to add a few more lines to his presidential resume was too tempting. His response also showed how important he thought Moscow would be in the remaining months of his presidency.[34] In addition, with the party so deeply divided, a successful summit with the Soviets might be all that was needed to ignite a "Draft Johnson" movement on the convention floor.[35] Clifford recalled that when Johnson mentioned this plan, "for a moment both Rusk and I were silent," shocked that the president seriously planned to upstage the convention by going to Moscow.[36] They were able to persuade him to move the trip to the first week of October, but after the Soviet invasion of Czechoslovakia, it had to be canceled.[37]

The invasion also complicated the Paris peace talks because many Democrats had endorsed the Soviet proposal for an unconditional bombing halt.[38] But after Czechoslovakia, no one wanted to appear too close to the Soviets.[39] They entered Prague virtually unopposed and arrested Alexander Dubček, the national leader who had grown too independent for Moscow's liking, as well as his liberal allies in the National Assembly. The Soviets claimed they were in Prague "on invitation."[40] When Johnson announced that the plan for a summit with the Soviets was canceled, Clifford said, "the saddest person in a sad room was Vice President Humphrey." Instead of proceeding triumphantly to Chicago, Humphrey would represent an administration with few foreign policy achievements that he could continue into his presidency.[41] His advisors said the stage was set for him to win the Democratic nomination but lose in the fall.[42] Meanwhile, Richard Nixon was saying nothing that might embarrass Johnson, further bolstering their nonaggression pact.[43]

Appearing on *Meet the Press* on August 25 on the eve of the convention, Humphrey sounded more like a man who had conceded defeat than like one near the pinnacle of his political career. He arrived in Chicago under cover of darkness, with no crowd to welcome him and no cameras, only a bagpipe band. Eugene McCarthy had been greeted by a crowd of ten thousand supporters. Even Mayor Daley—who still hoped the convention would draft Johnson—wanted nothing to do with Humphrey.[44] He had hoped to use an FBI "special team" as his personal intelligence service during the campaign, as Johnson had in 1964.[45] But J. Edgar Hoover shut down the idea after concluding that Deke DeLoach's eagerness to ingratiate himself with Humphrey was because he hoped a President Humphrey would make him director.[46] One reason for Hoover's decision could have been that he favored Nixon; but he did pass along intelligence about possible disturbances.[47] Near the International Amphitheater, protesters set up tents, walked around naked, smoked pot, and urinated and defecated where they chose. "We were a public display of filth and shabbiness, living-in-the-flesh rejects of middle-class standards," Jerry Rubin wrote in his memoirs.[48] In a little noticed op-ed in the *Chicago Sun Times*, not published until 1976, after the statute of limitations had expired, Rubin wrote: "We WANTED disruption. We PLANNED it. We WERE NOT innocent victims. . . . Guilty as hell. Guilty as charged."[49] The conflict to come marked the end of peaceful resistance to the war. From then on, protesters were increasingly willing to take direct action, not just against American involvement in Vietnam, but against the system that had produced the war.[50]

The protesters in Chicago were not the poor or downtrodden but white radicals, many from middle- and upper-middle-class backgrounds.[51] "We Shall Overcome" had been replaced by Black Power and Students for a Democratic Society.[52] They chanted "the whole world is watching" on the assumption that television viewers supported them. But most Americans did not identify with them.[53] All of the protest groups fit within the umbrella term the New Left.[54] "I supported the Vietcong and selective violence here at home," Rubin wrote. "Though I am a white middle-class American, who enjoys a good meal and the luxury of comfort, I nevertheless share the feelings of extremist revolutionaries."[55] However, Rubin, more inclined to use the convention to cement the celebrity status given to him, did not speak for all other protesters. Many were under twenty-one and thus unable to vote. They were not there to influence the convention but to state their refusal to accept the American political system.[56] Yet the press coverage—who the protesters were, where they came from, and what they sought—encouraged them.[57] The attention glamorized the mob. It made news; you couldn't look at the television, but you couldn't look away. Even though only ten thousand protesters showed up—far below the original estimate of fifty thousand—millions of Americans got their image of a typical protester from the coverage of the Chicago convention, and they did not like what they saw.[58] The protest leaders were brilliant at turning a political demonstration into theater designed for television.[59] Tom Hayden and Rennie Davis had begun their planning in December 1967, and they opened an office in Chicago in February—six months before the convention.[60] "I played into the hands of the theatrical media who compete against each other to dramatize their stories," Rubin wrote later.[61] According to Edgar Berman, Humphrey "never understood why so many mature minds, especially the press, failed to see the protesting for what it was: a mass childish tantrum."[62]

Humphrey's attention in Chicago was diverted from the protests to even greater problems inside the convention hall, starting with McCarthy. "I had an understanding with Gene McCarthy," Humphrey said, "but he never delivered." Instead, he went to the French Riviera on vacation, without endorsing anyone or giving his supporters a place to go.[63] They could vote for Eldridge Cleaver or Dick Gregory or write in McCarthy, but there were few other options.[64] To say that he did not live up to his supporters' expectations was the understatement of the year.[65] McCarthy later provided accounts of his campaign that exaggerated the lonely heroism of being the first to challenge Johnson. "It is even possible that he remembers things that way," Richard Goodwin wrote.[66]

Johnson was equally intransigent. Humphrey had no idea whether he would make an appearance—or for what purpose. "On the eve of the convention," Clifford wrote in his memoirs, "the President began to talk about going to Chicago to defend his record."[67] The bully pulpit of a sitting president was still powerful, and many of the nearly three thousand delegates owed the president some degree of loyalty. All of the politically appointed state and party leaders, especially in the South, certainly did.[68] John Connally threatened to start a "Draft Johnson" movement and reminded everyone how powerful the 527 Southern delegates were.[69] "I can make a very strong case," he told fellow Democrats, "that, notwithstanding his statement of withdrawal, he very much hoped he would be drafted by the convention in 1968."[70] Johnson's people controlled the state parties and conventions, the Democratic National Committee, its fundraising and spending, much of the detail that went into the convention, the distribution of convention tickets, and Mayor Daley himself.[71] "Our people organized the convention and virtually dictated the platform," Joseph Califano wrote in his memoirs. Long after it was known that Johnson would not be a candidate, Daley still planned to honor him and plan for his visit.[72] According to Lady Bird's diary, Daley had aggressively lobbied Johnson to come to Chicago—and possibly to make himself available for a draft. "I have not the slightest doubt," Johnson recalled, "that if I'd wanted to, I could have been reelected."[73]

The president had his speech ready and a Jetstar presidential aircraft fueled and waiting on the runway at the LBJ Ranch, ready to take him to Chicago. Members of his inner circle were all asked for their input on the speech, and a few submitted partial or even entire texts. An alternate ending suggested that he was receiving an honor, or that the speech was to be paired with a film that honored him, and at least one version ended with a nomination acceptance—either an actual acceptance or a signal that he was available for a draft. Another version made clear he would not be available for a draft.[74] Yet another sidestepped the issue and allowed listeners to draw their own conclusions. "My friends, let me speak of unity," one version read. "I believe we must continue to work for that unity . . . and I pledge that so long as I have breath in my body, I shall use it to encourage my country in its journey toward a freer, braver, more responsible and united America."[75] These are not the words of a retired politician content to sit on the sidelines. Califano was tasked with compiling the different versions of the speech, but he claimed in an interview that Johnson desired only to be honored in Chicago, or, if he was nominated, to turn it down.[76] "On Sunday afternoon, August 25, I joined Joe Califano and Harry McPherson at the White House," Clifford recalled, "where we worked until after midnight on a speech that none of us believed should be delivered."[77]

Johnson obviously planned to go to Chicago at some point: he had Billy Graham on hand to deliver a prayer at the convention on the day he was supposed to arrive.[78] "I was very happy to do this because this would give me an opportunity to be bipartisan," Graham recorded in his diary. "I did not want to become involved in open partisan politics if at all possible, even though in my heart I knew I was going to be pro-Nixon, especially with President Johnson out of the race."[79] Only at the last minute did Johnson decide not to go. Instead, he had a sixtieth birthday gathering of friends and family in Austin while he kept a close eye on the development of the platform.[80] "We were going to Chicago until the moment I was told we were not going," LBJ assistant Jim Jones said in an interview.[81] It is not clear why Johnson changed his mind. Based on the available documentation, the most likely explanation is that he hoped to go to Chicago to be honored by Daley on his birthday at Soldier Field, in the further hope that a draft movement would take hold once he was onsite.[82] What would have happened after that is anyone's guess. No matter what Johnson's true intentions were, the swirling rumors that he might show up in Chicago probably accelerated his lame duck status in a party in which the insurgents wanted nothing to do with him.[83]

One factor in Johnson's turnaround was the release of a Harris poll on August 26 that tested Nixon against Johnson, Humphrey, and McCarthy. It showed all three running behind Nixon by about six points. Harris, who had typically been closer to Democrats than Gallup, advised Johnson that if he tried to speak at the convention, he might be booed.[84] Another factor may have been the proposal to modify the unit rule, which could change how state delegations voted for a presidential candidate. As it stood, the rule required that each delegation give all its votes to one candidate. A particularly persuasive delegation chair could control a large and perhaps decisive voting bloc, especially if they teamed up with other delegation leaders. Together only a few people could control all of the delegates from an entire part of the country, which was partly how John-son came to and retained power. In July, however, Humphrey had tried to deflate McCarthy's charge of a rigged convention by proposing that del-egates be allowed to vote individually if their state party chose to rescind the unit rule.[85] Humphrey could easily afford the minor loss of delegates the rule change would entail.[86] But after John Connally made clear to the Rules Committee that the Southern governors did not support any change to the unit rule, the committee voted to keep it as it was.[87] Hum-phrey, breaking a promise to Connally that he would not challenge that decision, helped broker a compromise by which the rule stayed in place for the 1968 convention but was loosened for 1972. With his nomination assured, he simply wanted to prevent another divisive floor battle.[88] But in liberals' eyes, he had compromised himself even further.[89]

When he decided not to go to Chicago, Johnson released the South-ern governors and their blocs of delegates, who began to get in line behind Humphrey in order to prevent a move by the peace candidates.[90] It is un-likely any of the Democratic hopefuls could have united such an unusually divided party that year. The real question for the party was whether it was still flexible enough to hold the three Georges: George McGovern, who represented the liberals; George Wallace, who represented the conserva-tives; and George Meany, who represented the traditional labor strong-hold. The war in Vietnam was often blamed, but the division went much deeper than that. The McCarthy-Kennedy-McGovern flank was antiwar. According to Joseph Califano, McGovern also espoused abortion, "homo-sexual lifestyles," and legalizing marijuana—all values that were offensive to many middle Americans, whose sons were fighting the war and who would be named *Time* magazine's "Person of the Year" for 1968.[91] These citizens still believed in loyalty to the president and the military.[92] Finally, there were the Wallacites, who numbered 15 million and were conser-vative on social, cultural, and economic issues.[93] This group was already drifting away from the Democratic Party toward the Republicans.

Images of police beatings became the one thing that most people would remember or learn about the convention. There is no question they used excessive force, that it violated the civil rights of innocent protesters, and it was likely sanctioned by Daley himself. Humphrey's physician, Ed-gar Berman, saw it differently. "The baiting of the police was incredible," he wrote later. "There was no doubt police brutality in Chicago, plenty of it, but I saw provocation that few men could tolerate."[94] A Gallup poll showed that a commanding majority of Americans supported the police, 56 percent to 31 percent.[95] Most of the protesters believed Humphrey was the wrong candidate at the wrong time.[96] When they were denied access to sleep in parks during the convention, open conflict between them and police broke out.[97] Such provocations included spitting in the face of officers, throwing bags of urine and condoms filled with feces, defacing the interior of the Hilton with human excrement, and dropping beer bottles and cans containing urine and feces from open windows onto those below. "We were dirty, smelly, grimy, foul, loud, dope-crazed, hell-bent and leather-jacketed," Jerry Rubin wrote in his memoirs. "We pissed and shit and fucked in public."[98] Abbie Hoffman also sought to create the greatest political theater possible in Chicago, and understood that the cost would be borne later. "Because of our actions in Chicago, Richard Nixon will be elected," he said.[99]

Attorney General Ramsey Clark had no interest in pursuing any of the protesters, and instead wanted to prosecute the police for using excessive force against the protesters.[100] That was not likely to happen with J. Edgar Hoover at the FBI or Lyndon Johnson in the White House. A total of 668 people were arrested during convention week, including 8 protest leaders charged with federal crimes that included traveling to Chicago for the purpose of conspiring to incite a riot: Abbie Hoffman, Jerry Rubin, David Dellinger, Tom Hayden, Rennie Davis, John Froines, Lee Weiner, and Bobby Seale.[101] Eight police officers were indicted "for depriving civilians of their civil rights by assaulting them."[102] The Walker Report, the result of an official government inquiry led by Daniel Walker of the Chicago Crime Commission, largely blamed Daley's police for the get-tough approach adopted following King's assassination in April.[103]

Inside the convention hall, the movements of Johnson's lieutenants haunted the Humphrey leadership, who were not sure what the president would do next.[104] But once the threat of Johnson turning up passed, there was no doubt that Humphrey would get the nomination. The real question is whether Humphrey wanted it. He would have to spend a great deal of campaign energy patching up differences within the party. His advisors urged him to issue his statement on Vietnam so he could begin separating himself from Johnson.[105] Drew Pearson told him he would always be harmed by proximity to the president.[106] Averell Harriman encouraged him to "get out from under" Johnson's Vietnam policy by making a dramatic nomination acceptance speech that would include his resignation from the vice presidency.[107] "I am appalled at the calamity to our country if Richard Nixon should be elected," Harriman wrote to Humphrey, a preview of the political turn the negotiations in Paris were about to take. "Aside from the setback to our country of his reactionary policies and those of the Republican Right wing he represents, unfortunately around the world he has aroused a personal distrust."[108]

Harriman later said that an early version of Humphrey's nomination acceptance speech contained a resignation statement, for the purpose of doing whatever it took to deny Richard Nixon the presidency.[109] Such a bold move would have helped Harriman, too, since the invasion of Czechoslovakia had lessened Soviet involvement in the peace talks, leaving them stalled.[110] Resigning as vice president would have allowed Humphrey to break from Johnson so he could campaign freely as the party's nominee, rather than in the more restrained way that Harriman believed the vice presidency imposed upon him. Humphrey had been in a funk since Kennedy's death and needed something to break him out of it. He had had little to say for two months. His support for Johnson's Vietnam policy alienated his liberal base, his labor stronghold was under attack by Wallace, and there was lawlessness on the streets that everyone had an opinion about. Humphrey had too many staff and was too nice to fire or reorganize them. A bout of Hong Kong flu had shut him down for two weeks in July.[111]

His absence from the spring primaries plus a campaign that never really got going in the summer did not prepare Humphrey for the convention. It would have been out of character for him to make a bold break with Johnson in Chicago solely to make himself look better. "It would not look like an act based on principle or conviction," Humphrey said. "It would look like a gimmick. It would seem strange. And it will enrage the President."[112] Only one vice president, John Calhoun, had ever resigned, and that was in 1832 over his support for the discredited idea that states can nullify federal laws they consider unconstitutional. It was hardly a noble cause.[113] Besides, being vice president had been the path to the White House for Truman and Johnson.[114] "As nasty as he's been, I just can't quit Lyndon now," Humphrey said. "I have no doubt in the world he'd cut me up and out of the nomination if it was a matter of my spoiling his policy on the war. But that's not what holds me back. He's suffering like no president I've seen before, and I just can't add to that."[115]

Humphrey was scheduled tightly with time-wasting, mind-consuming meetings in his two-bedroom suite at the Conrad Hilton. He had no one like a Kenny O'Donnell, a Marvin Watson, or a Bob Haldeman to keep control of his commitments and make sure he kept his eye on the prize.[116] He felt the need to micromanage his Chicago team, including the number of staff, their grooming habits, and their use of hospitality bars.[117] No one in the party seemed to be looking out for him, certainly not Johnson.[118] Neither he nor Daley considered the convention to be about the nominee. Humphrey's son-in-law, Bruce Solomonson, had to stand in line to plead for tickets so Humphrey's family could watch his acceptance speech from the visitors' gallery.[119] "I'm the Vice President of the United States and I'm being treated like a Yugoslavian peasant," Humphrey said.[120] In a sense, his most important challenger at the convention was Johnson himself.[121] "Now don't get me wrong," Johnson told Humphrey. "If I want the nomination, I can get it. There's no two ways about it."[122] LBJ confidant John Roche later told Edgar Berman that Johnson considered getting back in the race up until the moment Humphrey was nominated.[123] Given his more than two decades of service to the Democrats, Humphrey deserved better. He was more than a party loyalist; he did what he thought was best for the nation, even when it risked his career. Now he was on the threshold of being the leader of the Democratic Party, at least in title.[124] "I thought it was sad that his party treated him so badly," Nixon wrote in his memoirs.[125]

The Vietnam debate was moved back from primetime on August 27 to noon the next day when few people would be paying attention.[126] Perhaps it was Johnson who had it moved, in order to blunt the opportunity for criticism of his policies or himself. Humphrey was scheduled to present his views on Vietnam to the convention. "For the first time in my life," he said to Berman during the drive to the International Amphitheater, "I'm scared to give a speech."[127] His proposal for ending the war contained four central elements: (1) an unconditional bombing halt; (2) a phased mutual withdrawal of troops; (3) a demand that Saigon negotiate with the NLF to create a "broadly representative" government; and (4) reduced U.S. military action in Southeast Asia.[128] This platform satisfied most of Kennedy and McCarthy's demands but would not cause an outright break with Johnson.[129] Humphrey downplayed the differences between this plan and Johnson's, saying he could support either.[130] He had consulted with Johnson about it and also run it by Dean Rusk, but they agreed to keep their conversation secret.[131] "Do you know what [Johnson] told me?" Humphrey said to an aide in advance of the convention. "'Hubert, don't try to pull the rug out from under my policy. The Vietnam plank will be mine—not yours.' He didn't give a damn about pulling the rug out."[132]

After the debate, Johnson summoned the convention and platform committee chairs, Carl Albert and Hale Boggs, as well as West Virginia Senator Jennings Rudolph, to the White House, ostensibly for a briefing about the crisis in Czechoslovakia. Instead, Johnson read them the riot act about the recklessness of Humphrey's peace plank, bolstering his tirade by reading from cables by Creighton Abrams, who argued that a bombing halt would vastly increase North Vietnamese military capabilities in the DMZ region and facilitate Hanoi's third major offensive of the year.[133] Albert and Boggs returned to Chicago determined to defeat the measure. Johnson's version, which was simply a rubber stamp on White House policy, won by a 65–35 margin in the Platform Committee and a full vote of the delegates, before a television audience of some 89 million, by 1567 ¾–1041 ¼. "I could have fought it out on the floor of the convention," Humphrey recalled, "but it would have been suicidal. It was a tough decision, but I was sure to lose the battle, and the president would have crippled me to boot."[134]

Johnson's victory in the platform committee was a disaster for Humphrey, Clifford wrote in his memoirs. It was "more evidence of his own weakness."[135] The result in Chicago made no one happy; Humphrey had failed to unite even the left wing of the party.[136] McCarthy withheld his endorsement, disgusted that Humphrey was not tougher on Vietnam, or even on the police brutality against the protesters outside.[137] Humphrey had asked for the support of disaffected liberals but gave them no reason to compel their support.[138] He achieved no more with the moderates and conservatives.

Once the battles over the platform were settled, Connally—on Johnson's behalf—made peace with Humphrey. "We've been playing games," he said during a visit to Humphrey headquarters in Chicago. "Let's forget this nonsense. We're with you."[139] The delegates got the message. In alphabetical order starting with Alabama, voting began for the presidential nomination. Humphrey did not need beyond *P*, for Pennsylvania, as the state's ninety votes put him over the top. The final vote was 1,760¼ for Humphrey, 601 for McCarthy, and 146 for McGovern. Neither McCarthy nor anyone else had ever posed a serious threat to his nomination.[140] The former mayor of Minneapolis, always known for emotional reactions that helped Americans connect with him, broke down crying, and both Johnson and Nixon called to congratulate him. That moment must have felt important for Humphrey, after his old friends abandoned him in 1956 to support Estes Kefauver as Adlai Stevenson's running mate, and after the bruising primary battles against Kennedy in 1960. While 1964 had seemed like a victory at the time, what was supposed to be a political marriage with Johnson left him more often in the position of a son living in fear of a punitive father.[141] This year, for all its conflicts, had brought redemption.[142]

The protests outside, however, hardly made it a smooth proceeding. While Cleveland Mayor Carl Stokes was seconding Humphrey's nomination, NBC broke away to cover the gathering crowds in Grant Park.[143] It was a major disservice to Humphrey, a great American who deserved better. Five thousand people marched across Michigan Avenue in the warm night air to their confrontation with Chicago police. Images of blue-helmeted police chasing, pushing, and beating protesters were seen by millions of Americans on television. Yet the majority sided with the police, a sign of how exhausted the nation was from the experiences of the 1960s. "The Democrats are finished," Theodore White wrote while looking down at the chaos from room 307 at the Blackstone Hotel.[144] Drew Pearson predicted that divisions in the Democratic Party would kill their chances in the fall. "Everybody's saying that Humphrey will get the nomination but lose to Nixon," he wrote in his diary.[145] "The disruptive methods of the radicals of the 'new Left,' at the Chicago convention and on university campuses," Johnson wrote in his memoirs, "offended the majority of American citizens and pushed them to the right."[146]

Inside, the focus turned to the vice-presidential running mate. Outgoing Texas Governor John Connally, wounded while sitting in front of President Kennedy in the limousine as he was assassinated in Dallas, was a lead choice for the nomination and the favorite of the Southerners who were not thrilled with Humphrey. The talk of putting Connally on the ticket surely had Johnson's blessing and may have been an attempt by Johnson to keep control over Humphrey. But Billy Graham intervened to prevent any split in the conservative vote. He passed along a message from Nixon, promising an appointment in his administration if Connally withdrew.[147] At any rate, Humphrey tolerated no serious discussion of Connally, and instead backed a nominee closer to his own image. He did not want a Southerner, which ruled out North Carolina Governor Terry Sanford. The Kennedys did not want him to choose U.S. Ambassador to France

Sargent Shriver, which would have been a backdoor to getting a Kennedy. Governor Richard Hughes of New Jersey did not have enough popular support outside his state.[148] Humphrey pursued Edward Kennedy, who would have been an obvious choice, but Kennedy refused to talk with him directly and avoided giving a firm answer.[149] Humphrey settled on Senator Edmund Muskie from Maine. Muskie brought a calming and serious presence to the Democratic ticket after the hysteria of Chicago, which made the national press corps swoon.[150] "A former governor who had shown great political skill in getting reelected in a traditionally Republican state, Muskie was a strong addition to the ticket," Nixon wrote in his memoirs.[151] "The Democratic ticket is Humphrey-Muskie—and I want to underscore that," Humphrey instructed. "Both names are to be used in everything we do."[152] Humphrey saw Muskie as a Kennedy surrogate, and Johnson's preference for someone else did not matter.[153] He would bring stability to the ticket, executive experience as a previous governor, and an interest in tackling the budget, and would be able to take over as president in an emergency.[154] "Don't forget," Humphrey said, "he's also a Pole, a Catholic, and he looks enough like Abe Lincoln."[155] The Humphrey campaign felt that Muskie brought more to Humphrey than Agnew brought to Nixon.[156] If he had any real shortcomings, it was that he did not appeal to any of the disaffected groups of Democrats that Humphrey hoped to unite, whether African Americans, antiwar liberals, or young people.[157]

In his speech accepting the nomination, Humphrey did his best to calm the chaos both inside and outside the hall. But it was not the radical, gauntlet-hurling speech that many wanted him to make. It was an elegant address, a classic Humphrey speech that had something for everyone. He paid tribute to his political heroes, including Franklin D. Roosevelt, Harry Truman, Adlai Stevenson, and John F. Kennedy. He thanked Johnson, called for party unity, praised Eugene McCarthy and George McGovern, and reminded Democrats that "we need a state of law and order."[158] Earlier, he had thought it would be a nice touch to include a quote from St. Francis of Assisi. When Van Dyk stripped it out in a late round of editing, Humphrey did not take issue. Instead, he reinserted it from memory during his delivery:

Where there is hatred, let me sow love
Where there is injury, pardon
Where there is doubt, faith

Where there is despair, love
Where there is darkness, light.[159]

Reaching a rhetorical peak, Humphrey said, "I say to America: Put aside recrimination and dissension. Turn away from violence and hatred. Believe in what American can do, and believe in what America can be . . . and . . . with the help of this vast, unfrightened, dedicated, faithful majority of Americans, I say to this great convention tonight, and to the great nation of ours, I am ready to lead our country!"[160]

Humphrey used the convention period to plan and retool a campaign that badly needed it.[161] Labor Day, the traditional start of the campaign high period, was just two days away.[162] He had no money and no campaign materials, and was about to face a fifteen-point deficit in the polls.[163] Lacking surrogates to speak on his behalf, he urged family members to quit their jobs and head out on the campaign trail. "God damn it, I want some action!" he ordered. "These well-kept family secrets should be open to the public. I don't know how you get the publicity, but somebody better figure it out."[164] Theodore White wrote that compared to the orderly Nixon campaign, the Humphrey organization resembled a "gypsy encampment."[165]

Humphrey recruited Lawrence "Larry" O'Brien to be his campaign manager for the fall. O'Brien warned him that being a Democrat that fall was a liability. "If Hubert Humphrey is elected President," he advised, "it will be on your merits—not on the reputation of the Democratic Party. In other words, run Humphrey the man, not Humphrey the Democrat."[166] O'Brien had managed the great Democratic victories of 1960 and 1964.[167] He had started the year with Johnson, then moved on to Kennedy after Johnson declared he would not run, and now was managing Humphrey— making him perhaps the only person in U.S. history to manage three different presidential campaigns in the same year.[168] Trying to bring order to what had been a chaotic campaign, he drafted a "very basic . . . flying by the seat of your pants" plan for the fall. But it was obvious that any plan would need more money than the little that Humphrey had.[169]

Humphrey invited Kenneth O'Donnell, also a Kennedy associate, to join his campaign as a troubleshooter.[170] Both moves were a way of appealing to Kennedy supporters, whom Humphrey needed badly if he was to have a serious shot at the White House. But those campaign acquisitions made his relationship with Johnson even worse. After being cut off from attending National Security Council meetings as of September 4, he began to look elsewhere for foreign policy information—by calling on administration officials who were moonlighting for him, including Harriman, George Ball, Nicholas Katzenbach, and Benjamin Read.[171] "The bullet that killed Bobby wounded Hubert Humphrey," reporters liked to say. It sounded pretty close to what Muriel Humphrey told her husband right after the tragedy. In other words, the key question in the fall campaign would be whether the young people who so enthusiastically backed Kennedy would transfer their support to Humphrey, or withdraw from politics.[172]

CHAPTER EIGHT

Pittsburgh

GEORGE WALLACE'S CAMPAIGN IN 1968 represented his first full attempt at the presidency after his limited effort in 1964 convinced him it would be worth trying again. Rather than run as a Democrat, however, he chose to run on the American Independent Party ticket and he got on the ballot in all fifty states, the first noteworthy intrusion on a two-party election in twenty years.[1] The only place the AIP was not successful was the District of Columbia.[2] "The party had been born in protest," Wallace wrote later.[3] Less an autonomous political party than a vehicle for Wallace's political ambition, the AIP was a magnet for dissidents.[4] Wallace found so much early popularity from supporters whom he later described as "solid, hard-working, God-fearing people" that it simply overwhelmed the campaign.[5] Compared to the Wallace operation, the disorganized Humphrey campaign was a model of efficiency.[6]

The national press found it easier to insult the campaign than to try to understand it. Reporters depicted Wallace as a barefoot country boy. Anyone who made a campaign issue of growing federal involvement in housing and business, ballooning welfare programs, and increasing crime was, at minimum, a closet racist.[7] "Racist" fairly described Wallace's rhetoric in the 1962–63 period, when he said and did what it took to become governor. But he had shifted, and even further since his first run for president in 1964. By 1968, he was a populist conservative, and on the campaign stump there were few overt mentions of race and no derogatory language used toward racial minorities—although concerns related to race often lay beneath the surface. He did not want the support of groups like the Ku Klux

Klan. A first-time supporter of Wallace might have been a retired U.S. Army enlisted man, an assembly line worker at the Buick plant in Flint, Michigan, or a taxi driver from Baltimore.[8] His critics, by remaining focused on his racist origins, missed the deeper bonds he was forming with anti-establishment supporters.[9] The polls consistently showed that Wallace received high marks for "saying it the way it really is," and for having "the courage of his convictions."[10]

It was the white workingmen who were perhaps the most disturbed by the events of the second half of the 1960s—factory workers, farmers, steelworkers, longshoremen, police, firefighters, and others. Their concerns were not always rational, but they were real and had been growing prior to Wallace's 1968 presidential campaign. As these Americans saw it, government social scientists were no longer content with simply interpreting the results of government efforts and had pushed the Great Society to the limit with untested utopian programs, the burden of which fell on the working class. It was their neighborhoods that were infiltrated by public housing, their sons who fought in the war, their children who had to be bused to newly integrated schools, their streets that were no longer safe. Their paychecks were being eaten away by taxes and rising inflation—reaching about 4 percent, the highest since the Korean War—even though they saved and lived within their means.[11] They believed they had lost social status, and they blamed those and the institutions they thought had taken things from them—elites, intellectuals, Washington bureaucrats, even African Americans. Americans who supported the Civil Rights Act of 1964 and the Voting Rights Act of 1965 withdrew their pledge to ensure these new rights after the liberal state began to lose credibility.[12] Wallace was the only candidate who spoke directly to them. A Gallup poll showed 46 percent of Americans believed that "big government" posed the greatest threat to the nation's future.[13] "Not since the Know-Nothings in the 1850s," Theodore White wrote, "has there been a significant national eruption of the right."[14]

The nation's ongoing turmoil prompted an eclectic group of organizations to express support, including the Fraternal Order of Police, American Legion, Veterans of Foreign Wars, and Disabled American Veterans. Ezra Taft Benson, who had been Eisenhower's Secretary of Agriculture, endorsed Wallace and sponsored an appearance at the Mormon Tabernacle. Union members fled Humphrey to support Wallace.[15] Young working people in the industrial cities listened to him.[16] Some national writers did not understand—and may not have wanted to understand—what was going on. Drew Pearson called Wallace a "psychoneurotic" who "used the tactics of Adolf Hitler."[17] Garry Wills said his working-class followers "vomit together." Wallace himself, the "Anti-Christ," was called "the old crotch-scratcher," "dingy," and a "handsome garage attendant" whose rallies included "honey-faced somewhat stupid 'Wallace Girls'" with teased and sprayed bouffant hairdos.[18] While there had always been divisions between the elites and the populists in the Democratic Party, Wallace in 1968 came under concentrated attack by the elites. It made for colorful coverage of his campaign but did little to explain to readers why millions of Americans were attracted to him.

Navigating fifty sets of statutes to get on the ballot in all states was a significant challenge. Wallace staffer Ed Ewing assigned John Paul De-Carlo to divide the nation into groupings of fourteen to fifteen states each and sent a team of freshly minted lawyers out to learn the procedures for getting Wallace on the ballot in those states. They opened offices, organized armies of volunteers, collected signatures, filed paperwork with each state's secretary of state, navigated the bureaucracy—such as whether a state required a running mate or a convention, whether the AIP existed in the state or an existing party could be renamed—and fended off legal challenges from the state government and the two major political parties. The number of signatures required ranged from 300 in South Dakota to 433,000 in Ohio. Often the signatories also had to be registered for AIP party membership, and some of the state deadlines were very early. In California, where the filing deadline was December 31, 1967, Wallace was required to have each signatory complete a two-page legal form to register as a member of the AIP.[19] One of the most difficult states was Ohio, where he had to obtain more than a hundred thousand additional signatures because Secretary of State Ted Brown declared so many invalid. Due to different rules for naming a third party, the AIP in 1968 was known by six different names. It was the Conservative Party in Kansas, the George Wallace Party in Connecticut, and the Courage Party in New York. Some state election boards challenged whether it was a real political party and required Wallace to have a convention, issue a party platform, and declare a running mate—all things he otherwise might not have done.[20] His staff, who faced all kinds of hurdles, were given the latitude to address them with energy and creativity. They helped establish credibility for the campaign and for Wallace.[21] The difficulty of organizing a national campaign under a third party was arguably why Wallace returned to running as a Democrat in 1972.[22] "Very few people will ever realize the magnitude of a national campaign," he wrote to staffer Joe Fine. "I do not think that the Press ever knew what was required to get on the ballot throughout the country."[23] He did not have a single campaign director and instead split the duties between several young attorneys. It was Wallace's first genuine national campaign and still largely directed by Alabamians whom he trusted.

Wallace was used to flying solo, so much of the message of the campaign was tied directly to its central personality. His success demonstrated that millions of Americans were tired of both major parties and that anti-establishment ideas had penetrated the mainstream of politics on the right as well as the left.[24] "He had denounced the hippies, rioters, and campus anarchists with a populist rhetoric Nixon could not match," Pat Buchanan wrote later. "He was a demon campaigner with a brutal but effective humor."[25] Despite Wallace's complaints about government overreach, the AIP platform called for greater government involvement in almost every aspect of American life, including more spending for job training, transportation, education, space exploration, social security, the elderly, and health care. Wallace called for a more generous welfare state than the platform passed by Democrats in Chicago.[26] He also endorsed the Equal Rights Amendment. "I feel a special kinship with your organization," he wrote to National Woman's Party founder Alice Paul, "because a native Alabamian, Mrs. Alva E. Belmont, was your first president and also because I feel that my wife, Lurleen, through her service contributed to the status of women in our Nation."[27] "The platform in 1968 was neither revolutionary nor extreme," he wrote later. "It called for equity: curtailment of foreign aid to our enemies even if that meant loss of profit, reform of our welfare program to eliminate abuses, an end to the federal government's encroachment in areas belonging to the states, an end to busing of little children to achieve racial quotas, and an end to judicial usurpation."[28]

Some states required him to declare a running mate so early that he used former Georgia Governor Marvin Griffin's name until a formal choice could be made.[29] Griffin did not give the ticket either geographical or ideological balance, but few mainstream politicians were willing to run with him.[30] The ideal running mate for Wallace would have been someone like Texas Governor John Connally, but he was not interested. Another campaign aide suggested FBI Director J. Edgar Hoover.[31] When finally forced to choose someone, Wallace wanted Albert Benjamin "Happy" Chandler. The former Kentucky governor was from a border state, and his background as former Major League Baseball commissioner would have broadened the campaign's appeal, if at the expense of ideological purity.[32] For one thing, Jackie Robinson had broken baseball's color barrier during Chandler's tenure. On September 9, however, Wallace withdrew the offer after some of his more conservative donors complained that Chandler was too moderate.[33] A wealthy contributor from Indiana suggested retired Air Force General Curtis LeMay. Wallace, who had served under LeMay in the Pacific, was intrigued.[34] LeMay was best known for two military accomplishments, each of them controversial. During World War II, he led the brutal B-29 firebombing of Japan, which helped force Japan to surrender and avoid the need for a land invasion, which would have cost tens of thousands of American lives. He also played a leading role in the creation of the Strategic Air Command (SAC) during the most dangerous phase of the Cold War. In between, he coordinated air operations for the Berlin Airlift in 1948–49.[35] While LeMay was often caricatured as a war-monger, leaders like him may have done more to prevent a nuclear holocaust than to increase the risk of one.[36] By 1968, LeMay was less potent: a heart patient who had to watch his weight as well as his temper. But he continued to write about military policy. "Gobbledygook has become the union card of defense intellectuals," he wrote in a 1968 book that surely got Wallace's attention.[37] He had been approached about running for the Senate in 1968 as a conservative Republican but was turned off by the idea of raising money. When the Wallace team approached him, he said he was not interested in running on a third-party ticket. He had never been involved in politics, did not like giving speeches, did not like reporters or their probing questions, and did not particularly like Wallace. Privately, LeMay was for Nixon and felt no need to become personally involved in the race. "I firmly believed we had to have a conservative government or we might never have another chance," he recalled.[38] Seymore Trammell of the Wallace team did not take no for an answer, emphasizing a point that resonated with LeMay: the campaign might deny Humphrey a victory and put an end to the Kennedy-McNamara-Johnson policies in Vietnam.[39]

LeMay had a long talk with Wallace on September 27 in Chicago, at which they settled their differences.[40] The appeal for LeMay was that Wallace pledged to return leadership of the Vietnam War to the military commanders, and would stand up to antiwar protesters and anarchists.[41]

Wallace believed that even if his way of talking about nuclear weapons scared a lot of people, LeMay would appeal to soldiers and veterans, give his campaign new credibility to talk about the Vietnam War, and provide the foreign policy muscle that Wallace lacked. Unlike Humphrey or Nixon, Wallace thought the United States could win in Vietnam if the politicians would listen to their military leaders. He understood that a large number of Vietnam veterans were about to vote for a president for the first time and were likely to view LeMay favorably.[42] He was not a segregationist or doctrinaire conservative. As a resident of Los Angeles who was born and raised in Ohio, LeMay was certainly not Southern, a fact that was sure to broaden Wallace's reach.[43] Despite the widespread perception of Wallace as a racist, LeMay came away from their conversation convinced he was not.[44] He had heard enough to persuade him to sign on. "I was more than pleased with the choice the American Independent Party made for my running mate," Wallace wrote later. "General Curtis LeMay was a distinguished gentleman with an outstanding military and civilian record."[45]

Wallace never seemed interested in the formalities of a national presidential campaign—holding a convention, issuing a platform, and declaring a running mate—perhaps because he was never confident his campaign would get to that point, or perhaps because it was part of his anti-establishment ethos. That never stopped the fund-raising machine. By October 1 he had raised $6.2 million in mostly small donations, against expenditures of $5.8 million. "The American Independent Party's success at the polls in 1968 astounded professional politicians in both parties," he wrote later.[46] A *New York Times* survey projected that Wallace would win more than fifteen million votes, and twice as many electoral votes as Humphrey. Gallup said Wallace was the seventh most admired man in the country, ahead of Nixon and just behind Pope Paul VI, while Humphrey did not make the list.[47] His success landed him on the covers of *Life*, *Time*, and *Newsweek*.

Lacking a traditional national convention, Wallace scheduled a press conference for October 3 in the grand ballroom of the Pittsburgh Hilton to unveil his running mate.[48] The event was to be followed by the official release of the American Independent Party platform.[49] The location was chosen because western Pennsylvania was a place where Wallace could expect to pick up votes. Polls showed him leading in seven key states. As his poll numbers topped 20 percent, there was a chance he could keep both Humphrey and Nixon from getting 270 electoral votes, throwing the election to Congress for the first time since 1876, when, as part of the Compromise of 1877, an electoral commission gave the presidency to Rutherford B. Hayes, who had finished second behind Samuel Tilden.[50]

Despite the high expectations for the unveiling of the American Independent Party candidates—broadcast live by all three television networks—the Wallace campaign went downhill from that point forward. His staff were still not sure LeMay would actually show up in Pittsburgh, so they had a last-minute replacement standing by: Jimmie H. Davis, the former governor of Louisiana and composer of the song "You Are My Sunshine." LeMay did show up, however, and after Wallace's introduction, he gave his acceptance speech. Explaining why he finally agreed to run, he said that while he did not miss eighteen-hour days, "nobody cared where I was going any more. Nobody wanted to know." He had been a part of the action for two decades, and he missed it.[51] Largely reading from the statement prepared by Wallace staffers, LeMay looked like a polished veteran of many high-level briefings. "I have decided to join him in this fight," LeMay concluded, "and eagerly dedicate myself to proving his judgment in my selection as a running mate."[52] Jack Nelson of the *Los Angeles Times* then asked him whether winning in Vietnam required the use of nuclear weapons.[53] The event quickly became the strangest political press event since Richard Nixon's "last press conference" in 1962. Rather than explain why Wallace was preferable to Humphrey or Nixon, LeMay used his first public appearance in three years to explain his philosophy of war and why every available weapon, including nuclear weapons, should be used to win and end the prolonged fighting going on in Vietnam. He claimed that despite what many said, nuclear weapons did not cause permanent damage. He was familiar with Bikini Atoll, where some atomic tests had been conducted in the 1950s, and while some of the land crabs were still "a little hot," he assured reporters that the fish, birds, and coconut trees were back, while the rats were "bigger, fatter, and healthier than they ever were before." Wallace began to squirm. "General LeMay hasn't advocated the use of nuclear weapons, not at all," he interjected. He no more wanted to be seen as radical on nuclear weapons than on race.[54] But LeMay was not deterred. "I gave you a discussion on the phobia that we have in this country about the use of nuclear weapons," he replied, and seemed prepared to continue.[55] Wallace had heard enough. He said, "General, we got to go," and ended the press conference.[56]

Everyone knew LeMay was no politician, and he might have been naïve to sign up for Wallace's campaign, but the national press seized an opportunity it seemed to have been waiting for all year. Up to that point, Wallace had arguably not made any mistakes.[57] "I still maintain the highest respect for General LeMay," Wallace wrote later, "and my only regret is that a man of his stature and forthrightness had to learn the hard way that candid answers to loaded questions are not always the best political strategy."[58] The *Los Angeles Times* compared LeMay to Hermann Göring standing by Hitler. For the final weeks of the campaign, with the press watching LeMay carefully, he continued to utter gaffes that not only made the news but shaped people's views about Wallace. Asked during an appearance at the Yale School of Forestry what he thought about abortion and birth control, LeMay responded without missing a beat: "I favor them both." He praised the usefulness of abortion to control population growth and protect national resources.[59]

The *New York Times*, which had aggressively attacked Wallace throughout the campaign, now had even more reason to attack.[60] In addition to reproductive rights, LeMay proved to be well to the left of Wallace on environmental issues, referring on the stump to the "savage orgy of ecological rape of mother nature." He told friends that he did not care what people said about him. He had a policy of not talking to reporters, so they stopped calling.[61] He was simply not prepared for the actual dirty work of a difficult campaign, especially to face an aggressive and hostile press corps. Wallace was used to it, but LeMay was not. Nor did he expect that as Wallace's running mate, he would be branded publicly as endorsing Wallace's past and present views on race.[62]

LeMay's brief and disastrous political career probably cost Wallace whatever chance he had to be a decisive factor in the election.[63] No matter how much briefing Wallace provided, the media knew exactly how to handle the man some had nicknamed "Bombs Away LeMay."[64] "I felt strongly about avoiding extremist views that could only hurt the party's image," Wallace wrote later.[65] When the American Independent Party platform was released to the press on October 14, nothing in its official points sounded remotely extreme. There was no mention of race and certainly not of nuclear weapons. The emphasis was on the needs of the working class: expanding education, job training, fiscal responsibility, and a restrained federal government. But this effort to attract more moderate voters was overshadowed by LeMay's debut in Pittsburgh.

While Wallace clearly believed LeMay had admirable qualities, it appeared that he would never be a politician. Years later, LeMay was asked whether joining the campaign had been a mistake. "Maybe it was," he said. "It was a miserable mess. But I considered this my last chore for the public."[66] At rallies in Indianapolis and Dayton, Wallace introduced LeMay but did not let him speak.[67] Then he packed LeMay up and sent him on a fact-finding trip to Vietnam, with stops in Guam and Wake Island, keeping him away from American reporters for the rest of the campaign.[68] The fiasco did not stop Wallace from ending his campaign on a high note in front of twenty thousand people at Madison Square Garden, which some called the biggest crowd there since an FDR rally in 1936.[69] He predicted an upset win and proclaimed that "after November 5, you anarchists are through in this country, I can tell you that."[70]

On election eve, Wallace returned, alone, to the home where he and Lurleen had planned to live. The American Independent Party had somewhere between $1 million and $2 million in unspent campaign funds. There had simply not been enough time or enough ways to spend it all. Long before the polls closed on the West Coast, Walter Cronkite announced that Wallace had "gone down to ignominious defeat."[71] Yet while less than 1 percent of Northerners had supported Strom Thurmond's campaign in 1948, about 8 percent supported Wallace in 1968. In some ways, he owed what success he had to Lyndon Johnson, the first successful Southern politician in the modern era. But while Johnson governed according to issues popular in the North, Wallace was still a little too Southern. Wallace represented the transition of the Old South to the New South, a move beyond regional concerns such as an obsession with race to an anti-elite, anti-Establishment message that all populist candidates would come to echo.[72]

PART III

Autumn Disquiet

CHAPTER NINE

Messenger

I N EARLY SEPTEMBER, THE Rev. Billy Graham requested a private meeting with President Lyndon Johnson.[1] When presidential assistant Jim Jones asked him what the purpose was, Graham would say only that it was a matter of "some importance" and should be off the record.[2] "This was the first time that I had ever asked President Johnson for an appointment," Graham recorded in his diary.[3] He was offered a thirty-minute slot at 1:20 P.M. on September 13.[4] When he arrived, Graham said he carried a message from a higher power, but it was not what Johnson thought. He brought a political offer from Richard Nixon.[5] He later described the meeting as "a bit of history in the making."[6]

Johnson and Nixon had communicated more frequently since Robert Kennedy's death, with Graham often serving as their go-between. As a longtime personal friend of both, he could talk freely to them, and they to him, without worrying about leaks. The messages were almost always exchanged orally, leaving no records.[7] "Some said I was instrumental in the transfer of authority from Johnson to Nixon," Graham wrote in his memoir. "As a friend to both, I might have said or done some things that helped in the transition, but I served in no official or even implied capacity."[8] John Connally was one of the few who ever joined these conversations. "He made an unusual political courier," Connally wrote in his memoirs. "He had Nixon's trust, and not many did."[9] Nixon sympathized with Johnson and saw that they had critics in common—the media, elites, liberals. "My opinion of Johnson," Nixon told Connally, "is a helluva lot higher than that of many others. He got a bad rap because of Vietnam."[10]

He understood how much extra weight his message would have if it came to Johnson from someone he loved as much as Graham.[11]

Graham had never been closer to a president than he was to Lyndon Johnson. "LBJ was impulsive and unpredictable," he wrote in his memoirs. "His speech could be as overbearing as his behavior. From my reading about past presidents, I would say he was in the same mold as Andrew Jackson—rough and brilliant, with plenty of natural ability."[12] Graham, who saw a side of Johnson that few others did, noticed how rapidly he had aged under the strain of the presidency. "The essential bond between us," he recalled later, "was not political or intellectual; rather, it was personal and spiritual."[13] When Johnson, who had a family history of heart problems, was trying to decide whether to run again, he told Graham about his chest pains before he even told his doctor. "He said to me that he had done a lot of things of which he was ashamed, although he refused to go into detail," Graham wrote in his memoirs. "One thing the President did confide in me, though, a full year before his term ended, was his decision not to run again."[14] Graham may have done more than anyone else to help Johnson feel comfortable with the decision: "I will always treasure a letter Johnson wrote to me when he got back to Texas: 'No one will ever fully know how you helped to lighten my load.'"[15]

Graham had become increasingly disturbed by the year's events, calling them a "dramatic indication that we have tens of thousands of mentally deranged people in America. . . . In some respects it has become an anarchy."[16] While he had never endorsed a presidential candidate before, he felt compelled to rethink that stance. "I might find I will," he said about the possibility of an endorsement. "I do believe I could influence a great number of people."[17] During the meeting in the Oval Office, however, he sought to influence only one voter. He pulled out his notes and read off a list of Nixon's commitments. First, Graham read, Nixon as president would never embarrass Johnson. He respected him both as a man and as the president, and considered Johnson the hardest-working and most dedicated president in 140 years—since Andrew Jackson, a president Nixon admired.[18] Nixon meant that sincerely; Johnson was a politician's politician who gave everything to the job.[19] Second, Nixon wanted a working relationship with Johnson and would seek his advice often. Johnson would be to Nixon what Eisenhower had been to Johnson. Third, Nixon proposed to use Johnson for special assignments after the election, including sending him to foreign countries. Johnson would remain the nation's top

Democrat and the most important leader of the opposition, something he strongly desired. Fourth, while Nixon would have to point out some of the weaknesses and failures of the Johnson administration, he promised never to focus on Johnson personally. Fifth, when Vietnam was settled, Nixon pledged to give Johnson a major share of the credit because he deserved it. Finally, Nixon would do everything possible to secure Johnson's place in history, again because Johnson deserved it.[20]

"As I read the points off to the President I could see that he was deeply moved and touched by this gesture on the part of Mr. Nixon," Graham wrote in his diary. Johnson had never heard anything like it in forty years in politics. Nixon's move was a "cunning piece of political marksmanship," Graham biographers Nancy Gibbs and Michael Duffy wrote, and it prompted Johnson to think even more highly of Nixon.[21] "He was not only appreciative, but I sensed that he was touched by this gesture on Mr. Nixon's part," Graham recalled. "The President asked me to read him these points twice."[22] While Johnson continued to offer public reassurances that he supported Humphrey, from that day forward his private actions conveyed another message. Johnson's position (which he would adopt again in 1972) was that he would continue to support the Democratic Party at all levels. At the same time, as Nixon later noted, "he found himself in sharp disagreement with the nominees of his party," and therefore did not discourage friends or family from overtly supporting Nixon.[23] Veteran diplomat Robert Murphy, who was close to Johnson, told Clifford's assistant, George Elsey, that if Humphrey did not stand firm on Vietnam, a Nixon victory "would be better for the country."[24]

Graham sensed how unusual his role was as election-year emissary between the two men. "It was my private judgment," he wrote in his diary, "that this might be unprecedented in history between two leaders of the Democratic and Republican parties in these particular circumstances."[25]

Graham's home base of Charlotte, North Carolina, was increasingly contested political territory. In many ways it symbolized the shift from the Old South to the New South. There were fewer and fewer conservative Democrats trying to make political headway into the upper South, which had been dominated by Democrats for generations.[26] While always insisting he remained a registered Democrat, Graham was seen more and more in the company of Republicans. But he resisted partisanship and always said he voted for the man, not the party.

In the late 1960s, Graham was at the peak of his influence, both within the evangelical world and politically.[27] He had never been so close to so many competing political figures and had known Johnson, Humphrey, Nixon, and Eisenhower for two decades.[28] He was even friendly with George Wallace, having once called him "one of the finest orators of the twentieth century."[29] His relationships with all of them were personal and even pastoral. Nothing leaked from their conversations. They looked to Graham for personal and political advice and saw him as a civil rights leader. His crusades had been desegregated even in officially segregated venues, beginning with Chattanooga in 1953.[30] By appealing to Graham, politicians hoped to unlock the support of his followers—largely evangelicals and white Southerners, many with politically moderate leanings.[31] With so many of his friends at the center of the 1968 presidential campaign, the real question was where he would throw his support. He avoided offering outright endorsements, but joint public appearances could be just as useful.

Graham regretted not having done more for Nixon during his 1960 presidential campaign and believed his inaction might have played a role in his narrow defeat. He hoped a Nixon presidency would revive the spiritual progress he believed the nation had made in Eisenhower's second term.[32] "The restlessness of the sixties generation burdened me greatly, and I was determined to do whatever I could," he wrote in his memoirs.[33] Prior to the emergence of the New Christian Right, Graham represented a movement that had been made increasingly anxious by the political, economic, and cultural trends of the 1960s.[34] He believed Nixon was the right leader for his time. Had Johnson run for reelection against Nixon, it would have presented a real test of loyalties, but once Johnson decided not to run, he was determined to go all out for Nixon. "Nixon's manner in conversation was very instructive to me," Graham wrote in his memoirs. "For one thing, he had a quality of attentiveness I have noticed also in royalty. When he talked with someone, he often looked them right in the eye, listened intently to what they said, and made them feel they were the only person in the world."[35] Before he could realize his wish of seeing Nixon in the White House, however, he first had to unify the Republicans behind him.

Graham's first stop was a visit to Dwight Eisenhower in August 1967. Eisenhower had been the first president to actively seek Graham's counsel; Graham had advised him during the Little Rock desegregation crisis in 1957, on civil rights generally, and on placing a greater emphasis on spiritual and religious matters in public life. Nixon's admiration of Eisenhower bordered on hero worship, but the feeling was not fully reciprocated. "Whatever Nixon felt about the slights from the man he served so loyally and so long, he still thought Eisenhower's endorsement and support could be decisive," Pat Buchanan reflected later. "Ike denied Nixon what he sought most: an acknowledgment of his achievements and his comeback in the face of an opposition Ike never knew."[36] He liked Nixon and respected him greatly as a politician, but as a five-star general and the hero of D-Day, Ike did not especially need politicians. He still viewed Nixon as the failed candidate from 1960, and there were other issues as well.[37] "I have always felt since 1956 that there has been a little something between Dick and me," Eisenhower told Graham. "I have never been able to put my finger on it but I think it goes back to the day I called him in and told him that I wanted him to decide whether he wanted to be my running mate that year or not."[38] He was referring to his suggestion in early 1956 that Nixon be dropped from their reelection ticket to take some other post, such as secretary of state, to broaden his experience—which the latter viewed as a demotion—and to Nixon's resentment at having to ask Ike to keep him as his vice president. Graham was concerned that another rift had occurred in the Eisenhower-Nixon relationship since 1961, and he made it his mission to bring the families together.[39] "I am convinced that America is facing the greatest crisis since the Civil War," he wrote to Eisenhower in 1968. "It is unbelievable how the situation has deteriorated both at home and abroad since you left office."[40]

Graham was troubled by a March 1967 Associated Press wire story about Eisenhower and Reagan sharing a round of golf at El Dorado Country Club, which carried a quote from Eisenhower that seemed to suggest he favored Reagan for the Republican nomination in 1968.[41] The story was carried widely, even by Walter Cronkite on the evening news, but Eisenhower said it was inaccurate.[42] "The reporters present obviously did not hear Mr. Nixon's name included in the question and therefore reported my answer as referring to Governor Reagan," Eisenhower wrote in his diary.[43] He thought he was only being asked about governors who were potential candidates.[44] The oversight was never corrected, so the myth continued. "In truth, Dwight Eisenhower did think Nixon was a loser," Pat Buchanan recalled.[45] Graham, thinking that Nixon needed to unite Republicans behind him to have a shot at the presidency, was determined to mend the Eisenhower-Nixon relationship. Yet even Eisenhower had never united all factions of the party behind him.[46]

At Eisenhower's home in Palm Desert, California, Graham urged the former president to consider endorsing Nixon: "I believe that your early endorsement of Nixon would be decisive," he implored. "I cannot press this upon you too strongly."[47] In a year of violence and turbulence, he believed Eisenhower could be a critical moderating influence. "The future of this country is at stake," he said, "even more drastically and decisively than it was at Normandy or Sicily. Once again you are the 'General in Command,' I have every confidence you will do what is right and best for America."[48] After the meeting, at Eisenhower's request, Graham brought him and Nixon together for "a protracted conversation" of "several hours" on October 17, 1967. "We discovered no major item of difference in our thinking and attitudes toward today's political scene," Eisenhower wrote.[49]

Graham made another unplanned visit to El Dorado Country Club in March 1968, when it looked as though Eisenhower might endorse Rockefeller. He was on the way to Australia for a crusade but deemed another intervention with Eisenhower important enough to interrupt his plans. "I spoke to him rather strongly as to why I believed he should support Nixon," Graham recorded in his diary, adding that he told Ike that "Nixon loves you like a Daddy." "Before I left, I felt he had pretty well committed himself to come out strongly for Nixon at the proper time."[50]

On Graham's advice, Eisenhower also encouraged the relationship between Julie Nixon and David Eisenhower. She had made her society debut with David at her side at the International Debutante Ball on December 30, 1966.[51] Less than a year later, Graham was delighted to see the front-page headline of the *New York Times* on December 1, 1967: "Eisenhower's Grandson to Wed a Nixon Daughter."[52] Graham emphasized the importance of their relationship to both Eisenhower and Nixon. "He loves David like his own flesh and blood and is so very proud of him," Graham wrote to Eisenhower about Nixon.[53] In May 1968, at a crusade in Portland that coincided with the Oregon primary, Graham introduced David and Julie from the podium, telling the crowd, "there is no American I admire more than Richard Nixon."[54] The young couple were struck that someone so influential behaved with such humility at his own crusade. Graham made no formal entrance, and no one introduced him as speaker. "These people were not responding to a man," Julie wrote later about the massive crowds at Graham's crusades that sometimes stretched as far as one could see. "Something far greater was at work."[55]

According to Graham's diary, when planning began for the Portland crusade two years earlier, no one thought about the Oregon primary or anticipated that the election would be a wide-open contest with Johnson not running for reelection. Publicly, Graham had to stay out of politics in Oregon, but he did what he could after hours. For example, Senator Mark Hatfield, well known as a Rockefeller supporter and possible running mate, was the honorary chairman of the crusade. Over breakfast at the Portland Hilton, Hatfield asked Graham about his support of Nixon. "I told him about my long friendship and my conviction that he was the best prepared man morally, spiritually and intellectually to be President of the United States," Graham recorded in his diary. "A few days later the entire political world was surprised when Senator Mark Hatfield, the strong Rockefeller booster, was now supporting Richard Nixon. This was a very important turning point in Nixon's campaign for the nomination."[56]

Graham also had worked on Ronald Reagan, hoping to head off a split in the party like the one that hurt Barry Goldwater in 1964. Graham admired Reagan and followed his campaign and election as governor of California in 1966. The Grahams had a vacation home on the fourth green of the Pauma Valley Country Club in San Diego County, which made it convenient for them to visit with the Reagans. "Certainly we are living in dangerous times," Graham wrote Reagan. "Perhaps God has raised you up for such a time as this."[57] Reagan spoke out forcefully against the decade's counterculture movements in a way that made Graham smile. "We have some hippies in California," Reagan said at a $100 a plate dinner in Milwaukee. "For those of you who don't know what a hippie is, he's a fellow who has hair like Tarzan, who walks like Jane and who smells like Cheetah."[58] Nixon was never so bold.

Reagan intrigued many Republicans, including Eisenhower, and that worried Graham. Privately, Eisenhower thought it would be a good move to nominate a governor, especially one from a large state like California.[59] The fact that in 1966 Reagan had defeated Pat Brown, who had defeated Nixon in 1962, suggested to Eisenhower that perhaps the political moment was Reagan's and not Nixon's. While visiting Reagan during the fall of 1967, Graham talked with the governor about the upcoming campaign and a possible clash between him and Nixon.[60] "It would be a great tragedy," he wrote Reagan afterward, "if you and Mr. Nixon should face each other in the primaries and divide the conservative vote—thus handing the nomination on a silver platter to one of the liberals." But "if in the primary he should stumble and fail, then you would have his considerable support and strength for the nomination."[61]

Nixon arrived in Portland on May 17 to campaign for the primary, which was scheduled for the 28th. He had breakfast on the 19th with Graham at the Benson Hotel, where they talked for nearly two hours. "No politician in Oregon ever had the crowds you are getting," Nixon said. He confided that he was very worried about the threat posed by George Wallace. "It seemed to occupy his thinking more than the possibility of not getting the nomination," Graham recorded in his diary. "At this point he felt that he definitely had the inside track for the nomination, and that unless he made some great mistake, he probably would get it."[62] A strong third-party contender could threaten his candidacy by drawing away the support of conservatives and Southerners.

Nixon wanted Graham to find out if Wallace might withdraw from the race. Graham paid Wallace a visit on May 27, just after the end of the Oregon crusade and right before the primary. "The moment I walked in he asked me how our meetings were in Oregon," he reported to Nixon on his meeting with "our friend in Alabama." "I immediately sensed that he thought I was your emissary."[63] Graham admitted that the timing of the meeting, so soon after his breakfast with Nixon and on the eve of the primary, was not wise. "I could see that he was already on the defensive," he reported. "When I left him I am convinced that he was uncertain about the motive of my visit."[64] There was no point, he realized, in trying to persuade Wallace to drop out. "I must confess that a lot of his arguments made sense," Graham recorded in his diary. "He did not mention the race problem the entire time."[65] His diaries do not reveal exactly what he said to Wallace, but one can imagine it was much like what he said to Reagan: dividing the conservative vote could hand the election to a liberal Democrat. Whereas Graham was not yet maneuvering actively for Nixon when he met with Reagan, he was by the time he saw Wallace, and it could only have undermined his message.

Nixon shrewdly used Graham to take advantage of splits in the Democratic Party between the liberals and the moderates, as well as splits among both Democratic and Republican conservatives.[66] The weekend after Labor Day, Graham was in Pittsburgh for a weeklong crusade. Nixon flew in for a political rally on September 7, staying in the same hotel as Graham.[67]

Later that day he appeared with Graham at his crusade, calling his crusade attendance "one of the most moving religious experiences of my life." Graham, during his introductory remarks, described his friendship with Nixon as "one of the most cherished I have ever had."[68] He also read a telegram of greetings from Hubert Humphrey, but it was Nixon whom he invited to sit in the VIP section.[69] Over breakfast the next day, Nixon asked Graham if he was willing to visit Johnson and give him a message intended to make Johnson comfortable with the idea of a Nixon presidency. It was one of the riskiest political moves in American history. "Nixon asked me if I would be willing to visit President Johnson privately and give him a private message from him," Graham recorded in his diary.[70] "'Billy, you are the only one that could do this,' Nixon said. I immediately agreed that I would, with the understanding there would be no publicity."[71] He agreed to carry out the mission because of the state of the country. While the 1860s had seen an actual Civil War, he felt that the 1960s were a kind of proxy civil war, and he could not envision how the nation would emerge from such a disorderly decade. Graham saw the disturbances in Chicago at the Democratic Convention as symptomatic of the nation's spiritual crisis. It was an orgy of violence in which the police had participated. Graham wondered how much lower civilization could go. The nation needed a healer, he thought, and Wallace could not be a healing figure, though he could be useful given his growing following. Graham also liked Humphrey but concluded that his ongoing need for support from the left wing of the Democratic Party limited his ability to act as a bridge.

Nixon had something the others did not. Because he had left politics earlier in the decade, he didn't owe anyone anything. In 1960 he had had an administration to defend, obligations to provide jobs for Eisenhower acolytes, and policy promises to keep. Now he had none of that. Unlike Humphrey or Wallace, he was beholden to no movement. He had crawled back from political oblivion on his own, making a comeback that had no precedent in American political history. That was why Graham decided to support Nixon: he was the stronger man. He had worked with Eisenhower on the world stage and had been close to Johnson since 1949. As Graham explained to his friend Hubert Humphrey later in the year, it did not mean he agreed with Nixon on everything. But he felt that Nixon had the best opportunity to heal the nation.

Between Labor Day and Election Day, the Nixons and Grahams were regularly seen together. By then most of Graham's work was done—

ensuring Nixon's nomination and a united Republican front behind him. Perhaps their most prominent appearance together that fall was in Atlanta, where Nixon took part in a televised town hall on October 2. The Grahams were shown several times during the program, seated next to the Nixon family. While Graham did not say anything during the event and did not applaud during the more partisan statements, his mere presence sent a message and helped establish a friendlier, warmer image for Nixon, who had long gotten a bad rap for being a sourpuss. Not counting gatherings of family members, Nixon and Graham appeared together in wire service photographs three times in the final two months of the campaign.[72]

Graham went as far as he could without making a public endorsement. When the press asked him whether he endorsed Nixon, he answered: "Absolutely not. He and I are personal friends of long standing and I do not intend to make a public endorsement. By endorsement I take it to mean that I not only come out publicly for him in the press but that I make speeches for him and urge others to vote for him. I do not intend to go any further."[73] Privately, he kept talking with Johnson. On October 10, he called the president to reassure him that Nixon stood behind his message of September 13. Without using Nixon's name, Graham said, "The friend we talked about the other day called me, and he asked me to call you. I'm just going to relay it. Everything I said to you, he wanted to reconfirm it all." Johnson responded much as he had done a few weeks earlier in the Oval Office. "I'm going to do just what I told you I'd do," he said. "As the leader of my party and the country, I'm going to do what I think's right, but I'm going to be just and reasonable and fair with every person." "Well, I think you have been," Graham replied, "and he really appreciates your stances on Vietnam."[74]

In the final days of the campaign, Graham saw how confident Nixon was, but also how tired. According to the polls, Humphrey was right on his heels, and the fatigue from running a campaign from New Hampshire to the finish line was beginning to set in. Graham offered reassurance. Nixon attended Sunday church service at Calvary Baptist Church in New York in late October with Graham and his son Franklin. When the service was over, Nixon and Graham walked the several blocks back to the former's apartment at 810 5th Avenue. Photographers followed them the entire way, a few well-wishers waved and offered encouragement, and they stopped and shook hands with a little boy. Just as Nixon said goodbye and was about to go up to his apartment, he turned to Graham aide Thomas Walter Wilson and said, "T.W., what do you know good?" T.W. responded, "I know two things. I know my relationship to Almighty God, and I know for whom I have already voted by absentee ballot." A smile momentarily brightened Nixon's tired expression. "That's one I have in the bag," he said.[75]

CHAPTER TEN

Stalemate

FTER FINDING SUCH UNITY at the Honolulu Conference, Washington and Saigon would spend the remainder of the year with more differences of opinion than similarities. Whatever optimism Johnson had at the start of the Paris talks in May that some step toward peace could be achieved during the remaining months of his presidency, it gradually depleted as Election Day neared. "The Paris talks dragged on through the summer," he wrote in his memoirs. "The formal sessions were sterile propaganda exercises. Informal talks during the breaks and elsewhere were of little more value."[1] Clark Clifford announced that since the beginning of the year, North Vietnam had successfully infiltrated 150,000 additional military personnel into the South, providing a sobering check on what could be realistically accomplished.[2] Johnson pressed on, with lower expectations. If he could not complete a peace agreement in Vietnam during his presidency, he could at least get the process started and receive credit for leaving his successor a better situation. Johnson could not have expected that the talks, rather than remain in the distant background of the presidential campaign, would become part of an effort by Harriman to elect Humphrey.

On September 3, after the party conventions, Harriman and Vance regrouped. In his National Day address a day earlier, North Vietnamese Premier Pham Van Dong called for more substantive discussions in Paris, presumably because the latest communist offensive in Vietnam did not produce the desired results. By this point, the Russians were as involved in the talks as any American. Harriman and Vance met again with the Soviet ambassador to France, Valerian Zorin, who said that Hanoi no longer believed it could win through military means alone and was now prepared to invest more in the negotiations—meaning they would in effect bring the "battle" to Paris.[3] The NLF planned to have some staff move from Prague to open a Paris office by the end of the month.[4] In addition, Zorin said, Hanoi was paying close attention to American politics. If Humphrey wanted to win, he would have to modify his party's position on the bombing halt, moving away from Johnson's and toward the peace plank advocated by some insurgents.[5] Hanoi understood that the longer the peace talks went on, the more their fate would be tied to the election result.[6]

The North Vietnamese were interested in additional private meetings that would include Le Duc Tho for the first time since he was recalled to Hanoi for consultations.[7] The U.S. delegation suggested convening at a CIA safe house on Rue Boileau before agreeing to meet instead at the North Vietnamese residence in Vitry-sur-Seine. On September 7, both sides agreed on the importance of stopping the bombing but bogged down on how such an agreement would affect the "serious" talks to follow.[8] The two sides did not seem that far apart on the issue of restoring the DMZ, with the North Vietnamese stating they "would know what to do" even if the specific steps were not spelled out. Harriman moved on to Saigon's participation in the talks, which he said "is a must." At that, Le Duc Tho subjected the Americans to what Harriman called "an endless harangue" about how the United States had already lost on the battlefield and failed in the negotiations. Cut off only by the scheduled end of the session, Tho said that he agreed to additional meetings for "many hours a day and many days a week." Harriman reported to Washington that this statement about future meetings seemed to be an important shift.[9]

At the next meeting, on September 12, Tho continued his "harangue."[10] Harriman reminded him that the United States had already agreed to an unconditional bombing halt as well as the participation of the NLF, and simply wanted to know what would happen after the bombing was stopped. "If you persist in having a solution as you want it to be," Tho said, "then the war will continue."[11] This firm restating of the North Vietnamese position seemed intended to determine whether the U.S. position had softened or shifted during the weeks that the talks had been bogged down. Hanoi seemed unconcerned that the communist side had lost 140,000 men since the beginning of the year. While Tho made it clear Hanoi was eager for additional dialogue, he again affirmed that the U.S.

two-phase proposal could not be accepted because it implied reciprocity. The North Vietnamese would not negotiate from a position of weakness, even if their latest offensive in Vietnam had not been successful. Ha Van Lau showed Vance a September 6 *New York Times* article by William Beecher that included three points raised in a previous plenary session—although points raised during private meetings were not included. That the article contained any points at all was a warning about the risks of leaks from the talks.[12]

The next secret meeting, on September 15, saw a minor breakthrough.[13] It was unusual both for the detailed level of the negotiations and for each side's lack of animosity toward the other. It also showed how Harriman and Vance pushed their guidance as far as they could without causing a breach with Washington. Johnson insisted he could not maintain the limited bombing halt, let alone order an expanded one, unless the American people saw that it was followed by movement toward peace.[14] Yet on September 15, Harriman and Vance raised the issue of restoring the DMZ without mentioning infiltration, attacks on Southern cities, or a freeze on force levels in the South. While Hanoi had not rejected these elements outright in previous meetings, neither had they given much positive response. They seemed most receptive on the DMZ issue, so the Americans pursued it, suggesting only the specific acts they had in mind following the bombing halt without linking them in a reciprocal way. Xuan Thuy took a softer position than in the two previous private meetings, promising that "on the very next day after the cessation of the bombing, we'd start the discussion of other issues, if necessary."[15] Harriman also made an "important and new" offer that eventually became a proposal for mutual withdrawal. United States and allied forces would be withdrawn from Vietnam as long as Hanoi also withdrew "all personnel infiltrated" in the South. All foreign forces would be removed no later than six months after the cessation of hostilities, and no further troops would be introduced. The North Vietnamese showed much interest in this idea, which had not been vetted by Saigon in advance.[16]

It was the first time in the negotiations that Harriman and Vance offered anything like a precise timetable for the American exit from Vietnam. The offer also tacitly signaled the Americans' willingness to abandon their earlier two-phase proposal and their insistence that Saigon be present during all discussions of the South's future. The North Vietnamese asked many questions about what level of decreased violence counted as "cessation of hostilities," how violence was defined, and the details of the six-month timing before withdrawal. "Even the President seemed impressed with the news of the first break in Paris," Clifford recalled.[17] Yet as interested as the North Vietnamese were in these new proposals, they still saw them as assuming reciprocity from Hanoi—which they continued to reject in principle. The Americans must stop the bombing unconditionally, and then the North Vietnamese would agree to substantive negotiations with "serious intent and goodwill." At that point, and not before or linked to a halt in the bombing, the agenda for items to be negotiated would be drawn up and agreed to. Harriman and Vance reported to Washington that as a result of this conversation, "we have concluded that if the bombing is stopped, the DRV will know what to do in and around the DMZ." Harriman then left Paris for consultations in Washington.[18]

He received new instructions for future negotiating sessions and then saw Johnson on September 17.[19] Previously, the U.S. delegation had focused on two "critical points": inclusion of Saigon in the negotiations according to the our side / your side formula, and restoration of the DMZ. Harriman apparently convinced Washington that Hanoi now understood the point about the DMZ and the United States did not need to raise it further, even though nothing in the record suggests there had been anything but disagreement on this point. In the most recent discussion, Le Duc Tho had specifically rejected restoring the DMZ as an American demand for reciprocity. Nonetheless, Harriman was authorized to simply note "Tho's apparent understanding of our views on the subject and the importance we attach to it," without going into the details. Harriman and Vance were also authorized to tell the North Vietnamese that the inclusion of Saigon in the talks was key to stopping the bombing. That was now the sole American request; all others had been dropped.

In the next secret meeting, on September 20, the matter of Saigon's role was brought forward as "a major factor" in agreeing to a bombing halt.[20] Xuan Thuy asked whether the United States had now abandoned the previous two-phase proposal and replaced it with a proposal to include Saigon, or whether Saigon was being added to the two-phase proposal. No solution in the South, he added, would be possible without a coalition government involving the NLF.[21] The Americans responded that there could not be a bombing halt without including Saigon. According to Vance's summary of the meeting, "the U.S., in effect, dropped its demand for prior verbal agreement in any form by the DRV on military restraint."[22] Hanoi asked whether, if they reached agreement on this point, the bombing would stop, but Harriman had been instructed to go no further. He said the United States planned to withdraw forces from the DMZ, and while the North "had not specifically agreed to any action on their part," Hanoi gave the impression that the American position was understood. Harriman pointed out that he was no longer pressing the issue, but offered clarification only so the North knew where the United States stood on the DMZ—even though the North continued to take the position that the United States should stop the bombing unconditionally, without any assumptions or understandings.[23]

Based on the number of questions they asked, the North Vietnamese were obviously interested in these latest proposals. But the American ambiguity over whether Saigon's inclusion would be the only additional condition for a bombing halt or whether they perhaps reserved the right to raise additional conditions made the North Vietnamese nervous. The delegation cabled Hanoi that they were convinced Harriman was sympathetic to the inclusion of the NLF at the talks.[24] Hanoi did not reject these proposals but, again, insisted they could be taken up only after an unconditional bombing halt.[25] Xuan Thuy told Harriman and Vance that while the United States was no longer seeking open reciprocity, it sought conditions that were "tantamount" to reciprocity.[26] Hanoi continued to demand an unconditional bombing halt.

The Americans again sought Soviet counsel. Vance briefed Oberemko and said the talks were at a critical juncture: it was time for the Soviet government to break the impasse. Vance was eager to see the United States move forward so that the bombing halt and the first meeting of the expanded talks could take place on the eve of the American presidential election.[27] Oberemko said that he would report on the talks' status to Moscow but that he believed the bombing, not Hanoi's refusal to agree to Saigon's inclusion, remained the roadblock to a settlement.[28]

There is no evidence that Saigon knew what the Americans were up to, or that even Bunker was being informed. To his thinking, the silence from his superiors meant that Washington was reexamining its position and might soon decide to stop the bombing in order to move from procedural talks to more substantive ones. In an unpublished memoir, he wrote that he believed the Chicago Democratic Convention was an important turning point. The chaos in Chicago and the terrible state of Humphrey's campaign, Bunker thought, had led Harriman to seek some kind of a deal with Hanoi that would enable Humphrey to establish himself as a statesman while forearming millions of voters with a glimpse of how a Humphrey administration would wind down the unpopular war.[29] He was surprisingly close to the truth. Bunker cabled Rusk and Rostow on September 24, ensuring he got the White House's attention, to say that "a variety of factors" and "instincts" led him to this conclusion. He thought the most important issue was the inclusion of Saigon in the talks. The longer that remained unresolved, the more suspicious Thieu would become, putting the United States "in trouble of the most serious kind" with Saigon.[30] Thieu's suspicion would spike even higher as Election Day approached, since it was assumed the administration would precede it with some breakthrough in Paris.[31] Johnson had engineered a similar "October surprise" only two years before, following the Manila Conference with Thieu on the eve of the 1966 midterm elections.

"If the GVN did not have a role in the negotiations from the time they start," Bunker argued, "this would strike at something that is basic to our whole military effort in South Vietnam, namely the cooperative relationship between the United States and South Vietnamese military leaders and forces." If one side lost confidence in the other, the entire military effort would be jeopardized. Bunker did not understand why the American negotiators in Paris said Saigon's inclusion "could" lead to a bombing halt. He believed the United States should be much more direct about the importance of giving Saigon a central role in the talks and that if it held to that position, Hanoi would have no choice but to come to terms.[32]

Bunker's concerns obviously struck a nerve, because in a telephone call with Rusk as well as a follow-up cable, Bunker expressed regret for any "misunderstanding." He said he and General Abrams merely wanted to be sure that the goal of including Saigon in the talks had not been lost, since he had not heard anything in advance of the rumor circulating about a forthcoming bombing halt. He was happy to learn that all remaining negotiating points, including the DMZ, infiltration, and attacks on Southern cities, in addition to Saigon's participation in the talks, remained important to Washington. That Rusk considered it important enough to call him about it probably suggested Washington's desire to make sure Bunker remained on message in his discussions with Thieu and other South Vietnamese officials. In fact, however, Bunker had good reason to be worried about the increasingly desperate negotiating tactics being pursued in Paris as the election neared.[33]

Harriman continued down the precise path that caused Bunker so much concern. He and Vance continued to press Washington for more flexibility on the inclusion of Saigon in the Paris talks. They were told they could strengthen the U.S. promise by changing "could" to "would": now, bringing in South Vietnam "would be a major factor" leading to a bombing halt.[34] The Americans notified the North Vietnamese of this change on September 25, the same day the NLF opened an office in Paris and thus became a presence in the background of the negotiations.[35] Tho responded that the modified position still implied reciprocity and the North Vietnamese definition of serious talks had nothing to do with including Saigon. Harriman said he was getting a strong impression that the North Vietnamese would not allow Saigon representation at the talks; Tho replied that Hanoi had not yet decided the issue and a bombing halt would allow both sides the opportunity to discuss it further.[36] The situation was serious enough that the task of prodding the Soviets to act was bumped up to Rusk, who met with Minister of Foreign Affairs Andrei Gromyko a few days later in New York. Rusk said he was counting on the Soviets to get North Vietnamese agreement on the inclusion of Saigon in the talks, while the American negotiators in Paris would focus on military issues in the coming negotiating sessions.[37]

Six weeks out from the U.S. election, time was getting short, both for President Johnson to show some accomplishments from the peace talks and for the presidential candidates to turn them into a campaign issue. "I'd quit if I thought I was just being used in Paris to hold the line until Nixon takes over," Harriman said to Clifford, who wrote in his memoir that Harriman "hated the war in Vietnam, he hated Richard Nixon, and he was determined to fight for his beliefs."[38] On September 27, the State Department asked for comment from both the negotiators in Paris and from Bunker in Saigon on two new possible approaches to the inclusion of Saigon in the talks. The first option was to notify the North Vietnamese, about five days in advance, that the bombing would stop and that serious discussions, with Saigon in attendance, would begin the next day; if they did not, the bombing would resume. A variation of that would have given the North Vietnamese the additional option of allowing Saigon to join the talks the day after the bombing halt or the week following. The State Department thought that offering these approaches would give the United States the minimum of what it insisted on yet would allow the North Vietnamese to concede without any discussion of reciprocity. The second option was that following a bombing halt, representatives of all sides, including the NLF and Saigon, would meet at the DMZ to discuss "the total cessation of hostilities, that is, a true ceasefire."[39]

Harriman and Vance responded that the first option carried an exceptional risk: if the United States showed up with Saigon's representatives at the first serious negotiating session without Hanoi's prior approval, the North Vietnamese might walk out. The variation, giving Hanoi a say in when Saigon could take part, probably would not help since the former might see a decision about whether to include the latter as another form of reciprocity—and the North Vietnamese had thus far not taken a position on the inclusion of Saigon. Harriman and Vance thought both Hanoi and Saigon would reject the second option as well, since it did not settle the matter of formally accepting Saigon's role in the talks. Instead, they suggested two options of their own: (1) a variation of the first, in which Saigon representatives would join the Americans at the first private negotiating session following the bombing halt, and (2) the United States would inform the Soviets that the United States would stop the bombing in exchange for Soviet word that the North Vietnamese would agree to immediate serious talks involving Saigon, and the North Vietnamese could tell the Soviets their decision if they did not wish to tell the Americans directly.[40]

Bunker saw no value in any of the proposals. As he saw it, each option involved the likelihood of embarrassing either Saigon or Hanoi and thus irreparably damaging the prospects for the talks. He did not think anything useful would be accomplished at a plenary session because it gave no side the option to be flexible about positions taken up to that point. In addition, the proposal of ceasefire was pointless since neither the United States nor Saigon had begun to work out what kind of ceasefire each could live with. Bunker preferred Harriman and Vance's idea of a private meeting, but he doubted anything could be kept secret since the world would soon know the bombing had stopped. Given the time it would take Washington, Paris, and Saigon to coordinate a bombing halt, members of the press would quickly discover what was going on. Finally, Bunker doubted that the North Vietnamese were really interested in serious discussions; they only wanted to look like they were working toward peace, "rather than operating from a cold calculation of how they can best wring benefit from the United States with minimal concessions on their part." He assumed they realized any concessions they made would soon be discovered.[41]

After meeting with the North Vietnamese on September 25, Vance flew to New York to huddle with Rusk.[42] He also saw Johnson on October 3. That meeting produced a modified set of instructions that the American side pitched to the North Vietnamese during the next tea break on the margins of the October 9 plenary meeting. This time, the inclusion of Saigon in the substantive talks to follow the bombing halt was "utterly indispensable." The North Vietnamese did not reject the proposal but said they would like to discuss the subject further in another private meeting. They would not have to wait long: a meeting was set for October 11. Both sides felt they had built some momentum.[43]

CHAPTER ELEVEN

Allies

IN HIS OWN MIND, Johnson was staying out of politics and focusing instead on his legacy and completing as many tasks as he could before his term ended. He might be out of the presidential campaign, but he had a great interest in influencing the choice of his successor. Those around him, meanwhile, were actively maneuvering for Humphrey. Johnson was especially incensed by the involvement of Averell Harriman, George Ball, and Clark Clifford. "The delegation should put aside all questions of domestic politics and keep out of them," Johnson said to Harriman in an attempt to bring him and the rest of the Paris delegation "back in line."[1] But the president had less and less control of his staff; some had already left to work full-time on Humphrey's campaign, while others moonlighted from the White House.[2] Johnson had resented the departures of people like George Reedy, Bill Moyers, and Jack Valenti, and as his presidency drew to a close, he resented subsequent departures even more—especially if a staffer was leaving to work for another politician.[3]

Rumors swirled that Harriman might resign to advise Humphrey.[4] He provided substantial financial help to Humphrey's campaign, including making his residences at 16 East 81st Street in New York and 3038 N Street, NW, in Washington available for fundraising.[5] "If nothing happens over there before November 6," Humphrey campaign aide Robert Nathan said to Harriman about the Paris talks, "the odds are going to go overwhelmingly against us." "I have got that very much in mind—will see what I can do," Harriman responded.[6] He convinced Humphrey that Johnson was not sharing enough information with him about the Paris talks, which started a pattern of Humphrey seeking information directly from Paris.[7] It dawned on Harriman that the reason Johnson was not sharing more information was that he actually wanted Humphrey to lose.[8] "If you agree it is just between you and me," Clifford told Harriman, "I believe you are right."[9] Johnson defended himself against charges that he was undermining Humphrey. "Look, I want the Vice President to win," he told his top aides, including Clifford. "I want the Democratic Party to win. They are better for the country . . . Where I help depends on where the Vice President wants me to help."[10] Yet his actions suggested the opposite: that Johnson was far more motivated to do what was best for his own legacy. Even *Time* magazine speculated that "the President might even prefer a Nixon victory."[11] About Humphrey, Johnson said he would respect him more if he "showed he had some balls." According to Clifford's memory of the conversation, Johnson doubted whether "Humphrey had the ability to be President."[12]

Humphrey faced an impossible climb—not against liberals or Nixon, but against Johnson, who continued to withhold support. He repeatedly failed to find any compromise with Johnson, and with each failure, he became a little less timid about distancing himself from the president. "In early September, I was awakened one night at 2:30 a.m. by a telephone call from a worried Hubert Humphrey, who wanted advice," Clifford wrote in his memoirs. "He had just said publicly he would start bringing American troops home in 1969, and, once again, had been reprimanded by Presidential aides for his statement." Clifford helped Humphrey find a way to deviate from Johnson's position safely, by framing his statements as being consistent with what Thieu had said. Humphrey proposed to Harriman that they use former Ambassador Arthur Goldberg as a liaison to improve information sharing, but Harriman thought it would do more harm than good, especially with the White House.

Harriman proposed that Humphrey come to Paris for direct meetings with Harriman and Vance, after which, in response to the inevitable outrage from the White House, Harriman would dramatically resign in protest to join the Humphrey campaign. But Humphrey vetoed the idea.[13] The *Wall Street Journal* was ready to run with the story until reporter Henry Gemmill got a firm denial from the State Department.[14] Instead, George Ball quit his post as ambassador to the UN on September 26 after only a short tenure, a role he had not been thrilled about anyway but which Johnson had talked him into.[15] "I cannot permit myself to remain quiet any longer about Nixon. He is a liar, dishonest, and a crook," Ball said, according to the version Clifford shared with Johnson.[16] "My new job was exactly as I knew it would be," Ball wrote in his memoirs. "Though I went to Washington every week and sat in on meetings, I was a bit player rather than a major actor."[17] Ball had been moonlighting for Humphrey since May, including contributing speech content, coordinating foreign policy experts to advise the campaign, making campaign appearances, hosting events for Humphrey, and making financial contributions.[18] According to Harriman's authorized biographer, Ball visited Harriman just before the decision to resign, and they discussed a draft of what would become Humphrey's Salt Lake City speech of September 30, in which he would finally articulate an independent position on the war.[19] "This will be our last chance before the election, and I feel action now is essential to give Hubert a fighting chance," Harriman said in a handwritten letter to Ball.[20] After the election, he wrote to Humphrey: "I am sure you realize how disappointed I was that I couldn't do a George Ball, but it seemed obvious that I should stick to the task here."[21]

One account contends that Ball quit because he was about to be investigated for maintaining a second office at Lehman Brothers, the investment bank where he had worked, while at the UN.[22] But Ball was a man of passions, like Humphrey, especially about Vietnam. The difference between them was that Ball spoke out publicly.[23] In his final day as UN ambassador, he sharply disagreed with Johnson and Rusk during a National Security Council meeting. "We are needlessly continuing the bombing and the war, without testing the chances for a settlement," he said, defending Clifford's position.[24] While Ball insisted that his departure should not be read as a break with the administration, Clifford and Rusk were not so sure. Johnson felt that "the time when he should have decided this was when he agreed to serve."[25]

Ball's decision to sign on as Humphrey's top political and foreign policy advisor was a viscerally partisan move with three clear purposes: to break from LBJ over Vietnam, to win the liberal voters who had supported Humphrey throughout much of his career but had sat on their hands since Chicago, and most importantly, to block a victory in the election by Ball's longtime enemy Richard Nixon. Humphrey's campaign kickoff on September 9 took place at John F. Kennedy Plaza in Philadelphia, the site of Humphrey's political coming-out twenty years earlier.[26] The event drew ten thousand, although Nixon's kickoff event, a parade in Chicago on

September 4, drew forty times as many.[27] "I did not think for a moment he could win," Ball wrote in his memoirs, "but at least we might deny Nixon an overwhelming victory."[28] Ball immediately launched an advertising program attacking Nixon and Agnew, calling them "Tricky Dick" and a "fourth-rate political hack." In his memoir, Ball wrote that "I planned to attack Nixon so outrageously as to force people to stop and think."[29] The nonpartisan Fair Campaign Practices Committee later called his attacks "vilification and defamation" and "dishonest and unethical statements."[30]

The last weekend of September was the roughest of the campaign for Humphrey. He was getting very little help from the Johnson administration. The campaign staff was still a mess; too many people spoke for Humphrey and to him, and he still lacked a central theme.[31] By wasting so much time formulating a Vietnam policy, he had allowed Nixon to focus on the issue of law and order. He hit rock bottom in the polls, too. On September 29, Gallup showed Nixon with 43 percent of the voters, Humphrey with 28, and Wallace right behind him with 21. "Let's face it," O'Brien had told Humphrey on September 16 while planning his arrival on the campaign, "as of now we've lost. It's on every newsman's lips."[32] The situation did not look any better two weeks later. Wallace could siphon as many as 20 million votes from the major-party candidates, denying an outright victory to either Nixon or Humphrey and leaving the race decided in the House of Representatives.

But rather than assume a Democratic-controlled House would throw the race to Humphrey, Wallace was savvy enough to realize that he could make a deal with Republicans and conservative Democrats, tip the result to Nixon, and emerge with the image of a kingmaker.[33] If the election had gone to the House, each state delegation would have had one vote. The Democrats controlled twenty-six delegations, but five of those were states that were strong for Wallace.[34] The Republicans controlled nineteen, and five others were evenly divided.[35] The wrangling would have been intense.[36] Cutting a deal with Republicans, preferably before the House of Representatives took up the matter, was a surer path to promoting what Wallace believed in.[37]

The rally at the Seattle Center Arena on September 29 was the worst of Humphrey's entire campaign.[38] Hecklers almost drowned out his remarks. "We have come not to talk with you, Mr. Humphrey. We have come to arrest you," a protester yelled.[39] "Hitler, Hubert, and Hirohito," a sign said.[40] Signs with the taunting message "Dump the Hump" drew attention to images of him with exaggerated features: popping eyes, dimpled chin, high forehead, bags under his eyes, and wrinkles. "I was constantly harassed by some of the student militants," Humphrey reflected later. "The division in the Democratic party in 1968 gave plenty of evidence that there was a growing tide of opposition."[41] Many on the left saw him as having all of Johnson's liabilities but none of his strengths.[42] The hecklers Humphrey faced "were the saddest aspect of the 1968 campaign," Nixon wrote in his memoirs.[43] David Schumacher of *CBS News* tracked down some of the protesters and interviewed them on camera. When Schumacher asked what it was about Humphrey or his campaign that displeased them, one of the leaders shouted into the camera, "Man, we don't care about where he's going or what he's done. We don't even care about the war. All we want to do is break up this fucking meeting." The hecklers, wearing sandals and torn T-shirts, were young, with maybe a third still in high school. They did not seem to Berman to be part of any organized movement. Many could not articulate informed positions on policy issues, but that did not stop journalists like Tom Wicker and Anthony Lewis from turning them into celebrities.[44]

After arriving in Salt Lake City from Seattle, Humphrey and his staff battled all night in his suite at the Hilton over the final text of his Vietnam speech. Ball told Humphrey it was essential that he break with the White House over Vietnam. He had spoken with Harriman and Vance in Paris, he said, and "they're willing to come out for you 1,000 percent if you do it."[45] Clifford recalled that Ball had been working on a draft of a statement "almost identical to recommendations Ball, Harriman, Vance, and I had made unsuccessfully for weeks."[46] In the hope of avoiding a conflict with Johnson, the draft was framed as what Humphrey would do after becoming president.[47] When asked if, with Humphrey's proposal, "we might be reaching a point of an honorable political solution to the war," Ball answered, "I think the answer is clearly yes."[48] As president, Humphrey would settle the war within a year.[49] The Salt Lake City speech, Ball wrote, was aimed at "commentators, editorial writers and the universities. I do not think the man in the street will form an independent judgment as to whether or not the proposals are sound."[50] He arranged for a Lehman Brothers friend, Harry Fitzgibbons, to secretly travel to Paris to seek Harriman's input.[51] "Harriman listened, made some suggestions, and said the speech was OK," Humphrey wrote in his memoirs.[52] But Harriman did more than that: his personal papers contain heavily annotated drafts of Humphrey's proposed speech.[53]

O'Brien told Humphrey the first draft was "not worth the expenditure of $100,000," the cost of television airtime for broadcasting the speech.[54] Humphrey's staff and other advisors were split between declaring independence from Johnson versus taking a more conciliatory approach that sought to remain within the general framework of Johnson's policy, minimizing any differences and reducing the risk of a break with the White House. Bill Connell, Bill Welsh, and James Rowe urged Humphrey to remain close to Johnson, while Edgar Berman, Fred Harris, and Larry O'Brien all pushed for a break from Johnson, arguing that the president did not support the campaign anyway. Ted Van Dyk and Norman Sherman were swayed back and forth by the arguments on each side. "I don't want a lot of hawk-dove debate taking place around me," Humphrey said.[55] "Whatever was said," Berman recalled, "it must imply that Humphrey had gotten out from under—was 'his own man.'" Harris asked Humphrey if he would seek Johnson's approval before giving the speech. "Hell, no," the candidate replied. "I'm not going to ask. I did that once."[56] Instead, after recording the speech for the national primetime broadcast, he called Johnson to give him advance notice of what it would say. "I gather you're not asking my advice," Johnson said.[57] Humphrey promised not to call for a unilateral withdrawal and said any proposals would be framed as what he would do as a "new President" facing "new circumstances." What he did not say was that it had already been taped.[58] What Johnson did not say, in turn, was that someone on Humphrey's team had left a draft of the speech in the studio, where it was found by a Republican staffer, who forwarded it to the Nixon campaign. Nixon had then tipped off Johnson.[59]

According to Humphrey's memoirs, Harriman had previously insisted that Humphrey not make any proposal related to the peace talks, but now he "no longer raised that objection, having, I suppose, lost heart himself that the negotiations would really succeed."[60] While talking about the peace talks no longer posed a risk with Harriman, a break with LBJ over Vietnam would also be a break with South Vietnam, or at least it would make such a break difficult to avoid. The key line in the speech, "As President, I would be willing to stop the bombing of the North as an acceptable risk for peace," meaning that Humphrey supported a bombing halt without conditions, had been drafted by Ball based on Fitzgibbons's consultations in Paris.[61] That was the prepared text issued to the press.[62] Yet when he delivered the speech, Humphrey dropped the words "be willing to" and simply said: "As President, I would stop the bombing of the North as an acceptable risk for peace." The change went largely unnoticed.[63]

Johnson was enraged.[64] Those around the president who were pulling for Humphrey emphasized that he had said nothing that deviated from Johnson's own positions. "I also know about the deep backgrounder that George Ball gave the newspapermen the next morning," Johnson told Rowe. "There are lots of differences," adding that if he were Hanoi, he would ask himself, "Can I get a better deal out of Humphrey than I can Johnson?"[65] All North Vietnam had to do was wait for a Humphrey victory, he said, and "they're in clover."[66] He was convinced that Humphrey was really saying that he would stop the bombing with no strings attached.[67]

George Ball told Clifford that Humphrey would waive all of Johnson's remaining conditions, including the presence of South Vietnam at the negotiations, and simply stop the bombing.[68] Humphrey was abandoning not only Johnson but the Democratic nominating convention.[69] "As President I would sever all relations with the South Vietnamese and leave them on their own," he said.[70] It was a carefully worded way of proposing the unconditional bombing halt that Johnson would never table in Paris.[71] By taking that stance, Humphrey made it difficult for the negotiators in Paris to maintain Johnson's position. Since Harriman had offered substantive input on Humphrey's speech and had also been pressing Johnson to weaken his conditions, presumably Harriman got what he wanted. As Ball hoped, the speech dramatically transformed media coverage of the campaign. "Humphrey's speech was shrewd," Nixon recalled later. "While it scarcely differed from Johnson's position, he made it sound like a major new departure."[72] But Nixon did not know about the maneuverings behind the scenes. The speech established Humphrey as his own man, no longer bound to Johnson.[73] Humphrey, often recognized as one of the few decent men in politics, used the hardball tactics he felt had been used against him throughout his career. He must have known that was how George Ball operated during the Kennedys' campaigns, but even if he did not, he surely found out once Ball was running his campaign. The shift by the Humphrey campaign politicized the U.S. delegation in Paris even more than they already were. Humphrey had taken advantage of access to private information about the negotiations and utilized it in his speeches, which were made not as vice president but as a political candidate.[74]

To add symbolism to substance, Humphrey gave the Salt Lake City speech without using the vice-presidential seal that always appeared on the front of the podium when he gave an address—and he did not use it for the remainder of the campaign. The decision was a nod to those who called on him to resign the vice presidency so that he could be truly independent from Johnson for the rest of the campaign. "It was enormously important for the political signal it sent," Clifford wrote in his memoirs.[75] Ball wrote that "no one asked Humphrey how his views on the war differed from those of Nixon. The thrust of every inquiry was, how did Humphrey's differ from Lyndon Johnson's?"[76]

It was a critical moment for the Humphrey campaign, and he risked losing Texas and even the election because of it. While it was not part of the speech, Ball said Humphrey would try to end the war on January 21, 1969, his first full day in office, and in any case it would be over by April. It was a direct appeal to the left wing of the party, even if it meant losing some of Humphrey's blue-collar supporters to Wallace or Nixon. Having someone of Ball's status now speaking for Humphrey, Berman wrote later, caused the bulk of the press to switch from earlier support of McCarthy or Kennedy to positive coverage of Humphrey.[77]

Humphrey did not know that the text of his Salt Lake City speech remained in the studio teleprompter after the taping. Thomas Korologos, a staffer for Senator Wallace Bennett, discovered it while working on Bennett's campaign taping later that day. The speech had been embargoed until the evening telecast, but Korologos immediately called Richard Allen, Nixon's lead advisor on foreign policy. It was not the first time he had shared intelligence from the Humphrey campaign; he had a source close to the vice president who periodically leaked details.[78] Allen passed this latest tip up the chain of command. "Reports from friendly source watching HHH taping operating in Salt Lake City say that there is great confusion surrounding the operation," he cabled to Pat Buchanan that afternoon.[79] Buchanan reached Nixon in Detroit with the news and Nixon placed a call to Lyndon Johnson at 6:45 P.M., tipping him off about what the vice president planned to say.[80] If Nixon had been looking for a way to warn a suspicious president that his own vice president planned to betray him, it could not have been better scripted. The tip prompted Johnson to obtain a copy of the speech from the DNC before it was broadcast.[81]

Nixon asked Johnson for reassurance that Humphrey's speech did not reflect a new administration policy, and after Johnson confirmed that it did not, Nixon put the knowledge to use. "Put yourself in the position of the enemy," he said on the campaign stump. "He is negotiating with

Plate 1. Johnson shocked the nation when he declared on nationwide television on March 31, 1968, that he would not run for reelection. Here, he studies the next day's newspapers while aboard Air Force One. (Courtesy of Lyndon B. Johnson Presidential Library)

Plate 2. Humphrey and Johnson were a great team, especially on civil rights, but the latter questioned whether the former was sufficiently loyal—especially after the former staked out independent positions to make a run for the presidency. (Courtesy of Lyndon B. Johnson Presidential Library)

Plate 3. Senator Eugene McCarthy of Minnesota was the first to challenge Johnson for the presidency within the Democratic Party. (Courtesy of Lyndon B. Johnson Presidential Library)

Plate 4. Both John-
son and Dr. Martin
Luther King Jr.
were frustrated by
increasingly tense
race relations in the
nation, even after the
Civil Rights Act of
1964 and the Voting
Rights Act of 1965. It
only got worse after
King's assassination
in Memphis, Tennes-
see on April 4,
1968. (Courtesy of
Lyndon B. Johnson
Presidential Library)

Plate 5. Johnson surveyed from a helicopter the damage done to Washington, DC, during the riots that occurred in the aftermath of King's death. (Courtesy of Lyndon B. Johnson Presidential Library)

Plate 6. Senator Robert F. Kennedy's late entry into the presidential race wooed young people and members of the national press, raising hope that the mystique of Camelot might be restored five years after his older brother was slain in 1963. (Courtesy of John F. Kennedy Presidential Library)

Plate 7. Johnson and Nixon were arguably the most intense political rivals of their generation. However, in 1968 they came to see they could help each other, and had more in common when not facing each other on a ballot. (Courtesy of Lyndon B. Johnson Presidential Library)

Plate 8. California Governor Ronald Reagan was the choice of many conservatives in 1968, especially those who were disappointed by Barry Goldwater's loss in 1964. Here, Reagan shakes hands with Johnson while Humphrey looks on. (Courtesy of Lyndon B. Johnson Presidential Library)

Plate 9. Johnson was intrigued by the possibility of being succeeded by New York Governor Nelson Rockefeller, but their relationship soured after the liberal Republican became more critical of Johnson's Vietnam policy during the spring of 1968. (Courtesy of Lyndon B. Johnson Presidential Library)

Plate 10. Alabama Governor George C. Wallace rose to power in 1962 as a leader of the segregationist wing of the Democratic Party. By 1968, he broadened his appeal beyond the South by focusing on an anti-elite, anti-Washington message. Here, he shakes hands with Johnson following a White House meeting in 1965. (Courtesy of Lyndon B. Johnson Presidential Library)

Plate 11. The Paris negotiations to end American military involvement in Vietnam began on May 13, 1968. Here, at Camp David a month before, key members of Johnson's team, including, from left to right: Ambassador to South Vietnam Ellsworth Bunker, Johnson, Averell Harriman, and Press Secretary George Christian. (Courtesy of Lyndon B. Johnson Presidential Library)

Plate 12. Johnson's key collaborator in the Vietnam War was Republic of Vietnam President Nguyen Van Thieu, pictured here at the Honolulu Conference in July 1968. (Courtesy of Lyndon B. Johnson Presidential Library)

Plate 13. At the Republican National Convention in Miami Beach, Florida, Nixon chose Rockefeller-protégé Maryland Governor Spiro Agnew as his running mate. Candidates for vice president rarely add to a ticket, and, most importantly for Nixon, Agnew was not seen as subtracting from it either. (Courtesy of Richard M. Nixon Presidential Library)

Plate 14. As former President Dwight Eisenhower's health declined, he spent most of 1968 at Walter Reed Hospital in Washington, DC. Johnson regularly consulted Eisenhower during the difficulties of that year, and Johnson hoped he would be to his successor what Eisenhower had been to him. (Courtesy of Lyndon B. Johnson Presidential Library)

Plate 15. Vice President Hubert Humphrey sealed his political rise that began twenty years earlier with his nomination at the chaotic convention in Chicago. For his running mate, Senator Edmund Muskie of Maine added experience and calm to the ticket. (Courtesy of National Museum of American History, Smithsonian Institution)

Plate 16. Up until the last moment, there was speculation that Johnson would make a surprise appearance at the Democratic National Convention in Chicago to coincide with his sixtieth birthday on August 27, 1968. Here, Johnson watches the convention from his bedroom at the Ranch. (Courtesy of Lyndon B. Johnson Presidential Library)

Plate 17. Perhaps the most memorable aspect of the convention in Chicago for many Americans was the violent standoff between protesters and Mayor Richard Daley's police. Here, a man puts on a helmet emblazoned with the word "Yippie!" under the watchful eyes of the police. (Courtesy of Lyndon B. Johnson Presidential Library)

Plate 18. Former Alabama Governor George Wallace chose General Curtis LeMay as his running mate on the American Independent Party ticket. While it was a major accomplishment for a third-party challenger to get on the ballot in all fifty states, it was all downhill after LeMay's appointment. (Courtesy of National Museum of American History, Smithsonian Institution)

Plate 19. The Rev. Billy Graham had a lot in common with Johnson—fellow Southerners, civil rights supporters, and a shared awareness that political loyalties in the South were beginning to shift. During the 1968 campaign, Graham also served as an informal messenger between Johnson and Nixon. (Courtesy of Lyndon B. Johnson Presidential Library)

Plate 20. Anna Chennault, widow of General Claire Chennault, was a Washington socialite who lobbied presidents from John F. Kennedy through George H. W. Bush for political access. She never got what she really wanted, a policy-making job that would force insiders to treat her like one of them. (Courtesy of John F. Kennedy Presidential Library)

Plate 21. On October 31, 1968, the eve of the presidential election, Johnson announced a bombing halt over North Vietnam. Here, Patrick Lyndon Nugent kisses one of the three televisions in the Oval Office as his grandfather's address is broadcast. (Courtesy of Lyndon B. Johnson Presidential Library)

Plate 22. Humphrey's mid-October shift back to traditional Democratic prosperity issues helped the campaign to end in a photo finish with the Nixon campaign. The November 3 event at the Astrodome, at which he and Johnson are pictured here, was as much a political farewell for Johnson as it was a rally for Humphrey. (Courtesy of Lyndon B. Johnson Presidential Library)

Plate 23. When the election was called for Nixon, daughter Julie presented him with a crewel embroidery of the presidential seal. Pictured at the Waldorf Astoria alongside campaign manager John Mitchell, Nixon seemed almost in a state of shock after completing his long road to political recovery. (Courtesy of Richard M. Nixon Presidential Library)

Plate 24. Johnson gave everything he had to the presidency. At the same time, he seemed visibly relieved when Nixon was sworn in as his successor on January 20, 1969. (Courtesy of Richard M. Nixon Presidential Library)

Lyndon Johnson and Secretary Rusk and then he reads in the paper that, not a senator, not a congressman, not an editor, but a potential *President of the United States* will give him a better deal than President Johnson is offering him. What's he going to do? It will torpedo those deliberations. The enemy will wait for the next man."[82] Once again, Nixon was able to demonstrate that he was more in accord with Johnson's Vietnam policy than Humphrey.

Humphrey's speech brought in about $300,000 in desperately needed campaign funds, although not from Johnson-Connally benefactors, who had not been released to support Humphrey.[83] NBC had demanded $100,000 for thirty minutes of airtime—in advance, because the network knew the terrible shape of the campaign finances.[84] The DNC barely scraped together the funds.[85] The campaign had burned through $700,000 for preconvention television spots—arguably not needed, since Humphrey's nomination was not in doubt—and was now in desperate straits.[86] In one of the more bizarre moments of the campaign, even the Soviets offered support and money to Humphrey.[87] Entirely separately, Soviet Ambassador Anatoly Dobyrnin also offered Humphrey campaign cash.[88] There is no evidence that Humphrey accepted either offer, but the fact that they were tendered is remarkable.[89] Moscow saw Nixon as far too unpredictable in how he would end the Vietnam War.[90] Berman writes that the Soviets offered encouragement at other times as well. Dobrynin pulled Humphrey aside three times at a White House diplomatic reception to say that both Aleksei Kosygin and Leonid Brezhnev felt they could cooperate with him.[91]

This was hardly the first time the Soviets had taken a stance in an American presidential election, although it is the first documented offer of cash. The Soviets also publicly favored Kennedy over Nixon in 1960. "We did not think very well of him," Soviet diplomat Valentin Zorin reflected about Nixon.[92] Sergei Khrushchev recalled that some in the Kremlin came to see that as a mistake; they came to realize that "Nixon was a good politician" with whom they could make a deal.[93] "And so our initial attitude towards Nixon as President turned favorable," Zorin said.[94] Marvin Kalb, perhaps the most experienced Soviet watcher alive as of this writing, doubts whether the Soviet leadership truly would have favored Humphrey. While his positions were closer to theirs, they thought the Democrats had a history of inconsistency. The Soviet leaders would rather make a deal with the devil; at least you know where the devil stands.[95]

While I could not verify the details surrounding the Soviet offer of cash to Humphrey, as it appeared in Dobrynin's memoirs, there is no reason to doubt the ambassador's account.[96] Some senior U.S. figures at the time thought the Soviets would insert themselves into the presidential election. In his memoirs, Clifford recalled "Harriman's prediction that Moscow would try to prevent a victory by Nixon, whom they still regarded as an unreconstructed Cold Warrior."[97]

At the campaign stop after Salt Lake City, in Nashville, Humphrey's hecklers were gone. The formerly harassing signs and placards now held messages like "If You Mean It, We're With You" and "Stop the War—Humphrey, We Trust You." While the content of the speech was not dramatic, Humphrey's aides played up his intention to break with Johnson. "The goddamn thing had a magical effect," Bill Connell recalled. "Instead of the students getting up and raising hell, people were cheering for him."[98] The Americans for Democratic Action endorsed him by a vote of its full board, 73–13, after previously withholding its endorsement, and Humphrey's campaign tone became more aggressive, not just with respect to Johnson, but directly attacking Nixon and Wallace for the first time. Comparing his two challengers in a Ball-inspired line, Humphrey said, "My Republican opponent appeals to the same fear, the same passions, the same frustrations which can unleash in this country a torrent of unceasing hate and repression."[99]

To get through the long days of the campaign, Humphrey had needed tranquilizers and sleeping pills prescribed by Dr. Berman, and after Salt Lake City, he put even more stops on his daily schedule, coming closer to working almost around the clock in the final weeks.[100] Lady Bird Johnson and daughters Lynda and Luci loyally supported and even campaigned for the Democratic nominee, even as Johnson continued to resist the pleas of James Rowe and Terry Sanford to campaign.[101]

One major repercussion from the Salt Lake City speech was that it probably created an irreconcilable break between Humphrey and Saigon. Even if President Nguyen Van Thieu was suspicious of Nixon's call to draw down American involvement in Vietnam, siding with Nixon promised better odds of survival for his government. "The Vietnamese leaders made no secret of their unhappiness with the Humphrey campaign and its efforts to corral the doves," George Christian wrote in his memoirs. Johnson believed that Saigon would never agree to make peace until they knew the winner of the presidential election. There was no incentive to move until they knew the direction of American policy.[102] The speech also caused an immediate ripple in Paris.[103] "The period from now to the presidential election is a propitious time to make the U.S. de-escalate the war," Nguyen Duy Trinh instructed Hanoi's delegation.[104] But the speech gave the negotiators no guidance about Saigon's role in the talks. It was surely confusing to the North Vietnamese to have the top officials of the United States speak in uncoordinated ways about what must have seemed like competing terms for peace. Harriman said he had not talked with Humphrey, and what presidential candidates said was not important: Johnson remained in charge of foreign policy decisions until January 20.

Johnson's control, however, was undermined further when former national security advisor McGeorge Bundy gave a speech at DePauw University in Indiana on October 12, in which he strongly urged a unilateral bombing halt.[105] According to American intelligence intercepts, Hanoi was elated.[106] Johnson wrote in his memoirs that he believed the speech "created further concern in Saigon. Bundy called for the next administration to 'steadily, systematically, and substantially reduce the number of Americans in Vietnam and the cost of the war.'"[107] Bundy was the epitome of an Establishment figure who had once strongly urged intervention in Vietnam but had since become loudly critical of the war.[108] He defended his role in the initial build-up of 1964–65 while endorsing Humphrey's proposal for an unconditional bombing halt, saying the United States could "not go on as we are going."[109] While many Americans would have heard his remarks as those of a conscientious objector, free to speak now that he was no longer part of the Johnson administration, speeches like Bundy's and Humphrey's only confused Hanoi, Saigon, and the other interested parties.[110] "Both speeches shook our allies," Johnson reflected later, "and, I am convinced, created doubts and anxiety in Saigon."[111] The speeches created doubts about Johnson's continued ability to lead, since even his inner circle seemed to be breaking apart. "The Humphrey and Bundy statements, taken in tandem, appeared to be two big chinks in the Johnson armor," Christian wrote later.[112]

While Humphrey's prospects improved once the calendar flipped to October, Lady Bird's campaign appearances did not leave her feeling optimistic. "In spite of the warmth of my welcome," she wrote in her diary after an appearance in Louisville, "I left feeling uneasy about Democratic chances in November."[113]

PART IV

October Surprises

CHAPTER TWELVE

Home Stretch

A	S THE CAMPAIGN ENTERED its final phase, domestic issues over-
took Vietnam and foreign policy in voters' minds.[1] Humphrey and
Nixon both called for an end to American involvement in Vietnam, effectively neutralizing the issue, and Wallace was seen
as speaking increasingly to the fringe even though he struck a deep chord
with his voters. Even Hanoi recognized that Humphrey and Nixon "had
fundamentally similar campaigning programs."[2] It was much easier to differentiate their views on domestic issues, with the result that these ended
up being the decisive factor according to most polls.[3] Issues like safety in
the streets, crime, and riots regularly polled among Americans' top concerns and almost always ranked higher than the war in Vietnam.[4]

The shift occurred after the assassinations of Martin Luther King
Jr. and Robert Kennedy. In May, Gallup showed the war as Americans'
number one concern, with 42 percent. But the individual law-and-order
categories, including race relations, crime and lawlessness, poverty, and
general unrest, polled at a combined 47 percent.[5] Polls taken on August 4,
August 18, and September 8 showed similar results. "Crime in streets is
real fear of U.S. voters," Gallup reported.[6] "As this campaign draws to a
close," Nixon scribbled in shorthand on a yellow pad found by Dwight
Chapin in 2020, "there is no issue on which a clear-cut choice . . . than
that of restoring law and order."[7] Overwhelming majorities believed
crime and violence were the most important issues facing the country,
and they wanted a strong president to restore order.[8] Nixon's stance was
substantially closer to most Americans' concerns on these issues than

Humphrey's—a fact conceded even by Humphrey's inner circle.[9] "The Democrats had lost the confidence of the nation," Theodore White wrote, referring not just to the Humphrey campaign but the party that had been at the helm for almost the entire decade.[10] Erron Kirkpatrick, Humphrey's former political science professor and chief public opinion analyst, advised the campaign that "Humphrey is soft in the area of law and order, and this softness is hurting him more than anything else. Crime prevention is at the top of what people—as many as 89 percent—want."[11]

It was no coincidence that Nixon kicked off his fall campaign on September 4 in Chicago, less than two weeks after the chaos of the Democratic Convention. "In some respects," he wrote in his memoirs, "this was a risk because the city was still tense and reeling from the Democratic Convention and from the criticism being leveled against Mayor Richard Daley and the Chicago police force. The risk paid off. As our motorcade passed through Chicago's loop at noontime, an estimated half-million people turned out in genuine good cheer, with frequent outbursts of enthusiastic support. The contrast with the bitter confrontation that Humphrey was tied to could not have been greater."[12] Nixon's appearance was effectively a defense of Daley, the police, and the city. Standing defiantly in a Democratic stronghold, the one that possibly denied him a victory in 1960, Nixon made a case for a new, more populist majority with anti-Establishment overtones, by appealing for center-right Democrats to join his centrist Republican core.[13] He said protesters deserve the right to be heard but not to be violent, and that police needed better training to handle "provocateurs" but should not be trampled upon.[14] Even Arthur Goldberg, one of Humphrey's campaign managers, allowed that "a few years of Nixon wouldn't be so bad."[15]

Nixon soon learned that, as the front-runner, he would become a target for both the left and the right—both the Humphrey and Wallace campaigns. With turmoil on the political extremes, supporting Nixon became surprisingly mainstream. Arthur Schlesinger Jr. was amazed at how many New York intellectuals had gone "soft" on Nixon, whether out of disgust for Humphrey or because, as Walter Lippmann suggested, they were drawn to a "maturer and mellower" Nixon.[16] Lippmann, America's foremost liberal columnist, described the Republican candidate as the personification of the middle American, with grit, tenacity, and hope.[17] "The Democratic Party needs a period of rest and recuperation," he wrote, "away from the seat of power after its overlong tenure of power."[18] Columnist Joseph Kraft believed Nixon was also likely to end the war faster, since he was not wedded to the policy that created it.[19] "The new campaign of 1968 reflected much that Nixon had learned since 1960, a capacity for growth undeniable," Theodore White wrote.[20] For example, rather than attempt a fifty-state campaign, as he had done in 1960, in 1968 he focused on the handful of battleground states. Rather than endless days campaigning from east to west, followed by a red-eye flight east to start all over the next day, Nixon used media like radio and television to reach more people.[21] In a campaign without major weaknesses, critics focused on soft spots such as the lack of excitement in the campaign or on Nixon's gaffe-prone running mate, Spiro Agnew. He represented exactly what Nixon wanted on the ticket, a piece of the Goldwater anti-Establishment embedded in an Establishment campaign, but he was not battle-tested and kept drawing attacks from the press.[22] "I tried to reassure him," Nixon wrote in his memoirs, "telling him that these efforts were mainly a way of using him to get to me."[23]

A whistle-stop tour through Ohio on October 22 was the most intensive day of Nixon's entire campaign.[24] The "Nixon Victory Special," a fifteen-car train pulled by a pair of diesel locomotives, began the day in Cincinnati and stopped in Middletown, Dayton, Springfield, London, Columbus, Marion, Lima, and Deshler, before ending in Toledo.[25] The event was designed for television, so viewers could see Nixon campaigning the old-fashioned way, talking to people in small towns across the state in a style reminiscent of Harry Truman's campaign from 1948.[26] Theodore White, who traveled with the campaign, noted that Nixon looked fresh, unworried, and smiling. He passed signs along the way with messages like "Nixon Is Next," "Nixon's My Man," and "Nixon Is Groovy."[27] In Deshler, Ohio, where the crowd numbered five times the town's population, a sign said "Bring Us Together Again."[28] White had also accompanied Nixon through Ohio in 1960—his only close look at Nixon's campaign that year—and he reflected: "The Richard Nixon whom I had followed up the same tracks in 1960 had been a divider, one of the most intensely partisan, sharply competitive men in American politics. The Richard Nixon who traveled along the same tracks, through the same towns, in 1968 remembered most sharply of the year: BRING US TOGETHER, and had decided he would be a healer. Rather than divide, he would risk his election."[29]

Virtually every telling of the 1968 presidential campaign indicates that the Humphrey campaign turned around after his Salt Lake City speech on September 30, but that is not borne out by the evidence. Humphrey turned negative on Nixon in order to chip away at his lead, focusing on his refusal to debate.[30] "Debate challenges are for losing candidates," Pat Buchanan said of the Nixon campaign strategy.[31] Nixon had written in favor of presidential debates in *Six Crises* and had encouraged Johnson to debate in 1964.[32] The only presidential debate in 1968 had been between Eugene McCarthy and Robert Kennedy on the eve of the California primary; there had been none during a general election since those between John F. Kennedy and Nixon in 1960. Humphrey refused to debate his primary challengers or enter any primaries.[33] "Naturally my unwillingness to debate gave Humphrey a major campaign issue," Nixon wrote in his memoirs.[34] But he did so presumably with the knowledge, or at the least on the assumption, that Johnson would not criticize him. Johnson had refused to debate Goldwater in 1964 and understood that you do not accept a debate challenge when you are ahead. The president also did Nixon a favor by treating Wallace as a major presidential candidate, including giving him a version of the same CIA briefing that Nixon received.[35] That gave Nixon an additional degree of protection. "As Humphrey knew," he recalled later, "there was no way that he and I could have a debate without including George Wallace."[36] That is what the Fairness Doctrine of the Federal Communications Commission would have required.[37]

The Gallup poll of October 9 showed Humphrey trailing Nixon 44 percent to 29 percent, with Wallace at 20 percent.[38] There had been barely any movement since Humphrey's Salt Lake City speech, when Gallup showed Nixon with 43, Humphrey with 28, and Wallace at 21.[39] While for liberals, whose support Humphrey already largely had, the speech helped to separate his Vietnam position from Johnson's, the difference was opaque for a national electorate already convinced both he and Nixon would bring the war to an end. The Humphrey campaign reached for the panic button. "We're going down the drain!" Clifford cried out.[40] Gallup reported privately that the issues that had dominated the campaign up to that point were "*not* natural Democratic issues, but are somewhat against the grain of the Democratic liberal tradition."[41] Democrats had always been torn between the elites and conservatives; the two wings of the party often despised each other.[42] By the late 1960s, liberals were arguing with radicals, the old left with the New Left, and all groups argued among themselves.[43] Since Franklin D. Roosevelt, successful candidates had been those who could straddle both wings, which together formed the New Deal coalition. The road to victory for a Democratic presidential candidate was almost always eased by taking the populist path.

Humphrey started experimenting with a law-and-order message—a delicate balance for a Democratic candidate.[44] Yet he was no stranger to the issue, or guilty of "appeasement," as Agnew suggested. As mayor of Minneapolis, Humphrey had been one of the toughest anticrime city leaders. In a speech on October 12 in New York City, he proposed the massive sum of $1 billion to hire more police, speed trials, and upgrade prisons.[45] Larry O'Brien hired political consultant Joseph Napolitan to overhaul campaign messaging, including removing Black people from campaign advertisements because they were not seen as consistent with Humphrey's new law-and-order theme.[46] With Nixon and Wallace focused in their own ways on imagery of urban violence and lawlessness, Humphrey took a more philosophical approach, emphasizing the link between poverty and crime rather than evoking racism or the failure of Great Society programs.[47] He needed every liberal and Black vote he could get, and he did not forget that Nixon had won 30 percent of the African-American vote in 1960.[48] Unable to separate the issues of crime and race, he did not want to alienate loyal African-American voters by digging into the causes of crime, the reasons for urban decay, or whether the policies enacted during the 1960s were (as Wallace charged) making the situation worse.[49] *Time* magazine called crime a "national disgrace" that Democrats sought to avoid talking about. When Attorney General Nicholas Katzenbach dismissed the chance of being "raped by a stranger" as akin to that of being "hit by lightning," Americans were not reassured.[50] No one could doubt the rise in crime that had occurred during two Democratic presidencies. A law-and-order message did not move the needle for Humphrey.

On October 15, Democratic consultant Vic Fingerhut, working on his first presidential campaign, fired off a thirteen-page "final plea" to Humphrey and his senior staff arguing for a completely new strategy.[51] Recognizing that Salt Lake City had not had the desired impact, Fingerhut made a series of bold suggestions in the memorandum, which he titled "Two Weeks to a Humphrey Victory . . . What Must Be Done."[52] Humphrey should stop talking about foreign policy, which had been a Republican strength since the Eisenhower years. He should not even mention Vietnam, because doing so would remind voters that Democrats started the war and that Nixon and the Republicans were better equipped to end it since they were not wedded to past policy. Fewer than 10 percent of voters had a family member in Vietnam. As late as October 31, Americans disapproved of a bombing halt by a margin of two to one.[53] Humphrey should drop the appeals to elites, who would probably come around to him eventually because they had nowhere else to go.[54] Instead, he needed to focus on ideas that mattered to working people, creating nostalgia for the New Deal and Fair Deal era, and remind voters what Democrats had done historically.[55] He needed the voters who had photos of Roosevelt and Kennedy on their walls. "The blue-collar worker, the lower-middle income white feels that the government has no interest in him," Orville Freeman advised Humphrey. "The group that we have often depended upon as the backbone of the Democratic vote is leaving us by the droves."[56] Finally, the character attacks on Nixon were not gaining much traction. His 43 percent was fairly solid, and other polls showed that he was respected even by those who disliked him. Nixon had a commanding lead over Humphrey on who could better handle Vietnam, who was the better candidate on television, who was more likeable, who was more sincere and believable, and who had a better command of world affairs. He led Humphrey in all regions of the country and among all community sizes, ages, occupations, and education levels.[57] Humphrey had to focus on Wallace's 20 percent—about 8 to 10 million voters.[58] As a third-party candidate, he had drawn every single one of his supporters from one of the two major parties. Fingerhut surmised that many were Democrats. That was where the votes were.[59] Nixon understood that, too, and was not taking on Wallace but instead saying that a vote for him was a wasted vote.[60]

Assuming turnout would be low, since Nixon commanded greater support but it was not considered enthusiastic support, Fingerhut argued that Humphrey needed to stop listening to elites and refocus on "late switchers" by using traditional Democratic prosperity issues: domestic economic policy, education, and unemployment. "It is precisely this kind of low turnout which enabled Harry Truman to 'squeeze by' Thomas Dewey in 1948," Fingerhut argued. "The late changers toward Truman were characterized by a marked shift in the basis of decision from the matter of personality to that of 'economic' interests."[61] The campaign picked up on a theme that emerged from a John Chancellor interview with a blue-collar voter: "Every time the Republicans get in, I'm out of a job. Every time the Democrats get in, I seem to make more money than when the Republicans are in."[62] This message needed to be reinforced to a generation three decades removed from the New Deal. "Franklin Roosevelt and the Democratic Party addressed themselves to the problems of the blue-collar worker, the farmer, the common man," Jack McNulty wrote to Harry McPherson. "Now he is not so common; he doesn't work on a farm anymore; he lives in a white-collar society. Just as a man 'moves up to Schlitz,' the common man of the Thirties has been pushed toward the Republican Party."[63]

Traditional Democratic voters who were unenthusiastic about Humphrey personally would vote for him if he started talking about their issues.[64] Harriman's effort to use the Paris negotiations to elect Humphrey was not helping as much as thought, because the negotiations were a subtle reminder of which party was responsible for the deployments of Americans. Humphrey, like Truman in 1948, had to refocus his campaign on domestic issues. As Nixon began using a calculated law-and-order message, promising to appoint an attorney general who would be tough on crime and hinting to Southerners that he would try to appoint a Southerner to the Supreme Court, Humphrey's appeals for "traditional Democrats" began to eat into Wallace's numbers.[65] Humphrey's strategy was simply to promise everything: more spending on education, social security, Medicare, jobs, housing, and health care, and a Marshall plan for cities. In a blitz of campaign rallies in Democratic strongholds in the Rust Belt and on the Eastern Seaboard, he questioned whether Nixon could be trusted to maintain the achievements of the New Deal, Fair Deal, and Great Society.[66] He emphasized things would get worse under a Republican presidency—exactly what Truman said about rival Thomas Dewey and Republicans in 1948.[67]

The second factor in Humphrey's two-pronged attack was organized labor. "We desperately need to activate organized Labor right down to the local union level," he urged his staff.[68] "We can win this campaign if people will quit bellyaching and go to work."[69] Appalled at the performance of the Humphrey campaign, the AFL-CIO assumed the responsibility to get out the vote itself.[70] The AFL-CIO Committee on Political Education (COPE) went all out, spending $10 million to persuade its membership not to waste a vote on Wallace, whom it described as no friend of labor.[71] "In the near-miracle of the Humphrey comeback in October," Theodore White wrote, "no single factor was more important than the army of organized labor, roused to the greatest political exertion of its history."[72] While labor leadership had supported Humphrey throughout his career, Wallace had whittled away at rank-and-file union members. The

AFL-CIO made four million calls to union households from telephone banks in 638 locations, using 8,055 telephones, by 24,611 union members and their families. In addition, 72,555 door-to-door canvassers registered 4.6 million new voters. Some 125 million pamphlets were distributed at plant gates, emphasizing that wages in Wallace's Alabama were among the lowest in the country and Alabama was one of just sixteen states without even the basic worker protection of a minimum-wage law. A total of 94,457 union volunteers were recruited to serve as car-pool drivers, baby-sitters, poll watchers, and callers to get out the vote on Election Day.[73] "All Humphrey had was us," George Meany said.[74]

The AFL-CIO emphasized, as well, that Alabama was 49th in the nation in welfare payments. The International Ladies' Garment Workers' Union (ILGWU) persuaded Johnson to record a carefully worded statement of support for Humphrey that emphasized their long relationship and his "unique" foreign policy experience.[75] These efforts were aimed at pushing down Wallace and propping up Humphrey just at the moment when voters got more serious and less emotional as Election Day approached.[76] Wallace's record of using the state police to bust unions was set against Humphrey's long pro-labor record. Every new non-union shop in the South, labor leaders stressed, meant less protection for workers. The popularity of Wallace, who had been polling as high as 23 percent of voters up to then, threatened not only Democrats but the leadership of labor itself.[77] The attack on Wallace was the most vicious of the entire 1968 presidential campaign. It was devastating for Wallace's new base of supporters in the North, who were more easily swayed than his more deeply committed followers in the South. "One could trace labor's efforts all across the country," Theodore White wrote: "steel workers, packaging-house workers, auto workers in Illinois; auto workers, machinists and service trades in California; oil workers in Texas; garment workers, building trades and electricians in New York."[78] Humphrey felt good again, and regional poll numbers started to go his way. Wallace supporters began to move in droves back to Humphrey—the liberal on civil rights and Vietnam.[79]

The first Gallup poll since Vic Fingerhut's memo, on October 24, showed a big bump for Humphrey, from 29 to 36 percent, while Nixon held steady at 44 percent.[80] The big shift was in the polling for Wallace, who slipped from 20 to 15 percent. The poll confirmed that Humphrey was picking up Wallace supporters as well as undecided voters.[81] Labor's effort had ravaged the Wallace working-class base, while those who stuck with him would probably have voted for Nixon in a two-way contest with Humphrey.[82] Those who left him went almost entirely to Humphrey, not Nixon. Fingerhut estimated that of Wallace's eight-point drop in the final three weeks of the campaign, seven of eight came over to Humphrey.[83] Organized labor's intervention was the major turnaround in his campaign, not the Salt Lake City speech. The New Deal coalition held but was split between two longtime New Deal Democrats, Humphrey and Wallace.[84] Humphrey's shift to a partisan, Democratic, common-man, populist economic message gave him momentum. The question would be whether it would be enough, with time short and the Nixon campaign running out the clock.

Things were going so well for Humphrey that the one area where he desperately needed help stood out all the more sharply: his relations with Johnson. "You know that Nixon is following my policies more closely than Humphrey," Johnson told James Rowe, who was close to both Johnson and Humphrey. "Humphrey started out as the leader of the Green Bay Packers and then he turned around and went into the opposite direction. To win elections, you've got to be for something and you've got to stand up for it."[85] Johnson was not impressed by Humphrey's inconsistent positions. When Nixon criticized the administration, he kept his promise and did not focus on Johnson, showing that he really did stand closer to the president than the vice president did. George Christian described Nixon's tightrope walk as "a masterful political approach to a difficult situation."[86]

Humphrey had to make peace with Johnson, and the only way to do that was to beg. He made an appointment, and Jim Jones confirmed it, for Saturday, October 19, at 2:00 P.M. Coming from a campaign rally in Landover, Maryland, Humphrey stopped at his apartment. He wanted to show respect for Johnson by shaving and changing into a clean shirt. As he entered the White House grounds at 2:05 p.m., Jones called Van Dyk to say that Humphrey was late, so his appointment was canceled. "That bastard Johnson," Humphrey said to Van Dyk. "I saw him sitting in his office. Jim Jones was standing across the doorway, and I said to him. 'You tell the president he can cram it up his ass.' I know Johnson heard me," he said.[87] It was another humiliating slight. Part of the problem for the White House was that Johnson considered the meeting with Humphrey off-the-record, yet word of it had leaked to the press.[88] Humphrey's staff denied being the source, but obviously reporters found out somehow. "Humphrey believed in everything I believed, until I announced I wouldn't run," Johnson recalled. "You can't be all over the court. He's a wonderful human being. But you can't be all things to all people."[89] "Shit, I am tired," Humphrey told Jones. "I am the Vice President. If you won't give me an appointment with the President, then never mind."[90]

Perhaps Johnson realized he had gone too far, because the following night Humphrey was invited back for another opportunity to meet with him. This time Humphrey kept Johnson waiting for over a half-hour.[91] In Jim Jones's telling, the meeting was a scotch-fueled screaming match that went until nearly midnight.[92] "The expression on the Vice President's face told all about his campaign troubles," Jones recalled. He estimated that Johnson had more than twenty scotch and waters—no matter how many he drank, he never seemed to show it. Humphrey tried to keep up. "By the end," said Jones, "Humphrey was a good four sheets to the wind. But I think they really got some things settled."[93]

Nixon was moving at a much less frantic pace. He was the odds-on favorite to win, had led by a safe margin for the entire campaign, and had far more campaign funds than Humphrey, who was embarrassed to ask even wealthy friends for money.[94] "No matter what we did in September, it didn't seem to come out right," Humphrey wrote in his memoirs. "We were broke."[95] His financial problems were compounded when much of the Texas money that had gone to Johnson in 1964 supported Nixon in 1968; supporters like Ross Perot withheld critical funding for the Humphrey campaign.[96] Johnson himself froze $700,000 raised by the DNC and suggested that it be returned to donors after the election.[97]

The national press concluded that Nixon ran a lazy campaign that did not articulate positions on many issues, but that is an oversimplification. "While masterfully, even flawlessly, run in the primaries, ours was a campaign that rarely took risks," Pat Buchanan wrote later. "And it had failed to capture the heart of the country. We had not bonded with the country, as happens in great fighting causes."[98] In a September 24 memo to staff, Nixon complained that his statements and releases needed to be more "meaty and quotable," more current, "livelier," not "cute or gimmicky," and no longer than a page and a half.[99] "Operation Extra Effort" was announced on October 15, previewing a surge of Nixon activity in the campaign's final weeks that even included unscripted media appearances.[100] One constant, however, was that even as the pressure built, Nixon continued to speak favorably of Johnson and make statements in support of his policies.[101]

Humphrey and Nixon were both keeping an eye on Wallace, but they were also competing for Johnson's affection, which was a powerful force.

Because Humphrey had to differentiate himself from the White House in order to attract the liberal vote, Nixon was left in the comfortable position of sitting in the middle, not disagreeing with anything Johnson said, and appearing reasonable on issues like Vietnam. Wallace stayed to Nixon's right, letting Nixon seem like the centrist candidate on the key domestic issue of law and order. Not only did Nixon not need to articulate many clear positions, it was in his interest not to do so. He was able to avoid head-to-head fights with Humphrey or Wallace and could focus on his image, appear presidential, and expand his following by going after groups like white ethnics, including Polish Catholics, white Protestants from the upper South, and rural Americans.[102]

The race tightened in the final month because of improvements in Humphrey's campaign organization and messaging, which brought many protest voters who had pledged support to Wallace coming home to the Democratic Party as Election Day drew near. One can only imagine where Humphrey might have found himself in October if he had used a populist strategy for the entire campaign instead of focusing so much time and energy on Vietnam and, in the process, damaging his relationship with Johnson.

CHAPTER THIRTEEN

Bombing Halt

I<small>T IS DEBATABLE WHETHER</small> the bombing halt and the flurry of activity leading up to it were motivated more by Harriman's, Clifford's, and Ball's urgent wish to pull Humphrey across the finish line ahead of Nixon, or by a genuine chance for peace. President Johnson did not want either side to accuse him of playing politics. According to George Christian, the president was irritated that the peace talks had dragged on so close to the election.[1] "Everyone will think we're working toward electing Humphrey by doing this," Johnson said. "But this is not what motivates us. I want to take it slow. . . . I would rather be viewed as stubborn and adamant than be seen as a tricky, slick politician." Johnson's motivation was his legacy, not politics. The North Vietnamese "know the Vice President would be softer," he added.[2] Those around Johnson questioned why a legendary politician, who had almost always acted politically, now refused to do so. "All of you know how much I want peace," he said to Clifford during a four-and-a-half-hour private conversation the evening of September 24, "but we don't have anything to show for it." "Mr. President," Clifford responded, "it's not your opportunity; it's your *responsibility* to stop bombing!"[3] Johnson did not need to get the process started and turn it over to Nixon; he could settle it himself.

The rumors of a bombing halt to come just before Election Day, in addition to the leaks coming out of Paris, Washington, and especially Saigon, put everyone, especially Republicans, on full alert. "Our unsuccessful attempt at secrecy seemed to validate the Republican charge that LBJ was planning some kind of last-minute surprise for political purposes," Clifford wrote in his memoirs.[4] Nixon was alarmed at both the secrecy and the political ramifications of the backstage maneuvering. Harriman wrote for his private files that "for several years, I have taken the position that Viet-Nam was important in U.S. policy, but that other things were more important. When asked what was more important, I always gave as my first point, not permitting it to elect Nixon as President."[5]

Unlike Humphrey, who had started inching away from Johnson as soon as he had the nomination in hand, Nixon had been consistent about the conditions he thought were necessary to justify a bombing halt.[6] A poll by International Research Associates conducted in six anticommunist nations and Hong Kong showed that 49 percent of respondents preferred Nixon to 25 percent for Humphrey, with the remainder split between Wallace and undecided.[7] According to Assistant Secretary of State for Far Eastern Affairs William Bundy, all American "clients" in Asia would welcome a Nixon victory except Laos—a legacy of Eisenhower's policy of interfering in its government to support anticommunists, which his former vice president was expected to continue. In mid-October, Bundy was already beginning to work on a transition to a Nixon administration so the new president would not have problems "when he takes office."[8] It is extremely unlikely that an Asian leader like Thieu would not already have preferred Nixon over Humphrey.

In Washington's view, the bombing halt would be unconditional even if it were not called that, and even the one significant concession the United States had gotten from Hanoi, agreement for Saigon's participation in the talks, was unraveling because of Thieu's concerns. On October 29, Johnson sent a message to Thieu that was a combination of exhortation and threat.[9] He expressed sympathy for Thieu's domestic problems, but said Saigon should understand that the United States planned to move forward no matter what. Thieu replied that his difficulties with the American proposal were not secondary but crucial to Vietnam's national security. Unless Hanoi provided assurances that the NLF would not be admitted as a separate delegation, Saigon would not participate. If Hanoi genuinely believed in peace, it would agree to negotiate directly with Saigon.[10]

"I decided then, with genuine regret, that we had to go forward with our plans," Johnson wrote in his memoirs.[11] He could not wait on Thieu any longer, and he had already informed the three presidential candidates, all of whom enthusiastically endorsed his decision. Because he felt a head cold coming on, Johnson would prerecord his speech announcing the bombing halt and the start of serious negotiations in Paris, and hold it for broadcast at approximately eight o'clock in the evening on October 31 in Washington, which was nine in the morning on November 1 in Saigon. The halt would take effect twelve hours later. Bunker was charged with discouraging Thieu from making any statement that could jeopardize the talks.[12] Thieu was not told that Johnson had already taped his address, using a nonnetwork television crew in order to avoid leaks.[13]

Since his address was recorded at a time when it was not clear that Thieu would agree to come to the peace talks, Johnson had to leave a few phrases loose. He used language about Saigon's participation that could stand whether or not Thieu came through with last-minute assent.[14] Later, he made a second recording of three sentences regarding Saigon that were inserted into the final broadcast.[15] They addressed the concern that the timing of the speech was to boost Humphrey, who was then just three points behind Nixon in the latest Harris poll: "I do not know who will be inaugurated as the 37th President of the United States next January. But I do know that I shall do all that I can in the next few months to try to lighten his burdens as the contributions of the Presidents who preceded me have greatly lightened mine. I shall do everything in my power to move us toward the peace that the new President—as well as this President and, I believe, every other American—so deeply and urgently desires."[16] Johnson could have delayed the announcement, but his aides convinced him that if he wanted to be viewed as a peacemaker it was time to act. The United States would move forward without its ally.[17] Johnson breathed a sigh of relief when he finished the taping, calling it the most important decision he had ever made.[18] The news media, perhaps too eager to boost Humphrey's chances, at first misreported the story. The *New York Times* city edition, for instance, used the headline "Saigon and the NLF will Join in the Enlarged Paris Discussions."[19] Johnson received 267 telegrams in response to his speech. A little more than half, or 153 according to Johnson, either said the bombing halt was "lousy" or that Johnson was a "no good political son of a bitch."[20] According to Tom Wicker, Johnson called Richard Nixon right before the speech aired. By tipping him off that he had been unable to persuade Thieu to go along, Johnson gave Nixon the evidence to charge that he had acted prematurely.[21]

As morning broke in Saigon on November 1, 1968, the National Day holiday, news spread not only of the bombing halt but also a Vietcong rocket attack on a Catholic Church that had killed nineteen worshippers. Few were reassured by the repeated American promise that Hanoi would stop these kinds of attacks once the bombing actually ended.[22] A CIA wiretap inside Thieu's office documented that he believed the United States "was trying to dupe" him on the eve of the election.[23] Thieu went to Radio Saigon and to seven different newspapers, with the announcement that Johnson had "unilaterally" stopped the bombing and that Thieu would address a joint session of the National Assembly the next day. His speech made the break in relations with the United States even worse: he said the conditions for serious talks with Hanoi did not yet exist, so South Vietnam would not be present at the November 6 meeting in Paris. The speech unified the South Vietnamese people. "This was a Vietnamese declaration of independence," Nguyen Phu Duc recalled, "and the South Vietnamese were proud of themselves again."[24] Members of the National Assembly and the South Vietnamese military referred to Johnson's action as a "betrayal" and a "surrender." Twelve senators telegrammed Johnson to protest "the breaking of the Honolulu agreement."[25]

Almost immediately, aerial reconnaissance flights detected that violations of the DMZ and attacks on smaller cities continued. Thirty-three rocket and mortar attacks were carried out against South Vietnamese cities the week after Johnson's announcement, causing 326 ARVN and 213 civilian deaths. In Paris, Xuan Thuy confirmed on November 2 that the bombing halt had indeed been unconditional and referred to the upcoming November 6 meeting as a "four-party conference." In an interview published in *L'Express* on November 19, the Hanoi delegation denied ever agreeing to any U.S. conditions on the composition of the parties. "The Americans did make such proposals," he said, "but we rejected them, and finally we agreed on the formula of the four-party conference."[26] The leader of the newly arrived NLF delegation, Nguyen Thi Binh, opened her first press conference by noting that "the party has sent me here to Paris to take part in the preparatory conference to the four-party conference which opens on November 6, as was agreed to by President Johnson in his speech of October 31." The NLF group had its own staff and diplomatic facility, and it behaved like a completely independent delegation that was the legitimate voice of the South Vietnamese people.[27]

While the number of American war dead would near thirty-seven thousand by the end of 1968, Vietnamese on both sides, both soldiers and civilians, suffered more by multiples.[28] Saigon was asking only for some assurance for the South Vietnamese people that it was not being forced to negotiate with the NLF. "The Vietnamese people," Ky said, ". . . see no reason for such a hasty move, unless you can explain that this is to our advantage."[29]

If the United States had brought a Saigon delegation into the Paris talks in May or found a way to consult with the South Vietnamese government as openly as Harriman did with the North Vietnamese or the Soviets, the outcome could have been different. "I think when the history of those days is written, it will perhaps reveal one of the less glorious chapters of our diplomacy," Bunker wrote to Clifford. "The United States had no problem preparing its political leadership and population for the bombing halt, which was easily accepted in our country. Yet when it came to allowing Thieu to prepare his political leadership and public opinion for the bombing halt and the negotiations, we imposed the most rigid security restrictions on him, refused to give him any time to line up the necessary support, and later used public pressure on him."[30]

Ky wrote later that Humphrey missed an opportunity.[31] If he did not favor some kind of vague coalition between Saigon and the NLF, he could have said so.[32] He could have offered reassurance to the South Vietnamese that might have persuaded them to go to Paris before the presidential election, and he could have taken credit for it. Reassurance that Humphrey planned to continue Johnson's policy in some form could have spared their own relationship, too. Yet Humphrey did not do that, leaving Americans and South Vietnamese guessing at what motivated Johnson to announce another bombing halt. "Those who have badgered, belittled, and second-guessed Lyndon Johnson must know that he wanted peace in Vietnam *desperately*," Humphrey wrote in his memoirs. "Those who deny him that bit of humanity are wrong."[33]

Johnson's October 31 speech has been misinterpreted even more than the one he gave on March 31. "Some people will call it a cheap political trick," he said to Christian.[34] The Humphrey side believed it was Johnson's way to finally do something, even begrudgingly, to give him a boost. For the Paris negotiators, the speech removed a major obstacle to substantive negotiations with the North Vietnamese.[35] The Nixon side believed Johnson was showing his true colors—supporting the Humphrey campaign. Nixon's approval of the bombing halt gave the proposal a bipartisan halo—but according to Clifford, the only reason Nixon went along was that Johnson lied and said Thieu had agreed to it. (Thieu's own speech to the National Assembly on November 2 makes it clear that he never did.)[36]

The most likely explanation, however, is that Johnson did it for Johnson. Even though it looked less likely than ever that the announcement would lead to a peace agreement—and certainly not during his presidency—at least he could say he got the process started and left his successor in a better position. As the grains of sand slipped through the hourglass, he seized his best remaining chance to establish a legacy as a peacemaker before he left the White House.[37]

After the election, none of the principals ever argued that a genuine chance for peace had been lost. As far as outcome of the election went, those who were for Humphrey defended Humphrey, and those who were for Nixon defended Nixon.

CHAPTER FOURTEEN

Dragon Lady

W HEN PRESIDENT JOHNSON TOLD Senate Minority Leader
Everett Dirksen that he was concerned about "treason" in
the final two weeks of the campaign, he was referring to
what has become known as the Chennault Affair, in which
Richard Nixon was accused of interfering in the Paris negotiations by encouraging Saigon to refuse to join the peace talks. He is supposed to have
assured them that under his administration, they would get a better deal.
The scandal was named after Anna Chennault, the Chinese-born socialite
and widow of Major General Claire Chennault of the 14th U.S. Air Force.
Anna Chennault's role in Nixon's campaign has been exaggerated, but the
complete story of that campaign cannot be told without discussing her.

To the extent that Anna Chennault had any political views, they were a
mix of her late husband's anti-communism, Southern Democratic conservativism, and her companion Thomas Corcoran's New Deal connections.
She had deep contacts on both sides of the aisle—especially among those
with strong anticommunist views and an interest in Southeast Asia—and
was famous for elegant parties at her Watergate penthouse apartment
featuring internationally known guests and multicourse dinners that she
helped prepare.[1] Chennault had become wealthy through United States
and foreign government shipping contracts, and she had a financial incentive to keep them going, which meant American involvement in Southeast
Asia needed to remain consistent. She used her regular business trips to
Southeast Asia to maintain personal relationships with many of the key
political and military leaders of the anticommunist American allies. Her

appointment books and personal correspondence are filled with invitations to CIA headquarters, records of letters exchanged, and CIA briefings before many of her Asian tours. The FBI investigated Claire Chennault for being a foreign agent on Taiwan's payroll in 1951.[2] Following his death in 1958, Anna picked up with his former business and social connections. While the available evidence remains heavily redacted, it appears that FBI surveillance of her began in 1962.[3] She regularly reported on the American and South Vietnamese political scenes to Taiwanese leader Chiang Kai-shek.[4]

The first president she met was John F. Kennedy. "When Democratic friends invited me to the Kennedy Inaugural Ball at the Stadium Armory, I went with almost teenage exuberance," she wrote in her memoirs.[5] In return for her loyal support of the Kennedy-Johnson administration, Kennedy appointed her to the Chinese Refugee Relief Association. When she visited Asia and sought audiences with political and military leaders, she sometimes had messages to convey from American leaders, and she would bring messages back. Often she asked for letters to carry back, which would validate her claim of being an informal diplomat. If she was asked to carry a substantive message, she could claim it was a government trip and seek reimbursement of expenses. Sometimes these messages were authorized, while other times she took them on her own initiative in order to build up her credentials. More than one White House caught on to this pattern and limited her contact with the president and top officials.[6] That her trips were primarily for personal business meant that the U.S. government did not want to be seen endorsing her actions.[7]

In the 1960s, scrutiny of Chennault's comings and goings, and her friendships with Asian diplomats in Washington, increased with U.S. troop levels in Vietnam.[8] The Johnson administration invited her to official functions, including lunches and state dinners. She also attended congressional events at the White House as the guest of both Democratic and Republican senators. She kept Humphrey informed of her travels to Asia, and he sent personal responses.[9] When Humphrey announced his 1967 visit to Saigon to attend Thieu's inauguration—one stop in a tour of allied nations—Chennault volunteered to join the bipartisan delegation and asked the CIA whether there was any business she could conduct for them on the trip. "Had we asked for her assistance in any way she no doubt would have then asked that we underwrite her trip to the Far East," an internal CIA memorandum documented.[10]

Chennault's faith in Johnson and Humphrey began to falter after Johnson announced he wouldn't run for reelection. Humphrey's pledges to stop the bombing, fears that Johnson was giving in to the dovish members of his party, and the general American desire to disengage from Vietnam concerned her greatly. As someone who had lost almost everything in the communist takeover in China in the late 1940s, Chennault was especially sensitive to U.S. leaders' apparent willingness to abandon South Vietnam.[11] She received regular reminders from friends in South Korea and Taiwan that the Americans would go home once they got tired of Vietnam.

Chennault first met Nixon while he was out of office in the 1960s, at a reception in Taiwan hosted by President and Madame Chiang Kai-shek. She met him again at another reception, although there is no evidence they ever had a substantive conversation.[12] The fact that she was a woman and Chinese-American were reasons, however, to give her honorary roles in the campaign related to fundraising and to outreach to what were then called "ethnics."[13] She boasted of having raised $250,000 for the Nixon campaign, although no documentation has surfaced to support the claim.[14] Chennault was a member of Citizens for Nixon and Agnew; she sat on the Republican Issues Committee and served as the Far Eastern consultant to the Key Issues Committee chaired by John Tower; she was also part of Women for Nixon-Agnew and served as chairman of the National Republican Women's Finance Committee.[15] "Because of my knowledge of Asia and because I have many friends not only in the Far East but in Southeast Asia," she said in 1969, "I was given the assignment to collect information regarding the situation in Asia, and in particular, the situation in Vietnam."[16] But she was not a substantive aide and never had a formal policy making role in Nixon's campaign. She wrote Nixon several times, but if she received a response, it was usually a form letter, sometimes with her name mangled.[17] Chennault was not rebuffed easily, and when she did not receive the desired response, she followed up with various campaign officials.[18] Theodore White described her as "a chairman of several Nixon citizen committees, wearing honorific titles which were borne by many but which she took more seriously than most."[19]

On July 12, Chennault went to New York as part of a meeting between Nixon and South Vietnamese Ambassador Bui Diem. It was the only such meeting she attended during the campaign, and it has been used to show collusion between Chennault, the South Vietnamese, and the Nixon campaign. But Bui Diem knew he was being wiretapped and surveilled, and his mail monitored, so he reported meetings with Republicans to the Johnson White House in advance.[20] Since he saw nothing inappropriate about communicating with the Nixon campaign, he notified his closest friend in the administration, William Bundy, that the meeting would take place.[21] "Bundy understood my position and accepted my assurances that I would limit myself to a general discussion with Nixon and would not go into details about the peace talks," he wrote in his memoirs.[22] Clifford wrote in his memoirs that "Bundy raised no objections. It was quite appropriate for an Ambassador to meet with a former Vice President."[23]

When Bui Diem arrived at the Hotel Pierre in New York to see Nixon, Chennault was waiting in the lobby. She wanted to make sure she got credit for setting up the meeting.[24] She had tried unsuccessfully in May to get "an hour" with Nixon, and tried again in June.[25] It took the meeting with Bui Diem for her to finally get her audience with the candidate. According to Chennault's account, Nixon arrived a half hour late, and then immediately left her and went into a conference room with Diem.[26] Diem wrote that they discussed the need for new military equipment for South Vietnamese armed forces, Hanoi's dependence on Moscow and Beijing, and turning more of the fighting over from Americans to the South Vietnamese. He maintained that he was never told to convey any specific message to Thieu, other than that if Nixon were elected, he would be supportive of Saigon.[27] It is not clear what Bui Diem would have known about the Paris negotiations, since South Vietnam was frequently kept in the dark and in any case, Harriman and Bundy believed Diem was "not cut in" by Thieu.[28] No evidence has surfaced that Nixon or Chennault knew what was going on in Paris.

According to Chennault's published version of events, Nixon referred to her as "my good friend" in front of Bui Diem and John Mitchell and told them that "she knows all about Asia. I know you also consider her a friend, so please rely on her from now on as the only contact between myself and your government."[29] This is not confirmed by any other source. When Bui Diem published his account of the meeting a few years later, he did not mention Nixon saying Chennault should be "the only contact" between him and South Vietnam.[30] Chennault's original dictation, in 1969, says something quite different from her published account: "Mr. Nixon remarked to Ambassador Bui Diem, which I remember, and I quote, 'Anna is a very good friend and certainly we rely on her information and her knowledge of Asia. In fact, sometimes I need her to come and brainwash me a little.'"[31] Chennault later complained to her publisher that her ghost-writer, Wendy Seagraves, had produced a manuscript that was not factually accurate.[32]

Chennault went to Vietnam at the end of July, just after Johnson and Thieu's Honolulu Conference, to remind government leaders of what they already knew: that Nixon was the stronger anti-communist.[33] The South Vietnamese knew who she was and that she was motivated by significant business interests, so they did not trust her. "My impression was that she may well have played her own game in encouraging both the South Vietnamese and the Republicans," Bui Diem wrote in his memoirs.[34] There is no evidence in her communications with South Vietnamese leaders that she ever claimed to be acting on Nixon's or Mitchell's authority. She had substantive contact with the Nixon campaign only twice in the fall: once to discuss fundraising and once to recommend John Tower as Secretary of State in a future Nixon presidency.[35]

Nixon wrote in his memoirs that during the second week of October, "rumors became rampant that something big was about to happen in Paris."[36] Chennault wrote a one-and-a-half-page report to this effect on October 16, which she hoped to deliver to him during his campaign stop in Kansas City, when he planned to meet with members of the Women's Advisory Committee.[37] The report touched on the likelihood of a bombing halt and the need to de-Americanize the war, and is arguably the closest thing she ever wrote to a policy paper during the campaign.[38] She repeatedly complained that she was never able to speak to Nixon directly after the convention; the only staffer she could reach was Richard Allen.[39] By the end of the campaign she was calling Allen "4–5 times daily" hoping to reach Nixon but was always denied access.[40] Her issue was that Nixon had promoted a Vietnam peace plank at the convention that leaned toward negotiations, which she opposed. In her eyes, any peace agreement that involved U.S. withdrawal while allowing the communists to remain in South Vietnam was tantamount to surrender.[41] She was likewise concerned about Nixon's willingness to establish a new relationship with the People's Republic of China at the cost of betraying Taiwan.[42]

In an October 22nd memo to Nixon, Bryce Harlow described active maneuvering around Johnson to announce a bombing halt on election eve in order to help the Humphrey campaign.[43] Nixon was not so sure.[44] "He promised he would not," he said about Johnson. "He has sworn he would not."[45] But after he read the memo, Nixon's suspicions reached full height. Each time he re-read it, he became angrier.[46] "I fired off a battery of orders," he wrote in his memoirs. "Have Mitchell check with Kissinger; have Dirksen and Tower blast the moves by the White House; have Dirksen call Johnson and let him know we were on to his plans."[47] Nixon was unsure what Johnson's motives were but felt he was either playing politics with the war or letting others around him do so.[48] Either way, it was a break with Nixon's previous understanding with Johnson. He continued, warily now, to refrain from attacking the president. "I sent a memo to my key staff thinkers and writers ordering them to put the Vietnam monkey on Humphrey's back, *not* Johnson's," he wrote in his memoirs. "I wanted to make it clear that I thought it was Humphrey rather than the President who was playing politics with the war."[49]

On the evening of October 22, Nixon discussed the status of the campaign with Bob Haldeman, whose notes from the conversation have been cited as "proof" that Nixon ordered Chennault to interfere in the peace talks.[50] They suggest that Nixon was reacting to the Harlow memo, including the rumors that Johnson's advisors were using the Paris peace talks to boost Humphrey's election chances, as well as that Humphrey wanted to soften the three conditions Johnson insisted on prior to an expanded bombing halt. It takes effort to decipher the notes, which are reproduced in an Appendix. Occasionally they contain quotes, unclear acronyms and abbreviations, and Haldeman's unique shorthand. They do not entirely record what Nixon said but are a running to-do list for his chief of staff to follow up.

"How do you want him to hit HH—how hard?" in Haldeman's notes reflected Nixon's frustration with Humphrey. The line "keep Anna Chennault working on SVN" is often cited to prove Nixon's sabotage: it shows, according to *The New York Times* and other news outlets, that Chennault was delivering Nixon's advice that the South Vietnamese not cooperate in the Paris talks. But the next line, overlooked, says "insist publicly on the 3 Johnson conditions." Nixon was not separating himself from Johnson but insisting that the administration stick to the president's conditions. He wanted those involved in the peace talks, including Saigon, to be reminded of Johnson's three conditions prior to the granting of a bombing halt.[51] What he was asking Chennault to do is unclear, since there is no record that any instruction was passed to her—or that she passed on any instruction to the South Vietnamese.

The next section of the notes cited by those arguing for Nixon's guilt is "re V.N. bomb halt memo," meaning the Harlow memo, "Harlow—

have Dirksen + Tower blast this," meaning the two senators should attack those who were trying to soften Johnson's conditions. "Dirksen call LBJ + brace him w/this" means that Dirksen should warn Johnson that Nixon was about to take action against those around Johnson who were no longer under his control. "Any other way to monkey wrench it? Anything RN can do," is often cited as further evidence that Nixon interfered with the peace talks. But the entire passage has to do with Nixon's strategy for responding to administration figures who were trying to separate themselves from Johnson after Humphrey's Salt Lake City speech. It has nothing to do with Chennault, the Paris peace talks, or trying to establish a Vietnam policy different from Johnson's. It was Nixon, not Humphrey, who maintained Johnson's Vietnam policy throughout the campaign.[52]

The next section cited to prove Nixon's treason is "Rose—get her friend Louis Kung—going on the SVN—tell him hold firm," meaning that Nixon's secretary, Rose Mary Woods, should tell a friend of hers, businessman Louis Kung, to remind Thieu to hold firm on Johnson's three conditions. Then there is "Rebozo—have Smathers threaten J," "N has learned staffers are dealing w/H + N is going to blast him—the bets are off + N very disappointed," "hard evidence W/house is giving H stuff he's not giving N," "will blast in major speech on V.N. on Thursday." The approximate meaning of this passage is that Charles G. "Bebe" Rebozo, a friend of both Nixon and Johnson, should tell Florida Senator George Smathers, also a mutual friend, that Nixon learned via the Harlow memo that those around Johnson are helping Humphrey, presumably against Johnson's wishes or without his knowledge. If Johnson did not take action, Nixon would criticize Johnson, and their understanding on Vietnam up to that point would be off.[53]

The notes reveal the actions Nixon proposed to take. "Harlow fly to V.N.—see Goodpaster" reflects Nixon's doubt that the military commanders in Vietnam favored a bombing halt. "This might make SVN govt. fall" suggests Nixon was concerned that a unilateral bombing halt could topple Thieu, given his growing domestic pressures. "Tomorrow RN blandly say US shld pause under condition J laid down in N Orleans ie go further than present position if conditions are met that J laid down then we would approve bomb pause but H is wrong in saying pause period to give away trump card w/o getting this much would be bad": Nixon wanted to make sure Humphrey and those around Johnson stuck to the conditions Johnson had laid out in his speeches in San Antonio and New

Orleans. "They're selling out SVN—leave new admin to hdle," which was exactly what Nixon feared. "WHouse staffers (name) Clifford, Califano + L. Thompson are now talking to H giving info they're not giving N . . . talking to H & working w/Ball." About the Johnson-Nixon relationship, Haldeman wrote, "Thot that at Al Smith dinner they had an understanding . . . now is going to blast LBJ." Reasonable people can debate whether, as the sitting vice president, Humphrey was entitled to have more information than Nixon, who enjoyed that advantage against Kennedy in 1960. But Nixon was on target that Ball was the conduit between the Paris peace talks delegation and Humphrey.[54]

Nixon never proposed a new Vietnam policy and only sought to compel Johnson to ensure that his staff and Humphrey went no further than Johnson's conditions for a bombing halt. He was angry that he remained more loyal to Johnson than Johnson's own people. Haldeman's notes do not suggest that Nixon had any inside information about the negotiations in Paris, let alone Saigon. The notes, now in the National Archives, were never given even the lowest national security classification— "Confidential"—even though other records about the peace talks were regularly classified "Secret" or "Top Secret." If Nixon were seeking to scuttle the peace talks, he would have needed to know what was taking place so he would know what to scuttle. But Haldeman's notes show he was kept in the dark. Read in full, they reveal Nixon trying to rally people toward Johnson's Vietnam position, not commit treason against it.

In two messages sent from the South Vietnamese Embassy in Washington to Saigon, intercepted by the National Security Agency on October 23 and 27, Bui Diem reported that Chennault encouraged the South Vietnamese to "hold on" for better terms for peace under a presumptive Nixon presidency. Despite her concern that Nixon no longer supported a military victory in Vietnam, she considered him the better option than Humphrey. In the wiretapped message, she spoke of "her boss" in New Mexico during a conversation with Bui Diem, presumably a reference to Spiro Agnew, who had made a campaign stop in Albuquerque, although it made little sense that Agnew would be involved.[55] There was also confusion as to whether Chennault actually said New Hampshire, which made more sense, since John Mitchell was there.[56] Johnson could not be sure, so he ordered the FBI to check the telephone records of Agnew's campaign plane as it sat on the tarmac to see whether there had been a conversation with Chennault.[57] The check turned up nothing relevant. Chennault did have contact with the South Vietnamese, but the contact did not seem to amount to anything.[58]

On October 28, Beverly Deepe of the *Christian Science Monitor* passed along a tip to her editor, Hank Hayward: Bui Diem had told his Foreign Ministry that Nixon aides approached him to say the Saigon government should hold firm, because once Nixon became president he would back the Thieu government in its demands.[59] Deepe never identified her sources—when I asked her decades later, she said she did not remember—so Saville Davis, the newspaper's Washington correspondent, tried to track down the necessary confirmations.[60] One of his first stops was Bui Diem at the South Vietnamese Embassy in Washington. "I knew for sure that there was no secret deal, but I could not imagine how such a misunderstanding could have started," Bui Diem wrote in his memoirs. "On the other hand, it was well known that Thieu had had plenty of reasons to oppose the expanded talks without making any deals with anyone."[61]

In his memoirs, Johnson wrote that "we had received information that people who claimed to speak for the Republican candidate were still trying to influence the South Vietnamese to drag their feet on the peace talks."[62] That information had arrived on October 28 courtesy of Alexander Sachs, an eminent Wall Street banker.[63] His warning, from an anonymous source, was that Nixon was "trying to frustrate the President, by inciting Saigon to step up its demands."[64] Clifford watched the situation closely. "Gradually we realized that President Thieu's growing resistance to the agreement in Paris was being encouraged, indeed stimulated, by the Republicans," he wrote in his memoirs, "and especially by Anna Chennault, whom we referred to as the 'Little Flower.'"[65] A complicating factor for the Johnson administration was the U.S. government's ongoing interest in Chennault's activities. One does not have regular audiences at Langley unless there is business to discuss.

On October 29, Johnson ordered twenty-four-hour-a-day surveillance and a wiretap on Anna Chennault. Because she was an American citizen acting in a private capacity, this was controversial and probably illegal. Attorney General Ramsey Clark claimed he did not authorize it.[66] "Those familiar with LBJ's use of the FBI as a personal Pinkerton agency during the 1964 campaign," wrote Nixon aide Tom Huston, "can't really be surprised at anything the former President did. He was not a man to leave a stone unturned when some tool was available to do the digging."[67] The justification for this surveillance was the Logan Act of 1799, which criminalizes negotiation with foreign governments by unauthorized American citizens. Since its passage it has never been used to secure a single conviction, arguably because it is arcane and unconstitutional.[68] In any case, the wiretap was not implemented because the FBI determined it was too risky to install at the busy switchboard at the Watergate, where Chennault lived.

Other electronic as well as physical surveillance of Chennault picked up frequent social contact between her and the South Vietnamese embassy in Washington, but it was the same pattern of contact, acting as an unofficial liaison while promoting herself and her business, that she had maintained for years. Chennault sometimes spoke in a kind of code, did not identify herself or use the names of those she spoke with, and talked with people who did the same because they assumed they were being wiretapped.[69] For someone unfamiliar with her routine, her communications could have looked suspicious.

Johnson held a conference call with the three presidential candidates on October 31, shortly before his bombing halt announcement.[70] "Some of our folks, even including some of the old China lobbyists," he said, thought Saigon could get a better deal under a different president. He did not go so far as to name Chennault, but the point was made. "Our refusal to send a delegation to the Paris meeting infuriated the American side," Thieu's spokesman Hoang Duc Nha wrote. "The Johnson administration, and most of the American media, thought that South Vietnam had been influenced by Mrs. Anna Chennault."[71]

"Once you win an election," Nixon reflected in a private letter, "you will find any number of people who will insist that they played a decisive role in the victory. In the case of Anna Chennault, she along with any number of others, used to bend John Mitchell's ear as to what was going on in Vietnam and what our position should be."[72] Shortly after the election, Chennault began saying at social gatherings that she had won it for Nixon.[73] But her name is not mentioned even once in the wiretapped conversations of officials in Saigon.[74] The FBI continued its surveillance of Chennault after the election but did not turn up anything meaningful.[75] Whatever her role was, when she had a financial incentive from publishers to tell her story, the resulting book, *The Education of Anna*, did not provide much illumination.[76] The most we can say about Chennault's influence on Thieu and the South Vietnamese is that, as William Bundy put it to Theodore White, "she worked on their fears, and some of the people in SVN no doubt thought that Nixon's election would be better for them than Hubert's would."[77] Those fears were already present; Chennault did not create them. "Look, John, all I've done is to relay messages," Chennault told Mitchell on October 31. "Thieu has told me over and over again that going to Paris would be walking into a smoke screen that has nothing to do with reality."[78] Virtually every account of the Chennault Affair underestimates the North and South Vietnamese governments and their knowledge of American politics.[79]

To suggest that Nixon somehow masterminded the outcome of the 1968 election gives him too much credit; he certainly did not have those skills in 1960 or 1962.[80] "Nixon personally had no hand in what [Chennault] was doing," William Bundy wrote, "if only because he would have been too smart and too aware of our intelligence resources."[81] Humphrey concluded in his memoirs that there was no solid connection between Chennault's activities and Nixon. He had been pressured by some to speak out publicly about the issue, but according to Christian, he concluded that "it would not be proper to do so. He had no proof that Nixon had anything to do with Saigon's reluctance to enter the peace talks, and to accuse the Republican candidate of prolonging the war would be a quite serious matter."[82] "The GVN withheld its consent to the Paris conference not because of any of Richard Nixon's promises," Nguyen Phu Duc wrote later, "but because of its apprehensions of Johnson's hasty plans aiming presumably at the formulation in South Viet-Nam of a coalition government with the Communists as a prelude to the U.S. unilateral withdrawal."[83] Theodore White ultimately concluded that the matter hurt Nixon's campaign rather than helped it.[84]

If Johnson had been on the ballot, perhaps he might have reacted differently to Chennault's actions. He never spoke of "treason" again; it was something said in the heat of the moment. "I never shared the intense dislike of Richard Nixon felt by many of my fellow Democrats," he reflected later. "I had served with him in the House of Representatives and in the Senate, and I was Senate Majority Leader during most of his term as President of the Senate. I considered him a much-maligned and misunderstood man."[85] According to George Christian, what made Johnson feel betrayed about the Chennault Affair was not Nixon's involvement—he determined there was no direct link to Nixon—but that Thieu seemed to believe that he could get a better deal from the Republicans than from Johnson.[86] "President Johnson had sacrificed his political career as a result of his efforts to save South Vietnam," Clifford wrote in his memoirs.[87] He felt betrayed that Thieu would not trust him.

CHAPTER FIFTEEN

Photo Finish

T HE BOMBING HALT ANNOUNCEMENT did not create the surge for Humphrey that some had hoped for. In the closing days of the campaign, the polls showed the race tightening nationally, but not enough in the states Humphrey needed to win in the Electoral College. In an appearance on ABC's *Issues and Answers*, he sounded like someone bracing for a defeat.[1] Eugene McCarthy finally gave his long-awaited endorsement in the campaign's final week, even while other prominent Democrats, such as Pat Brown, Jay Rockefeller, and John McKeithen, continued to withhold support. McCarthy had made vague promises of supporting Humphrey "when the time was ripe."[2] While his Vietnam policy "falls far short of what I think it should be," McCarthy said in his endorsement, Humphrey had "a better understanding of our domestic needs and a strong will to act."[3]

Johnson was under great pressure from fellow Democrats to help Humphrey's campaign, or at least make an appearance with him. James Rowe and North Carolina Governor Terry Sanford asked Johnson whether he would take a whistle stop through the border states, ending in Texas.[4] "Why?" Johnson replied. "Nixon is supporting my Vietnam policy stronger than Hubert."[5] Nixon had even offered to go to Saigon if the White House thought it would help. The weekend before Election Day, Johnson finally agreed to appear with Humphrey at the Astrodome, but he didn't make it easy. Plagued by a lingering cold, Johnson did not even confirm he would be there until four hours before the event. After making stops in West Virginia, Kentucky, and New York—no more or less than Eisenhower had done for Nixon in 1960, Johnson reasoned—he flew to Houston.[6] He and Humphrey strolled the field while fifty thousand lights on the world's largest scoreboard flashed a giant "H H H."[7] But the candidate was an afterthought: the rally was a showcase for Johnson. Before a capacity crowd of fifty-eight thousand, by far the largest of the entire campaign, the president gave his farewell to politics before the home crowd. They went wild. They knew they were witnessing a passing of the torch. That the dais included not only Johnson and Humphrey but Ralph Yarborough and Robert Strauss, while John Connally declined to attend—all of whom owed Johnson something, and some of whom were barely on speaking terms—was meant to show that the party was not divided as critics said it was.[8] Johnson gave a lukewarm endorsement of Humphrey and encouraged Texans to support him. The endorsement had originally been stronger, according to the version Drew Pearson saw, but the president asked Tom Johnson to water it down.[9] The event, and the endorsement, were a reminder to Humphrey that he could have never done it on his own. "Though it came late, the effort was more in the form of sparing Lyndon Johnson's pride than electing Hubert," Connally wrote in his memoirs.[10]

Afterward, on the campaign plane to Los Angeles, a buoyant Humphrey let loose. "As President, I would sever all relations with the South Vietnamese and leave them on their own," he said. The remark was toned down in the statement released to the press: "If the Vietnamese do not come to the conference table as promised, the United States should go on without them."[11] The bombing halt had brought Humphrey back to the issue of Vietnam, rather than to the emphasis on domestic issues that had helped him close the gap in the polls during the second half of October.

Humphrey and Nixon worked feverishly in the campaign's final stretch. "I was campaigning eighteen and twenty hours a day," Nixon wrote in his memoirs. "I felt it was essential to take the battle to Humphrey after his weeks of much harsher rhetorical assaults."[12] Nixon focused on issues related to crime and justice, where his differences with Humphrey were greater, and continued to say little about Vietnam except that he supported Johnson's policy. "Whatever the reason," he wrote in his memoirs, "sympathy for his temporary underdog status; preference for his liberal views; or simply his likability—Humphrey benefitted from favorable press coverage."[13] This was especially true in the final weeks of the campaign, when the Nixon camp was growing increasingly nervous.[14]

Gallup showed Nixon still leading, 42 percent to 40, but Harris, for the first time in the campaign, showed Humphrey ahead 43 percent to 40. (Wallace held the remaining 13 to 14 percent in each.)[15] "I felt that Harris might have weighted his sample in the metropolitan areas and that Gallup, whose last poll showed me still leading by two points, was more accurate," Nixon recalled later.[16] Lou Harris had been close to John F. Kennedy, and his sample was known to be skewed toward city dwellers—especially Robert Kennedy and Gene McCarthy supporters. His earlier models showed Nelson Rockefeller losing to the presidency to McCarthy.[17] Even Harris, however, said late in the campaign that Humphrey's rise occurred in parallel to, and was dependent on, Johnson's rise in popularity.[18] "To be on the low end of a Harris poll usually means to be on the high end of an election vote," Nixon spokesman Herb Klein said.[19] Regardless of what the true split was, the race was a nail-biter all the way to the finish line. Nixon wound up his campaign in Los Angeles on the eve of the election, conducting a telethon at the Ambassador Hotel. For four hours, he took questions from callers across the country and showed himself to be at the top of his game.[20] He later called the event "my best campaign decision. Had we not had that last telethon, I believe Humphrey would have squeaked through with a close win on Election Day."[21]

Wallace arguably never recovered from his one serious mistake of the entire campaign—choosing LeMay as his running mate. From July until October, he polled around 20 percent, but he only went down from there. If he was guilty of a second mistake, it was allowing others to define his campaign. He could have bypassed the national media, the way Nixon did, by using television to speak directly to voters and set the record straight.[22] Still, he ran a quality campaign that far exceeded expectations. He survived constant personal attacks from the national media, but his campaign did not survive organized labor's destruction of his Northern base.[23] It would be a mistake, however, to dismiss his effort as little more than a regional campaign. "What George Wallace demonstrated," wrote Theodore White, "was that of all those alienated with the set of American government, perhaps the largest group were the white workingmen of America; and in so demonstrating, George Wallace uncovered a reality that will be of concern for years."[24] The Democratic Party has steadily lost ground with these voters ever since.

Humphrey expected defeat when his chartered Boeing 707 landed at Minneapolis–St. Paul International Airport on the morning of Tuesday,

November 5. While the race had tightened nationally, the gaps were in-surmountable in the decisive states. Humphrey admitted that he had lost "some of my personal identity and personal forcefulness" during his ten-ure as vice president.[25] With Humphrey and Nixon each pledging to end the war, Vietnam was largely neutralized as a campaign issue, putting the spotlight on race relations, crime and lawlessness, poverty, and general un-rest. Law and order, as an issue of concern, had consistently polled higher than the war since the deaths of King and Kennedy. Wallace was blamed for fanning the flames of racism, but the media never understood his pop-ularity. He was dramatically underestimated as a campaigner. He took advantage of people's fears but did not create those fears. Elites viewed him with a mixture of amusement and disgust, but he struck a deep chord with blue-collar voters. All three candidates in 1968 came from working-class backgrounds, and those voters decided the outcome. They started the year in Johnson's column, and he was the last Democrat to win them as a voting bloc.

On his way home from the airport, Humphrey stopped to vote at Maryville Township Hall, which had a single voting booth. From there, he went home and slept until four o'clock in the afternoon. His top po-litical strategist, James Rowe, did not even make the trip with him. He said there was no point. Not a single member of Humphrey's entourage believed they would win. Rowe had been asked to send his suggestions for Cabinet appointments, but he did not have the heart do it. He had gone through the political map dozens of times and found no way Humphrey could win the Electoral College.[26] "We had a list of twenty-four states we had written off, and lost twenty-three of them—all except Washington," campaign consultant Joe Napolitan reflected.[27] George Ball, Humphrey's closest campaign aide, was so certain he would lose that he had booked a six-week trip to France and Spain departing the morning after the elec-tion.[28] "Richard M. Nixon is a strong favorite to win the Presidency to-morrow despite a late rally by Vice President Humphrey that has tight-ened the race considerably," the front page of the *New York Times* reported the day before the election. "The check of political opinion in all 50 states by representatives of *The New York Times* showed Mr. Nixon leading in 30 states with a total of 299 electoral votes. A majority of the 538 electoral votes, or 270, is required to win."[29]

Humphrey arrived just after eleven in the evening at his campaign headquarters at the Leamington Hotel in Minneapolis and promptly asked for a tranquilizer.[30] He studied the results as they came in.[31] Critical swing states like Illinois and Ohio did not look good for Nixon. NBC reported that New York, Pennsylvania, and Michigan looked good for Humphrey. "By golly, we might do it!" he proclaimed.[32] "Just after 10 P.M., Humphrey pulled even with me in the national returns," Nixon wrote in his memoirs. "The network commentators had begun playing with the numbers and speculating about a possible Humphrey upset."[33] "Texas had gone for Hubert, and that was of primary concern for us," Lady Bird wrote in her diary.[34] But if he lost California or any two of the other "big eight," plus Illinois, there was no way to make up those electoral votes.[35] One by one, as the state returns came in, Humphrey's odds fell: Wisconsin, New Jersey, Ohio, California—run by Kennedy boss Jesse Unruh—and Illinois did not look good. "They could not, they knew, win a majority of the electoral vote," Theodore White wrote.[36] By two in the morning, Humphrey recalled, "it looked as if we had lost it." He went down to the Hall of States to rally the faithful with a pep talk. "We're full of optimism," he said. Then he went back upstairs, took a sleeping pill, and went to bed.[37]

"As Ohio and California moved more solidly into my column," Nixon wrote in his memoirs, "the balance seemed to hang in Illinois."[38] After widespread allegations that the state had been stolen from him in 1960, leading to his narrow loss against Kennedy, it must have been difficult to see Illinois again decide his fate. He studied the results in his suite at the Waldorf Towers in New York; Bill Safire, Pat Buchanan, Dwight Chapin, Ray Price, Len Garment, and other staffers were in an adjacent suite.[39] "We all stayed busy working the phones and dealing with messages for Nixon, letting him know who had checked in," Chapin recalled.[40] Around midnight, when it looked as though Humphrey was surging forward, Nixon insisted on being alone, but he welcomed company again once it looked as though he was winning.[41] He had asked Billy Graham to watch the returns with him, telling him, "I'll need your prayers if I win and I'll need your prayers even more if I lose."[42] Since achieving his goal of uniting the Republican Party behind Nixon at the convention—and then uniting Johnson and Nixon—Graham had kept a lower profile. He let it be known that he had voted for Nixon by absentee ballot, but that was as close as he came to an official endorsement.[43] He thought being seen with Nixon on election night would make them appear too close—especially since it was not clear who would win.[44] "The bombing pause had made a tremendous impact," he recorded in his diary, "though by Sunday I began to feel that the tide was turning once again in Nixon's favor."[45] He and assistant T. W. Wilson agreed to stay nearby, at the Hilton Midtown, and to be available if needed.[46]

Nixon became increasingly confident during the overnight hours. He asked Mitchell to place a call to Mike Wallace of CBS to press Daley to release the Illinois results.[47] "You tell the mayor for every ballot box they bring in, we will bring in one. This isn't going to happen again," Mitchell said, referring to 1960.[48] Almost instantly, the Illinois totals were released and showed a Nixon victory. "At 8:30 the door burst open and Dwight Chapin rushed in. 'ABC just declared you the winner!' he shouted."[49] "T.W. and I immediately got a cab to the hotel," Graham wrote in his memoirs. "Rebozo met us and led us into Nixon's suite. Only he, Pat, Tricia, and Julie were in the room."[50] After a short prayer and conversation, Nixon needed to begin planning the rest of his day.[51] "I returned to my room and took an hour's nap," he wrote in his memoirs. "I got up at ten o'clock and shaved and dressed. There was still no word from Humphrey, and I could not do anything until he conceded. At 10:35 Haldeman came in with the news that NBC had finally projected my victory. A few minutes later CBS did the same.[52] At about 11:30, Hubert Humphrey called. His voice, usually so cheerful and confident, was full of fatigue and disappointment.[53] But he was as gracious in defeat as he had been tenacious in combat."[54]

"I have done my best," Humphrey said in his characteristically gracious concession speech. "I have lost. Mr. Nixon has won. The democratic process has worked its will, so now let's get on with the urgent task of uniting our country."[55] McCarthy, acerbic to the end, referred to Humphrey's loss as "a time for visiting the sick and burying the dead."[56] Nixon knew the feeling. "I knew from experience how bitter and crushing defeat is for the people one loves," he wrote.[57]

The conventional wisdom is that it was one of the closest elections in history, decided by a half million popular votes. But the Electoral College vote of 301–191, plus Wallace's 46, was a powerful rebuke of a decade of liberalism and government overreach.[58] Nixon took thirty-two states, with Humphrey and Wallace splitting the remaining eighteen.[59] Humphrey carried only six states with a clear majority, and two of those—Minnesota and Maine—were his and Muskie's home states.[60] Wallace won five states that otherwise probably would have gone to Nixon.[61] Together, Nixon and Wallace virtually annihilated Democratic presidential voting in the South, which had been gradually weakening ever since the emergence of the Dixiecrats in 1948.[62] Republicans picked up four governors, for a total of thirty-one; five Senate seats; and four House seats, although they remained in the minority in both chambers.[63] "Hubert lost to Nixon yesterday partly because of a large amount of money, partly because of a better 'advance' organization, and partly because of disunity in the Democratic Party," Drew Pearson wrote in his diary.[64] "Maybe Nixon is right for the country now," Humphrey wrote in his memoirs. "There's been such misery since John Kennedy's death."[65]

In his victory speech, Nixon emphasized bringing the country together. He recalled the sign he saw in Deshler, Ohio, on the whistle stop through the Buckeye State: "Bring Us Together Again." "The one great objective of the administration at the outset," he said, would be "to bring the American people together."[66] It was a theme that played well on both sides of the aisle. "I thought Nixon's speech was also wise and hopeful," Lady Bird reflected.[67] In Saigon, Thieu also liked it. He sent a telegram of congratulations: "The Vietnamese government, the Vietnamese people, and soldiers fighting in the front lines against Communist aggression will be most happy to receive on Vietnamese soil a staunch defender of freedom, which you have been for many years."[68]

While the popular vote was close, it was not nearly as close for Humphrey when you consider other measurements: the Electoral College result, the percentage of popular votes cast against him (57 percent for Nixon and Wallace combined), or what it meant in terms of the nation's shift to the right in response to violence and disorder, Vietnam, big government, the Great Society, and the Democratic majority that had dominated for almost the entire decade.[69] The 57 percent vote for Nixon and Wallace came just four years after Johnson had won 61 percent of the popular vote in defeating Barry Goldwater.[70] Humphrey received 12 million fewer votes than Johnson in 1964, even though the country's population grew by 8 million in those years and Democrats retained a significant advantage in party registration.

"What the tiny margin of victory concealed," Theodore White wrote, "was the fact of a landslide—for the election of 1968 was the first landslide of its kind in American history, a negative landslide. Americans turned against the whole set of Democratic policy and leadership of the previous four years—but could not make up their minds in which new direction they would move. Of the 43 million Americans who voted for Lyndon Johnson and the Democrats in 1964, 28 percent, or 12 million, repudiated him, a repudiation greater than that suffered by any President except Herbert Hoover."[71] Veteran political analysts Richard Scammon and Ben Wattenberg concluded that 8 percent of Wallace supporters in the South and 60 percent in other regions in the country would have gone to Nixon in a two-way race against Humphrey.[72]

"When one adds the Wallace and Nixon votes together," wrote White, "their combined total of 56.9 percent to 42.7 percent for Humphrey is a historic turning-of-the-back on all the great promises and domestic experiments of one of the most visionary administrations ever to hold the helm in America."[73] Had Wallace not been in the race, the result would probably have been a decisive victory for Nixon.[74] As much as 40 percent of Nixon's votes came from Johnson's supporters in 1964, showing how much of the center Nixon captured while conceding conservatives to Wallace.[75] Whereas two-thirds of the Southern Congressional districts that went for Goldwater in 1964 supported Wallace in 1968, Nixon performed far better with districts that backed Johnson four years earlier.[76] What Humphrey had lacked most during the campaign was the spirit and courage he had as a young man, the kind he summoned during the 1948 convention when he changed the way his party and the nation thought about civil rights. Had he been able to do the same in 1968, he might have won.[77]

Only slightly more than half of Wallace's votes came from the South. Unlike other insurgencies, his campaign in 1968 was not a sectional movement.[78] Wallace demonstrated more than any other figure, except possibly Billy Graham, that millions of Southern votes were in play, and that the South did not vote as a monolith. For example, on the safe assumption that a majority of Wallace's very conservative supporters would have voted for Nixon over Humphrey—who represented what Wallace was campaigning against—then Arkansas and Georgia, states that Wallace won decisively, would have gone to the Nixon column were Wallace not in the race. In addition, the states in which he won enough votes to change the result by a good margin, including Alabama, Louisiana, Maryland, Mississippi, Texas, and Washington, would likely also have gone to Nixon, since he and Wallace split the conservative vote. Wallace took his 46 electoral votes and 9,901,118 popular votes primarily from Nixon, not Humphrey.[79]

Nixon was the first president since Zachary Taylor in 1849 to take office without carrying either chamber of Congress.[80] He inherited an executive branch saturated with New Deal and Great Society Democrats, and the national press corps mostly loathed him.[81] "The net result was a blurred mandate for Richard M. Nixon rising chiefly from Americans' consideration of their condition at home," Theodore White wrote. "The mood was undeniably a swing to the right, an expression of a vague sentiment for a government oriented to caution and restraint."[82] Wallace's message about runaway government was here to stay. Working-class Americans did not necessarily vote the way their union voter guides instructed them. Regions and voting blocs were shifting, including African Americans, differences between the upper South and the Deep South marked the end of de facto single party dominance, big cities were in decline and suburbs were rising in importance, and many liberal supporters of the Great Society had become disenchanted that the results did not measure up to the original intentions.[83] "Abandoned by the liberal voices, and the intellectual sponsors who made the workingmen of America their wards in the 1930's, white workingmen find now, in the public dialogue of America, almost no expression of their problems," Theodore White wrote.[84]

At almost no time during the year did most Americans seem to be voting *for* someone or something. They almost always seemed to vote *against*.[85] The electorate was denied a true debate on Vietnam: only Humphrey, the candidate most allied with Johnson's administration, broke from Johnson's policy, and he did it late and not everyone believed in his sincerity or conviction. The great debate of the campaign, the issue that consistently struck the nation's nerve and where there were the greatest differences among the three candidates, was law and order.[86] The 1968 presidential election marked the beginning of the end of the New Deal era. At the beginning of that era, in 1932, government was the solution; by its end, President Ronald Reagan declared in his first inaugural address, "government is the problem." A majority had serious concerns about the nation's biggest foreign policy issue, the Vietnam War, and at home the 1960s saw extreme wings of both major parties exert themselves in new ways.[87]

Epilogue

I F ANYONE REMAINED IN control of the chaotic year 1968, it was Lyndon Johnson. He betrayed Humphrey—but not in a way that got him blamed for Humphrey's performance. Humphrey betrayed Johnson, too, in order to woo McCarthy and Kennedy voters, but he lost millions of moderate and conservative votes to Nixon and Wallace. Wallace, winning the Deep South and 10 million popular votes, started a sustained movement that migrated into and eventually came to dominate the Republican Party. Humphrey, going after voters on the left, and Wallace, pursuing them on the right, together conceded the broad center to Nixon. In a year in which all four major figures were battered by forces on their right and left, sometimes simultaneously, Nixon found the optimal lane between the two. He united both sides of the Republican Party as the only candidate acceptable to each, and defeated a divided Democratic party—with Johnson's help.

By the end of the year, North Vietnam had still not shown any serious interest in de-escalating the war. Perhaps the same could be said of the United States, although Hanoi did not suffer the consequences of deteriorating public opinion as Washington did. More than any other factor, the popular divisions over the war were why Johnson could not achieve peace by the end of his presidency. "I regretted more than anyone could possibly know," he wrote, "that I was leaving the White House without having achieved a just, an honorable, and a lasting peace in Vietnam." He knew the lengths he had gone to in order to broker peace and protect Thieu and Saigon. In his memoirs, he described seventy-one different "major peace initiatives" that he pursued between 1964 and 1968, using seventeen different overt and covert channels to the North Vietnamese.[1] He could take some credit for leaving Nixon in a better position than he otherwise would have been in—including establishing Paris as the site of the talks the format of public plenary sessions, private talks and tea breaks; insisting on South Vietnam's inclusion and establishing the four sides; crafting the negotiating formula; and recruiting the best officials to serve on the U.S. delegation. "I felt I was turning over to President Nixon a foreign policy problem that, although serious, was improving; an ally that was stronger than ever before; an enemy weakened and beaten in every major engagement; and a working forum for peace," Johnson reflected later.[2] Only someone with Johnson's consistent ambition could consider that a failure.

Johnson did not order the bombing halt with the idea of helping Humphrey. "I happen to *know* LBJ didn't end the bombing on October 31st just to elect Humphrey," Clifford said, "because I've never believed he wanted Humphrey to win!"[3] He ordered it because he hoped it might soften Hanoi's negotiating position—but the opposite occurred. North Vietnam used the halt to rehabilitate its economy and transportation infrastructure.[4] "From the time the Paris talks started until the day I left the White House," Johnson wrote in his memoirs, "we never received a clear unequivocal statement from Hanoi's representatives as to what they would do to lower the level of fighting in Vietnam or to bring the war to an end."[5] His dashed hopes, and those of millions of Americans, reflected a fundamental misunderstanding about the peace talks in 1968. The United States was the only side that wanted out, yet as George Christian wrote, the American people were "lulled into thinking peace was just around the corner."[6] That was exactly what Johnson was afraid of, and why he worked to keep expectations low with each report from Paris. The North Vietnamese, National Liberation Front, and South Vietnamese all saw an advantage in keeping the fighting going. "It became clear to most of the world," Johnson reflected later, "that Hanoi was merely using the sessions for propaganda purposes."[7] Nor did Saigon have any reason to want a peace agreement in which the United States left it to defend itself against the communists. "I was now absolutely certain that the South Vietnamese government did not want the war to end," Clifford recalled.[8] "Part of Saigon's foot-dragging about attending the Paris talks," Johnson wrote in his memoirs, "stemmed from the Vice President's foreign policy speech in Salt Lake City on September 30, a speech that was widely interpreted as a refutation of the administration's Vietnam policy, particularly with respect to bombing. That interpretation was not discouraged by several Humphrey aides who briefed the press after the speech."[9]

Did Johnson want Humphrey to win? "The answer is 'no,'" Humphrey biographer Arnold Offner writes. "Johnson was highly ambivalent toward Humphrey . . . he humiliated and denigrated him to others from the day he became his vice president and deliberately undermined his campaign."[10] While there is a good chance Nixon would have won anyway, given all the factors favoring Republicans in 1968, there is now no doubt that Johnson assisted him in many ways, both publicly and privately. "I told Nixon every bit as much, if not more, as Humphrey knows," Johnson said. "I've given Humphrey nothing."[11] He preferred Nixon as his successor because he believed it would be better for his own legacy.[12] A Democratic successor would relegate Johnson to a minor role. But if Nixon won, then Johnson would remain the nation's top Democrat and could become an elder statesman, like Eisenhower.[13] "If I had my druthers, I would be U.S. Senate Leader for life," Johnson said to Tom Johnson.[14] Late in life, Clark Clifford said to George Elsey, "I've never in my life said this to anyone, but I'll say it to you now. If Hubert had been elected, he would have been 'Mr. Democrat.' With Nixon in the White House, Lyndon was still head of the Democratic Party. Remaining party head meant *everything* to him!"[15]

While those around him focused on the short-term goal of getting Humphrey elected, Johnson played the long game. He saw the rightward shift of the nation and came to believe that a President Nixon would be better for Lyndon Johnson's legacy. The conventional wisdom is that Nixon won the White House by dishonorable and possibly even treasonous means. But in their memoirs, neither Johnson nor Humphrey took this view.

Hubert Humphrey would have made a great president in a relatively tranquil era in which the nation had the means to expand the Great Society programs.[16] The late 1960s were not that time. Humphrey's loss was the end of an era: he was the last traditional liberal to come close to winning the presidency. Heightened partisanship on both sides of the aisle following Watergate and Vietnam wiped away the liberal order that had dominated the leadership of both parties throughout the postwar period. With Humphrey, you could disagree without being disagreeable, and a difference in opinion did not mean a break in friendship.

Humphrey did not win enough votes in the states he needed, and he fell far short of Nixon in the electoral college. "I'd climbed that damned ladder of politics rung by rung and there wasn't an easy one in the lot," he said after the loss. "Yet there wasn't a campaign I didn't enjoy and profit by. But I slipped on the big ones—and once I almost hit bottom. I know now it was never in the cards."[17] After the election, Humphrey surfaced after his vacation in the U.S. Virgin Islands to comment on how he had spent time since the loss: "You don't wear shoes and you get over being mad."[18]

Humphrey and Nixon were the first two vice presidents since Martin Van Buren to run for the presidency while their bosses were still in office. After witnessing the transitions, or lack of them, from Hoover to Roosevelt and Truman to Eisenhower, Johnson wrote in his memoirs, "I believe that the dignity of the Office of the Presidency demanded cooperation and respect between the incumbent and his successor."[19] He respected Nixon and thought he was presidential timber. "One never knows what it is to be a President until you are a President," he said.[20]

Between the Republican Convention and Election Day, Johnson officially met with Nixon twice. Dwight Chapin recalled another late-night secret meeting, in addition to seven official telephone calls between August and November. Richard Whalen wrote about yet another secret meeting on July 26 between Nixon and Johnson, "the opponent whom Nixon had so carefully avoided."[21] They also spoke on the two conference calls with all of the candidates, on October 16 and 31. "After the election," Johnson wrote in his memoirs, "there was no reason for restraint on anyone's part and many reasons for establishing a close working relationship." On November 11, President-elect and Mrs. Nixon arrived at the White House South Portico for lunch and nearly four hours of conferences and briefings.[22] In the Cabinet Room, Rusk asked Nixon to appoint a foreign policy liaison. Nixon wanted Henry Cabot Lodge Jr., but he was already serving as ambassador to West Germany, and recalling him would offend the Germans, so he settled on Robert Murphy, the veteran diplomat and former undersecretary of state.[23] Johnson encouraged Nixon to keep Richard Helms as director of central intelligence—with Helms present during the briefings—and Nixon ultimately did.[24] Another person present in the room was Marvin Watson. "Mr. Nixon turned to Marvin," Lady Bird recalled, "and asked him if he was as good a man as Billy Graham said he was. Marvin made a modest, discreet reply. Lyndon told Mr. Nixon he could look to Marvin for any interim help."[25] When the discussion turned to Vietnam, Nixon emphasized the importance of achieving a negotiated settlement that did not look like a defeat for the United States and its allies.[26]

Then it was time to tour the White House. "Mrs. Johnson and I took the Nixons on a tour of the second-floor living quarters of the Executive Mansion. I was surprised to learn that it was the first time either of them had seen that part of the White House, in spite of the eight years they had spent in the Eisenhower administration," Johnson wrote in his memoirs.[27] "It was a long visit, lasting nearly four hours," Lady Bird wrote in her diary, "proper, circumspect and cordial throughout. Lyndon, I thought, was generous and rather fatherly."[28] Nixon recalled the tour as a "room-by-room inspection of the entire mansion."[29]

Johnson and Nixon also had a brief private conversation in the Oval Office. "He talked with a sense of urgency," Nixon recalled. "'There may be times when we disagree, and, if such time comes, I will let you know privately,' he said. 'But you can be sure that I won't criticize you publicly. Eisenhower did the same for me. I know what an enormous burden you will be carrying.'"[30] Johnson said he wanted to do everything he could to ensure Nixon's success. "'The problems at home and abroad are probably greater than any President has ever confronted since the time of Lincoln,'" Nixon recalled Johnson saying. "Johnson and I had been adversaries for many years, but on that day our political and personal differences melted away."[31]

After their tête-à-tête, Johnson and Nixon walked through the press lobby and spoke to the White House press corps together. After Johnson gave an update on the transition, Nixon made one of the most gracious spontaneous gestures that had been exchanged between them, telling the press that "if progress is to be made on matters like Vietnam, the current possible crisis in the Mideast, the relations between the United States and the Soviet Union with regard to certain outstanding matters—if progress is to be made in any of these fields, it can be made only if the parties of the other side realize that the current administration is setting forth policies that will be carried forward by the next administration. . . . I gave assurance in each instance to the Secretary of State and, of course, to the President, that they could speak not just for this administration but for the nation, and that meant for the next administration as well."[32] In effect, Nixon gave Johnson carte blanche to speak for the next administration on foreign policy matters, a move Johnson told Christian was totally unexpected.[33] "Although I was determined to hold the reins of government firmly while I was still in office," he wrote in his memoirs, "I was just as determined not to take any last-minute action that would tie the hands of the new administration or lock it into a program, unless that action were absolutely necessary."[34]

The Johnson and Nixon people did not exactly trust each other, but Johnson ordered everyone to cooperate.[35] They were not friends, but they were friendly. "So smoothly had the personal relations gone," he wrote, "that on the evening of December 12 an unprecedented event took place. While the Nixon family met with the Johnson family in the Executive Mansion, my Cabinet held a reception for the Nixon Cabinet at the State Department, and my personal staff held a reception for the Nixon staff in the White House mess."[36] Nixon praised Johnson for his historic presidency. "He said Lyndon would be remembered for two things," Lady Bird wrote in her diary: "his stand on Vietnam, which was the only thing he could have done—and right—and his achievements for Negroes. An accurate judgment as far as it went, I thought."[37] The departing and incoming presidents also remarked that while they had followed different paths and pursued different policies, they had been seared by some of the same enemies. "I heard Mr. Nixon use the expression, 'Georgetown dinner parties,' with an inflection of voice reminiscent of Lyndon's," Lady Bird wrote in her diary.[38]

Later that evening, Nixon aide Bryce Harlow called Jim Jones to say how thankful Nixon was to Johnson and his staff.[39] Johnson continued to reciprocate. "We immediately made available to Mr. Nixon a Presidential jet for his use," Johnson wrote in his memoirs. "We gave his staff members a suite of rooms in the new Executive Office Building across Pennsylvania Avenue from the White House. We gave them the use of the White House cars and the White House switchboard, the most efficient and effective telephone operation in the world."[40] Nixon recalled that "after I won the election in 1968, and through the remaining years of Johnson's life, I saw what some have described as the 'better side' of his character. He was courteous, generally soft-spoken, and thoughtful in every way. He was not the pushing, prodding politician or the consummate partisan of his earlier career."[41]

Billy Graham and his wife Ruth spent the final night of the Johnson administration in the Pineapple Bedroom. "Billy told us of Mr. Nixon's plans to hold religious services in the East Room, with a different minister each Sunday," Lady Bird wrote in her diary. "Billy was going to conduct the first service next Sunday—a final interesting touch to the transition."[42] Graham, who had helped facilitate a partnership between Johnson and

Nixon during the fall, served as a ceremonial bridge between the two administrations.

After his inauguration, one of Nixon's first requests to the military aide's office was to offer Air Force One to take the Johnsons home to the Ranch in Texas.[43] "From the Clifford residence we drove to Andrews Air Force Base, where we were to board Air Force One. President Nixon had graciously made it available for our return trip home," Johnson wrote in his memoirs.[44] "It was a quiet flight down," Lady Bird recalled. "One of the first things I saw in the plane was a big bunch of yellow roses with a card from the Nixons. What a thoughtful thing to do!"[45] Nixon also offered the Humphreys the use of a presidential aircraft to take them home to Minnesota, something Kennedy had not offered to Nixon in 1961.

It must have been a jarring, emotional day for Johnson to wake up in the White House, see his successor inaugurated, and spend the evening under the great open skies of Texas. Was it really over? His presidency had begun in crisis five plus years earlier, and much of his final year in office had been besieged by crises. "I tried to reassure him and encourage him," Billy Graham recorded in his diary. "I know what a tremendous agony of spirit any man would have who is suddenly coming to the end of 38 years of public service."[46] Somehow Johnson made it out alive, and he left his successor in the best possible position to carry on in his spirit. It was a fitting cap to a long political career. "On this night," Johnson wrote of those first hours as a former president, "I knew I had been there. And I knew also that I had given it everything that was in me."[47] "Maybe Nixon will do a better job than I did," he confessed to Billy Graham. "I tried awfully hard, but I made some mistakes."[48]

It was Nixon's America.

Appendix
Haldeman's Notes and the Chennault Affair

10/22
late

Z — indicate tomorrow
— preparing & recording 2 radio speeches
Harlow — Harlow monitoring V. Nam

RL— Andrews — if take a poll — inform us immy.

✓ Rhodes says we've dropped on older people
done — use radio for Soc Sec spot
— a newspn ad — nail the lie

RW — sit down w/ RW + Moore etc. —
in terms of their thot on tempo + content
how do you want him to hit HHH — how hard?

✗? maybe have to bite V.N.

→! USI — keep Chennault Anna working on SVN
— insist publicly on the 3
Johnson conditions

✓ say for Fri — doing 3 hrs of TV spots

Moore-etal- get a reading on how they thk we're doing

Harlow — be sure ce of defense goes to DOD

RN – how do you want him to hit (HHH?)
       how hard shld he go?

re V.N. bomb halt news

Harlow – have Dirksen & Tower blast this
        Dirksen call LBJ & brace him w/this
        – any other way to monkey wrench it?
        anything RN can do.

Rose – get her fed Louie Kenny –
        zing on the SUN – tell him told him

Dirksen – or someone

Rebozo – have Smathers threat a J
        N has learned toppers are dealing up H
        & N is going to blast him –
        the lets are off & N very disapptd
        hard evidence W/ there is going to
              stuff he's not giving N
        will blast in major speech on V.N.
              on Thurs –

add Harlow

— Harlow fly to U.N. — see Goodpaster
  RN sure military not for it.
— this might make SVN govt. fall

— Tomorrow RN blandly say US should pause
  under condition J laid down in N Orleans
  i e go further than present position
  if conditions are met that J laid down
        then we would approve bomb pause
  but H is wrong in saying pause period
  to give away our trump card w/o
        getting this much would be bad

— they're selling out SVN — leave new admin to help
  make a communist Asia —
  will have to go into Thailand.

Bebe — N mad as hell —   (Adams) Clifford   Califano
  W House staffers are now talking to H   + J. Thompson
        giving in, they're not giving N
  thot that at Al Smith dinner they had
        an understanding
  now is going to blast LBJ — Thurs.
  (Bebe — our private polls show we lead in
        every one of critical states.)

Hal — Harlow - try Burke, Radford, Greenthu
    find out what's going on
    Les Arends — Mel Laird
    have Dirksen call J

Hal — Scranton call Vance
    heard rumor — N very distressed
    what's going on

Hal — tell Dirksen if don't get 3 conditions
    N will last bomb halt

Agnew — go see Helms -
    tell him we want the truth —
    or he hasn't got the job.

These four pages of notes made by Nixon campaign aide H. R. "Bob" Haldeman on the evening of October 22, 1968, have been widely cited as proof that Richard Nixon scuttled the Vietnam peace negotiations, obstructed peace, and was guilty of treason.[1] They first received attention when John A. Farrell described them in his book *Richard Nixon: The Life*. In that book, Farrell is appropriately modest in assessing their meaning: "The droves of variables forestall a conclusion that Nixon's meddling cost the United States an opportunity to end the war in the fall of 1968."[2] But in the *New York Times*, he concluded differently: "A newfound cache of notes left by H. R. Haldeman, [Nixon's] closest aide, shows that Nixon directed his campaign's efforts to scuttle the peace talks, which he feared could give his opponent, Vice President Hubert H. Humphrey, an edge in the 1968 election. On Oct. 22, 1968, he ordered Haldeman to 'monkey wrench' the initiative."[3] This interpretation has been widely repeated by other authors, including Garrett Graff, Ken Hughes, and Kyle Longley and documentary filmmaker Ken Burns.

Farrell's op-ed caused sufficient public interest that *New York Times* Chief White House Correspondent Peter Baker followed it with a story of his own, and because of my background as a historian of the Nixon presidency, he asked me for a comment.[4] At the time, however, I did not know enough about the incident to say much, so I limited myself to this: "Because sabotaging the '68 peace efforts seems like a Nixon-like thing to do, we are willing to accept a very low bar of evidence." It turned out to be a prescient remark.

I had known for some time that Farrell was writing a book on Nixon, since he introduced himself to me by email on September 8, 2012. Having read his biographies of Clarence Darrow and Tip O'Neill, I was interested in his work and admired his polished writing. We met in Washington, DC, a few weeks later to discuss themes he might explore regarding Nixon. During that conversation he said one of his goals was to find something "worse than Watergate," in part because that scandal seemed less and less serious with the passage of time. We exchanged dozens of emails—while he worked on the manuscript, after the book was published, and about needed corrections in the paperback—and many telephone calls.

Galleys of his Nixon biography became available in late 2016, shortly after the presidential election. Accusations were already circulating that President-Elect Donald Trump had colluded with a foreign power (Russia) in order to win the election, and the cascade of stories gave Farrell the opportunity to use history to illuminate the present. If Nixon had also colluded with a foreign power (South Vietnam) in order to win an election, those convinced of Trump's guilt could point to a relevant historical antecedent. Using Haldeman's notes to draw a line from Nixon to Trump allowed Farrell's book, which otherwise contained no significant new findings, to reach a large audience. The story took off, and Farrell's book became a sensation. It won the Barbara and David Zalaznick Book Prize in American History from the New-York Historical Society and was a finalist for the 2018 Pulitzer Prize in Biography.

The charges against Nixon have actually been in the public record since January 1969, and I have been familiar with the story for my entire career. It is called "the Chennault Affair" because he purportedly used the socialite Anna Chennault as his conduit to South Vietnam. Like other people, I believed the charges or at least thought they must be mostly true. The Haldeman notes, however, were a new piece of the puzzle. When Farrell emailed me on December 23, 2016, to say he had sent me a galley and that he would offer important new evidence regarding the Chennault Affair, my first thought was that I knew too little about it. But the fact that so many records were still restricted raised immediate suspicions about what was "known."

Embarrassed by having nothing but a vague comment to give Peter Baker when he called, I began a deep dive into the Chennault Affair, which eventually became a book on the 1968 presidential election. The more I learned about the subject, the more I became convinced that it had never been seriously researched. For example, no historian had actually interviewed Anna Chennault or the South Vietnamese, put in Freedom of Information Act requests for the restricted documents, or scoured the Vietnamese archives. No one had tried to interview all the surviving principals from the Johnson, Humphrey, or Nixon sides. At the other end of this journey, I have not answered every question or solved every mystery. Numerous records remain restricted. I thus cannot prove Nixon did not do it—and in any case it is virtually impossible to prove a negative. Additional records related to the Chennault Affair will surely be released, and those records could change our understanding once again.

But I am comfortable saying that the four pages of Haldeman notes do not prove anything. They have been used selectively, piecing together shards of words from different pages on different subjects to make an argument. This is the worst kind of history.

Before getting to the details, I should make a methodological point. I have read many pages of Haldeman notes and have listened to many of his diary dictations. I have consistently found them to be a reliable source, and surprisingly unpartisan. They are an excellent guide to the Nixon presidency, especially when matched with other records. They are often easy to corroborate since we have Haldeman notes that cover White House meetings captured by Nixon's taping system. In other words, it is possible to listen to a recording of a meeting and compare what was said to what Haldeman recorded in his notes. In general, his notes contain four types of information: (1) things Nixon said, (2) things Haldeman said, (3) things someone else said, and (4) things that occurred to Haldeman during the conversation that he happened to write down. Rarely did he use actual quotations, although sometimes his notes contain verbatim content. There is not a recording of the conversation of October 22, 1968—Nixon was not yet president—but it seems likely that Haldeman's note taking followed the same methodology he used in White House meetings. The notes give one a sense of what was discussed but make it difficult to directly attribute anything to Nixon. That is the first problem with arguing that they prove Nixon gave any kind of order.

A second methodological question arises when we separate out the individual components of the Chennault Affair. The central idea is that there was some communication from Anna Chennault to the South Vietnamese that persuaded them not to take part in the peace talks in Paris. But this theory raises more questions than answers. For example:

- What was the message she passed along?
- To whom on the South Vietnamese side did she pass it?
- How do we know she claimed to represent Nixon?
- How do we know that what she said was approved by him?
- How do we know the message made it to Thieu?
- How do we know that it convinced him to stay away from Paris?
- How do we know that Thieu would have participated without Chennault's intervention?
- How do we know there was any peace agreement to scuttle?

Richard Nixon is probably the most investigated politician in U.S. history. Seemingly every part of his presidency was scrutinized in the aftermath of the Watergate break-in on June 17, 1972. If he had reached the presidency itself by dishonorable means, it would be deeply surprising if this were not investigated when virtually all the key witnesses were alive and could have been called to testify. The Chennault Affair is the latest effort by commentators to portray Nixon as a dishonest hustler—the kind you would not buy a used car from, to paraphrase a prominent advertisement by the Kennedy-Johnson campaign in 1960. But as a serious politician, Lyndon Johnson recognized that Nixon was serious too, which explains the nonaggression pact they developed in 1968, once it was clear they would not face each other on the ballot. Rather than being irrationally and myopically focused on some short-term electoral advantage, Nixon was a strategist who consistently took the long view during his career.

Looking at the pages of notes, one can see how creatively they were excerpted to support the Chennault Affair allegation. On the first page, "keep Anna Chenault working on SVN" is often cited to prove Nixon's sabotage: it shows, according to the *Times* and other news outlets, that Chenault was delivering Nixon's advice that the South Vietnamese not cooperate in the Paris talks. But the very next line, overlooked, says "*insist publicly* on the 3 Johnson conditions." These conditions appear three more times in the four pages. Nixon was not separating himself from Johnson but insisting that the administration stick to the president's policy. He wanted those involved in the peace talks, including Saigon, to be reminded of Johnson's three conditions for the granting of a bombing halt.[5] What he wanted Chenault to do is unclear, since there is no record that any instruction was given to her—or that she passed on any instruction to the South Vietnamese.

The next section of the notes cited by those arguing for Nixon's guilt is "re V.N. bomb halt memo" (meaning the Harlow memo, in which Bryce Harlow warned Nixon that those around Johnson were trying to use a bombing halt to elect Humphrey), "Harlow—have Dirksen + Tower blast this," meaning the two senators should attack those who were trying to soften Johnson's conditions. "Dirksen call LBJ + brace him w/this" means that Dirksen should warn Johnson that Nixon was about to take action against those around Johnson who were no longer under his control. "Any other way to monkey wrench it? Anything RN can do" is often cited as further evidence that Nixon interfered with the peace talks. But the entire passage has to do with Nixon's strategy for responding to administration figures who were trying to separate themselves from Johnson after Humphrey's Salt Lake City speech. It has nothing to do with Chennault, the

Paris peace talks, or trying to establish a Vietnam policy different from Johnson's. It was Nixon, not Humphrey, who maintained Johnson's Vietnam policy throughout the campaign.[6]

The next section cited to prove Nixon's treason is "Rose—get her friend Louis Kung—going on the SVN—tell him hold firm," meaning that Nixon's secretary, Rose Mary Woods, should tell a friend of hers, businessman Louis Kung, to remind Thieu to "hold firm." But hold firm on what? The most likely answer is the point Nixon keeps repeating throughout the call: Johnson's conditions for a bombing halt. Then there is "Rebozo—have Smathers threaten J," "N has learned staffers are dealing w/H + N is going to blast him—the bets are off + N very disappointed," "hard evidence W/house is giving H stuff he's not giving N," "will blast in major speech on V.N. on Thursday." The approximate meaning of this passage is that Charles G. "Bebe" Rebozo, a friend of both Nixon and Johnson, should tell Florida Senator George Smathers, also a mutual friend, that Nixon learned via the Harlow memo that those around Johnson are helping Humphrey, presumably against Johnson's wishes. If the president did not take action, Nixon would publicly criticize him, and their agreement not to attack each other on Vietnam would be off.[7]

The notes reveal the actions Nixon proposed to take. "Harlow fly to V.N.—see Goodpaster" reflects Nixon's doubt that the military commanders in Vietnam favored a bombing halt. "This might make SVN govt. fall" suggests that Nixon was concerned that a unilateral bombing halt could topple Thieu, given his growing domestic pressures. "Tomorrow RN blandly say US shld pause under condition J laid down in N Orleans ie go further than present position if conditions are met that J laid down then we would approve bomb pause but H is wrong in saying pause period to give away trump card w/o getting this much would be bad": Nixon wanted to make sure Humphrey and those around Johnson stuck to the conditions Johnson had laid out in his speeches in San Antonio and New Orleans. "They're selling out SVN—leave new admin to hdle," which was exactly what Nixon feared. "WHouse staffers (name) Clifford, Califano + L. Thompson are now talking to H giving info they're not giving N . . . talking to H & working w/Ball." About the Johnson-Nixon relationship, Haldeman wrote, "Thot that at Al Smith dinner they had an understanding . . . now is going to blast LBJ." Reasonable people can debate whether, as the sitting vice president, Humphrey was entitled to have more information than Nixon, who enjoyed that advantage against Kennedy in 1960.

But Nixon was on target that Ball was the conduit between the Paris peace talks delegation and Humphrey.[8]

If we want to know what was in Nixon's mind during the call with Haldeman, the best place to start is the phrase he repeats over and over: "3 conditions." Nixon never proposed a new Vietnam policy. He only sought to compel Johnson to ensure that his staff and Humphrey did not back off from Johnson's conditions for a bombing halt. He had a perfectly logical, even compelling reason for doing so: he expected to win the election, which means he expected to inherit responsibility for the Paris talks in just twelve weeks. The bombing campaign was the biggest bargaining chip the Paris delegation had, and he may well have seen Humphrey's proposal for a unilateral bombing halt as giving the game away. Johnson, by making the bombing halt conditional, would leave Nixon in a much stronger negotiating position. Rather than try to undermine the U.S. position in the talks, as Farrell's charge implies, he had every reason to try to strengthen it.

Moreover, he was angry that he remained more loyal to Johnson than Johnson's own people. Nothing in Haldeman's notes suggests that Nixon had any inside information about the negotiations in Paris, let alone Saigon. The notes, now in the National Archives, were never given even the lowest national security classification—"Confidential"—even though other records about the peace talks were regularly classified "Secret" or "Top Secret." If Nixon were seeking to scuttle the peace talks, he would have needed to know what was taking place so he would know what to scuttle. But Haldeman's notes show that he was in the dark. Read in full, they reveal Nixon trying to rally people toward Johnson's Vietnam position, not commit treason against it.

Acknowledgments

So much of what passes for history today is not based on rigorous research. Too often it is based on preconceived ideas, or conclusions in search of evidence. This comment is directed as much at those who write history as it is those who consume it. We should demand better. When it comes to diplomatic history, Americans often inflate our own role, underestimate the importance of the "other," overestimate what we know about them, and underestimate what they know about us. An author writing a work of modern history, especially on a contested or controversial subject, has a duty to review as many different kinds of evidence as is humanly possible. If a researcher does not challenge the outer limit of what is known about a subject, no one else will.

Being a historian is a morbid profession. We take information left by people, often after they die, and piece it together like a puzzle. While we do not always find every puzzle piece, hopefully we find enough to know what the finished puzzle is supposed to look like. This approach is flawed for another reason. Not everything is memorialized in the form of a record, not all records are preserved, and records can be incomplete, conflicting or lead a researcher astray. The impact of statutes, court orders, and political constraints create blind spots. All forms of evidence must be interpreted, triangulated, corroborated, and used with appropriate context and nuance. I have the highest respect for the energetic researchers I know, who in turn challenge me to be better. They understand that the more you know, the more you have to learn.

The National Endowment for the Humanities awarded me a Fellowship during 2020–21 in support of this work. (The views expressed in this work do not necessarily represent those of the NEH.) A number of other institutions also provided support, including Bowling Green State University and Texas A&M University-Central Texas. In the middle of this work, Chapman University became my new academic home. I am especially grateful to Daniele Struppa, Norma Bouchard, Jennifer Keene, Stephanie Takaragawa, Alexander Bay, and Lori Han. There are far too many archives and historic sites to thank them all individually. Without you, the research process described above would not be possible. Various National Archives and Records Administration (NARA) officials were extremely supportive. The archivists at the National Declassification Center are quickly becoming my new BFFs, in addition to my old BFFs—the Special Access/FOIA archivists.

If I had to single out just one archive, as unfair as it would be to the rest, I would recognize the Lyndon Baines Johnson Presidential Library and Museum (and Foundation) in Austin, Texas. For many years you have been my home away from home, driving down often on Fridays when I did not have to teach to see what was new. I have gotten to know some of you well enough to be chatty and share meals. Under the direction of Mark Lawrence, and previously Kyle Longley (and Mark Updegrove prior to that), you are exemplary and consistently provide the best researcher experience over the years. Special thanks are due to Claudia Anderson, Chris Banks, Siobhan Barbee, Jennifer Cuddeback, Allen Fisher, Jenna de Graffenried, Nicole Hadad, Lara Hall, Brian McNerney, Suzanne Mirabel, Alexis Percle, Ian Frederick Rothwell, Carrie Tallichet Smith, Liza Talbot, and John Wilson. Every single one of you helped me on this book, not to mention previous books. I will surely darken your doors again many times. Your presence on the University of Texas at Austin campus has allowed countless visitors and researchers to learn about one of the most significant periods of American history from the vantage point of Lyndon Johnson—warts and all, or, as he might have preferred, "with the bark off." In addition to keeping Austin Weird, keep showing us how an archive at the highest level operates.

A distinctive feature of this book is the official cooperation offered by all four major sides—Lyndon Johnson, Hubert Humphrey, Richard Nixon, and George Wallace. While the American people decided the outcome in 1968, I found the Johnson side had the best barbecue, the Humphrey folks the best home-cooked meals, the Nixon faithful the best business lunches, and the Wallaces the best informal conversations. Some

I met only once, others I returned to many times, and with some I have exchanged hundreds of emails. I have spent time with the "kids" and families on all sides. I made it my mission to learn as much as I could during the time I had, made some friends along the way, and filled in as many gaps in the archival record as was possible. Given the number who passed away since I started this research, I imagine no one will ever try what I was crazy enough to do again. I was struck by the number who told me they have never agreed to be interviewed before, or had done so very infrequently. I do not know whether to be more impressed with your discretion or the lack of thoroughness of those who came before me. Surely there will be things you disagree with, but my goal was to present your side in a way that you will recognize and think is fair. I am deeply grateful to you all and assure you there are no trick questions, snide remarks, or facetious comments. I tried to do justice to all sides.

Many scholars, writers, and thinkers read the manuscript, offered advice, and shared insights along the way: Kristina Agopian, Pierre Asselin, Peter Baker, William Baribault, Ryan Bayless, Robert Berg, Linda Black, Robert "Bobby" Blankenship, Thomas Blanton, Nigel Bowles, Douglas (and Anne) Brinkley, John David Briley, David Bruce, Jim Byron, James Campbell, Paul Carter, James and Esther Cavanaugh, Amilcar Challu, Leonard Colodny, Matthew Connelly, James Cooper, Michael Cotten, Manuel Rincon-Cruz, Gregory Daddis, John Dean, Joe Dmohowski, Niall Ferguson, Douglas Forsyth, Daniel Frick, Frank Gannon, Lloyd Gardner, Irwin Gellman, Liette Gidlow, Michael Gillette, Benjamin Greene, Walter Grunden, Timothy Hemmis, Gary Hess, Hugh Hewitt, Simon Hobson, Max Holland, Daniel Holt, Jim Hougan, Robert Jervis, Andrew Johns, Jerry Jones, David Kaiser, Jane Kamensky, Nancy Kassop, Curtis Keltner, James Kimble, Dean Kotlowski, Maarja Krusten, Brian Lamb, Heath Hardage Lee, Patrick Leech, Carmen Catena Lewis, Fredrik Logevall, Kyle Longley, William Martin, Allen Matusow, Cadra McDaniel, Jefferson Morley, Katy Morris, Richard Moss, Mark Moyar, Andrew Natsios, Justin Nelson, Lien-Hang Nguyen, Olav Njolstad, John O'Connor, Kipling Oren, Robert Pennoyer, Ronald Potter, John Prados, David Prentice, Lubna Qureshi, Allen Redmon, Amber Thomas Reynolds, Jason Rockett, James Rosen, John Rothmann, Nicholas Sarantakes, Jason Schwartz, Thomas Schwartz, Abbylin Sellers, Will Sellers, Geoff Shepard, Stephen Sherman, Rennie Silva, Melvin Small, Richard Norton Smith, Robert Stanton, Kathryn Statler, Paul Stone, Will Swift, John Taylor, Evan (and Oscie) Thomas, Timothy Thurber, Asle Toje, Robert Turner, Chase Untermeyer, George "Jay" Veith, Hasan Veli, Tuong Vu, Lee Weingart, Jonathan Winkler, Russell Witcher, and Kanisorn "Kid" Wongsrichanalai. Some of you might have no idea you influenced me at some point—a piece of information, an idea, or even an impression. I kept a list as a I progressed through the research.

At Yale University Press, Andrew Frisardi, Amanda Gerstenfeld, Brenda King, Brian Ostrander, Margaret Otzel, and Mary Pasti are the best in the business. If there is a publisher that produces a finer finished product, I have yet to work with them. Executive Editor William "Bill" Frucht, with whom I have now worked on two books, pushed me to be my best. Karen Olson is a terrific freelance editor; Fred Kameny and Marnie Wiss did a tremendous job preparing the index and proofreading. I respect those who have a skill I do not have! Alex Hoyt was the ideal agent for the project. Without his support and enthusiasm, it would never have come to fruition. Finally, Jennifer and Ava have stuck with me every step of the way. We have had some adventures together, and there are more ahead. Thank you for your consistent love, support, and friendship. Everyone mentioned here added value to the book you see. Errors and omissions are mine alone.

Notes

Introduction

1. Telephone Conversation #13706, November 2, 1968, 9:18 P.M., Recordings and Transcripts of Telephone Conversations and Meetings, Lyndon B. Johnson Presidential Library.
2. The figure used is from the Vietnam War U.S. Military Fatal Casualty Statistics maintained by the National Archives and Records Administration. For more information, see: www.archives.gov/research/military/vietnam-war/casualty-statistics (accessed July 25, 2022).
3. Melvin Small, "The Election of 1968," in Melvin Small, ed., *A Companion to Richard M. Nixon* (Malden, MA: Blackwell Publishing, 2011), 143.
4. Taylor Branch, *At Canaan's Edge: America in the King Years, 1965–1968* (New York: Simon & Schuster, 2006), 666; Max Hastings, *Vietnam: An Epic Tragedy, 1945–1975* (New York: Harper, 2018), 512.
5. Max Boot, *The Road Not Taken: Edward Lansdale and the American Tragedy in Vietnam* (New York: Liveright Publishing, 2018), 533.
6. David Paul Kuhn, *The Hardhat Riot: Nixon, New York City, and the Dawn of the White Working-Class Revolution* (New York: Oxford University Press, 2020), 19.
7. Frank Kusch, *Battleground Chicago: The Police and the 1968 Democratic National Convention* (Chicago: University of Chicago Press, 2008), vii.
8. Theodore H. White, *The Making of the President, 1968* (New York: Atheneum Publishers, 1969), 107.
9. Peter Baker, "White House Memo: Trump May Compare Himself to Nixon in 1968, but He Really Resembles Wallace," *New York Times*, June 9, 2020, A18.
10. Lewis L. Gould, *1968: The Election That Changed America*, 2nd edition (Chicago: Ivan R. Dee, 2010), viii.

11. Richard Vinen, *1968: Radical Protest and Its Enemies* (New York: Harper, 2018), 7.

12. Lewis Chester, Godfrey Hodgson, and Bruce Page, *An American Melodrama: The Presidential Campaign of 1968* (New York: Viking Press, 1969), xi.

Chapter 1. Johnson

1. Lyndon Baines Johnson, *The Vantage Point: Perspectives of the Presidency, 1963–1969* (New York: Holt, Rinehart and Winston, 1971), 425.

2. John W. Jeffries, *A Third Term for FDR: The Election of 1940* (Lawrence: University Press of Kansas, 2017), 117.

3. Author interview with Tom Johnson, January 23, 2019, Atlanta.

4. Randall B. Woods, *LBJ: Architect of American Ambition* (New York: Free Press, 2006), 767.

5. Johnson, *Vantage Point*, 425.

6. Theodore H. White, *The Making of the President, 1968* (New York: Atheneum Publishers, 1969), 111.

7. Johnson, *Vantage Point*, 425.

8. Michael A. Cohen, *American Maelstrom: The 1968 Election and the Politics of Division* (New York: Oxford University Press, 2016), 142.

9. Lady Bird Johnson, *A White House Diary* (New York: Holt, Rinehart and Winston, 1970), 643.

10. Ibid., 555.

11. Robert S. McNamara with Brian VanDeMark, *In Retrospect: The Tragedy and Lessons of Vietnam* (New York: Times Books, 1995), 316.

12. Lady Bird Johnson, *White House Diary*, 592.

13. White, *Making of the President, 1968*, 115.

14. George Reedy, *Lyndon B. Johnson: A Memoir* (New York: Andrews McMeel, 1982), xiii.

15. Earl Mazo, *Richard Nixon: A Political and Personal Portrait* (New York: Harper & Brothers Publishers, 1959), 260.

16. White, *Making of the President, 1968*, 116.

17. Irwin F. Gellman, *Campaign of the Century: Kennedy, Nixon, and the Election of 1960* (New Haven: Yale University Press, 2021), 258.

18. Bernard B. Fall, *The Two Viet-Nams: A Political and Military Analysis*, 2nd revised edition (New York: Frederick A. Praeger, 1967), 390.

19. Theodore H. White, *In Search of History: A Personal Adventure* (New York: Harper & Row, 1978), 530.

20. Walter LaFeber, *The Deadly Bet: LBJ, Vietnam, and the 1968 Election* (Lanham, MD: Rowman & Littlefield Publishers, 2005), 4.

21. Lisa McGirr, *Suburban Warriors: The Origins of the New American Right* (Princeton, NJ: Princeton University Press, 2001), 5.

22. White, *Making of the President, 1968*, 116.

23. Robert Dallek, *Flawed Giant: Lyndon Johnson and His Times, 1961–1973* (New York: Oxford University Press, 1998), 408.

24. David Halberstam, *The Best and the Brightest* (New York: Random House, 1969), 649.

25. White, *Making of the President, 1968*, 118.

26. Ibid., 221.

27. Lawrence F. O'Brien, *No Final Victories: A Life in Politics—from John F. Kennedy to Watergate* (Garden City, NY: Doubleday, 1974), 212–13.

28. White, *Making of the President, 1968*, 239.

29. Lady Bird Johnson, *White House Diary*, 595.

30. White, *Making of the President, 1968*, 234.

31. McGirr, *Suburban Warriors*, 5.

32. Peter B. Levy, *The Great Uprising: Race Riots in Urban America during the 1960s* (New York: Cambridge University Press, 2018), 9.

33. Billy Graham, *Just As I Am: The Autobiography of Billy Graham* (New York: HarperCollins, 1997), 413.

34. Nixon Diary, Notebook 15, VIP Notebooks, Records of the Billy Graham Evangelistic Association: Montreat Office, Billy Graham Archive and Research Center, Charlotte, NC.

35. Lady Bird Johnson, *White House Diary*, 556.

36. Dallek, *Flawed Giant*, 513.

37. Lady Bird Johnson, *White House Diary*, 612.

38. Ibid., 519.

39. Johnson, *Vantage Point*, 427.

40. Lady Bird Johnson, *White House Diary*, 643.

41. Ibid., 617–18.

42. Irving Bernstein, *Guns or Butter: The Presidency of Lyndon Johnson* (New York: Oxford University Press, 1996), 477.

43. Harry McPherson, *A Political Education: A Washington Memoir* (Austin: University of Texas Press, 1972), 445.

44. Nixon Diary, Notebook 15.

45. Bui Diem with David Chanoff, *In the Jaws of History* (Boston: Houghton Mifflin, 1987), 220.

46. Paul H. Nitze, *From Hiroshima to Glasnost: At the Center of Decision—A Memoir* (New York: Grove Weidenfeld, 1989), 279.

47. William Conrad Gibbons, ed., *The U.S. Government and the Vietnam War: Executive and Legislative Roles and Relationships, Part IV, July 1965-January 1968* (Princeton, NJ: Princeton University Press, 1995), 877.

48. George C. Herring, *LBJ and Vietnam: A Different Kind of War* (Austin: University of Texas Press, 1994), xii.

49. Lady Bird Johnson, *White House Diary*, 642.

50. Sunday, March 31, 1968, Lady Bird White House Diary, Lyndon B. Johnson Presidential Library.

51. Johnson, *Vantage Point*, 431–32.
52. Lady Bird Johnson, *White House Diary*, 555.
53. Julia Sweig, *Lady Bird Johnson: Hiding in Plain Sight* (New York: Random House, 2021), 342.
54. Clint Hill with Lisa McCubbin, *Five Presidents: My Extraordinary Journey with Eisenhower, Kennedy, Johnson, Nixon, and Ford* (New York: Gallery Books, 2016), 306.
55. Johnson, *Vantage Point*, 432.
56. Ibid.
57. Oral History with James R. Jones, June 11, 1972, p. 28, Lyndon B. Johnson Presidential Library.
58. Cohen, *American Maelstrom*, 141.
59. Don Oberdorfer, *Tet! The Turning Point in the Vietnam War* (Baltimore: Johns Hopkins University Press, 1971), 319–20.
60. Johnson, *Vantage Point*, 433.
61. Lady Bird Johnson, *White House Diary*, 645.
62. Drew Pearson, *Washington Merry-Go-Round: The Drew Pearson Diaries, 1960–1969*, edited by Peter Hannaford (Lincoln, NE: Potomac Books, 2015), 558.
63. Lyndon B. Johnson, "The President's Address to the Nation Announcing Steps to Limit the War in Vietnam and Reporting His Decision Not to Seek Reelection," online by Gerhard Peters and John T. Woolley, The American Presidency Project, www.presidency.ucsb.edu/node/238065 (accessed July 27, 2022).
64. Ibid.
65. Lady Bird Johnson, *White House Diary*, 645.
66. Dallek, *Flawed Giant*, 530.
67. Reminiscences of Lyndon B. Johnson, August 19, 1969, p. 34, Lyndon B. Johnson Presidential Library.
68. Johnson, *Vantage Point*, 435.
69. "Aboard Air Force One, April 1, 1968," Box 9, Tom Johnson Notes of Meetings, Personal Papers of Tom Johnson, Lyndon B. Johnson Presidential Library.
70. Hugh Sidey, *A Very Personal Presidency: Lyndon Johnson in the White House* (London: Andre Deutsch, 1968), 277.
71. Luke A. Nichter, *The Last Brahmin: Henry Cabot Lodge Jr. and the Making of the Cold War* (New Haven: Yale University Press, 2020), 311.
72. Clark Clifford with Richard Holbrooke, *Counsel to the President: A Memoir* (New York: Random House, 1991), 525.
73. Ibid., 481.
74. William C. Westmoreland, *A Soldier Reports* (Garden City, NY: Doubleday, 1976), 359.
75. Nguyen Phu Duc, *The Viet-Nam Peace Negotiations: Saigon's Side of the Story*, edited by Arthur J. Dommen (Christiansburg, VA: Dalley Book Service, 2005), 43.

76. Max Boot, *The Road Not Taken: Edward Lansdale and the American Tragedy in Vietnam* (New York: Liveright Publishing, 2018), 521.

77. Larry Berman, *Lyndon Johnson's War: The Road to Stalemate in Vietnam* (New York: W. W. Norton, 1989), 175.

78. Stanley Karnow, *Vietnam: A History* (New York: Viking Press, 1983), 541.

79. Author interview with Tom Johnson, January 23, 2019, Atlanta.

80. Peter Braestrup, *Big Story: How the American Press and Television Reported and Interpreted the Crisis of Tet 68 in Vietnam and Washington*, vol. 1 (Boulder, CO: Westview Press, 1977), xxiii.

81. Max Hastings, *Vietnam: An Epic Tragedy, 1945–1975* (New York: Harper, 2018), 464.

82. Cohen, *American Maelstrom*, 11.

83. W. Marvin Watson with Sherwin Markman, *Chief of Staff: Lyndon Johnson and His Presidency* (New York: Thomas Dunne Books, 2004), 279.

84. Dallek, *Flawed Giant*, 528.

85. Johnson, *Vantage Point*, 538.

86. Patrick J. Buchanan, *The Greatest Comeback: How Richard Nixon Rose from Defeat to Create the New Majority* (New York: Crown Forum, 2014), 217.

87. Albert Eisele, *Almost to the Presidency: A Biography of Two American Politicians* (Blue Earth, MN: Piper, 1972), 302.

88. Richard M. Scammon and Ben J. Wattenberg, *The Real Majority* (New York: Coward-McCann, 1970), 91.

89. Dominic Sandbrook, *Eugene McCarthy: The Rise and Fall of Postwar American Liberalism* (New York: Alfred A. Knopf, 2004), 182.

90. Eugene McCarthy, *Up 'Til Now: A Memoir* (New York: Harcourt Brace Jovanovich, 1987), 5.

91. Jeremy Larner, *Nobody Knows: Reflections on the McCarthy Campaign of 1968* (New York: Macmillan, 1969), 26.

92. Unpublished manuscript, p. 10, Box 13, Curtis B. Gans Papers, Lyndon B. Johnson Presidential Library.

93. Richard N. Goodwin, *Remembering America: A Voice from the Sixties* (Boston: Little, Brown, 1988), 496.

94. Eisele, *Almost to the Presidency*, 294.

95. Larner, *Nobody Knows*, 149.

96. Cohen, *American Maelstrom*, 53.

97. Arthur Herzog, *McCarthy for President* (New York: Viking Press, 1969), 293.

98. Eugene J. McCarthy, *Gene McCarthy's Minnesota: Memories of a Native Son* (Minneapolis: Winston Press, 1982), 131.

99. Edgar Berman, *Hubert: The Triumph and Tragedy of the Humphrey I Knew* (New York: G. P. Putnam's Sons, 1979), 158.

100. Sandbrook, *Eugene McCarthy*, 172.

101. Walter F. Mondale with David Hage, *The Good Fight: A Life in Liberal Politics* (Minneapolis: University of Minnesota Press, 2010), 70.

102. Larner, *Nobody Knows*, 22.

103. Herzog, *McCarthy for President*, 3.

104. Eugene McCarthy, *Frontiers in American Democracy* (Cleveland: World Publishing, 1960), 14.

105. Arthur M. Schlesinger Jr., *Robert Kennedy and His Times* (Boston: Houghton Mifflin, 1978), 830.

106. Cohen, *American Maelstrom*, 93–94.

107. Arthur Krock, *Memoirs: Sixty Years on the Firing Line* (New York: Funk & Wagnalls, 1968), 345.

108. Pearson, *Washington Merry-Go-Round*, 550.

109. Bill Connell Undated Notes, Box 148.B.15.8F, Hubert H. Humphrey Papers, Minnesota Historical Society.

110. Jules Witcover, *85 Days: The Last Campaign of Robert Kennedy* (New York: G. P. Putnam's Sons, 1969), 25.

111. Krock, *Memoirs*, 345.

112. David Halberstam, *The Unfinished Odyssey of Robert Kennedy* (New York: Random House, 1968), 5.

113. Schlesinger Jr., *Robert Kennedy and His Times*, 833.

114. Mondale with Hage, *Good Fight*, 71.

115. Pearson, *Washington Merry-Go-Round*, 550.

116. Scammon and Wattenberg, *Real Majority*, 127.

117. Buchanan, *Greatest Comeback*, 220.

118. Cohen, *American Maelstrom*, 79.

119. Evan Thomas, *Robert Kennedy: His Life* (New York: Simon & Schuster, 2000), 327.

120. David C. Hoeh, *1968, McCarthy, New Hampshire: "I Hear America Singing"* (Rochester, MN: Lone Oak Press, 1994), 69.

121. Ronald Steel, *In Love with Night: The American Romance with Robert Kennedy* (New York: Simon & Schuster, 2000), 18–19.

122. Cohen, *American Maelstrom*, 81.

123. Pearson, *Washington Merry-Go-Round*, 552.

124. Berman, *Hubert*, 158.

125. Halberstam, *Unfinished Odyssey*, 37.

126. Johnson, *Vantage Point*, 539.

127. Berman, *Hubert*, 167.

128. Dallek, *Flawed Giant*, 544.

129. Not including Panzer's research files on the candidates, such as Nixon, Wallace, and especially Robert Kennedy, his voluminous state-by-state memoranda to Johnson spread across Boxes 121 to 147, Fred Panzer Files, Lyndon B. Johnson Presidential Library.

130. Cohen, *American Maelstrom*, 318.

131. Reedy, *Lyndon B. Johnson*, 154.

132. Lady Bird Johnson, *White House Diary*, 518.

133. Johnson, *Vantage Point*, 437.

134. Clifford with Holbrooke, *Counsel to the President*, 470.

135. Remarks of the President before the National Legislative Conference, Villita Assembly Hall, San Antonio, Texas, September 29, 1967, Box 14, Charles Maguire Files, Lyndon B. Johnson Presidential Library.

136. Ilya V. Gaiduk, *The Soviet Union and the Vietnam War* (Chicago: Ivan R. Dee, 1996), 136.

137. Clifford with Holbrooke, *Counsel to the President*, 470.

138. San Antonio Formula, Undated, Box 520, W. Averell Harriman Papers, Manuscript Division, Library of Congress.

139. Walter Isaacson, *Kissinger: A Biography* (New York: Simon & Schuster, 1982), 121.

140. Johnson, *Vantage Point*, 494.

141. Luu Van Loi and Nguyen Anh Vu, *Le Duc Tho—Kissinger Negotiations in Paris* (Hanoi: Gioi Publishers, 1996), 16.

142. Johnson, *Vantage Point*, 496.

143. Arthur J. Dommen, *The Indochinese Experience of the French and the Americans: Nationalism and Communism in Cambodia, Laos, and Vietnam* (Bloomington: Indiana University Press, 2001), 672–73.

144. Henry A. Kissinger, *American Foreign Policy: Three Essays* (New York: W. W. Norton, 1969), 111.

145. Neil Sheehan, *A Bright Shining Lie: John Paul Vann and America in Vietnam* (New York: Random House, 1988), 732.

146. Harry G. Summers Jr., *On Strategy: A Critical Analysis of the Vietnam War* (Novato, CA: Presidio Press, 1982), 1.

147. Clifford with Holbrooke, *Counsel to the President*, 473.

148. Boot, *Road Not Taken*, 519.

149. David M. Barrett, *Uncertain Warriors: Lyndon Johnson and His Vietnam Advisers* (Lawrence: University Press of Kansas, 1993), 156.

150. Schlesinger Jr., *Robert Kennedy and His Times*, 850.

151. George H. Gallup, *The Gallup Poll: Public Opinion, 1935–1971*, volume 3, *1959–1971* (New York: Random House, 1972), 2115.

152. Lady Bird Johnson, *White House Diary*, 669.

153. Cohen, *American Maelstrom*, 114.

154. Thurston Clarke, *The Last Campaign: Robert F. Kennedy and 82 Days That Inspired America* (New York: Henry Holt, 2008), 129.

155. Immanuel Wallerstein and Paul Starr, eds., *The University Crisis Reader: Confrontation and Counterattack*, vol. 1 (New York: Random House, 1971), ixx.

156. Tom Wells, *The War Within: America's Battle over Vietnam* (Berkeley: University of California Press, 1994), 271.

157. Taylor Branch, *At Canaan's Edge: America in the King Years, 1965–1968* (New York: Simon & Schuster, 2006), 648.

158. Clarence B. Jones and Joel Engel, *What Would Martin Say?* (New York: Harper, 2008), 72.

159. Martin Luther King Jr., *Where Do We Go from Here? Chaos or Community?* (New York: Harper & Row, 1967), 3.
160. Johnson, *Vantage Point*, 538.
161. White, *Making of the President, 1968*, 243–44.
162. Author interview with Tom Johnson, January 23, 2019, Atlanta.
163. Pearson, *Washington Merry-Go-Round*, 560.
164. Phu Duc, *Viet-Nam Peace Negotiations*, 48.
165. White, *Making of the President, 1968*, 220.
166. George Christian, *The President Steps Down: A Personal Memoir of the Transfer of Power* (New York: Macmillan, 1970), 43.
167. Tom Wicker, "Introduction to the 1988 Edition," in *The Kerner Report: The 1968 Report of the National Advisory Commission on Civil Disorders* (New York: Pantheon Books, 1988), xiii.
168. White, *Making of the President, 1968*, 242.
169. William C. Sullivan with Bill Brown, *The Bureau: My Thirty Years in Hoover's FBI* (New York: W. W. Norton, 1979), 148.
170. David Paul Kuhn, *The Hardhat Riot: Nixon, New York City, and the Dawn of the White Working-Class Revolution* (New York: Oxford University Press, 2020), 19.
171. Richard J. Whalen, *Catch the Falling Flag: A Republican's Challenge to His Party* (Boston: Houghton Mifflin, 1972), 163–64.
172. Memorandum from Jim Jones to Lyndon Johnson, June 21, 1968, Box 1, James R. Jones Collection, Carl Albert Center, University of Oklahoma.
173. Thomas J. Schoenbaum, *Waging Peace and War: Dean Rusk in the Truman, Kennedy, and Johnson Years* (New York: Simon & Schuster, 1988), 481.
174. Buchanan, *Greatest Comeback*, 274.
175. Johnson, *Vantage Point*, 504.
176. Phu Duc, *Viet-Nam Peace Negotiations*, 25.
177. Lady Bird Johnson, *White House Diary*, 669.
178. Christian, *President Steps Down*, 1.
179. Joseph A. Califano Jr., *Inside: A Public and Private Life* (New York: Public-Affairs, 2004), 251.
180. David W. Reinhard, *The Republican Right since 1945* (Lexington: University Press of Kentucky, 1983), 213.
181. Christian, *President Steps Down*, 2.
182. Berman, *Hubert*, 170.
183. William Vanden Heuvel and Milton Gwirtzman, *On His Own: Robert F. Kennedy, 1964–1968* (Garden City, NY: Doubleday, 1970), 258.
184. Andrew L. Johns, *Vietnam's Second Front: Domestic Politics, The Republican Party, and the War* (Lexington: University Press of Kentucky, 2010), 203.
185. Michael Kramer and Sam Roberts, *"I Never Wanted to Be Vice-President of Anything!" An Investigative Biography of Nelson Rockefeller* (New York: Basic Books, 1976), 325.

186. Lady Bird Johnson, *White House Diary*, 672.
187. Thomas A. Schwartz, *Henry Kissinger and American Power: A Political Biography* (New York: Hill and Wang, 2020), 57.
188. Steel, *In Love with Night*, 181.
189. Schlesinger Jr., *Robert Kennedy and His Times*, 909–10.
190. "Drew Pearson and Jack Anderson on The Washington Merry-Go-Round," May 24, 1968, Box 62, Jack Anderson Papers, Special Collections Research Center, Gelman Library System, George Washington University, Washington, DC.
191. Memorandum for the Record, April 9, 1968, Box 12, Official and Confidential Subject Files, 1924–72, Office of the Director, J. Edgar Hoover, RG 65: Records of the Federal Bureau of Investigation, National Archives and Records Administration.
192. Notes, May 24, 1968, Box G11, Drew Pearson Papers, Lyndon B. Johnson Presidential Library.
193. Pearson, *Washington Merry-Go-Round*, 578.
194. Memorandum from C. D. DeLoach to Clyde Tolson, "Robert F. Kennedy: Denial of Knowledge Regarding Usage of Microphones by the FBI," December 13, 1966, FBI FOIA Request 1333813–001.
195. Memorandum from C. D. DeLoach to Clyde Tolson, May 21, 1968, Box 12, Official and Confidential Subject Files, 1924–72, Office of the Director, J. Edgar Hoover, RG 65: Records of the Federal Bureau of Investigation, National Archives and Records Administration.
196. Thomas, *Robert Kennedy*, 378.
197. Jules Witcover, *Party of the People: A History of the Democrats* (New York: Random House, 2003), 552.
198. Scammon and Wattenberg, *Real Majority*, 127.
199. McCarthy, *Up 'Til Now*, 192.
200. Ibid., 197.
201. Eisele, *Almost to the Presidency*, 312.
202. Bill Connell Undated Notes, Box 148.B.15.8F, Hubert H. Humphrey Papers, Minnesota Historical Society, St. Paul, MN.
203. Witcover, *85 Days*, 7.
204. Tom Wicker, *One of Us: Richard Nixon and the American Dream* (New York: Random House, 1991), 347.
205. Scammon and Wattenberg, *Real Majority*, 128.
206. Lady Bird Johnson, *White House Diary*, 680.
207. Clarke, *Last Campaign*, 7.
208. LaFeber, *Deadly Bet*, 96.
209. Witcover, *85 Days*, 320–21.
210. Dennis V. N. McCarthy with Philip W. Smith, *Protecting the President: The Inside Story of a Secret Service Agent* (New York: William Morrow, 1985), 133–34.

211. Schlesinger Jr., *Robert Kennedy and His Times*, xix.

212. Steel, *In Love with Night*, 192–93.

213. Lady Bird Johnson, *White House Diary*, 683.

214. Clarke, *Last Campaign*, 5.

215. Schlesinger Jr., *Robert Kennedy and His Times*, 1.

216. Nancy Gibbs and Michael Duffy, *The Preacher and the Presidents: Billy Graham in the White House* (New York: Center Street, 2007), 162.

217. Lady Bird Johnson, *White House Diary*, 707.

218. Joseph A. Califano Jr., *The Triumph and Tragedy of Lyndon Johnson: The White House Years* (New York: Simon & Schuster, 2015), 336.

219. Nixon Diary, Notebook 15.

220. Special interview with Billy Graham, p. 2, October 12, 1983, Lyndon B. Johnson Presidential Library.

221. William Martin, *A Prophet with Honor: The Billy Graham Story* (New York: William Morrow, 1991), 305.

222. Stephen P. Miller, *Billy Graham and the Rise of the Republican South* (Philadelphia: University of Pennsylvania Press, 2009), 5.

223. Special interview with Billy Graham, pp. 1–2, October 12, 1983, Lyndon B. Johnson Presidential Library.

224. Martin, *Prophet with Honor*, 305.

225. Graham, *Just As I Am*, 404.

226. Reedy, *Lyndon B. Johnson*, 155.

227. Gibbs and Duffy, *Preacher and the Presidents*, 123.

228. Graham, *Just As I Am*, 405–6.

229. Miller, *Billy Graham and the Rise of the Republican South*, 131.

230. Letter from Billy Graham to Hubert Humphrey, June 28, 1968, Notebook 9, VIP Notebooks, Records of the Billy Graham Evangelistic Association: Montreat Office, Billy Graham Archive and Research Center, Charlotte, NC.

231. Peter Baker, "White House Memo: Trump May Compare Himself to Nixon in 1968, but He Really Resembles Wallace," *New York Times*, June 9, 2020, A18.

232. Maurice Isserman and Michael Kazin, *America Divided: The Civil War of the 1960s* (New York: Oxford University Press, 2000), 237.

233. Lady Bird Johnson, *White House Diary*, 685.

234. Christian, *President Steps Down*, 31.

235. Nixon Diary, Notebook 15.

236. Nixon Diary, Notebook 1.

237. Martin, *Prophet with Honor*, 359.

238. Gibbs and Duffy, *Preacher and the Presidents*, 163.

239. Memorandum from James Rowe to Hubert Humphrey, July 31, 1968, Box 173, Larry O'Brien Papers, John F. Kennedy Presidential Library.

240. Nixon Diary, Notebook 15.

241. Dallek, *Flawed Giant*, 559.

242. Clifford with Holbrooke, *Counsel to the President*, 555.

243. Christian, *President Steps Down*, 21.

244. Califano Jr., *Inside*, 191.

Chapter 2. Humphrey

1. John G. Stewart, "When Democracy Worked: Reflections on the Passage of the Civil Rights Act of 1964," *New York Law School Law Review* 59, no. 1 (2014–15): 148.

2. Carl Solberg, *Hubert Humphrey: A Biography* (New York: W. W. Norton, 1984), 11–12.

3. Leslie H. Southwick, ed., *Presidential Also-Rans and Running Mates, 1788 through 1996*, volume 2, *1892–1996*, 2nd edition (Jefferson, NC: McFarland, 2008), 675.

4. Robert Sherrill and Harry W. Ernst, *The Drugstore Liberal* (New York: Grossman Publishers, 1968), 17–18.

5. Edgar Berman, *Hubert: The Triumph and Tragedy of the Humphrey I Knew* (New York: G. P. Putnam's Sons, 1979), 27.

6. Solberg, *Hubert Humphrey*, 54.

7. Southwick, *Presidential Also-Rans*, 676.

8. Sheldon D. Engelmayer and Robert J. Wagman, *Hubert Humphrey: The Man and His Dream* (New York: Methuen, 1978), 3.

9. "Hubert Humphrey the Man," Undated, Box 150.F.18.10F, Hubert H. Humphrey Papers, Minnesota Historical Society.

10. Sherrill and Ernst, *Drugstore Liberal*, 29.

11. Eugene McCarthy, *Up 'Til Now: A Memoir* (New York: Harcourt Brace Jovanovich, 1987), 5.

12. Andrew L. Johns, *The Price of Loyalty: Hubert Humphrey's Vietnam Conflict* (Lanham, MD: Rowman & Littlefield, 2020), 11.

13. Sherrill and Ernst, *Drugstore Liberal*, 11.

14. Stewart, "When Democracy Worked," 148.

15. Kari Frederickson, *The Dixiecrat Revolt and the End of the Solid South, 1932–1968* (Chapel Hill: University of North Carolina Press, 2001), 129.

16. Solberg, *Hubert Humphrey*, 12–13.

17. Marshall Frady, "The American Independent Party," in Arthur M. Schlesinger Jr., ed., *History of U.S. Political Parties: 1945–1972, The Politics of Change*, vol. 4 (Philadelphia: Chelsea House Publishers, 1973), 3434.

18. Frank M. Dixon, Keynote Address at Southern Democratic Convention, Birmingham, Alabama, July 17, 1948, in Schlesinger Jr., *History of U.S. Political Parties*, 3415–16.

19. Engelmayer and Wagman, *Hubert Humphrey*, 4.

20. Michael A. Cohen, *American Maelstrom: The 1968 Election and the Politics of Division* (New York: Oxford University Press, 2016), 75; Stewart, "When Democracy Worked," 148.

21. Sherrill and Ernst, *Drugstore Liberal*, 11.

22. Letter from Hubert Humphrey to George Ball, April 22, 1958, Box 58, George W. Ball Papers, The Seeley G. Mudd Manuscript Library, Princeton University.

23. Thomas L. Hughes, *Anecdotage: Some Authentic Retrievals* (self-pub. 2014), 24.

24. Johns, *Price of Loyalty*, 12.

25. Memorandum from Leonid Brezhnev to the Politburo of the Central Committee, Undated [July 1968], Fond 80, Inventory 1, Cause 314 [Ф. 80. Оп. 1. Д. 314], Russian State Archive of Contemporary History (RGANI) [Российский Государственный Архив Новейшей Истории]. Brezhnev's concerns were apparently based on a belief that American voters could shift right-wing in the coming election, which "increases the possibility of our influence on the political processes taking place in the United States." The election of Humphrey provided the best chance to avoid such a shift. According to RGANI archivists, the memo was discovered in Brezhnev's closed desk only after his death in 1982.

26. Solberg, *Hubert Humphrey*, 19–20.

27. Southwick, *Presidential Also-Rans*, 678.

28. Walter F. Mondale with David Hage, *The Good Fight: A Life in Liberal Politics* (Minneapolis: University of Minnesota Press, 2010), 71.

29. Berman, *Hubert*, 182.

30. Hubert H. Humphrey, *The Education of a Public Man: My Life and Politics* (Garden City, NY: Doubleday, 1976), 356.

31. Berman, *Hubert*, 55.

32. Author telephone interview with Ken and Patricia Gray, July 3, 2018.

33. Berman, *Hubert*, 33–34.

34. Letter from James Rowe to Ben Bradlee, June 4, 1968, Box 148.B.15.8F, Hubert H. Humphrey Papers, Minnesota Historical Society.

35. Berman, *Hubert*, 172.

36. Ted Van Dyk, *Heroes, Hacks, and Fools: Memoirs from the Political Inside* (Seattle: University of Washington Press, 2007), 33.

37. Berman, *Hubert*, 34.

38. Ibid., 35.

39. Sherrill and Ernst, *Drugstore Liberal*, 4.

40. Theodore H. White, *The Making of the President, 1968* (New York: Atheneum Publishers, 1969), 315.

41. Nelson W. Polsby, *The Citizens' Choice: Humphrey or Nixon* (Washington, DC: Public Affairs Press, 1968), 10.

42. Stewart, "When Democracy Worked," 157.

43. Ibid., 170.

44. Berman, *Hubert*, 87; Joseph A. Califano, Jr., *Inside: A Public and Private Life* (New York: PublicAffairs, 2004), 247.
45. Berman, *Hubert*, 40–41.
46. George McKee Elsey, *An Unplanned Life* (Columbia: University of Missouri Press, 2005), 238.
47. Johns, *Price of Loyalty*, 32.
48. Solberg, *Hubert Humphrey*, 242–43.
49. Van Dyk, *Heroes, Hacks, and Fools*, 33.
50. Johns, *Price of Loyalty*, 39.
51. Humphrey, *Education of a Public Man*, 427.
52. Mondale with Hage, *Good Fight*, 82.
53. Solberg, *Hubert Humphrey*, 278–80.
54. Telegram from Walt Rostow to Lyndon Johnson, October 30, 1967, CAP67917, Box 13, Confidential Files, Lyndon B. Johnson Presidential Library.
55. Remarks by Vice President Hubert H. Humphrey upon Presentation of Credentials, Saigon—October 30, 1967, Box 150.G.15.8F, Hubert H. Humphrey Papers, Minnesota Historical Society.
56. Vice President's Asian Trip Briefing Book, 10–11/67, Box 27, International Meetings, National Security File, Lyndon B. Johnson Presidential Library.
57. Memorandum from Bill Connell to Ted Van Dyk, October 13, 1967, Box 150.F.18.10F, Hubert H. Humphrey Papers, Minnesota Historical Society.
58. Murrey Marder, "Humphrey Widens Bid to Vietcong," *Washington Post*, December 8, 1967, A1.
59. Van Dyk, *Heroes, Hacks, and Fools*, 56.
60. Telegram from Ellsworth Bunker to Walt Rostow, October 26, 1968, CAS Channels 264, Box 61, Country File Vietnam, National Security File, Lyndon B. Johnson Presidential Library.
61. Telegram from American Embassy Saigon to Secretary of State, "Humphrey-Thieu Conversation," October 30, 1967, Saigon 9986, Box 2615, POL 7 US/HUMPHREY, Central Foreign Policy Files, 1967–69, RG 59: General Records of the Department of State, National Archives and Records Administration.
62. Nguyen Tien Hung and Jerrold Schecter, *The Palace File* (New York: Harper & Row, 1986), 21.
63. Nguyen Cao Ky, *Buddha's Child: My Fight to Save Vietnam* (New York: St. Martin's Press, 2002), 190.
64. Van Dyk, *Heroes, Hacks, and Fools*, 57.
65. "Vice President's Report to the President, Visit to South Vietnam, October 29–November 2, 1967," Box 150.F.18.10F, Hubert H. Humphrey Papers, Minnesota Historical Society.

66. Telegram from American Embassy Saigon to Secretary of State, November 1, 1967, Saigon 10177, Box 150.G.15.8F, Hubert H. Humphrey Papers, Minnesota Historical Society.

67. Cohen, *American Maelstrom*, 48.

68. Solberg, *Hubert Humphrey*, 311–12.

69. William Conrad Gibbons, ed., *The U.S. Government and the Vietnam War: Executive and Legislative Roles and Relationships, Part IV, July 1965–January 1968* (Princeton, NJ: Princeton University Press, 1995), 894–95.

70. Memorandum from Hubert Humphrey to Lyndon Johnson, November 7, 1967, Box 61, Country File Vietnam, National Security File, Lyndon B. Johnson Presidential Library.

71. Jeff Shesol, *Mutual Contempt: Lyndon Johnson, Robert Kennedy, and the Feud that Defined a Decade* (New York: W. W. Norton, 1997), 393.

72. Humphrey, *Education of a Public Man*, 8.

73. Cohen, *American Maelstrom*, 325.

74. Mark Atwood Lawrence, *The Vietnam War: A Concise International History* (New York: Oxford University Press, 2008), 117.

75. Berman, *Hubert*, 116.

76. Author telephone interview with Ken and Patricia Gray, July 3, 2018.

77. Sherrill and Ernst, *Drugstore Liberal*, 3–4.

78. Daniel Patrick Moynihan, "The Negro Family: The Case for National Action," Office of Policy Planning and Research, United States Department of Labor, March 1965. The full text is available here: www.dol.gov/general/aboutdol/history/webid-moynihan (accessed July 27, 2022).

79. Daniel P. Moynihan, *The Politics of a Guaranteed Income: The Nixon Administration and the Family Assistance Plan* (New York: Random House, 1973), 37.

80. Lee Rainwater and William L. Yancey, *The Moynihan Report and the Politics of Controversy* (Cambridge, MA: MIT Press, 1967), 141.

81. Godfrey Hodgson, *The World Turned Right Side Up: A History of the Conservative Ascendancy in America* (Boston: Houghton Mifflin, 1996), 130; Richard J. Whalen, *Catch the Falling Flag: A Republican's Challenge to His Party* (Boston: Houghton Mifflin, 1972), 38.

82. Rainwater and Yancey, *Moynihan Report*, 449–50.

83. Garry Wills, "From 'The Second Civil War,'" in Harold Hayes, ed., *Smiling Through the Apocalypse: Esquire's History of the Sixties* (New York: McCall Publishing, 1969), 705.

84. Steven R. Weisman, ed., *Daniel Patrick Moynihan: A Portrait in Letters of an American Visionary* (New York: PublicAffairs, 2010), 140.

85. Daniel P. Moynihan, *Maximum Feasible Misunderstanding: Community Action in the War on Poverty* (New York: Free Press, 1969), 179.

86. Arnold A. Offner, *Hubert Humphrey: The Conscience of the Country* (New Haven: Yale University Press, 2018), 270–71.

87. Ibid., 273.

88. Berman, *Hubert*, 56.

89. Ibid., 153.

90. Offner, *Hubert Humphrey*, 273.

91. Jules Witcover, *The Year the Dream Died: Revisiting 1968 in America* (New York: Warner Books, 1997), 142.

92. Berman, *Hubert*, 155.

93. Van Dyk, *Heroes, Hacks, and Fools*, 63.

94. Berman, *Hubert*, 160.

95. Ibid., 156.

96. Ibid., 157.

97. Offner, *Hubert Humphrey*, 274.

98. Cohen, *American Maelstrom*, 313.

99. White, *Making of the President, 1968*, 315.

100. Johns, *Price of Loyalty*, 82.

101. Offner, *Hubert Humphrey*, 279.

102. G. Scott Thomas, *Counting the Votes: A New Way to Analyze America's Presidential Elections* (Santa Barbara, CA: Praeger, 2015), 215.

103. Mondale with Hage, *Good Fight*, 72.

104. Tom Wicker, *One of Us: Richard Nixon and the American Dream* (New York: Random House, 1991), 320.

105. Polsby, *Citizens' Choice*, 28.

106. White, *Making of the President, 1968*, 316.

107. Mondale with Hage, *Good Fight*, 72–73.

108. Offner, *Hubert Humphrey*, 278.

109. Cohen, *American Maelstrom*, 144.

110. Witcover, *Year the Dream Died*, 182.

111. Notes on 1968 Presidential Campaign, Box 2M394, Walter Cronkite Papers, Dolph Briscoe Center for American History, University of Texas at Austin.

112. Richard Lowitt, *Fred Harris: His Journey from Liberalism to Populism* (Lanham, MD: Rowman & Littlefield Publishers, 2002), 67.

113. Offner, *Hubert Humphrey*, 277.

114. Lewis Chester, Godfrey Hodgson, and Bruce Page, *An American Melodrama: The Presidential Campaign of 1968* (New York: Viking Press, 1969), 168.

115. Rufus Phillips, *Why Vietnam Matters: An Eyewitness Account of Lessons Not Learned* (Annapolis: Naval Institute Press, 2008), 293.

116. Van Dyk, *Heroes, Hacks, and Fools*, 66.

117. Author email interview with Norman Sherman, October 28, 2017.

118. Berman, *Hubert*, 20.

119. Mondale with Hage, *Good Fight*, 76.

120. Berman, *Hubert*, 100.

121. Memorandum from Hubert Humphrey to Walter Mondale and Fred Harris, June 4, 1968, Box 150.F.18.10F, Hubert H. Humphrey Papers, Minnesota Historical Society.

122. Letter from Hubert Humphrey to Richard Nixon, August 2, 1955, Box 20, Special Files, PPS 320, Pre-Presidential Papers, Richard M. Nixon Presidential Library.

123. Letter from Richard Nixon to Hubert Humphrey, August 9, 1955, Box 20, Special Files, PPS 320, Pre-Presidential Papers, Richard M. Nixon Presidential Library.

124. Letter from Robert King to Senate Parliamentarian, February 17, 1956, Box 20, Special Files, PPS 320, Pre-Presidential Papers, Richard M. Nixon Presidential Library.

125. Memorandum from Rose Mary Woods to Richard Nixon, May 31, 1957, Box 20, Special Files, PPS 320, Pre-Presidential Papers, Richard M. Nixon Presidential Library.

126. Humphrey, *Education of a Public Man*, 355.

127. Berman, *Hubert*, 167.

128. Memorandum from Hubert Humphrey to Fred Harris, June 25, 1968, Box 150.F.18.10F, Hubert H. Humphrey Papers, Minnesota Historical Society.

129. Letter from Hubert to Humphrey to Arthur Schlesinger Jr., July 13, 1968, in Andrew Schlesinger and Stephen Schlesinger, eds., *The Letters of Arthur Schlesinger, Jr.* (New York: Random House, 2013), 365.

130. Richard N. Goodwin, *Remembering America: A Voice from the Sixties* (Boston: Little, Brown, 1988), 500.

131. George H. Gallup, *The Gallup Poll: Public Opinion, 1935–1971*, volume 3, *1959–1971* (New York: Random House, 1972), 2117.

132. Offner, *Hubert Humphrey*, 284.

133. Cohen, *American Maelstrom*, 146.

134. Albert Eisele, *Almost to the Presidency: A Biography of Two American Politicians* (Blue Earth, MN: Piper, 1972), 365.

135. Berman, *Hubert*, 161.

136. Ibid., 171.

137. Van Dyk, *Heroes, Hacks, and Fools*, 70.

138. Offner, *Hubert Humphrey*, 281.

139. Author interview with James R. Jones, October 17, 2017, Washington, DC.

140. Berman, *Hubert*, 174.

141. Memorandum from Orville Freeman to Hubert Humphrey, June 7, 1968, Box 148.B.15.8F, Hubert H. Humphrey Papers, Minnesota Historical Society.

142. White, *Making of the President, 1968*, 316.

143. Berman, *Hubert*, 176.

144. Memorandum for the Record from the Vice President, June 7, 1968, Box 148.B.15.8F, Hubert H. Humphrey Papers, Minnesota Historical Society.

145. Mondale with Hage, *Good Fight*, 76.

146. Berman, *Hubert*, 173; Van Dyk, *Heroes, Hacks, and Fools*, 72.

147. Memorandum from Hubert Humphrey to Fred Harris, June 27, 1968, Box 148.B.15.8F, Hubert H. Humphrey Papers, Minnesota Historical Society.

148. Offner, *Hubert Humphrey*, 282.

149. Berman, *Hubert*, 75.

150. Memorandum from Hubert Humphrey to Bob McCandless, October 8, 1968, Box 148.B.15.8F, Hubert H. Humphrey Papers, Minnesota Historical Society.

151. Max Frankel, *The Times of My Life and My Life with* The Times (New York: Random House, 1999), 311.

152. Berman, *Hubert*, 210–11.

153. Ibid., 152.

154. Offner, *Hubert Humphrey*, 286.

155. Ibid., 283–84.

156. Memorandum for the Record from the Vice President, June 7, 1968, Box 148.B.15.8F, Hubert H. Humphrey Papers, Minnesota Historical Society.

157. Offner, *Hubert Humphrey*, 282.

158. Eisele, *Almost to the Presidency*, 5.

159. Arthur Herzog, *McCarthy for President* (New York: Viking Press, 1969), 282.

160. Drew Pearson, *Washington Merry-Go-Round: The Drew Pearson Diaries, 1960–1969*, edited by Peter Hannaford (Lincoln, NE: Potomac Books, 2015), 584.

161. Letter from Bill Moyers to Hubert Humphrey, June 6, 1968, Box 148.B.15.8F, Hubert H. Humphrey Papers, Minnesota Historical Society.

162. Offner, *Hubert Humphrey*, 282.

Chapter 3. Nixon

1. Melvin Small, *The Presidency of Richard Nixon* (Lawrence: University Press of Kansas, 1999), 3.

2. Lewis Chester, Godfrey Hodgson, and Bruce Page, *An American Melodrama: The Presidential Campaign of 1968* (New York: Viking Press, 1969), 256.

3. Small, *Presidency of Richard Nixon*, 3.

4. William Martin, *A Prophet with Honor: The Billy Graham Story* (New York: William Morrow, 1991), 365.

5. Author interview with Edward C. Nixon, October 14, 2016, Newport Beach, CA.

6. Nick Thimmesch, *The Condition of Republicanism* (New York: W. W. Norton, 1968), 74.

7. Small, *Presidency of Richard Nixon*, 5.

8. Ibid., 9.

9. Ibid., 11.

10. Allen Weinstein, *Perjury: The Hiss-Chambers Case*, 3rd edition (Stanford, CA: Hoover Institution Press, 2013), 2; Herbert S. Parmet, *Richard Nixon and His America* (New York: Smithmark Publishers, 1990), 28.

11. Letter from Ruth Graham to Richard Nixon, July 3, 1979, Billy Graham, Post-Presidential Correspondence, Richard M. Nixon Presidential Library.

12. Patrick J. Buchanan, *The Greatest Comeback: How Richard Nixon Rose from Defeat to Create the New Majority* (New York: Crown Forum, 2014), 5.

13. Evan Thomas, *Being Nixon: A Man Divided* (New York: Random House, 2015), 78.
14. Small, *Presidency of Richard Nixon*, 14–15.
15. David Greenberg, *Nixon's Shadow: The History of an Image* (New York: W. W. Norton, 2003), 50–51.
16. Theodore H. White, *The Making of the President, 1968* (New York: Atheneum Publishers, 1969), 250.
17. Buchanan, *Greatest Comeback*, 7–8.
18. Irwin F. Gellman, *Campaign of the Century: Kennedy, Nixon, and the Election of 1960* (New Haven: Yale University Press, 2021), 316.
19. Chester, Hodgson, and Page, *American Melodrama*, 251.
20. John C. Lungren and John C. Lungren, Jr., *Healing Richard Nixon: A Doctor's Memoir* (Lexington: University Press of Kentucky, 2003), 65.
21. Greenberg, *Nixon's Shadow*, 39–40.
22. Buchanan, *Greatest Comeback*, 7.
23. Stephen Hess and David S. Broder, *The Republican Establishment: The Present and Future of the G.O.P.* (New York: Harper & Row, 1967), 145.
24. Buchanan, *Greatest Comeback*, 12.
25. Ibid., 12–13.
26. Hess and Broder, *Republican Establishment*, 141.
27. Jules Witcover, *The Year the Dream Died: Revisiting 1968 in America* (New York: Warner Books, 1997), 11.
28. Thomas W. Evans Oral History Interview with Richard Nixon, March 15, 1983, Box 3, Thomas W. Evans Papers, Richard M. Nixon Presidential Library.
29. Nancy Gibbs and Michael Duffy, *The President's Club: Inside the World's Most Exclusive Fraternity* (New York: Simon & Schuster, 2012), 224.
30. Irwin F. Gellman, "Richard M. Nixon: Bicoastal Practitioner," in Norman Gross, ed., *America's Lawyer-Presidents: From Law Office to Oval Office* (Evanston, IL: Northwestern University Press, 2004), 273.
31. Leonard Garment, *Crazy Rhythm: My Journey from Brooklyn, Jazz, and Wall Street to Nixon's White House, Watergate, and Beyond* (New York: Times Books, 1997), 58.
32. Victor Li, *Nixon in New York: How Wall Street Helped Richard Nixon Win the White House* (Vancouver: Fairleigh Dickinson University Press, 2018), xiv.
33. Hess and Broder, *Republican Establishment*, 162.
34. Garment, *Crazy Rhythm*, 59.
35. Richard J. Whalen, *Catch the Falling Flag: A Republican's Challenge to His Party* (Boston: Houghton Mifflin, 1972), 21.
36. Garment, *Crazy Rhythm*, 61.
37. Buchanan, *Greatest Comeback*, 27.
38. Ibid., 16.
39. Garment, *Crazy Rhythm*, 105.

40. Patrick J. Buchanan, *Nixon's White House Wars: The Battles That Made and Broke a President and Divided America Forever* (New York: Crown Forum, 2017), 9.

41. Rick Perlstein, *Before the Storm: Barry Goldwater and the Unmaking of the American Consensus* (New York: Hill and Wang, 2001), 515.

42. Memo for the Files from the Vice President, August 23, 1967, Box 76, White House Confidential Files, Lyndon B. Johnson Presidential Library; Tom Wicker, *One of Us: Richard Nixon and the American Dream* (New York: Random House, 1991), 278.

43. Richard Nixon, *RN: The Memoirs of Richard Nixon* (New York: Grosset & Dunlap, 1978), 266.

44. Buchanan, *Greatest Comeback*, 18.

45. Thimmesch, *Condition of Republicanism*, 87.

46. Buchanan, *Greatest Comeback*, 17–18.

47. David Steigerwald, *The Sixties and the End of Modern America* (New York: St. Martin's Press, 1995), 277.

48. Nixon, *RN: The Memoirs*, 266.

49. David S. Broder, "Election of 1968," in Arthur M. Schlesinger Jr., ed., *History of American Presidential Elections, 1789–1968*, vol. 4 (New York: McGraw-Hill, 1971), 3706.

50. Jules Witcover, *The Resurrection of Richard Nixon* (New York: G. P. Putnam's Sons, 1970), 340–41.

51. Daniel P. Moynihan, *The Politics of a Guaranteed Income: The Nixon Administration and the Family Assistance Plan* (New York: Random House, 1993), 66.

52. Nixon, *RN: The Memoirs*, 267.

53. Buchanan, *Greatest Comeback*, 252.

54. Lisa McGirr, *Suburban Warriors: The Origins of the New American Right* (Princeton, NJ: Princeton University Press, 2001), 11.

55. Nixon, *RN: The Memoirs*, 268.

56. Buchanan, *Greatest Comeback*, 31.

57. Garry Wills, *Nixon Agonistes: The Crisis of the Self-Made Man* (Boston: Houghton Mifflin, 1969), 312.

58. Richard Nixon, *Nixon Speaks Out* (New York: Nixon-Agnew Campaign Committee, 1968), 24.

59. Nixon, *RN: The Memoirs*, 271–72.

60. Buchanan, *Greatest Comeback*, 9.

61. David W. Reinhard, *The Republican Right since 1945* (Lexington: University Press of Kentucky, 1983), 215.

62. Alexander Bloom and Wini Breines, eds., *Takin' It to the Streets: A Sixties Reader* (New York: Oxford University Press, 1995), 294.

63. Bedroom-Second Floor, March 13, 1966, 9:25–10:20 A.M., Nixon Index Cards, Lyndon B. Johnson Presidential Library.

64. Nixon, *RN: The Memoirs*, 272.

65. Ibid., 754.

66. Gellman, *Campaign of the Century*, 49.

67. Frank Gannon Interview with Richard Nixon, June 13, 1983—Part 3, Walter J. Brown Media Archives and Peabody Awards Collection, Special Collection Libraries, University of Georgia.

68. Letter from Lyndon Johnson to Richard Nixon, October 5, 1954, Box 20, Special Files, PPS 320, Pre-Presidential Files, Richard M. Nixon Presidential Library.

69. Letter from C. G. "Bebe" Rebozo to Lyndon Johnson, August 24, 1966, Box 8, Trip File, Series II, PPS 347, Richard M. Nixon Presidential Library.

70. Earl Mazo, *Richard Nixon: A Political and Personal Portrait* (New York: Harper & Brothers Publishers, 1959), 260.

71. Letter from Richard Nixon to Lyndon Johnson, February 12, 1957, Box 21, Special Files, PPS 320, Pre-Presidential Files, Richard M. Nixon Presidential Library.

72. John Connally with Mickey Herskowitz, *In History's Shadow: An American Odyssey* (New York: Hyperion, 1993), 259.

73. Andrew L. Johns, *Vietnam's Second Front: Domestic Politics, the Republican Party, and the War* (Lexington: University Press of Kentucky, 2010), 220.

74. Letter from Richard Nixon to Lady Bird Johnson, January 22, 1973, Box 26, Alphabetical Name Files, White House Central Files, Richard M. Nixon Presidential Library.

75. David Halberstam, *The Best and the Brightest* (New York: Random House, 1969), 629.

76. Nixon, *RN: The Memoirs*, 272.

77. Thomas W. Evans Oral History Interview with Richard Nixon, March 15, 1983, Box 3, Thomas W. Evans Papers, Richard M. Nixon Presidential Library.

78. Garment, *Crazy Rhythm*, 79.

79. Gellman, "Richard M. Nixon: Bicoastal Practitioner," 274.

80. Richard G. Kleindienst, *Justice: The Memoirs of Attorney General Richard Kleindienst* (Ottawa, IL: Jameson Books, 1985), 40.

81. William Safire, *Before the Fall: An Inside View of the Pre-Watergate White House* (Garden City, NY: Doubleday, 1975), 35.

82. Nixon, *RN: The Memoirs*, 273.

83. Safire, *Before the Fall*, 37.

84. Michael A. Cohen, *American Maelstrom: The 1968 Election and the Politics of Division* (New York: Oxford University Press, 2016), 181–82.

85. Harry McPherson, *A Political Education: A Washington Memoir* (Austin: University of Texas Press, 1972), 448.

86. Nixon, *RN: The Memoirs*, 276.

87. Buchanan, *Greatest Comeback*, 88–89.

88. Gibbs and Duffy, *President's Club*, 226.

89. Nixon, *RN: The Memoirs*, 276–77.

90. Buchanan, *Greatest Comeback*, 89.

91. Mary C. Brennan, *Turning Right in the Sixties: The Conservative Capture of the GOP* (Chapel Hill: University of North Carolina Press, 1995), 119.

92. Robert Mason, *Richard Nixon and the Quest for a New Majority* (Chapel Hill: University of North Carolina Press, 2004), 1.

93. John Roy Price, *The Last Liberal Republican: An Insider's Perspective on Nixon's Surprising Social Policy* (Lawrence: University Press of Kansas, 2021), 109.

94. J. William Middendorf II, *A Glorious Disaster: Barry Goldwater's Presidential Campaign and the Origins of the Conservative Movement* (New York: Basic Books, 2006), 247.

95. Nixon, *RN: The Memoirs*, 277.

96. Cohen, *American Maelstrom*, 181–82.

97. Letter from Barry Goldwater to Richard Nixon, July 7, 1967, Box 2, PPS 501, Pre-Presidential Files, Richard M. Nixon Presidential Library.

98. Nixon, *RN: The Memoirs*, 278.

99. Ibid., 280.

100. Letter from Richard Nixon to Dwight Eisenhower, August 5, 1967, Box 14, Special Names, Post-Presidential Papers, Dwight D. Eisenhower Presidential Library.

101. White, *Making of the President, 1968*, 170.

102. Price, *Last Liberal Republican*, 108.

103. Hubert H. Humphrey, *The Education of a Public Man: My Life and Politics* (Garden City, NY: Doubleday, 1976), 382.

104. Eugene McCarthy, *Up 'Til Now: A Memoir* (New York: Harcourt Brace Jovanovich, 1987), 199.

105. Nixon, *RN: The Memoirs*, 287.

106. Buchanan, *Greatest Comeback*, 156–57.

107. Henry Kissinger, *Years of Renewal* (New York: Simon & Schuster, 1999), 48.

108. Brennan, *Turning Right in the Sixties*, 123.

109. Arthur M. Schlesinger Jr., *The Crisis of Confidence: Ideas, Power and Violence in America* (Boston: Houghton Mifflin, 1969), 276.

110. Whalen, *Catch the Falling Flag*, 15.

111. White, *Making of the President, 1968*, 170.

112. Buchanan, *Greatest Comeback*, 35.

113. Melvin Small and William D. Hoover, eds., *Give Peace a Chance: Exploring the Vietnam Antiwar Movement* (Syracuse, NY: Syracuse University Press, 1992), xv.

114. Nixon, *RN: The Memoirs*, 290.

115. Letter from Billy Graham to Richard Nixon, August 17, 1974, Name File, Post-Presidential Correspondence, Richard M. Nixon Presidential Library.

116. Billy Graham, *Just As I Am: The Autobiography of Billy Graham* (New York: HarperCollins, 1997), 443.

117. Letter from Billy Graham to Richard Nixon, August 17, 1974.

118. Introduction of Mr. Nixon at Pittsburgh Crusade, Notebook 10, VIP Note-books, Records of the Billy Graham Evangelistic Association: Montreat Office, Billy Graham Archive and Research Center, Charlotte, NC.

119. Letter from Julie Nixon Eisenhower to John C. Pollock, July 2, 1975, Note-book 14, VIP Notebooks, Records of the Billy Graham Evangelistic Association: Montreat Office, Billy Graham Archive and Research Center, Charlotte, NC.

120. Julie Nixon Eisenhower, *Special People* (New York: Simon & Schuster, 1977), 69.

121. Introduction of Mr. Nixon at Pittsburgh Crusade, Notebook 10, VIP Note-books, Records of the Billy Graham Evangelistic Association: Montreat Office, Billy Graham Archive and Research Center, Charlotte, NC.

122. Graham, *Just As I Am*, 445.

123. Ibid., 390–91.

124. Raymond Price, *With Nixon* (New York: Viking Press, 1977), 15.

125. Nixon, *RN: The Memoirs*, 291.

126. David Eisenhower with Julie Nixon Eisenhower, *Going Home to Glory: A Memoir of Life with Dwight D. Eisenhower, 1961–1969* (New York: Simon & Schuster, 2010), 233.

127. Martin, *Prophet with Honor*, 356.

128. Nixon Diary, Notebook 15, VIP Notebooks, Records of the Billy Graham Evangelistic Association: Montreat Office, Billy Graham Archive and Research Center, Charlotte, NC.

129. Nixon, *RN: The Memoirs*, 292.

130. Thomas, *Being Nixon*, 150.

131. Nixon Diary, Notebook 15.

132. Ibid.

133. Stephen P. Miller, *Billy Graham and the Rise of the Republican South* (Philadelphia: University of Pennsylvania Press, 2009), 131.

134. Nixon Diary, Notebook 15.

135. Graham, *Just As I Am*, 444.

136. Martin, *Prophet with Honor*, 356.

137. Nixon, *RN: The Memoirs*, 292–93.

138. Nixon Diary, Notebook 15.

139. Letter from Julie Nixon Eisenhower to John C. Pollock, July 2, 1975, Note-book 14, VIP Notebooks, Records of the Billy Graham Evangelistic Association: Montreat Office, Billy Graham Archive and Research Center, Charlotte, NC.

140. Nixon Diary, Notebook 15.

141. Nixon, *RN: The Memoirs*, 293–94.

142. Thomas, *Being Nixon*, 151.

143. Lloyd Gardner, ed., *The Great Nixon Turnaround: America's New Foreign Policy in the Post-Liberal Era* (New York: New Viewpoints, 1973), 3.

144. Buchanan, *Greatest Comeback*, 38.
145. Witcover, *Resurrection of Richard Nixon*, 231.
146. Buchanan, *Greatest Comeback*, 201.
147. Witcover, *Resurrection of Richard Nixon*, 215.
148. Whalen, *Catch the Falling Flag*, 77.
149. Nixon, *RN: The Memoirs*, 297.
150. Buchanan, *Nixon's White House Wars*, 10.
151. George Romney Interview, Lou Gordon's "Hot Seat," September 7, 1967, George Romney Papers, Bentley Historical Library, University of Michigan.
152. Witcover, *Resurrection of Richard Nixon*, 214.
153. Buchanan, *Greatest Comeback*, 209.
154. Stephen E. Ambrose, *Nixon, Volume Two: The Triumph of a Politician, 1962–1972* (New York: Simon & Schuster, 1989), 144.
155. Nixon, *RN: The Memoirs*, 298.
156. Wills, *Nixon Agonistes*, 20.
157. Seth Blumenthal, *Children of the Silent Majority: Young Voters and the Rise of the Republican Party, 1968–1980* (Lawrence: University Press of Kansas, 2018), 12.
158. Nixon, *Nixon Speaks Out*, 28.
159. Broder, "Election of 1968," 3712.
160. Brennan, *Turning Right in the Sixties*, 121.
161. Maurice H. Stans, *The Terrors of Justice: The Untold Side of Watergate* (New York: Everest House Publishers, 1978), 142.
162. Robert Dallek, *Flawed Giant: Lyndon Johnson and His Times, 1961–1973* (New York: Oxford University Press, 1998), 549; Richard M. Scammon and Ben J. Wattenberg, *The Real Majority* (New York: Coward-McCann, 1970), 88.
163. Stans, *Terrors of Justice*, 136–37.
164. Wills, *Nixon Agonistes*, 307.
165. Lewis L. Gould, *Grand Old Party: A History of the Republicans* (New York: Random House, 2003), 381.
166. Whalen, *Catch the Falling Flag*, 61.
167. Stephen Hess, *The Professor and the President: Daniel Patrick Moynihan in the Nixon White House* (Washington, DC: Brookings Institution Press, 2015), xiii.
168. Garment, *Crazy Rhythm*, 69.
169. Buchanan, *Greatest Comeback*, 115.
170. Richard Norton Smith, *On His Own Terms: A Life of Nelson Rockefeller* (New York: Random House, 2014), 512.
171. Buchanan, *Greatest Comeback*, 209.
172. Ibid., 213.
173. White, *Making of the President, 1968*, 264.
174. Smith, *On His Own Terms*, 513.
175. White, *Making of the President, 1968*, 264.

176. Cary Reich, *The Life of Nelson A. Rockefeller: Worlds to Conquer, 1908–1958* (New York: Doubleday, 1996), xi.

177. Buchanan, *Greatest Comeback*, 40.

178. Matthew Dallek, *The Right Moment: Ronald Reagan's First Victory and the Decisive Turning Point in American Politics* (New York: Oxford University Press, 2000), 241.

179. Perlstein, *Before the Storm*, 501.

180. Cohen, *American Maelstrom*, 211.

181. Brennan, *Turning Right in the Sixties*, 124.

182. Lou Cannon, *Governor Reagan: His Rise to Power* (New York: PublicAffairs, 2003), 257.

183. Cohen, *American Maelstrom*, 211.

184. Theodore White Interview with Bob Haldeman, June 18, 1968, Box 116, Theodore White Papers, Pusey Library, Harvard University.

185. Buchanan, *Greatest Comeback*, 234–35.

186. Richard Nixon, *Nixon on the Issues* (New York: Nixon-Agnew Campaign Committee, 1968), 174.

187. Buchanan, *Greatest Comeback*, 210.

188. Price, *With Nixon*, 28.

189. Whalen, *Catch the Falling Flag*, 98.

190. Ibid., 125.

191. Viet March 29, 1968 redraft, p. 1, Box 22, Richard V. Allen Papers, Hoover Institution Library and Archives.

192. Nixon, *RN: The Memoirs*, 300.

193. Whalen, *Catch the Falling Flag*, 141–42.

194. Eisenhower with Nixon Eisenhower, *Going Home to Glory*, 245.

195. Statement by Richard M. Nixon, April 1, 1968, Box 22, Richard V. Allen Papers, Hoover Institution Library and Archives.

196. Nixon, *RN: The Memoirs*, 300.

197. Whalen, *Catch the Falling Flag*, 143.

198. Gibbs and Duffy, *President's Club*, 223.

199. Nixon, *RN: The Memoirs*, 301.

200. Buchanan, *Greatest Comeback*, 240.

201. Ibid., 253.

202. T. George Harris, *Romney's Way: A Man and an Idea* (Englewood Cliffs, NJ: Prentice-Hall, 1967), 257.

203. Dean J. Kotlowski, *Nixon's Civil Rights: Politics, Principle, and Policy* (Cambridge, MA: Harvard University Press, 2001), 132.

204. Nixon, *Nixon Speaks Out*, 65.

205. Whalen, *Catch the Falling Flag*, 158.

206. Nixon, *Nixon on the Issues*, 109.

207. Kotlowski, *Nixon's Civil Rights*, 106.

208. Walter F. Mondale with David Hage, *The Good Fight: A Life in Liberal Politics* (Minneapolis: University of Minnesota Press, 2010), 95.

209. Timothy N. Thurber, *Republicans and Race: The GOP's Frayed Relationship with African Americans, 1945–1974* (Lawrence: University Press of Kansas, 2013), 270.

210. Nixon, *Nixon Speaks Out*, 86.

211. Kotlowski, *Nixon's Civil Rights*, 192–93.

212. Thurber, *Republicans and Race*, 266.

213. Earl Mazo and Stephen Hess, *Nixon: A Political Portrait* (New York: Harper & Row, 1968), 316.

214. Nixon, *RN: The Memoirs*, 754.

215. Nixon, *Nixon Speaks Out*, 73–74.

216. Kotlowski, *Nixon's Civil Rights*, 18–19.

217. Safire, *Before the Fall*, 49.

218. Randall B. Woods, *LBJ: Architect of American Ambition* (New York: Free Press, 2006), 813.

219. Peter Baker, "White House Memo: Trump May Compare Himself to Nixon in 1968, but He Really Resembles Wallace," *New York Times*, June 9, 2020, A18.

220. George H. Gallup, *The Gallup Poll: Public Opinion, 1935–1971*, volume 3, *1959–1971* (New York: Random House, 1972), 2164.

221. Thurber, *Republicans and Race*, 269.

222. Nixon, *RN: The Memoirs*, 302.

223. Smith, *On His Own Terms*, 522.

224. White, *Making of the President, 1968*, 275.

225. Robert Dallek, *Nixon and Kissinger: Partners in Power* (New York: HarperCollins Publishers, 2007), 63.

226. Broder, "Election of 1968," 3706.

227. Nixon, *RN: The Memoirs*, 303.

228. Smith, *On His Own Terms*, 529.

229. Nixon, *RN: The Memoirs*, 303.

230. Smith, *On His Own Terms*, 527.

231. Nixon, *RN: The Memoirs*, 303.

232. Buchanan, *Greatest Comeback*, 31.

233. Steigerwald, *The Sixties*, 282.

234. Peter Baker, "White House Memo: Trump May Compare Himself to Nixon in 1968, but He Really Resembles Wallace," *New York Times*, June 9, 2020, A18.

235. Harry S. Dent, *The Prodigal South Returns to Power* (New York: John Wiley & Sons, 1978), 3.

236. Kotlowski, *Nixon's Civil Rights*, 156.

237. Thurber, *Republicans and Race*, 268.

238. Witcover, *Resurrection of Richard Nixon*, 310.

239. Michael Kramer and Sam Roberts, *"I Never Wanted to Be Vice-President of Anything!" An Investigative Biography of Nelson Rockefeller* (New York: Basic Books, 1976), 326.

240. Buchanan, *Greatest Comeback*, 45.
241. Nixon, *RN: The Memoirs*, 304.
242. Witcover, *Resurrection of Richard Nixon*, 311.
243. Broder, "Election of 1968," 3726–27.
244. Nixon, *RN: The Memoirs*, 304–5.
245. John A. Farrell, *Richard Nixon: The Life* (New York: Doubleday, 2017), 328.
246. Nixon, *RN: The Memoirs*, 305.
247. Witcover, *Resurrection of Richard Nixon*, 310.
248. Nixon Diary, Notebook 15.
249. Buchanan, *Greatest Comeback*, 78–79.
250. White, *Making of the President, 1968*, 424.
251. Witcover, *Resurrection of Richard Nixon*, 343.
252. Wicker, *One of Us*, 343.
253. Scammon and Wattenberg, *Real Majority*, 203.
254. Farrell, *Richard Nixon*, 329.
255. Memorandum from Bill Safire to Pat Buchanan, June 21, 1968, Box 19, Papers of William Safire, Manuscript Division, Library of Congress.
256. Whalen, *Catch the Falling Flag*, 65.
257. Farrell, *Richard Nixon*, 322.
258. Nixon, *RN: The Memoirs*, 306.
259. Ibid., 305.
260. Neil Sheehan, *A Bright Shining Lie: John Paul Vann and American in Vietnam* (New York: Random House, 1988), 730.
261. Buchanan, *Greatest Comeback*, 261.
262. Drew Pearson, *Washington Merry-Go-Round: The Drew Pearson Diaries, 1960–1969*, edited by Peter Hannaford (Lincoln, NE: Potomac Books, 2015), 607.
263. Dwight Chapin, *The President's Man: The Memoirs of Nixon's Trusted Aide* (New York: William Morrow, 2022), 57.
264. John Ehrlichman, *Witness to Power: The Nixon Years* (New York: Simon & Schuster, 1982), 41.
265. Garment, *Crazy Rhythm*, 117–18.
266. Li, *Nixon in New York*, xv.
267. Whalen, *Catch the Falling Flag*, 168.
268. James Rosen, *The Strong Man: John Mitchell and the Secrets of Watergate* (New York: Doubleday, 2008), 40.
269. White, *Making of the President, 1968*, 167.

Chapter 4. Wallace

1. Stephan Lesher, *George Wallace: American Populist* (Reading, MA: Addison-Wesley Publishing, 1994), x.
2. Marshall Frady, *Wallace* (New York: New American Library, 1968), 6.
3. George Wallace Jr., *Governor George Wallace: The Man You Never Knew* (2011), iii.

4. Glenn T. Eskew, "George C. Wallace, 1963–1967, 1971–1979, 1983–1987," in Samuel L. Webb and Margaret E. Armbrester, eds., *Alabama Governors: A Political History of the State* (Tuscaloosa: University of Alabama Press, 2014), 250.

5. George C. Wallace, *Stand Up for America* (Garden City, NY: Doubleday, 1976), 10.

6. Wallace Jr., *Governor George Wallace*, 9.

7. The Life of George C. Wallace, Box 2, Ed Ewing Papers, Alabama Department of Archives and History.

8. Wallace, *Stand Up for America*, 18.

9. The Life of George C. Wallace, Box 2, Ed Ewing Papers, Alabama Department of Archives and History.

10. Wallace Jr., *Governor George Wallace*, 35.

11. The Life of George C. Wallace, Ed Ewing Papers.

12. Ibid.

13. Ibid.

14. Anita Smith, *The Intimate Story of Lurleen Wallace: Her Crusade of Courage* (Montgomery: Communications Unlimited, 1969), 75–76.

15. Eskew, "George C. Wallace," 250.

16. Anne Permaloft, "James E. Folsom, 1947–1951, 1955–1959," in Samuel L. Webb and Margaret E. Armbrester, eds., *Alabama Governors: A Political History of the State* (Tuscaloosa: University of Alabama Press, 2014), 232.

17. Morris Dees with Steve Fiffer, *A Season for Justice: The Life and Times of Civil Rights Lawyer Morris Dees* (New York: Simon & Schuster, 1991), 80.

18. Wallace Jr., *Governor George Wallace*, 12–13.

19. Author interview with George C. Wallace Jr., June 8, 2021, Montgomery, AL.

20. Nelson W. Polsby, *The Citizens' Choice: Humphrey or Nixon* (Washington, DC: Public Affairs Press, 1968), 7; Michael A. Cohen, *American Maelstrom: The 1968 Election and the Politics of Division* (New York: Oxford University Press, 2016), 221–23.

21. The Life of George C. Wallace, Ed Ewing Papers.

22. Peggy Wallace Kennedy with H. Mark Kennedy, *The Broken Road: George Wallace and a Daughter's Journey to Reconciliation* (New York: Bloomberg Publishing, 2019), 40.

23. Eskew, "George C. Wallace," 252.

24. Dan T. Carter, *The Politics of Rage: George Wallace, the Origins of the New Conservatism, and the Transformation of American Politics* (New York: Simon & Schuster, 1995), 297.

25. Peggy Wallace Kennedy with H. Mark Kennedy, *Broken Road*, 41.

26. Anne Permaloft and Carl Grafton, "John Patterson, 1959–1963," in Samuel L. Webb and Margaret E. Armbrester, eds., *Alabama Governors: A Political History of the State* (Tuscaloosa: University of Alabama Press, 2014), 244.

27. Peggy Wallace Kennedy with H. Mark Kennedy, *Broken Road*, 54.

28. Frady, *Wallace*, 127.

29. Dees with Fiffer, *Season for Justice*, 81.
30. Cohen, *American Maelstrom*, 223.
31. Wallace Jr., *Governor George Wallace*, 12.
32. Jeff Frederick, *Stand Up for Alabama: Governor George Wallace* (Tuscaloosa: University of Alabama Press, 2007), 182.
33. Smith, *Intimate Story of Lurleen Wallace*, 78.
34. Peggy Wallace Kennedy with H. Mark Kennedy, *Broken Road*, 54.
35. Wallace Jr., *Governor George Wallace*, 121.
36. Ibid., 6.
37. Author interview with Peggy Wallace Kennedy and Mark Kennedy, June 10, 2021, Montgomery, AL.
38. Carter, *Politics of Rage*, 299.
39. Eskew, "George C. Wallace," 253.
40. Peggy Wallace Kennedy with H. Mark Kennedy, *Broken Road*, 84.
41. Wallace, *Stand Up for America*, 76.
42. Lesher, *George Wallace*, 155–56.
43. Lewis Chester, Godfrey Hodgson, and Bruce Page, *An American Melodrama: The Presidential Campaign of 1968* (New York: Viking Press, 1969), 298.
44. Mike Wallace, "Larry King Live," *CNN*, August 25, 1998.
45. Author interview with Peggy Wallace Kennedy and Mark Kennedy.
46. Author interview with George C. Wallace Jr.
47. Wayne Greenhaw, *Fighting the Devil in Dixie: How Civil Rights Activists Took on the Ku Klux Klan in Alabama* (Chicago: Lawrence Hill Books, 2011), 275.
48. Richard M. Scammon and Ben J. Wattenberg, *The Real Majority* (New York: Coward-McCann, 1970), 186.
49. Wallace Jr., *Governor George Wallace*, ix.
50. Ibid., 18–19.
51. Chester, Hodgson, and Page, *American Melodrama*, 302.
52. Eskew, "George C. Wallace," 253.
53. Wallace Jr., *Governor George Wallace*, xi.
54. Carter, *Politics of Rage*, 313–14.
55. Peggy Wallace Kennedy with H. Mark Kennedy, *Broken Road*, 56.
56. Author interview with George C. Wallace Jr.
57. Memorandum from Burke Marshall to Robert Kennedy, "Re: University of Alabama," April 9, 1968, Box 18, Burke Marshall Personal Papers, John F. Kennedy Presidential Library.
58. Conversation between Attorney General Robert F. Kennedy and Governor Wallace, Montgomery, Alabama, April 25, 1963, Box 18, Burke Marshall Personal Papers, John F. Kennedy Presidential Library.
59. Ibid.
60. George C. Wallace Oral History Interview, May 25, 1967, John F. Kennedy Presidential Library.

61. Author interview with David Azbell, June 8, 2021, Montgomery, AL.
62. Peggy Wallace Kennedy with H. Mark Kennedy, *Broken Road*, 105.
63. Jody Carlson, *George C. Wallace and the Politics of Powerlessness: The Wallace Campaigns for the Presidency, 1964–1976* (New Brunswick, NJ: Transaction Books, 1981), 68.
64. Carter, *Politics of Rage*, 299.
65. Frady, *Wallace*, 18.
66. Lloyd Rohler, *George Wallace: Conservative Populist* (Westport, CT: Praeger, 2004), 55.
67. Lesher, *George Wallace*, xvii.
68. Eskew, "George C. Wallace," 249.
69. Frady, *Wallace*, 137.
70. Eskew, "George C. Wallace," 256.
71. Peggy Wallace Kennedy with H. Mark Kennedy, *Broken Road*, 131–32.
72. Cohen, *American Maelstrom*, 229–30.
73. Lesher, *George Wallace*, 358.
74. Glenn T. Eskew, "Lurleen B. Wallace, 1967–1968," in Samuel L. Webb and Margaret E. Armbrester, eds., *Alabama Governors: A Political History of the State* (Tuscaloosa: University of Alabama Press, 2014), 265.
75. Smith, *Intimate Story of Lurleen Wallace*, 10.
76. Eskew, "Lurleen B. Wallace," 256.
77. Frederick, *Stand Up for Alabama*, 182.
78. Peggy Wallace Kennedy with H. Mark Kennedy, *Broken Road*, 138.
79. Chester, Hodgson, and Page, *American Melodrama*, 302.
80. Carter, *Politics of Rage*, 294.
81. Frederick, *Stand Up for Alabama*, 186.
82. Smith, *Intimate Story of Lurleen Wallace*, 9.
83. Carter, *Politics of Rage*, 309.
84. Carlson, *George C. Wallace*, 71.
85. Ed Ewing Oral History, p. 1, November 11, 1988, Ed Ewing Papers, Alabama Department of Archives and History.
86. Lesher, *George Wallace*, 387–88.
87. Carter, *Politics of Rage*, 304.
88. Wallace Campaign Meeting Notes, January 6, 1968, Box 7, George C. Wallace Collection, Alabama Department of Archives and History.
89. Gov. George C. Wallace Declares Candidacy for President, February 8, 1968, Box 13, George C. Wallace Collection, Alabama Department of Archives and History.
90. Carlson, *George C. Wallace*, 77.
91. Rohler, *George Wallace*, 57.
92. Author interview with David Azbell.
93. Carter, *Politics of Rage*, 304.
94. Carlson, *George C. Wallace*, 79.

95. Kevin M. Kruse, *White Flight: Atlanta and the Making of Modern Conservativism* (Princeton, NJ: Princeton University Press, 2005), 6.

96. Author interview with David Azbell.

97. Paul Pierson and Theda Skocpol, "American Politics in the Long Run," in Paul Pierson and Theda Skocpol, eds., *The Transformation of American Politics: Activist Government and the Rise of Conservatism* (Princeton, NJ: Princeton University Press, 2007), 4.

98. Cohen, *American Maelstrom*, 233–34.

99. Smith, *Intimate Story of Lurleen Wallace*, 6.

100. Wallace, *Stand Up for America*, 116.

101. Wallace Jr., *Governor George Wallace*, 191.

102. Carter, *Politics of Rage*, 318–19.

103. Smith, *Intimate Story of Lurleen Wallace*, 108.

104. Wallace, *Stand Up for America*, 118.

105. Lesher, *George Wallace*, 383–84.

106. Frederick, *Stand Up for Alabama*, 221.

107. Eskew, "Lurleen B. Wallace," 269.

108. Author interview with David Azbell.

109. Carter, *Politics of Rage*, 322–23.

110. Lesher, *George Wallace*, 386.

111. Cohen, *American Maelstrom*, 238.

112. Peggy Wallace Kennedy with H. Mark Kennedy, *Broken Road*, 153–54.

113. Frady, *Wallace*, 2.

114. Peggy Wallace Kennedy with H. Mark Kennedy, *Broken Road*, 46–47.

115. Wallace Jr., *Governor George Wallace*, 109.

116. Lesher, *George Wallace*, xiii.

117. Al Fox, "Wallace 'Amateur' Aides Stage Hard-Hitting Third Party Drive," September 8, 1968, *Birmingham News*, A-34.

118. Peggy Wallace Kennedy with H. Mark Kennedy, *Broken Road*, 154.

119. Cohen, *American Maelstrom*, 238–39.

120. Rohler, *George Wallace*, 58.

121. Carter, *Politics of Rage*, 335–37.

122. Wallace Jr., *Governor George Wallace*, 125.

123. Lesher, *George Wallace*, xiii.

124. Wallace Jr., *Governor George Wallace*, 131.

125. Hubert H. Humphrey, *The Political Philosophy of the New Deal* (Baton Rouge: Louisiana State University Press, 1970), 39.

126. Herbert S. Parmet, *Richard Nixon and His America* (New York: Smithmark Publishers, 1990), 46.

127. William Graham Sumner, "The Forgotten Man," Address to Audiences in Brooklyn and New Haven, January 30 and February 8 (or 9), 1883. The text is available here: www.swarthmore.edu/SocSci/rbannis1/AIH19th/Sumner .Forgotten.html (accessed July 27, 2022).

128. Christopher Lydon, "18,000 Hear Wallace in Boston; He Jousts with Heck-lers, Raps Harvard on Common," October 9, 1968, *Boston Globe*, 1.

129. Carter, *Politics of Rage*, 338.

130. Cohen, *American Maelstrom*, 236.

131. Richard Nixon, *Nixon on the Issues* (New York: Nixon-Agnew Campaign Committee, 1968), 71.

132. Wallace Jr., *Governor George Wallace*, 125.

133. Frady, *Wallace*, 6.

134. Carter, *Politics of Rage*, 348.

135. David Farber, *The Age of Great Dreams: America in the 1960s* (New York: Hill and Wang, 1994), 219.

136. George H. Gallup, *The Gallup Poll: Public Opinion, 1935–1971*, volume 3, *1959–1971* (New York: Random House, 1972), 2128.

137. Carter, *Politics of Rage*, 338.

138. Cohen, *American Maelstrom*, 221.

Chapter 5. Paris

1. George C. Herring, *America's Longest War: The United States and Vietnam, 1950–1975* (Philadelphia: Temple University Press, 1979), 209.

2. Drew Pearson, *Washington Merry-Go-Round: The Drew Pearson Diaries, 1960–1969*, edited by Peter Hannaford (Lincoln, NE: Potomac Books, 2015), 571.

3. Arthur J. Dommen, *The Indochinese Experience of the French and the Americans: Nationalism and Communism in Cambodia, Laos, and Vietnam* (Bloomington: Indiana University Press, 2001), 681.

4. Clark Clifford with Richard Holbrooke, *Counsel to the President: A Memoir* (New York: Random House, 1991), 536.

5. Rudy Abramson, *Spanning the Century: The Life of W. Averell Harriman, 1891–1986* (New York: William Morrow, 1992), 17.

6. Nguyen Phu Duc, *The Viet-Nam Peace Negotiations: Saigon's Side of the Story*, edited by Arthur J. Dommen (Christiansburg, VA: Dalley Book Service, 2005), 26.

7. Lyndon Baines Johnson, *The Vantage Point: Perspectives of the Presidency, 1963–1969* (New York: Holt, Rinehart and Winston, 1971), 505.

8. Abramson, *Spanning the Century*, 15.

9. Vietnam Negotiations, April 15, 1968, Box 586, W. Averell Harriman Papers, Manuscript Division, Library of Congress.

10. Robert D. Schulzinger, *A Time for War: The United States and Vietnam, 1941–1975* (New York: Oxford University Press, 1997), 247.

11. Don Oberdorfer, *Tet! The Turning Point in the Vietnam War* (Baltimore: Johns Hopkins University Press, 1971), 313.

12. Abramson, *Spanning the Century*, 658.

13. Ibid., 659.

14. Nguyen, *Viet-Nam Peace Negotiations*, 25.

15. Ibid., 27.

16. Bui Diem with David Chanoff, *In the Jaws of History* (Boston: Houghton Mifflin, 1987), 230.

17. Robert K. Brigham, *Guerrilla Diplomacy: The NLF's Foreign Relations and the Viet Nam War* (Ithaca, NY: Cornell University Press, 1999), 78.

18. "Vietnam SVN-Alliance Leader Views Peace Prospects," July 8, 1968, Box 7, National Security Adviser, Gerald R. Ford Presidential Library.

19. Nguyen, *Viet-Nam Peace Negotiations*, 29.

20. Telegram from Secretary of State to American Embassy Paris, May 14, 1968, State 163605, Box 3, Paris Peace Conference Telegrams and Special Caption Messages, 1966–72, Office of the Executive Secretariat, RG 59: General Records of the Department of State, National Archives and Records Administration.

21. Pearson, *Washington Merry-Go-Round*, 578.

22. Background to the October 31 Announcement, p. 94, Box 1 (Accession 2015-M-027), Cyrus R. and Grace Sloane Vance Papers, Manuscripts and Archives, Yale University Library, Yale University.

23. Letter from Cyrus Vance to Henry Kissinger, December 31, 1968, Box 3, Henry A. Kissinger Office Files, National Security Council Files, Richard M. Nixon Presidential Library.

24. William Bundy, *A Tangled Web: The Making of Foreign Policy in the Nixon Presidency* (New York: Hill and Wang, 1998), 22.

25. "The Negotiations for a Bombing Cessation," May 13–October 31, 1968, by Tom Charles Huston, June 1, 1971, p. 2, Box 114, White House Special Files, Staff Member Office Files, H. R. Haldeman, Richard M. Nixon Presidential Library.

26. Johnson, *Vantage Point*, 501.

27. Nguyen, *Viet-Nam Peace Negotiations*, 29–30.

28. Robert Shaplen, *The Road from War: Vietnam, 1965–1970* (New York: Harper & Row, 1970), 210.

29. Dommen, *Indochinese Experience*, 673.

30. Nguyen, *Viet-Nam Peace Negotiations*, 33–34.

31. Johnson, *Vantage Point*, 508.

32. Ilya V. Gaiduk, *The Soviet Union and the Vietnam War* (Chicago: Ivan R. Dee, 1996), 172.

33. Jim Stockdale and Sybil Stockdale, *In Love and War: The Story of a Family's Ordeal and Sacrifice During the Vietnam Years*, revised and updated edition (Annapolis: Naval Institute Press, 1990), 295.

34. Pearson, *Washington Merry-Go-Round*, 579.

35. Shaplen, *Road from War*, 225.

36. Memorandum of Conversation, May 27, 1968, Box 558, W. Averell Harriman Papers, Manuscript Division, Library of Congress.

37. Cyrus Vance, *Hard Choices: Critical Years in America's Foreign Policy* (New York: Simon & Schuster, 1983), 122.

38. Memorandum of Conversation, May 19, 1968, Box 559, W. Averell Harriman Papers, Manuscript Division, Library of Congress.

39. Gaiduk, *Soviet Union and the Vietnam War*, 159.

40. Notes on Harriman-Oberemko Meeting on May 17, 1968, Box 557, W. Averell Harriman Papers, Manuscript Division, Library of Congress.

41. Telegram from American Embassy Paris to Secretary of State, May 27, 1968, Paris 14827, Box 559, W. Averell Harriman Papers, Manuscript Division, Library of Congress.

42. Memorandum of Conversation, May 31, 1968, Box 559, W. Averell Harriman Papers, Manuscript Division, Library of Congress.

43. "The Negotiations for a Bombing Cessation," May 13–October 31, 1968, by Tom Charles Huston, June 1, 1971, p. 3.

44. Memorandum from Woodruff Wallner to Averell Harriman, "Lunch with Oberemko," May 28, 1968, Box 559, W. Averell Harriman Papers, Manuscript Division, Library of Congress.

45. Telegram from Secretary of State to American Embassy Paris, May 14, 1968, State 163607, Box 3, Paris Peace Conference Telegrams and Special Caption Messages, 1966–72, Office of the Executive Secretariat, RG 59: General Records of the Department of State, National Archives and Records Administration.

46. Telegram from American Embassy Paris to Secretary of State, May 25, 1968, Paris 14709, Box 559, W. Averell Harriman Papers, Manuscript Division, Library of Congress.

47. "The Negotiations for a Bombing Cessation," May 13—October 31, 1968, by Tom Charles Huston, June 1, 1971, p. 4.

48. Telegram from Secretary of State to American Embassy Paris, June 3, 1968, State 175104, Box 3, Paris Peace Conference Telegrams and Special Caption Messages, 1966–72, Office of the Executive Secretariat, RG 59: General Records of the Department of State, National Archives and Records Administration.

49. "The Negotiations for a Bombing Cessation," May 13–October 31, 1968, by Tom Charles Huston, June 1, 1971, pp. 5–6.

50. Telegram from Secretary of State to American Embassy Paris, June 6, 1968, State 177491, Box 558, W. Averell Harriman Papers, Manuscript Division, Library of Congress.

51. Johnson, *Vantage Point*, 485.

52. Background to the October 31 Announcement, p. 1, Box 1 (Accession 2015-M-027), Cyrus R. and Grace Sloane Vance Papers, Manuscripts and Archives, Yale University Library, Yale University.

53. Gaiduk, *Soviet Union and the Vietnam War*, 148.

54. Abramson, *Spanning the Century*, 664.

55. Johnson, *Vantage Point*, 510.
56. Luu Van Loi and Nguyen Anh Vu, *Le Duc Tho–Kissinger Negotiations in Paris* (Hanoi: Gioi Publishers, 1996), 19.
57. General Review of Last Six Months, December 14, 1968, Box 558, W. Averell Harriman Papers, Manuscript Division, Library of Congress.
58. Johnson, *Vantage Point*, 510.
59. Telegram from Secretary of State to American Embassy Paris, June 12, 1968, State 180920, Box 558, W. Averell Harriman Papers, Manuscript Division, Library of Congress.
60. Dommen, *Indochinese Experience*, 676.
61. Telegram from American Embassy Paris to Secretary of State, May 31, 1968, Paris 15232, Box 166, Paris Talks/Meetings, National Security Council Files, Richard M. Nixon Presidential Library.
62. Loi and Nguyen, *Le Duc Tho*, 19.
63. Ibid., 19.
64. Telegram from American Embassy Paris to Secretary of State, June 18, 1968, Paris 16467, Box 7, Paris Peace Conference Telegrams and Special Caption Messages, 1966–1972, Office of the Executive Secretariat, RG 59: General Records of the Department of State, National Archives and Records Administration.
65. "The Negotiations for a Bombing Cessation," May 13–October 31, 1968, by Tom Charles Huston, June 1, 1971, p. 8.
66. Telegram from American Embassy Paris to Secretary of State, June 19, 1968, Paris 16568, Box 166, Paris Talks/Meetings, National Security Files, Richard M. Nixon Presidential Library.
67. Dommen, *Indochinese Experience*, 673.
68. Abramson, *Spanning the Century*, 665.
69. Diem with Chanoff, *In the Jaws of History*, 227–28.
70. Telegram from American Embassy Paris to Secretary of State, June 19, 1968, Paris 16633, Box 166, Paris Talks/Meetings, National Security Files, Richard M. Nixon Presidential Library.
71. Dommen, *Indochinese Experience*, 676.
72. "Phase A–Phase B Formula," June 3, 1968, Box 561, W. Averell Harriman Papers, Manuscript Division, Library of Congress.
73. Telegram from American Embassy Saigon to American Embassy Paris, August 19, 1968, Saigon 35677, Box 561, W. Averell Harriman Papers, Manuscript Division, Library of Congress.
74. Brigham, *Guerrilla Diplomacy*, 78.
75. Telegram from American Embassy Paris to Secretary of State, June 28, 1968, Paris 17153, Box 561, W. Averell Harriman Papers, Manuscript Division, Library of Congress.
76. "The Negotiations for a Bombing Cessation," May 13–October 31, 1968, by Tom Charles Huston, June 1, 1971, p. 24.

77. Background to the October 31 Announcement, p. 6, Box 1 (Accession 2015-M-027), Cyrus R. and Grace Sloane Vance Papers, Manuscripts and Archives, Yale University Library, Yale University.
78. Ibid.
79. "The Negotiations for a Bombing Cessation," May 13–October 31, 1968, by Tom Charles Huston, June 1, 1971, pp. 13–14.
80. Stockdale and Stockdale, *In Love and War*, 299–300.
81. Creighton Abrams, *Vietnam Chronicles: The Abrams Tapes, 1968–1972*, edited by Lewis Sorley (Lubbock: Texas Tech University Press, 2004), 15.
82. "The Negotiations for a Bombing Cessation," May 13–October 31, 1968, by Tom Charles Huston, June 1, 1971, p. 14.
83. "The Negotiations for a Bombing Cessation," May 13–October 31, 1968, by Tom Charles Huston, June 1, 1971, p. 17.
84. Telegram from American Embassy Paris to Secretary of State, July 10, 1968, Paris 17735, Box 561, W. Averell Harriman Papers, Manuscript Division, Library of Congress.
85. Memorandum of Conversation, July 13, 1968, Box 558, W. Averell Harriman Papers, Manuscript Division, Library of Congress.
86. Memorandum of Conversation, July 13, 1968, Box 559, W. Averell Harriman Papers, Manuscript Division, Library of Congress.
87. Loi and Nguyen, *Le Duc Tho*, 22.
88. "The Negotiations for a Bombing Cessation," May 13–October 31, 1968, by Tom Charles Huston, June 1, 1971, pp. 17–18.
89. Dommen, *Indochinese Experience*, 563.
90. Pierre Asselin, "Forgotten Front: The NLF in Hanoi's Diplomatic Struggle, 1965–67." *Diplomatic History* 45, no. 2 (2021): 338.
91. Background to the October 31 Announcement, p. 8, Box 1 (Accession 2015-M-027), Cyrus R. and Grace Sloane Vance Papers, Manuscripts and Archives, Yale University Library, Yale University.
92. "The Negotiations for a Bombing Cessation," May 13–October 31, 1968, by Tom Charles Huston, June 1, 1971, p. 18.
93. Dommen, *Indochinese Experience*, 563.
94. "The Negotiations for a Bombing Cessation," May 13–October 31, 1968, by Tom Charles Huston, June 1, 1971, p. 19.
95. Memorandum of Conversation, July 16, 1968, Box 558, W. Averell Harriman Papers, Manuscript Division, Library of Congress.
96. "The Negotiations for a Bombing Cessation," May 13–October 31, 1968, by Tom Charles Huston, June 1, 1971, pp. 20–21.
97. Memorandum of Conversation, July 19, 1968, Box 559, W. Averell Harriman Papers, Manuscript Division, Library of Congress.
98. Dommen, *Indochinese Experience*, 680.
99. Nguyen, *Viet-Nam Peace Negotiations*, 64–65.
100. "The Negotiations for a Bombing Cessation," May 13–October 31, 1968, by Tom Charles Huston, June 1, 1971, p. 37.

101. Honolulu Conference, July 1968, Statement of President Nguyen Van Thieu at the Joint Working Session, Box 38, Speeches and Statements by the Secretary of State, 1961–69, Records of Secretary of State Dean Rusk, RG 59: General Records of the Department of State, National Archives and Records Administration.

102. Clifford with Holbrooke, *Counsel to the President*, 552.

103. Pearson, *Washington Merry-Go-Round*, 597.

104. Telegram from Walt Rostow to Lyndon Johnson, July 23, 1968, Box 23, International Meetings, National Security File, Lyndon B. Johnson Presidential Library.

105. Notes from July 27, 1968, Box 1, George Elsey's Notes of Secretary of Defense Clark Clifford's Morning Staff Conference, May 1968–January 1969, George Elsey Papers, Lyndon B. Johnson Presidential Library.

106. Clifford with Holbrooke, *Counsel to the President*, 553.

107. Dommen, *Indochinese Experience*, 680.

108. "The Negotiations for a Bombing Cessation," May 13–October 31, 1968, by Tom Charles Huston, June 1, 1971, pp. 22–23.

109. Ibid., 26–27.

110. Clifford with Holbrooke, *Counsel to the President*, 567.

111. Memorandum for Personal Files, August 22, 1968, Box 477, W. Averell Harriman Papers, Manuscript Division, Library of Congress.

112. General Review of Last Six Months, December 14, 1968, Box 558, W. Averell Harriman Papers, Manuscript Division, Library of Congress.

113. Hedrick Smith, "'68 Shift on Vietnam—II," March 7, 1969, *New York Times*, 1, 14.

114. "The Negotiations for a Bombing Cessation," May 13–October 31, 1968, by Tom Charles Huston, June 1, 1971, pp. 28–29.

115. Abramson, *Spanning the Century*, 666.

116. Telegram from American Embassy Paris to Secretary of State, August 3, 1968, Paris 18977, Box 559, W. Averell Harriman Papers, Manuscript Division, Library of Congress.

117. Dommen, *Indochinese Experience*, 679.

118. "The Negotiations for a Bombing Cessation," May 13–October 31, 1968, by Tom Charles Huston, June 1, 1971, pp. 34–35.

119. Dommen, *Indochinese Experience*, 684.

120. Memorandum from Richard C. Holbrooke to Averell Harriman, December 24, 1968, Box 558, W. Averell Harriman Papers, Manuscript Division, Library of Congress.

121. "The Negotiations for a Bombing Cessation," May 13–October 31, 1968, by Tom Charles Huston, June 1, 1971, pp. 35–36.

122. Nguyen, *Viet-Nam Peace Negotiations*, 37.

123. Dommen, *Indochinese Experience*, 677.

124. Memorandum from Richard C. Holbrooke to Averell Harriman, December 24, 1968.

125. "The Negotiations for a Bombing Cessation," May 13–October 31, 1968, by Tom Charles Huston, June 1, 1971, pp. 36–37.

126. Clifford with Holbrooke, *Counsel to the President*, 508.

127. "The Negotiations for a Bombing Cessation," May 13–October 31, 1968, by Tom Charles Huston, June 1, 1971, pp. 37–38.

128. Ibid., 40–43.

129. George Christian, *The President Steps Down: A Personal Memoir of the Transfer of Power* (New York: Macmillan, 1970), 23.

130. "The Negotiations for a Bombing Cessation," May 13–October 31, 1968, by Tom Charles Huston, June 1, 1971, pp. 43–44.

131. Telegram from American Embassy Paris to Secretary of State, August 20, 1968, Paris 19629, Box 561, W. Averell Harriman Papers, Manuscript Division, Library of Congress.

132. Loi and Nguyen, *Le Duc Tho*, 24.

133. "The Negotiations for a Bombing Cessation," May 13–October 31, 1968, by Tom Charles Huston, June 1, 1971, p. 44.

134. Johnson, *Vantage Point*, 513.

Chapter 6. Miami

1. Theodore H. White, *The Making of the President, 1968* (New York: Atheneum Publishers, 1969), 162.

2. Maurice H. Stans, *The Terrors of Justice: The Untold Side of Watergate* (New York: Everest House Publishers, 1978), 142.

3. William Safire, *Before the Fall: An Inside View of the Pre-Watergate White House* (Garden City, NY: Doubleday, 1975), 57.

4. G. Calvin MacKenzie and Robert Weisbrot, *The Liberal Hour: Washington and the Politics of Change in the 1960s* (New York: Penguin Books, 2008), 367.

5. Daniel P. Moynihan, *The Politics of a Guaranteed Income: The Nixon Administration and the Family Assistance Plan* (New York: Random House, 1973), 69.

6. John Roy Price, *The Last Liberal Republican: An Insider's Perspective on Nixon's Surprising Social Policy* (Lawrence: University Press of Kansas, 2021), 117.

7. Steven R. Weisman, ed., *Daniel Patrick Moynihan: A Portrait in Letters of an American Visionary* (New York: PublicAffairs, 2010), 155.

8. John Roy Price, *The Last Liberal Republican: An Insider's Perspective on Nixon's Surprising Social Policy* (Lawrence: University Press of Kansas, 2021), 117.

9. Excerpts of Remarks of Richard Nixon, Gary, Indiana, May 2, 1968, Box 22, Richard V. Allen Papers, Hoover Institution, Library and Archives.

10. Thomas A. Schwartz, *Henry Kissinger and American Power: A Political Biography* (New York: Hill and Wang, 2020), 9.

11. Jules Witcover, *The Resurrection of Richard Nixon* (New York: G. P. Putnam's Sons, 1970), 302–3.

12. Leonard Garment, *Crazy Rhythm: My Journey from Brooklyn, Jazz, and Wall Street to Nixon's White House, Watergate, and Beyond* (New York: Times Books, 1997), 137.

13. Richard Nixon, *RN: The Memoirs of Richard Nixon* (New York: Grosset & Dunlap, 1978), 303.

14. Patrick J. Buchanan, *The Greatest Comeback: How Richard Nixon Rose from Defeat to Create the New Majority* (New York: Crown Forum, 2014), 200.

15. Joe McGinniss, *The Selling of the President, 1968* (New York: Trident Press, 1969), 63.

16. Buchanan, *Greatest Comeback*, 198–99.

17. McGinniss, *Selling of the President*, 28–29.

18. Norman Mailer, *Some Honorable Men: Political Conventions, 1960–1972* (Boston: Little, Brown, 1976), 134.

19. J. William Middendorf II, *A Glorious Disaster: Barry Goldwater's Presidential Campaign and the Origins of the Conservative Movement* (New York: Basic Books, 2006), 248.

20. Kevin P. Phillips, *The Emerging Republican Majority* (New Rochelle, NY: Arlington House, 1969), 25.

21. Buchanan, *Greatest Comeback*, 287.

22. White, *Making of the President, 1968*, 162.

23. Buchanan, *Greatest Comeback*, 291.

24. Nixon, *RN: The Memoirs*, 306.

25. Author interview with John Price, December 12, 2018, Yorba Linda, CA.

26. Jeffrey Frank, *Ike and Dick: Portrait of a Strange Political Marriage* (New York: Simon & Schuster, 2013), 303.

27. David Eisenhower with Julie Nixon Eisenhower, *Going Home to Glory: A Memoir of Life with Dwight D. Eisenhower, 1961–1969* (New York: Simon & Schuster, 2010), 255–56.

28. Letter from Bryce Harlow to Dwight Eisenhower, June 17, 1968, Box 8, Special Names, Post-Presidential Papers, Dwight D. Eisenhower Presidential Library.

29. Nixon, *RN: The Memoirs*, 307.

30. Eisenhower with Nixon Eisenhower, *Going Home to Glory*, 254.

31. Frank, *Ike and Dick*, 303.

32. Letter from Richard Nixon to Dwight Eisenhower, July 19, 1968, Box 14, Special Names, Post-Presidential Papers, Dwight D. Eisenhower Presidential Library.

33. Eisenhower with Nixon Eisenhower, *Going Home to Glory*, 258.

34. Briefing, July 26, 1968, 6:04–7:30 P.M., Nixon Index Cards, Lyndon B. Johnson Presidential Library.

35. Handwritten Notes from July 26, 1968, 7:00 P.M., meeting with Richard Nixon, Box 3, Tom Johnson Notes of Meetings, Personal Papers of Tom Johnson, Lyndon B. Johnson Presidential Library.

36. Nixon, *RN: The Memoirs*, 308.
37. Arnold A. Offner, *Hubert Humphrey: The Conscience of the Country* (New Haven: Yale University Press, 2018), 306.
38. Safire, *Before the Fall*, 84.
39. Nixon, *RN: The Memoirs*, 308.
40. White, *Making of the President, 1968*, 281.
41. Richard J. Whalen, *Catch the Falling Flag: A Republican's Challenge to His Party* (Boston: Houghton Mifflin, 1972), 193.
42. John Ehrlichman, *Witness to Power: The Nixon Years* (New York: Simon & Schuster, 1982), 45.
43. Whalen, *Catch the Falling Flag*, 192.
44. Norman Mailer, *Miami and the Siege of Chicago: An Informal History of the Republican and Democratic Conventions of 1968* (New York: Signet Books, 1968), 18.
45. White, *Making of the President, 1968*, 281–82.
46. Buchanan, *Greatest Comeback*, 221.
47. Michael A. Endicott, *Walking with Presidents: Stories from Inside the Perimeter* (BookSurge, 2009), 58.
48. Nixon, *RN: The Memoirs*, 309.
49. Drew Pearson, *Washington Merry-Go-Round: The Drew Pearson Diaries, 1960–1969*, edited by Peter Hannaford (Lincoln, NE: Potomac Books, 2015), 601.
50. Quote: White, *Making of the President, 1968*, 282; landing in Miami airport: Herbert G. Klein, *Making It Perfectly Clear: An Inside Account of Nixon's Love-Hate Relationship with the Media* (Garden City, NY: Doubleday, 1980), 156.
51. Press Conference of Richard M. Nixon, Hilton Plaza Hotel, August 6, 1968, Box 22, Richard V. Allen Papers, Hoover Institution, Library and Archives.
52. White, *Making of the President, 1968*, 284.
53. Vietnam Statement by Richard M. Nixon, August 1, 1968, Box 22, Richard V. Allen Papers, Hoover Institution, Library and Archives.
54. Richard M. Scammon and Ben J. Wattenberg, *The Real Majority* (New York: Coward-McCann, 1970), 94.
55. David Steigerwald, *The Sixties and the End of Modern America* (New York: St. Martin's Press, 1995), 281–82.
56. White, *Making of the President, 1968*, 298.
57. Godfrey Hodgson, *The World Turned Right Side Up: A History of the Conservative Ascendancy in America* (Boston: Houghton Mifflin, 1996), 219.
58. Jules Witcover, *The Resurrection of Richard Nixon* (New York: G. P. Putnam's Sons, 1970), 347.
59. Whalen, *Catch the Falling Flag*, 201.
60. Nixon, *RN: The Memoirs*, 310.
61. Ibid.
62. Jules Witcover, *The Year the Dream Died: Revisiting 1968 in America* (New York: Warner Books, 1997), 165–66.

63. Buchanan, *Greatest Comeback*, 319.

64. Memorandum from Bill Safire to H. R. Haldeman, "Campaign Assessment," November 20, 1968, Box 16, William Safire Papers, Manuscript Division, Library of Congress.

65. Nixon, *RN: The Memoirs*, 312.

66. Whalen, *Catch the Falling Flag*, 203.

67. Charles J. Holden, Zach Messitte, and Jerald Podair, *Republican Populist: Spiro Agnew and the Origins of Donald Trump's America* (Charlottesville: University of Virginia Press, 2019), 2.

68. Pearson, *Washington Merry-Go-Round*, 602.

69. George Christian, *The President Steps Down: A Personal Memoir of the Transfer of Power* (New York: Macmillan, 1970), 156.

70. Michael A. Cohen, *American Maelstrom: The 1968 Election and the Politics of Division* (New York: Oxford University Press, 2016), 316.

71. Nixon, *RN: The Memoirs*, 313.

72. Whalen, *Catch the Falling Flag*, 206.

73. David S. Broder, "Election of 1968," in Arthur M. Schlesinger Jr., ed., *History of American Presidential Elections, 1789–1968*, vol. 4 (New York: McGraw-Hill, 1971), 3730–31; Richard Nixon, *Nixon Speaks Out* (New York: Nixon-Agnew Campaign Committee, 1968), 290–91.

74. Nixon, *RN: The Memoirs*, 315.

75. John A. Farrell, *Richard Nixon: The Life* (New York: Doubleday, 2017), 323.

76. Deborah Davis, *Katharine the Great: Katharine Graham and the Washington Post* (New York: Harcourt Brace Jovanovich, 1979), 247.

77. Farrell, *Richard Nixon*, 324.

78. Hubert H. Humphrey, *The Education of a Public Man: My Life and Politics* (Garden City, NY: Doubleday, 1976), 382.

79. Stephen P. Miller, *Billy Graham and the Rise of the Republican South* (Philadelphia: University of Pennsylvania Press, 2009), 132.

80. Billy Graham, *Just As I Am: The Autobiography of Billy Graham* (New York: HarperCollins, 1997), 448.

81. William Martin, *A Prophet with Honor: The Billy Graham Story* (New York: William Morrow, 1991), 356.

82. Andrew L. Johns, *Vietnam's Second Front: Domestic Politics, the Republican Party, and the War* (Lexington: University Press of Kentucky, 2010), 214.

83. William Bundy, *A Tangled Web: The Making of Foreign Policy in the Nixon Presidency* (New York: Hill and Wang, 1998), 25.

84. Whalen, *Catch the Falling Flag*, 189.

85. Christopher Goscha, *Vietnam: A New History* (New York: Basic Books, 2016), 333.

86. Robert Mann, *A Grand Delusion: America's Descent into Vietnam* (New York: Basic Books, 2001), 607.

87. Johns, *Vietnam's Second Front*, 197–98.

88. Nixon, *RN: The Memoirs*, 298.

89. LBJ Ranch, August 10, 1968, 11:59 A.M. Arrival, Nixon Index Cards, Lyndon B. Johnson Presidential Library.

90. Clark Clifford with Richard Holbrooke, *Counsel to the President: A Memoir* (New York: Random House, 1991), 563.

91. Lady Bird Johnson, *A White House Diary* (New York: Holt, Rinehart and Winston, 1970), 703.

92. Notes from August 10, 1968, 12:25 P.M. President's Briefing of Former Vice President Nixon and Gov. Agnew, Box 3, Tom Johnson Notes of Meetings, Personal Papers of Tom Johnson, Lyndon B. Johnson Presidential Library.

93. John Helgerson, "Intelligence Support for Richard M. Nixon: A Difficult Relationship," *Studies in Intelligence* 39, no. 4 (1995): 103.

94. Nancy Gibbs and Michael Duffy, *The Preacher and the Presidents: Billy Graham in the White House* (New York: Center Street, 2007), 166.

95. Clifford with Holbrooke, *Counsel to the President*, 563.

96. Theodore White Interview with Richard Nixon, November 23, 1968, Box 119, Theodore White Papers, Pusey Library, Harvard University.

97. Offner, *Hubert Humphrey*, 288.

98. Nixon, *RN: The Memoirs*, 316.

99. Ibid.

100. Safire, *Before the Fall*, 84.

101. Notes from August 12, 1968, Box 1, George Elsey's Notes of Secretary of Defense Clark Clifford's Morning Staff Conference, May 1968—January 1969, George Elsey Papers, Lyndon B. Johnson Presidential Library.

102. Alexander M. Haig Jr. with Charles McCarry, *Inner Circles: How America Changed the World, A Memoir* (New York: Warner Books, 1992), 186.

103. Notes from August 12, 1968.

104. Offner, *Hubert Humphrey*, 288.

105. Steigerwald, *Sixties and the End of Modern America*, 282; Timothy N. Thurber, *Republicans and Race: The GOP's Frayed Relationship with African Americans, 1945–1974* (Lawrence: University Press of Kansas, 2013), 268.

106. Nixon, *RN: The Memoirs*, 316.

Chapter 7. Chicago

1. Michael A. Cohen, *American Maelstrom: The 1968 Election and the Politics of Division* (New York: Oxford University Press, 2016), 261.

2. Joseph A. Califano Jr., *Inside: A Public and Private Life* (New York: PublicAffairs, 2004), 248.

3. Jerry Rubin, *Do It! Scenarios of the Revolution* (New York: Simon & Schuster, 1970), 168.

4. Michael A. Endicott, *Walking with Presidents: Stories from Inside the Perimeter* (BookSurge, 2009), 60.

5. Ramsey Clark, *Crime in America: Observations on Its Nature, Causes, Prevention, and Control* (New York: Simon & Schuster, 1970), 12.

6. Norman Sherman, *From Nowhere to Somewhere, My Political Journey: A Memoir of Sorts* (Minneapolis: First Avenue Editions, 2016), 172.

7. Mike Royko, *Boss: Richard J. Daley of Chicago* (New York: E. P. Dutton, 1971), 165.

8. Adam Cohen and Elizabeth Taylor, *American Pharaoh: Mayor Richard J. Daley; His Battle for Chicago and the Nation* (Boston: Little, Brown, 2000), 461.

9. Theodore H. White, *The Making of the President, 1968* (New York: Atheneum Publishers, 1969), 304.

10. Arnold A. Offner, *Hubert Humphrey: The Conscience of the Country* (New Haven: Yale University Press, 2018), 291.

11. Edgar Berman, *Hubert: The Triumph and Tragedy of the Humphrey I Knew* (New York: G. P. Putnam's Sons, 1979), 170.

12. Letter from John Criswell to Walter Mondale, August 6, 1968, Box 172, Lawrence O'Brien Papers, John F. Kennedy Presidential Library.

13. Ted Van Dyk, *Heroes, Hacks, and Fools: Memoirs from the Political Inside* (Seattle: University of Washington Press, 2007), 73.

14. Andrew L. Johns, *The Price of Loyalty: Hubert Humphrey's Vietnam Conflict* (Lanham, MD: Rowman & Littlefield, 2020), 86.

15. Offner, *Hubert Humphrey*, 285.

16. Robert Mann, *A Grand Delusion: America's Descent into Vietnam* (New York: Basic Books, 2001), 612.

17. Drew Pearson, *Washington Merry-Go-Round: The Drew Pearson Diaries, 1960–1969*, edited by Peter Hannaford (Lincoln: Potomac Books, 2015), 598–99.

18. Johns, *The Price of Loyalty*, 87.

19. Offner, *Hubert Humphrey*, 286.

20. Van Dyk, *Heroes, Hacks, and Fools*, 73.

21. Carl Solberg, *Hubert Humphrey: A Biography* (New York: W. W. Norton, 1984), 348.

22. Van Dyk, *Heroes, Hacks, and Fools*, 73.

23. Offner, *Hubert Humphrey*, 287.

24. Solberg, *Hubert Humphrey*, 349.

25. Memorandum from Dean Rusk to Lyndon Johnson, August 8, 1968, Box 40, White House Correspondence Files, 1961–69, Records of Secretary of State Dean Rusk, RG 59: General Records of the Department of State, National Archives and Records Administration.

26. Pearson, *Washington Merry-Go-Round*, 604.

27. E. J. Dionne Jr., *Why Americans Hate Politics* (New York: Simon & Schuster, 1991), 44.

28. Lady Bird Johnson, *A White House Diary* (New York: Holt, Rinehart and Winston, 1970), 701.

29. Berman, *Hubert*, 94.
30. Offner, *Hubert Humphrey*, 288.
31. Anatoly Dobrynin, *In Confidence: Moscow's Ambassador to America's Six Cold War Presidents (1962–1986)* (New York: Times Books, 1995), 180.
32. George C. McGhee, *On the Frontline in the Cold War: An Ambassador Reports* (Westport, CT: Praeger, 1997), 180.
33. Matthew J. Ambrose, *The Control Agenda: A History of the Strategic Arms Limitation Talks* (Ithaca, NY: Cornell University Press, 2018), 21.
34. Ilya V. Gaiduk, *The Soviet Union and the Vietnam War* (Chicago: Ivan R. Dee, 1996), 174.
35. White, *Making of the President, 1968*, 326.
36. Clark Clifford with Richard Holbrooke, *Counsel to the President: A Memoir* (New York: Random House, 1991), 559.
37. Stephan Kieninger, *Dynamic Détente: The United States and Europe, 1964–1975* (Lanham, MD: Lexington Books, 2016), 59.
38. Letter from William P. Bundy to Cyrus Vance, August 26, 1968, Box 5, Cyrus R. and Grace Sloane Vance Papers, Manuscripts and Archives, Yale University Library, Yale University.
39. Notes on 1968 Presidential Campaign, Box 2M396, Walter Cronkite Papers, Dolph Briscoe Center for American History, University of Texas at Austin.
40. Thomas A. Schwartz, *Lyndon Johnson and Europe: In the Shadow of Vietnam* (Cambridge, MA: Harvard University Press, 2003), 217.
41. Clifford with Holbrooke, *Counsel to the President*, 562.
42. Offner, *Hubert Humphrey*, 290.
43. Ronald G. Shafer, "When Soviets Invaded Czechoslovakia, Nixon Promised Not To 'Embarrass' LBJ," *Washington Post*, March 1, 2022.
44. Cohen, *American Maelstrom*, 262–63.
45. Athan Theoharis, ed., *From the Secret Files of J. Edgar Hoover* (Chicago: Ivan R. Dee, Publisher, 1991), 240.
46. C. D. DeLoach to Mr. Tolson, "Democratic National Convention, Chicago Illinois, 8/26/68," August 7, 1968, with undated cover letter [circa 1973] from William Sullivan to Robert Mardian, Box 12, Department of Justice, 1967–78, Robert Charles Mardian Papers, Hoover Institution Library and Archives.
47. Letter from J. Edgar Hoover to Hubert Humphrey, August 19, 1968, Box 150.F.18.5B, Hubert H. Humphrey Papers, Minnesota Historical Society.
48. Rubin, *Do It!* 169.
49. Jerry Rubin, "Guilty As Hell, But Not Wrong: Rubin," *Chicago Sun-Times*, March 8, 1976, p. 4.
50. John Schultz, *The Chicago Conspiracy Trial*, revised edition (Chicago: University of Chicago Press, 2009), 384–85.
51. White, *Making of the President, 1968*, 334.
52. Jon Wiener, ed., *Conspiracy in the Streets: The Extraordinary Trial of the Chicago Eight* (New York: New Press, 2006), 5.

53. David Paul Kuhn, *The Hardhat Riot: Nixon, New York City, and the Dawn of the White Working-Class Revolution* (New York: Oxford University Press, 2020), 27.

54. David Farber, *Chicago '68* (Chicago: University of Chicago Press, 1988), xv.

55. Jerry Rubin, *Growing (Up) at Thirty-Seven* (New York: M. Evans, 1976), 85.

56. Farber, *Chicago '68*, 246.

57. Theodore White Notes, Undated, Box 117, Theodore White Papers, Pusey Library, Harvard University.

58. Frank Kusch, *Battleground Chicago: The Police and the 1968 Democratic National Convention* (Westport, CT: Praeger, 2004), 159–60.

59. Marly Jezer, *Abbie Hoffman: American Rebel* (New Brunswick, NJ: Rutgers University Press, 1992), xiv.

60. Tom Wells, *The War Within: America's Battle over Vietnam* (Berkeley: University of California Press, 1994), 237–38.

61. Rubin, *Growing (Up) at Thirty-Seven*, 95.

62. Berman, *Hubert*, 185–86.

63. Ibid.; Jeremy Larner, *Nobody Knows: Reflections on the McCarthy Campaign of 1968* (New York: Macmillan, 1969), 165.

64. Richard M. Scammon and Ben J. Wattenberg, *The Real Majority* (New York: Coward-McCann, 1970), 165.

65. Lewis Chester, Godfrey Hodgson, and Bruce Page, *An American Melodrama: The Presidential Campaign of 1968* (New York: Viking Press, 1969), 91.

66. Richard N. Goodwin, *Remembering America: A Voice from the Sixties* (Boston: Little, Brown, 1988), 491.

67. Clifford with Holbrooke, *Counsel to the President*, 565.

68. White, *Making of the President, 1968*, 317.

69. Offner, *Hubert Humphrey*, 293–94.

70. Evan Edward Laine, *Nixon and the Dragon Lady: Did Richard Nixon Conspire with Anna Chennault in 1968 to Destroy Peace in Vietnam?* (Champaign, IL: Common Ground Publishing, 2015), 11.

71. Cohen, *American Maelstrom*, 116.

72. Joseph A. Califano Jr., *The Triumph and Tragedy of Lyndon Johnson: The White House Years* (New York: Simon & Schuster, 2015), 319.

73. Reminiscences of Lyndon B. Johnson, August 19, 1969, p. 29, Lyndon B. Johnson Presidential Library.

74. Telegram from Ben Wattenberg to Jim Jones for the President, August 25, 1968, Box 77, Confidential File, Lyndon B. Johnson Presidential Library.

75. Telegram from Joe Califano to Lyndon Johnson, August 27, 1968, Box 86, Confidential File, Papers of Lyndon Baines Johnson, Lyndon B. Johnson Presidential Library.

76. Author interview with Joseph Califano, June 27, 2018, New York.

77. Clifford with Holbrooke, *Counsel to the President*, 565.

78. Billy Graham, *Just As I Am: The Autobiography of Billy Graham* (New York: HarperCollins, 1997), 448.

79. Nixon Diary, Notebook 15, VIP Notebooks, Records of the Billy Graham Evangelistic Association: Montreat Office, Billy Graham Archive and Research Center, Charlotte, NC.

80. Solberg, *Hubert Humphrey*, 360.

81. Author interview with James R. Jones, October 17, 2017, Washington, DC.

82. Offner, *Hubert Humphrey*, 297.

83. George Christian, *The President Steps Down: A Personal Memoir of the Transfer of Power* (New York: Macmillan, 1970), 45.

84. White, *Making of the President, 1968*, 327.

85. Memorandum from Stu Eizenstat to John Stewart, Bill Welsh, Dough Bennett [sic], Gerry Bush, Lew Rivlin, and Eiler Ravenholt [sic], Undated, Box 150.F.18.5B, Hubert H. Humphrey Papers, Minnesota Historical Society.

86. David S. Broder, "Election of 1968," in Arthur M. Schlesinger Jr., ed., *History of American Presidential Elections, 1789–1968*, vol. 4 (New York: McGraw-Hill, 1971), 3735.

87. Offner, *Hubert Humphrey*, 293.

88. Kyle Longley, *LBJ's 1968: Power, Politics, and the Presidency in America's Year of Upheaval* (New York: Cambridge University Press, 2018), 217.

89. Offner, *Hubert Humphrey*, 294–95.

90. White, *Making of the President, 1968*, 327.

91. Califano Jr., *Inside*, 251; Kuhn, *Hardhat Riot*, 3.

92. Walter F. Mondale with David Hage, *The Good Fight: A Life in Liberal Politics* (Minneapolis: University of Minnesota Press, 2010), 81.

93. Patrick J. Buchanan, *The Greatest Comeback: How Richard Nixon Rose from Defeat to Create the New Majority* (New York: Crown Forum, 2014), 328–29.

94. Berman, *Hubert*, 187.

95. George H. Gallup, *The Gallup Poll: Public Opinion, 1935–1971*, volume 3, *1959–1971* (New York: Random House, 1972), 2160.

96. Jezer, *Abbie Hoffman*, 180.

97. Nick Sharman, *The Chicago Conspiracy Trial and the Press*, (New York: Palgrave Macmillan, 2016), 1.

98. Rubin, *Do It!* 169.

99. Jezer, *Abbie Hoffman*, 172.

100. Lonnie T. Brown Jr., *Defending the Public's Enemy: The Life and Legacy of Ramsey Clark* (Stanford, CA: Stanford University Press, 2019), 107.

101. Karen Alonso, *The Chicago Seven Political Protest Trial: A Headline Court Case* (Berkeley Heights, NJ: Enslow Publishers, 2002), 16.

102. John Schultz, *No One Was Killed: Documentation and Meditation, Convention Week, Chicago, August 1968* (Chicago: Big Table Publishing, 1969), 286.

103. Cohen and Taylor, *American Pharaoh*, 485.

104. White, *Making of the President, 1968*, 317.

105. Offner, *Hubert Humphrey*, 288.

106. Pearson, *Washington Merry-Go-Round*, 615–16.

107. Offner, *Hubert Humphrey*, 286.
108. Letter from Averell Harriman to Hubert Humphrey, August 31, 1968, Box 148.B.15.8F, Hubert H. Humphrey Papers, Minnesota Historical Society.
109. Rudy Abramson, *Spanning the Century: The Life of W. Averell Harriman, 1891–1986* (New York: William Morrow, 1992), 667.
110. Memorandum of Conversation, September 3, 1968, Box 558, W. Averell Harriman Papers, Manuscript Division, Library of Congress.
111. White, *Making of the President, 1968*, 316.
112. Berman, *Hubert*, 94.
113. Rufus Phillips, *Why Vietnam Matters: An Eyewitness Account of Lessons Not Learned* (Annapolis: Naval Institute Press, 2008), 285.
114. Solberg, *Hubert Humphrey*, 361–62.
115. Berman, *Hubert*, 182.
116. White, *Making of the President, 1968*, 339.
117. Memorandum from Hubert Humphrey to Larry O'Brien, August 19, 1968, Box 148.B.15.8F, Hubert H. Humphrey Papers, Minnesota Historical Society.
118. Jack Valenti, *My Life: In War, the White House, and Hollywood* (New York: Harmony Books, 2007), 248.
119. White, *Making of the President, 1968*, 318.
120. Offner, *Hubert Humphrey*, 293.
121. Randall B. Woods, *LBJ: Architect of American Ambition* (New York: Free Press, 2006), 862.
122. Berman, *Hubert*, 156–57.
123. Ibid., 155.
124. Longley, *LBJ's 1968*, 207.
125. Richard Nixon, *RN: The Memoirs of Richard Nixon* (New York: Grosset & Dunlap, 1978), 755.
126. Solberg, *Hubert Humphrey*, 362.
127. Berman, *Hubert*, 190–91.
128. Offner, *Hubert Humphrey*, 295.
129. Johns, *The Price of Loyalty*, 95.
130. Broder, "Election of 1968," 3744.
131. Van Dyk, *Heroes, Hacks, and Fools*, 76.
132. Berman, *Hubert*, 180–81.
133. Offner, *Hubert Humphrey*, 296.
134. Berman, *Hubert*, 181.
135. Clifford with Holbrooke, *Counsel to the President*, 565.
136. Memorandum from Bill Welsh to Larry O'Brien, September 10, 1868, Box 150.G.5.2F, Hubert H. Humphrey Papers, Minnesota Historical Society.
137. White, *Making of the President, 1968*, 363.
138. Memo of Telcon with Bill Moyers, August 31, 1968, Box 458, W. Averell Harriman Papers, Manuscript Division, Library of Congress.

139. James Reston Jr., *The Lone Star: The Life of John Connally* (New York: Harper & Row, 1989), 365.

140. Berman, *Hubert*, 178.

141. Offner, *Hubert Humphrey*, 289.

142. Eugene McCarthy, *Gene McCarthy's Minnesota: Memories of a Native Son* (Minneapolis: Winston Press, 1982), 132.

143. Offner, *Hubert Humphrey*, 300.

144. White, *Making of the President, 1968*, 348.

145. Pearson, *Washington Merry-Go-Round*, 608.

146. Lyndon Baines Johnson, *The Vantage Point: Perspectives of the Presidency, 1963–1969* (New York: Holt, Rinehart and Winston, 1971), 549.

147. Letter from Billy Graham to Richard Nixon, June 1, 1968, Notebook #10, VIP Notebooks, Records of the Billy Graham Evangelistic Association: Montreat Office, Billy Graham Archive and Research Center, Charlotte, NC.

148. Offner, *Hubert Humphrey*, 301.

149. Berman, *Hubert*, 193.

150. Cohen, *American Maelstrom*, 317.

151. Nixon, *RN: The Memoirs*, 317.

152. Memorandum from Hubert Humphrey to Larry O'Brien, September 15, 1968, Box 219, Lawrence O'Brien Papers, John F. Kennedy Presidential Library.

153. Christian, *President Steps Down*, 157.

154. Leslie H. Southwick, ed., *Presidential Also-Rans and Running Mates, 1788 through 1996*, volume 2, *1892–1996*, 2nd edition (Jefferson, NC: McFarland, 2008), 687.

155. Berman, *Hubert*, 177.

156. Memorandum from William Connell to Larry O'Brien, October 30, 1968, Box 171, Lawrence O'Brien Papers, John F. Kennedy Presidential Library.

157. Offner, *Hubert Humphrey*, 302.

158. White, *Making of the President, 1968*, 358.

159. Berman, *Hubert*, 191.

160. White, *Making of the President, 1968*, 359.

161. Memorandum from Orville Freeman to Hubert Humphrey, August 19, 1968, Box 150.F.18.5B, Hubert H. Humphrey Papers, Minnesota Historical Society.

162. Memorandum from Bill Connell to Hubert Humphrey, August 17, 1968, Box 150.F.18.5B, Hubert H. Humphrey Papers, Minnesota Historical Society.

163. Joseph Napolitan, *The Election Game and How to Win It* (Garden City, NY: Doubleday, 1972), 34.

164. Memorandum from Hubert Humphrey to Al Spivak, September 15, 1968, Box 219, Lawrence O'Brien Papers, John F. Kennedy Presidential Library.

165. White, *Making of the President, 1968*, 381.

166. Memorandum from Larry O'Brien to Hubert Humphrey, August 24, 1968, Box 173, Lawrence O'Brien Papers, John F. Kennedy Presidential Library.

167. Memorandum from Larry O'Brien to Hubert Humphrey, "Presidential Campaign Plan," August 27, 1968, Box 173, Lawrence O'Brien Papers, John F. Kennedy Presidential Library.

168. Napolitan, *Election Game*, 21.

169. Offner, *Hubert Humphrey*, 307.

170. Berman, *Hubert*, 178.

171. Offner, *Hubert Humphrey*, 307–8.

172. Berman, *Hubert*, 179.

Chapter 8. Pittsburgh

1. Richard M. Scammon and Ben J. Wattenberg, *The Real Majority* (New York: Coward-McCann, 1970), 185.

2. G. Scott Thomas, *Counting the Votes: A New Way to Analyze America's Presidential Elections* (Santa Barbara, CA: Praeger, 2015), 221.

3. George C. Wallace, *Stand Up for America* (Garden City, NY: Doubleday, 1976), 121.

4. Jody Carlson, *George C. Wallace and the Politics of Powerlessness: The Wallace Campaign for the Presidency, 1964–1976* (New Brunswick, NJ: Transaction Books, 1981), 76.

5. Wallace, *Stand Up for America*, 11.

6. Dan T. Carter, *The Politics of Rage: George Wallace, the Origins of the New Conservativism, and the Transformation of American Politics* (New York: Simon & Schuster, 1995), 339.

7. Stephan Lesher, *George Wallace: American Populist* (Reading, MA: Addison-Wesley Publishing, 1994), 413.

8. Theodore H. White, *The Making of the President, 1968* (New York: Atheneum Publishers, 1969), 428.

9. Lesher, *George Wallace*, 417.

10. Lloyd Rohler, *George Wallace: Conservative Populist* (Westport, CT: Praeger, 2004), 65.

11. Mario Del Pero, *The Eccentric Realist: Henry Kissinger and the Shaping of American Foreign Policy* (Ithaca, NY: Cornell University Press, 2010), 34.

12. Jonathan Rieder, *Canarsie: The Jews and Italians of Brooklyn against Liberalism* (Cambridge, MA: Harvard University Press, 1985), 109.

13. Daniel P. Moynihan, *The Politics of a Guaranteed Income: The Nixon Administration and the Family Assistance Plan* (New York: Random House, 1973), 53.

14. White, *Making of the President, 1968*, 430.

15. Lesher, *George Wallace*, 405.

16. White, *Making of the President, 1968*, 409.

17. Drew Pearson and Jack Anderson, "Wallace Was Tagged Psychoneurotic," *Washington Post*, October 16, 1968, D19; and "Humphrey Drive Recalls Tru-

man in '48," *Washington Post*, October 10, 1968, H7, in Box F120, Papers of Drew Pearson, Lyndon B. Johnson Presidential Library.

18. Carter, *Politics of Rage*, 341.
19. Lesher, *George Wallace*, 397–98.
20. Carlson, *George C. Wallace*, 74.
21. Ed Ewing Oral History, pp. 1–2, November 11, 1988, Ed Ewing Papers, Alabama Department of Archives and History.
22. George Wallace Jr., *Governor George Wallace: The Man You Never Knew* (2011), 205.
23. Letter from George C. Wallace to Joe Fine, December 10, 1968, Box 24, George C. Wallace Collection, Alabama Department of Archives and History.
24. Wallace Jr., *Governor George Wallace*, 199.
25. Patrick J. Buchanan, *The Greatest Comeback: How Richard Nixon Rose from Defeat to Create the New Majority* (New York: Crown Forum, 2014), 291.
26. Michael A. Cohen, *American Maelstrom: The 1968 Election and the Politics of Division* (New York: Oxford University Press, 2016), 234.
27. Telegram from George C. Wallace to Alice Paul, July 19, 1968, Box 17, George C. Wallace Collection, Alabama Department of Archives and History.
28. Wallace, *Stand Up for America*, 122.
29. Ibid., 123.
30. Rohler, *George Wallace*, 56.
31. Warren Kozak, *LeMay: The Life and Wars of General Curtis LeMay* (Washington, DC: Regnery Publishing, 2009), 371.
32. Rick Perlstein, *Nixonland: The Rise of a President and the Fracturing of America* (New York: Scribner, 2008), 348.
33. Carter, *Politics of Rage*, 356.
34. Kozak, *LeMay*, 372.
35. Biography—General Curtis E. LeMay—United States, Air Force, Box 3, Ed Ewing Papers, Alabama Department of Archives and History.
36. L. Douglas Keeney, *15 Minutes: General Curtis LeMay and the Countdown to Nuclear Annihilation* (New York: St. Martin's Press, 2011), 320.
37. Curtis E. LeMay with Dale O. Smith, *America Is in Danger* (New York: Funk & Wagnalls, 1968), xii.
38. Thomas M. Coffey, *Iron Eagle: The Turbulent Life of General Curtis LeMay* (New York: Crown Publishing, 1986), 444–45.
39. Kozak, *LeMay*, 373.
40. Rohler, *George Wallace*, 56.
41. Carter, *Politics of Rage*, 337–58.
42. Kozak, *LeMay*, 372.
43. Cohen, *American Maelstrom*, 299.
44. Coffey, *Iron Eagle*, 445.
45. Wallace, *Stand Up for America*, 124.

46. Ibid., 123.

47. Lesher, *George Wallace*, 423.

48. Carter, *Politics of Rage*, 358.

49. Platform of the American Independent Party, Box 2, Ed Ewing Papers, Alabama Department of Archives and History.

50. Cohen, *American Maelstrom*, 298.

51. Kozak, *LeMay*, 374–75.

52. Statement of General Curtis LeMay, October 3, 1968, Box 3, Ed Ewing Papers, Alabama Department of Archives and History.

53. Rohler, *George Wallace*, 56.

54. Scammon and Wattenberg, *Real Majority*, 190.

55. Kozak, *LeMay*, 375–76.

56. Rohler, *George Wallace*, 57.

57. White, *Making of the President, 1968*, 429.

58. Wallace, *Stand Up for America*, 124.

59. Rohler, *George Wallace*, 57.

60. Cohen, *American Maelstrom*, 302.

61. Kozak, *LeMay*, 379–80.

62. Ibid., 374.

63. Jules Witcover, *The Year the Dream Died: Revisiting 1968 in America* (New York: Warner Books, 1997), 384.

64. Wallace Jr., *Governor George Wallace*, 202–3.

65. Wallace, *Stand Up for America*, 124.

66. Coffey, *Iron Eagle*, 446–47.

67. Witcover, *Year the Dream Died*, 387.

68. Memorandum from Stan Sikes to Cecil C. Jackson Jr., October 10, 1968, "General Curtis E. LeMay's Viet Nam Trip," Box 3, George C. Wallace Collection, Alabama Department of Archives and History.

69. Carter, *Politics of Rage*, 365.

70. Marshall Frady, "The American Independent Party," in Arthur M. Schlesinger Jr., ed., *History of U.S. Political Parties*, volume 4, *1945–1972: The Politics of Change* (Philadelphia: Chelsea House Publishers, 1973), 3491.

71. Carter, *Politics of Rage*, 367.

72. Ibid., 368.

Chapter 9. Messenger

1. "Billy Graham Notes," Box 8, Post-Presidential Ranch Files, Lyndon B. Johnson Presidential Library.

2. Memorandum from Bob Faiss to Jim Jones, September 10, 1968, Box 227, Name File, White House Central File, Lyndon B. Johnson Presidential Library.

3. Nixon Diary, Notebook 15, VIP Notebooks, Records of the Billy Graham Evangelistic Association: Montreat Office, Billy Graham Archive and Research Center, Charlotte, NC.

4. "The President's Remarks at a Buffet Dinner for Members of His Staff," September 13, 1968, Lyndon B. Johnson Presidential Library.

5. Andrew L. Johns, *Vietnam's Second Front: Domestic Politics, the Republican Party, and the War* (Lexington: University Press of Kentucky, 2010), 221.

6. Nixon Diary, Notebook 15, VIP Notebooks, Records of the Billy Graham Evangelistic Association: Montreat Office, Billy Graham Archive and Research Center, Charlotte, NC.

7. W. Marvin Watson with Sherwin Markman, *Chief of Staff: Lyndon Johnson and His Presidency* (New York: Thomas Dunne Books, 2004), 301.

8. Billy Graham, *Just As I Am: The Autobiography of Billy Graham* (New York: HarperCollins, 1997), 416.

9. John Connally with Mickey Herskowitz, *In History's Shadow: An American Odyssey* (New York: Hyperion, 1993), 231.

10. Ibid., 259.

11. Nancy Gibbs and Michael Duffy, *The President's Club: Inside the World's Most Exclusive Fraternity* (New York: Simon & Schuster, 2012), 233.

12. Graham, *Just as I Am*, 407.

13. Ibid., 454.

14. Ibid., 414.

15. Ibid., 416.

16. William Martin, *A Prophet with Honor: The Billy Graham Story* (New York: William Morrow, 1991), 357.

17. Ibid.

18. Rowland Evans Jr. and Robert D. Novak, *Nixon in the White House: The Frustration of Power* (New York: Random House, 1971), 5.

19. Stephen Hess and David S. Broder, *The Republican Establishment: The Present and Future of the G.O.P.* (New York: Harper & Row, 1967), 198.

20. Notes of Conversation between Billy Graham and Richard Nixon, September 8, 1968, Notebook 6, VIP Notebooks, Records of the Billy Graham Evangelistic Association: Montreat Office, Billy Graham Archive and Research Center, Charlotte, NC.

21. Gibbs and Duffy, *President's Club*, 233; Robert Dallek, *Flawed Giant: Lyndon Johnson and His Times, 1961–1973* (New York: Oxford University Press, 1998), 578.

22. Notes of Conversation between Billy Graham and Richard Nixon, September 8, 1968.

23. Memorandum from Richard Nixon to John Connally, July 24, 1972, Box 4, Memoranda from the President, 1969–74, President's Personal File, Richard M. Nixon Presidential Library.

24. Clark Clifford with Richard Holbrooke, *Counsel to the President: A Memoir* (New York: Random House, 1991), 564.

25. Notes of Conversation between Billy Graham and Richard Nixon, September 8, 1968.

26. Byron E. Shafer and Richard Johnston, *The End of Southern Exceptionalism: Class, Race, and Partisan Change in the Postwar South* (Cambridge, MA: Harvard University Press, 2006), 11.

27. Connally with Herskowitz, *In History's Shadow*, 231.

28. Gibbs and Duffy, *President's Club*, 232.

29. George Wallace Jr., *Governor George Wallace: The Man You Never Knew* (2011), 122.

30. Martin, *Prophet with Honor*, 318–19.

31. Stephen P. Miller, *Billy Graham and the Rise of the Republican South* (Philadelphia: University of Pennsylvania Press, 2009), 5.

32. Ibid., 138.

33. Graham, *Just As I Am*, 422.

34. Axel R. Schäfer, ed., *American Evangelicals and the 1960s* (Madison: University of Wisconsin Press, 2013), 4.

35. Graham, *Just As I Am*, 455.

36. Patrick J. Buchanan, *The Greatest Comeback: How Richard Nixon Rose from Defeat to Create the New Majority* (New York: Crown Forum, 2014), 159–60.

37. David Eisenhower with Julie Nixon Eisenhower, *Going Home to Glory: A Memoir of Life with Dwight D. Eisenhower, 1961–1969* (New York: Simon & Schuster, 2010), 234.

38. Nixon Diary, Notebook 15.

39. Miller, *Billy Graham*, 5.

40. Letter from Billy Graham to Dwight Eisenhower, March 20, 1968, Notebook 2, VIP Notebooks, Records of the Billy Graham Evangelistic Association: Montreat Office, Billy Graham Archive and Research Center, Charlotte, NC.

41. Associated Press, "Eisenhower Says He Admires Reagan," *New York Times*, March 14, 1967, p. 26.

42. Memorandum for the Record, March 14, 1967, Box 14, Special Names, Post-Presidential Papers, Dwight D. Eisenhower Presidential Library.

43. Dwight Eisenhower, *The Eisenhower Diaries*, edited by Robert H. Ferrell (New York: W. W. Norton, 1981), 396.

44. Letter from Dwight Eisenhower to Walter Williams, October 20, 1967, Box 14, Special Names, Post-Presidential Papers, Dwight D. Eisenhower Presidential Library.

45. Buchanan, *Greatest Comeback*, 157.

46. Lewis Chester, Godfrey Hodgson, and Bruce Page, *An American Melodrama: The Presidential Campaign of 1968* (New York: Viking Press, 1969), 249.

47. Letter from Billy Graham to Dwight Eisenhower, March 20, 1968.

48. Ibid.

49. Letter from Dwight Eisenhower to Walter Williams, October 20, 1967.

50. Nixon Diary, Notebook 15.
51. William Safire, *Before the Fall: An Inside View of the Pre-Watergate White House* (Garden City, NY: Doubleday, 1975), 43.
52. Jeffrey Frank, *Ike and Dick: Portrait of a Strange Political Marriage* (New York: Simon & Schuster, 2013), 292.
53. Letter from Billy Graham to Dwight Eisenhower, February 3, 1969, Notebook 2, VIP Notebooks.
54. Martin, *Prophet with Honor*, 357.
55. Julie Nixon Eisenhower, *Special People* (New York: Simon & Schuster, 1977), 55–56.
56. Nixon Diary, Notebook 15.
57. Letter from Billy Graham to Ronald Reagan, March 7, 1967, Notebook 24, VIP Notebooks.
58. Gibbs and Duffy, *President's Club*, 213.
59. Eisenhower with Nixon Eisenhower, *Going Home to Glory*, 238.
60. Miller, *Billy Graham*, 131.
61. Letter from Billy Graham to Ronald Reagan, September 27, 1967, Notebook 24, VIP Notebooks.
62. Nixon Diary, Notebook 15.
63. Letter from Billy Graham to Richard Nixon, June 1, 1968, Notebook 10, VIP Notebooks.
64. Ibid.
65. Nixon Diary, Notebook 15.
66. Arnold A. Offner, *Hubert Humphrey: The Conscience of the Country* (New Haven: Yale University Press, 2018), 310.
67. Miller, *Billy Graham*, 134.
68. Gibbs and Duffy, *President's Club*, 167.
69. Martin, *Prophet with Honor*, 359.
70. Nixon Diary, Notebook 15.
71. Ibid.
72. Miller, *Billy Graham*, 136.
73. Nixon Diary, Notebook 15.
74. Telephone Conversation #13530, October 10, 1968, 10:12 A.M., Recordings and Transcripts of Telephone Conversations and Meetings, Lyndon B. Johnson Presidential Library.
75. Nixon Diary, Notebook 15.

Chapter 10. Stalemate

1. Lyndon Baines Johnson, *The Vantage Point: Perspectives of the Presidency, 1963–1969* (New York: Holt, Rinehart and Winston, 1971), 510.
2. Nguyen Phu Duc, *The Viet-Nam Peace Negotiations: Saigon's Side of the Story*, edited by Arthur J. Dommen (Christiansburg, VA: Dalley Book Service, 2005), 92.

3. Telegram from American Embassy Paris to Secretary of State, September 3, 1968, Paris 20314, Box 559, W. Averell Harriman Papers, Manuscript Division, Library of Congress.

4. Telegram from American Embassy Paris to Secretary of State, September 9, 1968, Paris 20528, Box 561, W. Averell Harriman Papers, Manuscript Division, Library of Congress.

5. "The Negotiations for a Bombing Cessation," May 13–October 31, 1968, by Tom Charles Huston, June 1, 1971, pp. 48–49, Box 114, White House Special Files, Staff Member Office Files, H. R. Haldeman, Richard M. Nixon Presidential Library.

6. Luu Van Loi and Nguyen Anh Vu, *Le Duc Tho–Kissinger Negotiations in Paris* (Hanoi: Gioi Publishers, 1996), 27.

7. Telegram from American Embassy Paris to Secretary of State, September 4, 1968, Paris 20340, Box 561, W. Averell Harriman Papers, Manuscript Division, Library of Congress.

8. Telegram from American Embassy Paris to Secretary of State, September 7, 1968, Paris 20522, Box 561, W. Averell Harriman Papers, Manuscript Division, Library of Congress.

9. "Negotiations for a Bombing Cessation," 49–51.

10. Telegram from American Embassy Paris to Secretary of State, September 13, 1968, Paris 20789, Box 561, W. Averell Harriman Papers, Manuscript Division, Library of Congress.

11. Loi and Nguyen, *Le Duc Tho–Kissinger Negotiations*, 30.

12. "Negotiations for a Bombing Cessation," 51–53.

13. Telegram from American Embassy Paris to Secretary of State, September 14, 1968, Paris 20872, Box 561, W. Averell Harriman Papers, Manuscript Division, Library of Congress.

14. Background to the October 31 Announcement, p. 1, Box 1 (Accession 2015-M-027), Cyrus R. and Grace Sloane Vance Papers, Manuscripts and Archives, Yale University Library, Yale University.

15. Loi and Nguyen, *Le Duc Tho–Kissinger Negotiations*, 36.

16. "Negotiations for a Bombing Cessation," 53–55.

17. Clark Clifford with Richard Holbrooke, *Counsel to the President: A Memoir* (New York: Random House, 1991), 570.

18. "Negotiations for a Bombing Cessation," 55–57.

19. Background to the October 31 Announcement, 2.

20. Telegram from American Embassy Paris to Secretary of State, September 20, 1968, Paris 21178, Box 561, W. Averell Harriman Papers, Manuscript Division, Library of Congress.

21. Loi and Nguyen, *Le Duc Tho–Kissinger Negotiations*, 39.

22. Background to the October 31 Announcement, 10.

23. "Negotiations for a Bombing Cessation," 60–61.

24. Lien-Hang T. Nguyen, *Hanoi's War: An International History of the War for Peace in Vietnam* (Chapel Hill: University of North Carolina Press, 2012), 123.

25. Background to the October 31 Announcement, 10.
26. "Negotiations for a Bombing Cessation," 62–64.
27. Background to the October 31 Announcement, 12.
28. "Negotiations for a Bombing Cessation," 64–65.
29. Ellsworth Bunker, unpublished memoir, "Chapter 8: One Fist in the Tar Baby," 1. Courtesy of Steve Young.
30. Robert Shaplen, *The Road from War: Vietnam, 1965–1970* (New York: Harper & Row, 1970), 237.
31. "Negotiations for a Bombing Cessation," 67–68.
32. Ibid., 68–69.
33. Ibid., 69–71.
34. Telegram from American Embassy Paris to Secretary of State, September 25, 1968, Paris 21344, Box 561, W. Averell Harriman Papers, Manuscript Division, Library of Congress.
35. Étienne Manac'h, *Mémoires d'Extrême Asie: La face cachée du monde* (Paris: Fayard, 1977), 31.
36. "Negotiations for a Bombing Cessation," 72–73.
37. Ibid., 74.
38. Clifford with Holbrooke, *Counsel to the President*, 570.
39. "Negotiations for a Bombing Cessation," 74–76.
40. Ibid., 76–77.
41. Ibid., 78–80.
42. Background to the October 31 Announcement, 2.
43. "Negotiations for a Bombing Cessation," 81–82.

Chapter 11. Allies

1. Memorandum from Lyndon Johnson to Averell Harriman, October 3, 1968, Box 6, Walt Rostow Files, National Security File, Lyndon B. Johnson Presidential Library.
2. Memorandum from Jim Jones to Lyndon Johnson, October 21, 1968, Box 6, James R. Jones Collection, Carl Albert Center, University of Oklahoma.
3. Edgar Berman, *Hubert: The Triumph and Tragedy of the Humphrey I Knew* (New York: G. P. Putnam's Sons, 1979), 94.
4. Jules Witcover, *The Year the Dream Died: Revisiting 1968 in America* (New York: Warner Books, 1997), 364.
5. Letter from Hubert Humphrey to Averell Harriman, December 14, 1968, Box 150.F.16.2F, Hubert H. Humphrey Papers, Minnesota Historical Society.
6. Memo of Telcon with Robert Nathan, September 2, 1968, Box 458, W. Averell Harriman Papers, Manuscript Division, Library of Congress.
7. Arnold A. Offner, *Hubert Humphrey: The Conscience of the Country* (New Haven: Yale University Press, 2018), 287.

8. General Review of Last Six Months, December 14, 1968, Box 558, W. Averell Harriman Papers, Manuscript Division, Library of Congress.

9. Rudy Abramson, *Spanning the Century: The Life of W. Averell Harriman, 1891–1986* (New York: William Morrow, 1992), 668.

10. Clark Clifford with Richard Holbrooke, *Counsel to the President: A Memoir* (New York: Random House, 1991), 569–70.

11. Offner, *Hubert Humphrey*, 313.

12. Clifford with Holbrooke, *Counsel to the President*, 571.

13. Joseph Napolitan, *The Election Game and How to Win It* (Garden City, NY: Doubleday, 1972), 44–45.

14. Notes on Telephone Call to Frank Sieverts from Henry Gemmill, September 25, 1968, Box 458, W. Averell Harriman Papers, Manuscript Division, Library of Congress.

15. David DiLeo, *George Ball, Vietnam, and the Rethinking of Containment* (Chapel Hill: University of North Carolina Press, 1991), 171.

16. Notes of Meeting, September 25, 1968, 2:04–2:45 P.M., Box 4, Tom Johnson Notes of Meetings, Personal Papers of Tom Johnson, Lyndon B. Johnson Presidential Library.

17. George W. Ball, *The Past Has Another Pattern: Memoirs* (New York: W. W. Norton, 1982), 438.

18. Letter from Walter Mondale to George Ball, May 4, 1968, Box 54, George W. Ball Papers, Seeley G. Mudd Manuscript Library, Princeton University.

19. Abramson, *Spanning the Century*, 668–69.

20. Letter from Averell Harriman to George Ball, Undated, Box 434, W. Averell Harriman Papers, Manuscript Division, Library of Congress.

21. Letter from Averell Harriman to Hubert Humphrey, December 26, 1968, Box 470, W. Averell Harriman Papers, Manuscript Division, Library of Congress.

22. William Edwards, "Resignation by Ball Stirs Scandal Talk," *Chicago Sun-Tribune*, September 29, 1968, in Box 54, George W. Ball Papers, Seeley G. Mudd Manuscript Library, Princeton University.

23. Carl Solberg, *Hubert Humphrey: A Biography* (New York: W. W. Norton, 1984), 380.

24. Clifford with Holbrooke, *Counsel to the President*, 572.

25. Notes of the President's Weekly Luncheon Meeting, September 25, 1968, Box 4, Tom Johnson Notes of Meetings, Personal Papers of Tom Johnson, Lyndon B. Johnson Presidential Library.

26. Andrew L. Johns, *The Price of Loyalty: Hubert Humphrey's Vietnam Conflict* (Lanham, MD: Rowman & Littlefield, 2020), 106.

27. Theodore H. White, *The Making of the President, 1968* (New York: Atheneum Publishers, 1969), 390.

28. Ball, *Past Has Another Pattern*, 444.

29. Ibid., 444–45.

30. DiLeo, *George Ball*, 175.

31. White, *Making of the President, 1968*, 393.

32. Johns, *Price of Loyalty*, 111

33. Author interview with George "Ed" Ewing, January 25, 2019, Wetumpka, AL.

34. G. Scott Thomas, *Counting the Votes: A New Way to Analyze America's Presidential Elections* (Santa Barbara, CA: Praeger, 2015), 221.

35. Tom Wicker, *One of Us: Richard Nixon and the American Dream* (New York: Random House, 1991), 385.

36. How the House May Pick the Next President, Congressional Leadership Briefings, Undated, Box A4, Melvin Laird Papers, Gerald R. Ford Presidential Library.

37. Richard M. Scammon and Ben J. Wattenberg, *The Real Majority* (New York: Coward-McCann, 1970), 187.

38. Norman Sherman, *From Nowhere to Somewhere, My Political Journey: A Memoir of Sorts* (Minneapolis: First Avenue Editions, 2016), 170.

39. Jules Witcover, *Party of the People: A History of the Democrats* (New York: Random House, 2003), 565.

40. Witcover, *Year the Dream Died*, 284.

41. Letter from Hubert Humphrey to Henry Kissinger, October 11, 1969, Box 818, National Security Council Files, Richard M. Nixon Presidential Library.

42. Offner, *Hubert Humphrey*, 310.

43. Richard Nixon, *RN: The Memoirs of Richard Nixon* (New York: Grosset & Dunlap, 1978), 318.

44. Berman, *Hubert*, 182–83.

45. Theodore White Interview with George Ball, January 1969, Box 117, Theodore White Papers, Pusey Library, Harvard University.

46. Clifford with Holbrooke, *Counsel to the President*, 572.

47. Offner, *Hubert Humphrey*, 315.

48. George W. Ball Interview with Marvin Kalb, Peter Lisagor, and Richard C. Hottelet, *Face the Nation*, September 29, 1968, Box 130, George W. Ball Papers, Seeley G. Mudd Manuscript Library, Princeton University.

49. Interview with George W. Ball with Frank McGee, *The Today Show*, September 27, 1968, Box 130, George W. Ball Papers, Seeley G. Mudd Manuscript Library, Princeton University.

50. Letter from George Ball to the Humphrey Campaign, Undated, Box 54, George W. Ball Papers, Seeley G. Mudd Manuscript Library, Princeton University.

51. DiLeo, *George Ball*, 174.

52. Hubert H. Humphrey, *The Education of a Public Man: My Life and Politics* (Garden City, NY: Doubleday, 1976), 402.

53. "Confidential," Undated, Box 458, W. Averell Harriman Papers, Manuscript Division, Library of Congress.

54. Memorandum from Larry O'Brien to Hubert Humphrey, September 28, 1968, Box 173, Lawrence O'Brien Papers, John F. Kennedy Presidential Library.

55. Ted Van Dyk, *Heroes, Hacks, and Fools: Memoirs from the Political Inside* (Seattle: University of Washington Press, 2007), 86.
56. Offner, *Hubert Humphrey*, 316.
57. Humphrey, *Education of a Public Man*, 403.
58. George Christian, *The President Steps Down: A Personal Memoir of the Transfer of Power* (New York: Macmillan, 1970), 151.
59. Offner, *Hubert Humphrey*, 317.
60. Humphrey, *Education of a Public Man*, 401.
61. DiLeo, *George Ball*, 174.
62. "Release on Delivery (7:30 P.M.), September 30, 1968," Box 150.G.5.2F, Hubert H. Humphrey Papers, Minnesota Historical Society.
63. Telegram from Secretary of State to American Embassy Paris, State 247671, October 1, 1968, Box 470, W. Averell Harriman Papers, Manuscript Division, Library of Congress.
64. Ken Hughes, *Chasing Shadows: The Nixon Tapes, the Chennault Affair, and the Origins of Watergate* (Charlottesville: University of Virginia Press, 2014), 21.
65. Oral History with James H. Rowe Jr., November 10, 1982, pp. 13–14, Lyndon Johnson Presidential Library.
66. Offner, *Hubert Humphrey*, 318.
67. Notes from October 1, 1968, Box 1, George Elsey's Notes of Secretary of Defense Clark Clifford's Morning Staff Conference, May 1968–January 1969, George Elsey Papers, Lyndon B. Johnson Presidential Library.
68. Notes from October 17, 1968, Box 1, George Elsey's Notes of Secretary of Defense Clark Clifford's Morning Staff Conference, May 1968–January 1969.
69. William Bundy, *A Tangled Web: The Making of Foreign Policy in the Nixon Presidency* (New York: Hill and Wang, 1998), 29.
70. Robert Dallek, *Flawed Giant: Lyndon Johnson and His Times, 1961–1973* (New York: Oxford University Press, 1998), 591.
71. Witcover, *Party of the People*, 566.
72. Nixon, *RN: The Memoirs*, 318.
73. Theodore White Interview with George Ball, January 1969.
74. Solberg, *Hubert Humphrey*, 380.
75. Clifford with Holbrooke, *Counsel to the President*, 572.
76. Ball, *Past Has Another Pattern*, 446.
77. Berman, *Hubert*, 220.
78. Memorandum from Richard Allen to DC, "Senator Wallace Bennett, Utah," July 28, 1968, Box 1, Richard V. Allen Papers, Hoover Institution Library & Archive.
79. Telegram from Richard Allen to Pat Buchanan, September 30, 1968, 5:30 P.M., Box 24, Richard V. Allen Papers, Hoover Institution Library & Archive.
80. Author interview with Thomas Korologos and Richard Allen, December 2, 2019, Washington, DC.

81. Christian, *President Steps Down*, 151.

82. Nancy Gibbs and Michael Duffy, *The President's Club: Inside the World's Most Exclusive Fraternity* (New York: Simon & Schuster, 2012), 228.

83. Offner, *Hubert Humphrey*, 319.

84. Berman, *Hubert*, 212.

85. White, *Making of the President, 1968*, 414.

86. Napolitan, *Election Game*, 30.

87. Memorandum from Leonid Brezhnev to the Politburo of the Central Committee, Undated, Fond 80, Inventory 1, Cause 314 [Ф. 80. Оп. 1. Д. 314], Russian State Archive of Contemporary History (RGANI) [Российский Государственный Архив Новейшей Истории]. Breznhev was concerned that American voters could shift right-wing in the coming election, which "increases the possibility of our influence on the political processes taking place in the United States." The election of Humphrey provided the best chance to avoid such a shift. According to RGANI archivists, the memo was discovered in Brezhnev's closed desk only after his death in 1982.

88. Anatoly Dobrynin, *In Confidence: Moscow's Ambassador to America's Six Cold War Presidents (1962–1986)* (New York: Times Books, 1995), 176.

89. Offner, *Hubert Humphrey*, 308.

90. Ilya V. Gaiduk, *The Soviet Union and the Vietnam War* (Chicago: Ivan R. Dee, 1996), 181–82.

91. Berman, *Hubert*, 169.

92. Memorandum of Conversation, November 18, 1969, Box 832, National Security Council Files, Richard M. Nixon Presidential Library.

93. Author telephone interview with Sergei Khrushchev, December 15, 2017.

94. Memorandum of Conversation, November 18, 1969.

95. Author interview with Marvin Kalb, January 28, 2020, Washington, DC.

96. After applying for access to the relevant documents at the Archive of Foreign Policy (AVP) in Moscow in November 2017 and being granted access in February 2018, during another height of headlines about alleged Russian collusion in the 2016 American presidential election the AVP became unhelpful. In the same month I was approved for access, in February 2018, I was then denied. Curiously, I was approved again in October 2018, but the three files ("delo") they served had nothing to do with Hubert Humphrey. The AVP reading room staff blamed the storage room staff for pulling the wrong folders. After several more attempts, I gave up in early 2020 after spending more than two years on the effort. I was later told the AVP staff became spooked about any research topic that sounded like a request for records on Russian collusion in American presidential elections.

97. Clifford with Holbrooke, *Counsel to the President*, 575–76.

98. Michael A. Cohen, *American Maelstrom: The 1968 Election and the Politics of Division* (New York: Oxford University Press, 2016), 295–96.

99. Solberg, *Hubert Humphrey*, 386–87.

100. Berman, *Hubert*, 224.

101. Offner, *Hubert Humphrey*, 319–20.

102. Christian, *President Steps Down*, 77.

103. Telegram from American Embassy Paris to Secretary of State, October 2, 1968, Paris 21737, Box 561, W. Averell Harriman Papers, Manuscript Division, Library of Congress.

104. Luu Van Loi and Nguyen Anh Vu, *Le Duc Tho–Kissinger Negotiations in Paris* (Hanoi: Gioi Publishers, 1996), 44.

105. Chester L. Cooper, *In the Shadows of History: Fifty Years behind the Scenes of Cold War Diplomacy* (Amherst, NY: Prometheus Books, 2005), 278.

106. Notes from October 17, 1968, Box 1, George Elsey's Notes of Secretary of Defense Clark Clifford's Morning Staff Conference, May 1968–January 1969.

107. Lyndon Baines Johnson, *The Vantage Point: Perspectives of the Presidency, 1963–1969* (New York: Holt, Rinehart and Winston, 1971), 517.

108. Henry A. Kissinger, *Ending the Vietnam War: A History of America's Involvement in and Extrication from the Vietnam War* (New York: Simon & Schuster, 2003), 46.

109. Christian, *President Steps Down*, 50.

110. Jack Valenti, *My Life: In War, the White House, and Hollywood* (New York: Harmony Books, 2007), 250.

111. Johnson, *Vantage Point*, 517.

112. Christian, *President Steps Down*, 50.

113. Lady Bird Johnson, *A White House Diary* (New York: Holt, Rinehart and Winston, 1970), 716–17.

Chapter 12. Home Stretch

1. Walter LaFeber, *The Deadly Bet: LBJ, Vietnam, and the 1968 Election* (Lanham, MD: Rowman & Littlefield Publishers, 2005), 123.

2. Luu Van Loi and Nguyen Anh Vu, *Le Duc Tho–Kissinger Negotiations in Paris* (Hanoi: Gioi Publishers, 1996), 27.

3. Peter Baker, "White House Memo: Trump May Compare Himself to Nixon in 1968, but He Really Resembles Wallace," *New York Times*, June 9, 2020, A18.

4. LaFeber, *Deadly Bet*, 131.

5. George H. Gallup, *The Gallup Poll: Public Opinion, 1935–1971*, volume 3, *1959–1971* (New York: Random House, 1972), 2128.

6. Richard M. Scammon and Ben J. Wattenberg, *The Real Majority* (New York: Coward-McCann, 1970), 167.

7. Email by Dwight Chapin to the author, June 10, 2020. While writing his memoir, Chapin found a cache of original handwritten notes made by Nixon during the campaign. "All I can figure out is at the end of a visit to a city I would always check our hotel suite and then give any notes or memos found

to Rose Mary [Woods]," Chapin wrote. "Something happened, the notes ended up in a box here at the house that I opened yesterday, 52 years later!"

8. Memorandum from Jim Jones to Lyndon Johnson, September 12, 1968, Box 6, James R. Jones Collection, Carl Albert Center, University of Oklahoma.

9. Memorandum from Ed Cubberley to Larry O'Brien, Issues Meeting, Department of Agriculture, Monday, September 30, 1968, Box 164, Lawrence O'Brien Papers, John F. Kennedy Presidential Library.

10. Theodore H. White, *The Making of the President, 1968* (New York: Atheneum Publishers, 1969), 423.

11. Carl Solberg, *Hubert Humphrey: A Biography* (New York: W. W. Norton, 1984), 387.

12. Richard Nixon, *RN: The Memoirs of Richard Nixon* (New York: Grosset & Dunlap, 1978), 317.

13. Lisa McGirr, *Suburban Warriors: The Origins of the New American Right* (Princeton, NJ: Princeton University Press, 2001), 217.

14. Patrick J. Buchanan, *The Greatest Comeback: How Richard Nixon Rose from Defeat to Create the New Majority* (New York: Crown Forum, 2014), 328.

15. Drew Pearson, *Washington Merry-Go-Round: The Drew Pearson Diaries, 1960–1969*, edited by Peter Hannaford (Lincoln, NE: Potomac Books, 2015), 619.

16. Arnold A. Offner, *Hubert Humphrey: The Conscience of the Country* (New Haven: Yale University Press, 2018), 313.

17. John A. Farrell, *Richard Nixon: The Life* (New York: Doubleday, 2017), 325.

18. Walter Lippmann, *Newsweek*, October 7, 1968, in Box 107, PPS 500, Pre-Presidential Files, Richard M. Nixon Presidential Library.

19. Daniel Ellsberg, *Secrets: A Memoir of Vietnam and the Pentagon Papers* (New York: Viking Press, 2002), 217.

20. White, *Making of the President, 1968*, 381.

21. Joe McGinniss, *The Selling of the President, 1968* (New York: Trident Press, 1969), 81.

22. Charles J. Holden, Zach Messitte, and Jerald Podair, *Republican Populist: Spiro Agnew and the Origins of Donald Trump's America* (Charlottesville: University of Virginia Press, 2019), 8.

23. Nixon, *RN: The Memoirs*, 320.

24. Jules Witcover, *The Year the Dream Died: Revisiting 1968 in America* (New York: Warner Books, 1997), 400.

25. Detail Schedule, Richard M. Nixon—Monday, October 21, to Wednesday, October 23, 1968, Box 14, PPS 212, Pre-Presidential Files, Richard M. Nixon Presidential Library.

26. R. W. Apple Jr., "Nixon Intensifies Blows at Humphrey on Ohio Train Tour," *New York Times*, October 23, 1968.

27. Theodore White Notes, Undated, Box 117, Theodore White Papers, Pusey Library, Harvard University.

28. William Safire, *Before the Fall: An Inside View of the Pre-Watergate White House* (Garden City, NY: Doubleday, 1975), 82.

29. White, *Making of the President, 1968*, 437–38.

30. Campaign Policy Committee Minutes, September 16, 1968, Box 150.G.5.4F, Hubert H. Humphrey Papers, Minnesota Historical Society.

31. Buchanan, *Greatest Comeback*, 196.

32. Richard M. Nixon, "L.B.J. Should Debate on TV," *Saturday Evening Post*, June 27, 1964, pp. 12, 14.

33. Offner, *Hubert Humphrey*, 280.

34. Nixon, *RN: The Memoirs*, 319.

35. John Helgerson, "Intelligence Support for Richard M. Nixon: A Difficult Relationship," *Studies in Intelligence* 39, no. 4 (1995): 104.

36. Nixon, *RN: The Memoirs*, 319.

37. "Maneuvers Late in the Session Kill TV Debate Bill," in *Congressional Quarterly Almanac, 1968* (Washington, DC: Congressional Quarterly, 1969), 647.

38. Memorandum from William Connell to Hubert Humphrey, "Humphrey on the Upswing, Gallup or not!," October 9, 1968, Box 150.G.5.4F, Hubert H. Humphrey Papers, Minnesota Historical Society.

39. Jules Witcover, *The Resurrection of Richard Nixon* (New York: G. P. Putnam's Sons, 1970), 405.

40. Notes from September 20, 1968, Box 1, George Elsey's Notes of Secretary of Defense Clark Clifford's Morning Staff Conference, May 1968–January 1969, George Elsey Papers, Lyndon B. Johnson Presidential Library.

41. Memorandum from Jim Jones to Lyndon Johnson, September 12, 1968, Box 6, James R. Jones Collection.

42. E. J. Dionne Jr., *Why Americans Hate Politics* (New York: Simon & Schuster, 1991), 45.

43. Melvin Small and William D. Hoover, eds., *Give Peace a Chance: Exploring the Vietnam Antiwar Movement* (Syracuse, NY: Syracuse University Press, 1992), 3.

44. Campaign Policy Committee Minutes, September 18, 1968, Box 150.G.5.4F, Hubert H. Humphrey Papers, Minnesota Historical Society.

45. Scammon and Wattenberg, *Real Majority*, 167.

46. Offner, *Hubert Humphrey*, 320.

47. Solberg, *Hubert Humphrey*, 388.

48. Michael A. Cohen, *American Maelstrom: The 1968 Election and the Politics of Division* (New York: Oxford University Press, 2016), 309.

49. Memorandum from Evron Kirkpatrick to Orville Freeman, September 27, 1968, Box 150.G.5.4F, Hubert H. Humphrey Papers, Minnesota Historical Society.

50. Cohen, *American Maelstrom*, 29.

51. Author telephone interview with Vic Fingerhut, January 29, 2021.

52. Memorandum from Vic Fingerhut to Hubert Humphrey, "Two Weeks to a Humphrey Victory . . . What Must Be Done," October 15, 1968, Fingerhut / Granados Opinion Research Co. Provided by Vic Fingerhut.

53. Memorandum from Jim Jones to Lyndon Johnson, October 31, 1968, Box 6, James R. Jones Collection.

54. David Kusnet, *Speaking American: How the Democrats Can Win in the Nineties* (New York: Thunder's Mouth Press, 1992), 3.

55. Drew Pearson and Jack Anderson, "Humphrey Drive Recalls Truman in '48," *Washington Post*, October 10, 1968, H7, in Box F120, Papers of Drew Pearson, Lyndon B. Johnson Presidential Library.

56. Memorandum from Orville Freeman to Hubert Humphrey, September 18, 1968, Box 148.B.15.8F, Hubert H. Humphrey Papers, Minnesota Historical Society.

57. Gallup, *Gallup Poll*, 2162.

58. Memorandum from William Connell to Hubert Humphrey, October 25, 1968, Box 150.G.5.4F, Hubert H. Humphrey Papers, Minnesota Historical Society.

59. Author telephone interview with Vic Fingerhut.

60. Scammon and Wattenberg, *Real Majority*, 191.

61. Author telephone interview with Vic Fingerhut.

62. Memorandum from Charles Maguire to Ted Van Dyk, September 18, 1968, Box 10, Charles Maguire Files, Papers of Lyndon Baines Johnson, Lyndon B. Johnson Presidential Library.

63. Memorandum from Jack McNulty to Harry McPherson, September 28, 1967, Box 1, John W. McNulty Papers, Lyndon B. Johnson Presidential Library.

64. Campaign Policy Committee Minutes, October 11, 1968, Box 150.G.5.4F, Hubert H. Humphrey Papers, Minnesota Historical Society.

65. Lloyd Rohler, *George Wallace: Conservative Populist* (Westport, CT: Praeger, 2004), 66.

66. Offner, *Hubert Humphrey*, 328.

67. Cohen, *American Maelstrom*, 314.

68. Memorandum from Hubert Humphrey to Larry O'Brien, September 15, 1968, Box 148.B.15.8F, Hubert H. Humphrey Papers, Minnesota Historical Society.

69. Memorandum from Hubert Humphrey to Larry O'Brien, October 4, 1968, Box 148.B.15.8F, Hubert H. Humphrey Papers.

70. White, *Making of the President, 1968*, 426.

71. Buchanan, *Greatest Comeback*, 353.

72. White, *Making of the President, 1968*, 426.

73. Ibid., 427.

74. Cohen, *American Maelstrom*, 303.

75. Offner, *Hubert Humphrey*, 319.

76. Scammon and Wattenberg, *Real Majority*, 172.

77. Solberg, *Hubert Humphrey*, 388–89.

78. White, *Making of the President, 1968*, 427.

79. Stephan Lesher, *George Wallace: American Populist* (Reading, MA: Addison-Wesley Publishing, 1994), 414.

80. Memorandum from William Connell to Hubert Humphrey, October 25, 1968.

81. Lesher, *George Wallace*, 426.

82. Safire, *Before the Fall*, 57.

83. Author telephone interview with Vic Fingerhut.

84. Scammon and Wattenberg, *Real Majority*, 175.

85. Reminiscences of Lyndon B. Johnson, August 19, 1969, p. 29, Lyndon B. Johnson Presidential Library.

86. George Christian, *The President Steps Down: A Personal Memoir of the Transfer of Power* (New York: Macmillan, 1970), 79.

87. Solberg, *Hubert Humphrey*, 392.

88. President's Daily Diary Entry, October 19, 1968, President's Daily Diary Collection, Lyndon B. Johnson Presidential Library.

89. Reminiscences of Lyndon B. Johnson, August 19, 1969, p. 30.

90. Memorandum from Jim Jones to Lyndon Johnson, October 19, 1968, Box 6, James R. Jones Collection.

91. President's Daily Diary Entry, October 20, 1968, President's Daily Diary Collection.

92. Author interview with James R. Jones, October 17, 2017, Washington, DC.

93. Solberg, *Hubert Humphrey*, 392.

94. Edgar Berman, *Hubert: The Triumph and Tragedy of the Humphrey I Knew* (New York: G. P. Putnam's Sons, 1979), 75.

95. Hubert H. Humphrey, *The Education of a Public Man: My Life and Politics* (Garden City, NY: Doubleday, 1976), 5.

96. Solberg, *Hubert Humphrey*, 399.

97. Christian, *President Steps Down*, 157.

98. Buchanan, *Greatest Comeback*, 278.

99. Ibid., 345.

100. Witcover, *Year the Dream Died*, 392.

101. Pearson, *Washington Merry-Go-Round*, 620.

102. Cohen, *American Maelstrom*, 306–9.

Chapter 13. Bombing Halt

1. George Christian, *The President Steps Down: A Personal Memoir of the Transfer of Power* (New York: Macmillan, 1970), 82.

2. Arnold A. Offner, *Hubert Humphrey: The Conscience of the Country* (New Haven: Yale University Press, 2018), 325.

3. Notes from September 25, 1968, Box 1, George Elsey's Notes of Secretary of Defense Clark Clifford's Morning Staff Conference, May 1968–January 1969, George Elsey Papers, Lyndon B. Johnson Presidential Library.

4. Clark Clifford with Richard Holbrooke, *Counsel to the President: A Memoir* (New York: Random House, 1991), 579.

5. General Review of Last Six Months, December 14, 1968, Box 558, W. Averell Harriman Papers, Manuscript Division, Library of Congress.

6. Ken Hughes, *Chasing Shadows: The Nixon Tapes, the Chennault Affair, and the Origins of Watergate* (Charlottesville: University of Virginia Press, 2014), 19.

7. Memorandum from Dick Allen to Richard Nixon, "Poll in Far East," October 25, 1968, Box 1, Richard V. Allen Papers, Hoover Institution Library and Archives.

8. Memorandum from Bryce Harlow to H. R. Haldeman, October 13, 1968, Box 11, Richard V. Allen Papers, Hoover Institution Library & Archive.

9. Telegram from Secretary of State to American Embassy Paris, October 30, 1968, State 263693, Box 559, W. Averell Harriman Papers, Manuscript Division, Library of Congress.

10. Memorandum for Walt Rostow, "Presidential Views Concerning the Bombing Halt and the Paris Talks," October 29, 1968, Central Intelligence Agency, FOIA Request F-2019–25556.

11. Lyndon Baines Johnson, *The Vantage Point: Perspectives of the Presidency, 1963–1969* (New York: Holt, Rinehart and Winston, 1971), 524.

12. "The Negotiations for a Bombing Cessation," May 13–October 31, 1968, by Tom Charles Huston, June 1, 1971, p. 265, Box 114, White House Special Files, Staff Member Office Files, H. R. Haldeman, Richard M. Nixon Presidential Library.

13. Christian, *President Steps Down*, 97.

14. Office of the White House Press Secretary, Remarks of the President, October 31, 1968, Box 67, Harry McPherson Files, Lyndon B. Johnson Presidential Library.

15. Clifford with Holbrooke, *Counsel to the President*, 592–93.

16. Christian, *President Steps Down*, 107.

17. "The Negotiations for a Bombing Cessation," May 13–October 31, 1968, pp. 277–79.

18. Offner, *Hubert Humphrey*, 327.

19. William Safire, *Before the Fall: An Inside View of the Pre-Watergate White House* (Garden City, NY: Doubleday, 1975), 87.

20. Notes from November 1, 1968, Box 1, George Elsey's Notes of Secretary of Defense Clark Clifford's Morning Staff Conference, May 1968–January 1969.

21. Tom Wicker, *One of Us: Richard Nixon and the American Dream* (New York: Random House, 1991), 379–80.

22. Christian, *President Steps Down*, 100.

23. Memorandum for Walt Rostow, "Further Views of Vice President Ky on the Present Bombing Halt Negotiations," October 23, 1968, Central Intelligence Agency, FOIA Request F-2019–25556.

24. Nguyen Phu Duc, *The Viet-Nam Peace Negotiations: Saigon's Side of the Story*, edited by Arthur J. Dommen (Christiansburg, VA: Dalley Book Service, 2005), 159.

25. Arthur J. Dommen, *The Indochinese Experience of the French and the Americans: Nationalism and Communism in Cambodia, Laos, and Vietnam* (Bloomington: Indiana University Press, 2001), 693–94.

26. Nguyen, *Viet-Nam Peace Negotiations*, 162.

27. Dommen, *Indochinese Experience*, 695.

28. The figure used for Americans is from the Vietnam War U.S. Military Fatal Casualty Statistics maintained by the National Archives and Records Administration. For more information, see: www.archives.gov/research/military/ vietnam-war/casualty-statistics (accessed August 6, 2022). There are no authoritative Vietnamese figures, but for the entire period of 1954 to 1975 it is likely to be at least 2 million.

29. Nguyen, *Viet-Nam Peace Negotiations*, 116.

30. Letter from Ellsworth Bunker to Clark Clifford, July 7, 1969, Box 4, Ambassador Ellsworth Bunker's Subject Files, RG 84, Foreign Service Posts of the Department of State, National Archives and Records Administration.

31. Nguyen Cao Ky, *Twenty Years and Twenty Days* (New York: Stein and Day, 1976), 169.

32. Tran Ngoc Chau with Ken Fermoyle, *Vietnam Labyrinth: Allies, Enemies, and Why the U.S. Lost the War* (Lubbock: Texas Tech University Press, 2012), 328.

33. Hubert H. Humphrey, *The Education of a Public Man: My Life and Politics* (Garden City, NY: Doubleday, 1976), 354.

34. Christian, *President Steps Down*, 51.

35. Chester L. Cooper, *In the Shadows of History: Fifty Years behind the Scenes of Cold War Diplomacy* (Amherst, NY: Prometheus Books, 2005), 278.

36. Notes from November 4, 1968, Box 1, George Elsey's Notes of Secretary of Defense Clark Clifford's Morning Staff Conference, May 1968–January 1969.

37. Background to the October 31 Announcement, p. 90, Box 1 (Accession 2015-M-027), Cyrus R. and Grace Sloane Vance Papers, Manuscripts and Archives, Yale University Library, Yale University.

Chapter 14. Dragon Lady

1. David McKean, *Tommy the Cork: Washington's Ultimate Insider from Roosevelt to Reagan* (South Royalton, VT: Steerforth Press, 2004), 284.

2. Memorandum from the Director of the FBI to James M. McInerney, Assistant Attorney General, Criminal Division, Department of Justice, "Major

General Claire Chennault, Registration Act, China Lobby," July 23, 1951, FBI FOIA Request 1379638-000.

3. Memorandum from Special Agent in Charge, Washington Field Office, to the Director of the FBI, June, February 28, 1962, FBI FOIA Request 1372165-0.

4. George J. Veith, *Drawn Swords in a Distant Land: South Vietnam's Shattered Dreams* (New York: Encounter Books, 2021), 323–24.

5. Anna Chennault, *The Education of Anna* (New York: Times Books, 1980), 165.

6. Memorandum from David N. Laux to Robert C. McFarlane, "Request by Anna Chennault to Meet with the President," March 5, 1985, Box 5, David N. Laux Files, Ronald Reagan Presidential Library.

7. Memorandum from Robert C. McFarlane to Craig Fuller, "Anna Chennault's Request for Letters from the President to Chinese Leaders," January 18, 1985, Box 5, David N. Laux Files.

8. Catherine Forslund, *Anna Chennault: Informal Diplomacy and Asian Relations* (Wilmington, DE: SR Books, 2002), 47.

9. Letter from Hubert Humphrey to Anna Chennault, January 24, 1966, Box 38, Anna Chennault Papers, Schlesinger Library, Harvard University.

10. Memorandum from R. L. Bannerman to Richard Helms, "Anna Chennault," October 25, 1967, CIA Electronic Reading Room.

11. William Bundy, *A Tangled Web: The Making of Foreign Policy in the Nixon Presidency* (New York: Hill and Wang, 1998), 30.

12. Chennault, *Education of Anna*, 163.

13. Ibid., 164.

14. Jules Witcover, *The Year the Dream Died: Revisiting 1968 in America* (New York: Warner Books, 1997), 286.

15. Chennault, *Education of Anna*, 185.

16. Tape 4, Page 1, September 19, 1969, Box 26, Anna Chennault Papers, Schlesinger Library, Harvard University.

17. Forslund, *Anna Chennault*, 57–58; Letter from Richard Nixon to A. Chennault, December 2, 1968, Box 63, Anna Chennault Papers.

18. Letter from Anna Chennault to Richard Nixon, March 25, 1968, Box 11, Richard V. Allen Papers, Hoover Institution Library and Archives.

19. Theodore H. White, *The Making of the President, 1968* (New York: Atheneum Publishers, 1969), 444.

20. Author interview with Bui Diem, August 7, 2017, Rockville, MD.

21. Andrew L. Johns, *Vietnam's Second Front: Domestic Politics, the Republican Party, and the War* (Lexington: University Press of Kentucky, 2010), 230.

22. Bui Diem with David Chanoff, *In the Jaws of History* (Boston: Houghton Mifflin, 1987), 237.

23. Clark Clifford with Richard Holbrooke, *Counsel to the President: A Memoir* (New York: Random House, 1991), 581.

24. Letter from Anna Chennault to Richard Nixon, June 24, 1968, Box 11, Richard V. Allen Papers.

25. Memorandum from Shelley Scarney to Richard Nixon, May 6, 1968, Name Files, Wilderness Years, Richard M. Nixon Presidential Library; Memorandum from Pat Hitt to Richard Nixon, June 22, 1968, Name Files, Wilderness Years, Richard M. Nixon Presidential Library.

26. Chennault, *Education of Anna*, 175.

27. Witcover, *Year the Dream Died*, 409.

28. Telegram from American Embassy Paris to Secretary of State, July 28, 1968, Paris 18644, Box 561, W. Averell Harriman Papers, Manuscript Division, Library of Congress.

29. Chennault, *Education of Anna*, 175.

30. Letter from Anna Chennault to Bui Diem, January 7, 1985, Box 49, Anna Chennault Papers.

31. Tape 4, Page 3, September 19, 1969, Box 26, Anna Chennault Papers.

32. Letter from Anna Chennault to John J. Simon, May 17, 1979, Box 23, Anna Chennault Papers.

33. Nguyen Cao Ky, *Buddha's Child: My Fight to Save Vietnam* (New York: St. Martin's Press, 2002), 290.

34. Diem with Chanoff, *In the Jaws of History*, 245.

35. Witcover, *Year the Dream Died*, 442–43.

36. Richard Nixon, *RN: The Memoirs of Richard Nixon* (New York: Grosset & Dunlap, 1978), 325.

37. Letter from Anna Chennault to Richard Nixon, October 15, 1968, Box 32, William Safire Papers, Manuscript Division, Library of Congress.

38. Letter from Anna Chennault to Richard Nixon, October 15, 1968, Box 11, Richard V. Allen Papers.

39. Lewis Chester, Godfrey Hodgson, and Bruce Page, *An American Melodrama: The Presidential Campaign of 1968* (New York: Viking Press, 1969), 820; William Safire, *Before the Fall: An Inside View of the Pre-Watergate White House* (Garden City, NY: Doubleday, 1975), 90.

40. Memorandum for the File, Undated, Box 11, Richard V. Allen Papers.

41. Chennault, *Education of Anna*, 200–201.

42. Anna Chennault, "China Issue," enclosed with Letter from Anna Chennault to Robert Hartmann, June 1, 1976, Box 45, Robert T. Hartmann Files, Gerald R. Ford Presidential Library.

43. Stephen E. Ambrose, *Nixon, Volume Two: The Triumph of a Politician, 1962–1972* (New York: Simon & Schuster, 1989), 208.

44. Telephone Conversation #13587, October 23, 1968, 6:02 P.M., Recordings and Transcripts of Telephone Conversations and Meetings, Lyndon B. Johnson Presidential Library.

45. Oral History with Bryce Harlow, May 6, 1979, p. 58, Lyndon B. Johnson Presidential Library.

46. Witcover, *Year the Dream Died*, 401.

47. Nixon, *RN: The Memoirs*, 326.

48. Ambrose, *Nixon, Volume Two*, 208.

49. Nixon, *RN: The Memoirs*, 324.

50. Despite the attention paid to John A. Farrell's book when it was published in March 2017, it lacked a footnote identifying the Haldeman notes of October 22, 1968, in the discussion that begins on p. 342. The notes are located in Box 33, Folder 8, Nixon Presidential Returned Materials Collection, White House Special Files, Richard M. Nixon Presidential Library. When Farrell began the research that led to the book, he told the author during a conversation on October 4, 2012, in Washington, DC, about possible themes that he was looking for something "worse than Watergate," in part because the scandal seemed less and less serious with the passage of time; John A. Farrell, *Richard Nixon: The Life* (New York: Doubleday, 2017), 342–43. Farrell concludes: "The droves of variables forestall a conclusion that Nixon's meddling cost the United States an opportunity to end the war in the fall of 1968" (344). This more balanced conclusion has been overlooked by those who have used the book to argue that Nixon scuttled the Vietnam negotiations, obstructed peace, and was guilty of treason. The two most prominent pieces were John A. Farrell, "Nixon's Vietnam Treachery," *New York Times*, December 31, 2016; and Peter Baker, "Nixon Tried to Spoil Johnson's Peace Talks in '68, Notes Show," *New York Times*, January 2, 2017. Others used the timing of the book's publication in March 2017, starting shortly after the 2016 presidential election when galleys began to circulate, to argue it was reasonable to conclude that Donald Trump colluded with Russians to affect the outcome of the election, since Farrell's book proved it had been done before by Nixon and the South Vietnamese in 1968. Drawing a line from Nixon to Trump, who were friendly and the subject of many comparisons, allowed Farrell's book, which otherwise contained no new significant findings about Richard Nixon, to reach a much larger audience. Those convinced of Trump's meddling could explore its historical antecedents.

51. "RN 10/22 late," p. 1, HRH Handwritten Notes, Box 33, Folder 8, Nixon Presidential Returned Materials Collection, White House Special Files, Richard M. Nixon Presidential Library.

52. "RN 10/22 late," p. 2, HRH Handwritten Notes.

53. Ibid.

54. "RN 10/22 late," p. 3, HRH Handwritten Notes.

55. Michael A. Cohen, *American Maelstrom: The 1968 Election and the Politics of Division* (New York: Oxford University Press, 2016), 324.

56. Melvin Small, *The Presidency of Richard Nixon* (Lawrence: University Press of Kansas, 1999), 29.

57. Thomas Powers, *The Man Who Kept the Secrets: Richard Helms and the CIA* (New York: Alfred A. Knopf, 1979), 227.

58. Hoang Duc Nha, "Striving for a Lasting Peace: The Paris Accords and Aftermath," in Tuong Vu and Sean Fear, eds., *The Republic of Vietnam, 1955–1975: Vietnamese Perspectives on Nation Building* (Ithaca, NY: Cornell University Press, 2020), 60.

59. Beverly Deepe Keever, *Death Zones and Darling Spies: Seven Years of Vietnam War Reporting* (Lincoln: University of Nebraska Press, 2013), 223–24.

60. Author email interview with from Beverly Deepe Keever, January 22, 2019.

61. Diem with Chanoff, *In the Jaws of History*, 243–44.

62. Lyndon Baines Johnson, *The Vantage Point: Perspectives of the Presidency, 1963–1969* (New York: Holt, Rinehart and Winston, 1971), 521.

63. Memorandum from Eugene Rostow to Walt Rostow, October 29, 1968, Box 19, Files of Walt W. Rostow, National Security File, Lyndon B. Johnson Presidential Library.

64. Anthony Summers with Robbyn Swan, *The Arrogance of Power: The Secret World of Richard Nixon* (New York: Penguin Books, 2000), 301.

65. Clifford with Holbrooke, *Counsel to the President*, 583.

66. Powers, *Man Who Kept the Secrets*, 226–27.

67. Memorandum from Tom Charles Huston to Richard Nixon, February 25, 1970, Box 128, H. R. Haldeman Staff Member Office Files, White House Special Files, Richard M. Nixon Presidential Library.

68. Wilson C. Freeman, "The Logan Act: An Overview of a Sometimes Forgotten 18th Century Law," Congressional Research Service, January 12, 2018, p. 1–2.

69. For example, see the copies of her wiretapped communications contained in folders "Chennault, Anna—Reference File," "CHENNAULT ANNA—from folder 'South Vietnam and U.S. Policies' [1 of 2]," and "CHENNAULT ANNA—from folder 'South Vietnam and U.S. Policies' [2 of 2]," Box 19, Files of Walt W. Rostow, National Security File, Lyndon B. Johnson Presidential Library.

70. Telephone Conversation #13618, October 31, 1968, 6:05 P.M., Recordings and Transcripts of Telephone Conversations and Meetings, Lyndon B. Johnson Presidential Library.

71. Hoang, "Striving for a Lasting Peace," 60.

72. Letter from Richard Nixon to Jonathan Aitken, May 29, 1991, Box 10, Jonathan Aitken Collection, Post-Presidential Papers, Richard M. Nixon Presidential Library.

73. "Jan. 7, 1969, Tuesday Lunch," Box 11, Tom Johnson Notes of Meetings, Personal Papers of Tom Johnson, Lyndon B. Johnson Presidential Library.

74. For example, see Memorandum from Walt Rostow to Lyndon Johnson, October 31, 1968; Memorandum from Dean Rusk to Walt Rostow, "Presidential Views Concerning the Bombing Halt and the Paris Talks," October 29, 1968; and Memorandum from Dean Rusk to Walt Rostow, "President Thieu's Views Regarding the Issues Involved in Agreeing to a Bombing

Halt," October 26, 1968, Box 19, Files of Walt W. Rostow, National Security File, Lyndon B. Johnson Presidential Library.

75. Memorandum from Jim Jones to Lyndon Johnson, November 15, 1968, Box 6, James R. Jones Collection, Carl Albert Center, University of Oklahoma.

76. Correspondence related to her book, with publishers, with her literary agent, Morton Janklow, who ultimately ended his representation of her, and with her ghostwriter, Wendy Seagraves, with whom she ultimately had a dispute about factual content that appeared in the book, is located in Box 23, Anna Chennault Papers.

77. Theodore White Interview with William Bundy, January 5, 1969, Box 119, Theodore White Papers, Pusey Library, Harvard University.

78. Chennault, *Education of Anna*, 191.

79. Thomas A. Schwartz, *Henry Kissinger and American Power: A Political Biography* (New York: Hill and Wang, 2020), 60.

80. Lawrence Roberts, *Mayday 1971: A White House at War, a Revolt in the Streets, and the Untold History of America's Biggest Mass Arrest* (Boston: Houghton Mifflin Harcourt, 2020), 17.

81. Letter from William Bundy to Theodore White, September 10, 1969, Box 29, Theodore White Papers.

82. George Christian, *The President Steps Down: A Personal Memoir of the Transfer of Power* (New York: Macmillan, 1970), 94.

83. Nguyen Phu Duc, *The Viet-Nam Peace Negotiations: Saigon's Side of the Story*, edited by Arthur J. Dommen (Christiansburg, VA: Dalley Book Service, 2005), 166.

84. Cohen, *American Maelstrom*, 322.

85. Johnson, *Vantage Point*, 547–48.

86. Christian, *President Steps Down*, 94.

87. Clifford with Holbrooke, *Counsel to the President*, 583.

Chapter 15. Photo Finish

1. Carl Solberg, *Hubert Humphrey: A Biography* (New York: W. W. Norton, 1984), 398.

2. Edgar Berman, *Hubert: The Triumph and Tragedy of the Humphrey I Knew* (New York: G. P. Putnam's Sons, 1979), 166.

3. Solberg, *Hubert Humphrey*, 398.

4. "Jim Rowe—Terry Sanford, Oct. 18, 1968," Box 10, Tom Johnson Notes of Meetings, Personal Papers of Tom Johnson, Lyndon B. Johnson Presidential Library.

5. Berman, *Hubert*, 218.

6. George Christian, *The President Steps Down: A Personal Memoir of the Transfer of Power* (New York: Macmillan, 1970), 81.

7. Arnold A. Offner, *Hubert Humphrey: The Conscience of the Country* (New Haven: Yale University Press, 2018), 330.

8. James Reston Jr., *The Lone Star: The Life of John Connally* (New York: Harper & Row, 1989), 375.

9. Drew Pearson, *Washington Merry-Go-Round: The Drew Pearson Diaries, 1960–1969*, edited by Peter Hannaford (Lincoln, NE: Potomac Books, 2015), 622.

10. John Connally with Mickey Herskowitz, *In History's Shadow: An American Odyssey* (New York: Hyperion, 1993), 231–32.

11. Solberg, *Hubert Humphrey*, 400–401.

12. Richard Nixon, *RN: The Memoirs of Richard Nixon* (New York: Grosset & Dunlap, 1978), 320–21.

13. Ibid., 329.

14. Joe McGinniss, *The Selling of the President, 1968* (New York: Trident Press, 1969), 126.

15. Tom Wicker, "Nation Will Vote Today; Close Presidential Race Predicted in Late Polls," *New York Times*, November 5, 1968, p. 1.

16. Nixon, *RN: The Memoirs*, 330.

17. Patrick J. Buchanan, *The Greatest Comeback: How Richard Nixon Rose from Defeat to Create the New Majority* (New York: Crown Forum, 2014), 305.

18. Memorandum from Jim Jones to Lyndon Johnson, October 25, 1968, Box 6, James R. Jones Collection, Carl Albert Center, University of Oklahoma.

19. Jules Witcover, *The Resurrection of Richard Nixon* (New York: G. P. Putnam's Sons, 1970), 330.

20. Buchanan, *Greatest Comeback*, 360.

21. Ibid., 362–63.

22. Theodore H. White, *The Making of the President, 1968* (New York: Atheneum Publishers, 1969), 428.

23. Jules Witcover, *The Year the Dream Died: Revisiting 1968 in America* (New York: Warner Books, 1997), 388.

24. White, *Making of the President, 1968*, 430.

25. Offner, *Hubert Humphrey*, 334.

26. Ted Van Dyk, *Heroes, Hacks, and Fools: Memoirs from the Political Inside* (Seattle: University of Washington Press, 2007), 95.

27. Joseph Napolitan, *The Election Game and How to Win It* (Garden City, NY: Doubleday, 1972), 62.

28. George W. Ball, *The Past Has Another Pattern: Memoirs* (New York: W. W. Norton, 1982), 448.

29. Warren Weaver Jr., "Contest Tightens; G.O.P. Nominee Put Ahead in 30 States and His Rival in 8," *New York Times*, November 4, 1968, pp. 1, 36.

30. Solberg, *Hubert Humphrey*, 403–4.

31. White, *Making of the President, 1968*, 461.

32. Albert Eisele, *Almost to the Presidency: A Biography of Two American Politicians* (Blue Earth, MN: Piper, 1972), 392.

33. Nixon, *RN: The Memoirs*, 331.

34. Lady Bird Johnson, *A White House Diary* (New York: Holt, Rinehart and Winston, 1970), 732.

35. Tom Wicker, *One of Us: Richard Nixon and the American Dream* (New York: Random House, 1991), 374.

36. White, *Making of the President, 1968*, 461.

37. Solberg, *Hubert Humphrey*, 405–6.

38. Nixon, *RN: The Memoirs*, 332.

39. White, *Making of the President, 1968*, 457.

40. Dwight Chapin, *The President's Man: The Memoirs of Nixon's Trusted Aide* (New York: William Morrow, 2022), 84.

41. Raymond Price, *With Nixon* (New York: Viking Press, 1977), 36.

42. Nixon Diary, Notebook 15, VIP Notebooks, Records of the Billy Graham Evangelistic Association: Montreat Office, Billy Graham Archive and Research Center, Charlotte, NC.

43. Nancy Gibbs and Michael Duffy, *The Preacher and the Presidents: Billy Graham in the White House* (New York: Center Street, 2007), 170–71.

44. William Martin, *A Prophet with Honor: The Billy Graham Story* (New York: William Morrow, 1991), 360.

45. Nixon Diary, Notebook 15.

46. Billy Graham, *Just As I Am: The Autobiography of Billy Graham* (New York: HarperCollins, 1997), 449.

47. Price, *With Nixon*, 36.

48. Evan Thomas, *Being Nixon: A Man Divided* (New York: Random House, 2015), 186.

49. Nixon, *RN: The Memoirs*, 333.

50. Graham, *Just As I Am*, 449.

51. Martin, *Prophet with Honor*, 361.

52. Nixon, *RN: The Memoirs*, 334.

53. Nov. 6–11:30 [Nixon yellow pad notes], Box 98, PPS 208, Pre-Presidential Files, Richard M. Nixon Presidential Library.

54. Nixon, *RN: The Memoirs*, 334.

55. Hubert H. Humphrey, *The Education of a Public Man: My Life and Politics* (Garden City, NY: Doubleday, 1976), 3.

56. Berman, *Hubert*, 229.

57. Nixon, *RN: The Memoirs*, 334.

58. Melvin Small, *The Presidency of Richard Nixon* (Lawrence: University Press of Kansas, 1999), 30.

59. Mary C. Brennan, *Turning Right in the Sixties: The Conservative Capture of the GOP* (Chapel Hill: University of North Carolina Press, 1995), 133.

60. Richard M. Scammon and Ben J. Wattenberg, *The Real Majority* (New York: Coward-McCann, 1970), 178.

61. Peter Baker, "White House Memo: Trump May Compare Himself to Nixon in 1968, but He Really Resembles Wallace," *New York Times*, June 9, 2020, A18.

62. Kari Frederickson, *The Dixiecrat Revolt and the End of the Solid South, 1932–1968* (Chapel Hill: University of North Carolina Press, 2001), 238.

63. David S. Broder, "Election of 1968," in Arthur M. Schlesinger Jr., ed., *History of American Presidential Elections, 1789–1968*, vol. 4 (New York: McGraw-Hill, 1971), 3751.

64. Pearson, *Washington Merry-Go-Round*, 630.

65. Humphrey, *Education of a Public Man*, 13.

66. Melvin Small, "The Election of 1968," in Melvin Small, ed., *A Companion to Richard M. Nixon* (Malden, MA: Blackwell Publishing, 2011), 159–60.

67. Lady Bird Johnson, *White House Diary*, 732.

68. Christian, *President Steps Down*, 110.

69. Solberg, *Hubert Humphrey*, 407.

70. Offner, *Hubert Humphrey*, 335.

71. White, *Making of the President, 1968*, 462.

72. G. Scott Thomas, *Counting the Votes: A New Way to Analyze America's Presidential Elections* (Santa Barbara, CA: Praeger, 2015), 223.

73. White, *Making of the President, 1968*, 464.

74. Lewis L. Gould, *Grand Old Party: A History of the Republicans* (New York: Random House, 2003), 379.

75. Robert Mason, *Richard Nixon and the Quest for a New Majority* (Chapel Hill: University of North Carolina Press, 2004), 35.

76. Timothy N. Thurber, *Republicans and Race: The GOP's Frayed Relationship with African Americans, 1945–1974* (Lawrence: University Press of Kansas, 2013), 280.

77. Offner, *Hubert Humphrey*, 335.

78. White, *Making of the President, 1968*, 430.

79. Kevin P. Phillips, *The Emerging Republican Majority* (New Rochelle, NY: Arlington House, 1969), 33–34.

80. Robert Mann, *A Grand Delusion: America's Descent into Vietnam* (New York: Basic Books, 2001), 624.

81. Buchanan, *Greatest Comeback*, 365.

82. White, *Making of the President, 1968*, 465.

83. Michael A. Cohen, *American Maelstrom: The 1968 Election and the Politics of Division* (New York: Oxford University Press, 2016), 11.

84. White, *Making of the President, 1968*, 430–31.

85. Scammon and Wattenberg, *Real Majority*, 146.

86. White, *Making of the President, 1968*, 466–67.

87. Cohen, *American Maelstrom*, 7.

Epilogue

1. Lyndon Baines Johnson, *The Vantage Point: Perspectives of the Presidency, 1963–1969* (New York: Holt, Rinehart and Winston, 1971), 579–80, 591.

2. Ibid., 529.

3. Notes from November 17, 1968, Box 1, George Elsey's Notes of Secretary of Defense Clark Clifford's Morning Staff Conference, May 1968–January 1969, George Elsey Papers, Lyndon B. Johnson Presidential Library.
4. Pierre Asselin, *Vietnam's American War: A History* (New York: Cambridge University Press, 2018), 170–71.
5. Johnson, *Vantage Point*, 509.
6. George Christian, *The President Steps Down: A Personal Memoir of the Transfer of Power* (New York: Macmillan, 1970), 112.
7. Johnson, *Vantage Point*, 510.
8. Clark Clifford with Richard Holbrooke, *Counsel to the President: A Memoir* (New York: Random House, 1991), 551.
9. Johnson, *Vantage Point*, 548.
10. Arnold A. Offner, *Hubert Humphrey: The Conscience of the Country* (New Haven: Yale University Press, 2018), 324.
11. Ibid., 326.
12. Kate Andersen Brower, *First in Line: Presidents, Vice Presidents, and the Pursuit of Power* (New York: Harper, 2018), 146–47.
13. Brian VanDeMark, *Road to Disaster: A New History of America's Descent into Vietnam* (New York: Custom House, 2018), 496.
14. "Aboard Air Force One, April 1, 1968," Box 9, Tom Johnson Notes of Meetings, Personal Papers of Tom Johnson, Lyndon B. Johnson Presidential Library.
15. George McKee Elsey, *An Unplanned Life* (Columbia: University of Missouri Press, 2005), 241.
16. Leslie H. Southwick, ed., *Presidential Also-Rans and Running Mates, 1788 through 1996*, volume 2, *1892–1996*, 2nd edition (Jefferson, NC: McFarland, Publishers, 2008), 680.
17. Edgar Berman, *Hubert: The Triumph and Tragedy of the Humphrey I Knew* (New York: G. P. Putnam's Sons, 1979), 86.
18. Christian, *President Steps Down*, 133.
19. Johnson, *Vantage Point*, 553.
20. Nancy Gibbs and Michael Duffy, *The President's Club: Inside the World's Most Exclusive Fraternity* (New York: Simon & Schuster, 2012), 268.
21. Richard J. Whalen, *Catch the Falling Flag: A Republican's Challenge to His Party* (Boston: Houghton Mifflin, 1972), 184–85.
22. Johnson, *Vantage Point*, 555–56.
23. Luke A. Nichter, *The Last Brahmin: Henry Cabot Lodge Jr. and the Making of the Cold War* (New Haven: Yale University Press, 2020), 316; Christian, *President Steps Down*, 121.
24. Notes of the President's Meeting with the President-Elect Richard Nixon, November 11, 1968, Box 4, Tom Johnson Notes of Meetings, Personal Papers of Tom Johnson, Lyndon B. Johnson Presidential Library.

25. Lady Bird Johnson, *A White House Diary* (New York: Holt, Rinehart and Winston, 1970), 733.
26. John Helgerson, "Intelligence Support for Richard M. Nixon: A Difficult Relationship," *Studies in Intelligence* 39, no. 4 (1995): 104.
27. Johnson, *Vantage Point*, 556.
28. Lady Bird Johnson, *White House Diary*, 733.
29. Richard Nixon, *RN: The Memoirs of Richard Nixon* (New York: Grosset & Dunlap, 1978), 336.
30. Ibid., 337.
31. Ibid.
32. Johnson, *Vantage Point*, 556–57.
33. Christian, *President Steps Down*, 124.
34. Johnson, *Vantage Point*, 556–57.
35. Bill Gulley with Mary Ellen Reese, *Breaking Cover* (New York: Simon & Schuster, 1980), 104.
36. Johnson, *Vantage Point*, 558–59.
37. Gulley with Reese, *Breaking Cover*, 10
38. Lady Bird Johnson, *White House Diary*, 734.
39. Robert Dallek, *Flawed Giant: Lyndon Johnson and His Times, 1961–1973* (New York: Oxford University Press, 1998), 593.
40. Johnson, *Vantage Point*, 559.
41. Nixon, *RN: The Memoirs*, 754.
42. Lady Bird Johnson, *White House Diary*, 771.
43. Gulley with Reese, *Breaking Cover*, 104.
44. Johnson, *Vantage Point*, 567.
45. Lady Bird Johnson, *White House Diary*, 781–82.
46. Nixon Diary, Notebook 15, VIP Notebooks, Records of the Billy Graham Evangelistic Association: Montreat Office, Billy Graham Archive and Research Center, Charlotte, NC.
47. Johnson, *Vantage Point*, 569.
48. Nixon Diary, Notebook 15.

Appendix

1. H. R. "Bob" Haldeman's notes from "10/22"—October 22, 1968—can be accessed here: www.nixonlibrary.gov/sites/default/files/virtuallibrary/documents/whsfreturned/WHSF_Box_33/WHSF33-08.pdf. The relevant portion discussed here appears on pages 7–10.
2. John A. Farrell, *Richard Nixon: The Life* (New York: Doubleday, 2017), 344. The relevant discussion takes place on pages 342–44.
3. John A. Farrell, "Nixon's Vietnam Treachery," *New York Times*, December 31, 2016.

4. Peter Baker, "Nixon Tried to Spoil Johnson's Peace Talks in '68, Notes Show," *New York Times*, January 2, 2017.

5. "RN 10/22 late," p. 1, HRH Handwritten Notes, Box 33, Folder 8, Nixon Presidential Returned Materials Collection, White House Special Files, Richard M. Nixon Presidential Library.

6. Ibid., 2.

7. Ibid.

8. Ibid., 3.

Bibliography

1. The ground rules for the communication with Prime Minister Khiem were on background and through mutual intermediaries. Therefore, his reflections are included in this manuscript but are not cited.

Bibliography

Archival Sources

Alabama Department of Archives and History—Montgomery, AL
    Ed Ewing Papers
        1968 Presidential Campaign, 1967–68
        Oral History Collection
    Seymore Trammell Unpublished Prison Memoir
    George C. Wallace Collection
        Series I: Administrative Files
            B. 1960–69
        Series IV: Photographs, 1897–1986
Archive of Foreign Policy of the Russian Federation [Архива внешней политики
    Российской Федерации]—Moscow, Russia
    Fond (Ф.)
        Information on the USA (Ф. 129)
Arizona State University Libraries—Tempe, Arizona
    Arizona Collection
        Personal and Political Papers of Senator Barry M. Goldwater
            Series I: Personal
                Sub-Series F: Correspondence
Association for Diplomatic Studies and Training—Arlington, VA
    Foreign Affairs Oral History Collection
Baylor University—Waco, Texas
    University Libraries
        Texas Collection
            Leon Jaworski Papers
        Institute for Oral History
Billy Graham Archive and Research Center—Charlotte, NC

Records of the Billy Graham Evangelistic Association
    VIP Notebooks, 1946–2015 (Collection 685)
        Series I
            Notebook 6: Johnson I
            Notebook 9: Humphrey
            Notebook 10: Nixon I
            Notebook 14: Nixon V
            Notebook 15: Nixon Diary
            Notebook 24: Reagan I
George Bush Presidential Library—College Station, TX
    Presidential Records
        Alphabetical File
        Name File
        Subject File
            Gifts to the President
            Messages
                Sent to Groups/Organizations
            Office of Personnel
                Presidential Appointment Files—Priority Resume Files
    Vice Presidential Records
        Chief of Staff
            David Q. Bates Files
                Event Files
        Office of Operations, Administration, and Staff Secretary
            Thomas J. Collamore Files
                Personnel Files
        Office of Policy
            Subject Files
        Subject File
Central Intelligence Agency—Washington, DC
    Electronic Reading Room
        President's Daily Brief (1968)
Duke University—Durham, NC
    David M. Rubenstein Rare Book and Manuscript Library
        Clyde Roark Hoey Papers
            Correspondence, 1943–54
Dwight D. Eisenhower Presidential Library—Abilene, KS
    Dwight D. Eisenhower Papers
        Post-Presidential Papers, 1961–69
            1967 Principal File
            1968 Principal File
            Augusta-Walter Reed Series

Secretary's Series
Special Names
Gerald R. Ford Presidential Library—Ann Arbor, MI
Counsellors to the President
Robert T. Hartmann Files
General Correspondence
Gerald R. Ford Papers
National Security Adviser
Kissinger-Scowcroft West Wing Office Files, 1969–77
National Security Council
Vietnam Information Group
Intelligence and Other Reports, 1967–75
Saigon Embassy Files Kept by Ambassador Graham Martin
Gerald and Betty Ford Special Materials, 1941–2007
Gerald Ford Special Letters, 1956–2006
Condolence Letters Written to Betty Ford, 2006–7
Personal Papers
Melvin Laird Papers
Congressional Papers
Baroody Subject File
Campaign, 1968
Roy Wetzel Papers
Presidential Administrations File, 1963–98
Presidential Elections File, 1952–2004
Press Secretary's Office
Press Secretary to the President
Ronald H. Nessen Files
Press Secretary to the President Files
Press Secretary's Press Briefings
Public Liaison Office
Theodore C. Marrs Files
General Subject File
Ethnic Affairs
White House Central File
Name File
Subject File
George Washington University—Washington, DC
Gelman Library System
Special Collections Research Center
Jack Anderson Papers
Merry-Go-Round Columns
Other Anderson Publications

Georgetown University—Washington, DC
    Georgetown University Library
        Booth Family Center for Special Collections
           Richard M. Helms Papers I
                Correspondence with Individuals
Harvard University—Cambridge, MA
    Pusey Library
        Theodore White Papers
           Correspondence
           The Making of the President, 1968
                Interview Notebooks
                Notes and Interviews: Chapter 11
    Schlesinger Library
        Anna Chennault Papers
           Articles and Clippings
           Correspondence
                House of Representatives
                Name File
                Publicity and Contracts
                VIPs
           Daily Calendars
           Interviews and Television Appearances
           Press Correspondence
           Speeches
           Vietnam
Hoover Institution—Stanford, CA
    Library and Archives
        Richard V. Allen Papers
           Campaign and Transition Files, 1967–84
           Correspondence, 1962–87
           Speeches and Writings, 1961–99
        Stanley Karnow Papers
           Subject File, 1952–85
        Robert Charles Mardian Papers
           Department of Justice, 1967–78
        Robert D. Murphy Papers
           Biographical File, 1913–71
           Later Years, 1959–78
        Richard Nixon Campaign Notes
John F. Kennedy Presidential Library—Boston, MA
    Burke Marshall Personal Papers
    Lawrence F. O'Brien Personal Papers
        Series 4. 1968 Presidential Campaigns
        Series 5.5. Subject Files

Library of Congress—Washington, DC
    Asian Division
        Southeast Asian Collection
    Manuscript Division
        Papers of Thomas G. Corcoran
            General Correspondence, 1927–82
            Subject File, 1915–82
        Papers of W. Averell Harriman
            Subject File, 1906–54
            Special Files: Public Service, 1918–86
                Kennedy-Johnson Administrations, 1958–71
                    Subject File
                    Trips and Missions
                    Chronological File
                    Memoranda of Conversations
            Speeches and Statements, 1920–83
            Addition I
                Special Files
                Public Service
            Addition II
                Family Papers, 1891–1986
                Special Files
                    Public Service
                      Kennedy/Johnson Administrations, 1959–71
                      Postgovernment, 1901–88
        Papers of Curtis LeMay
            Campaign Papers, 1968–69
        Papers of Henry Luce
            Special Correspondence, 1935–67
        Papers of William Safire
            Public Relations File, 1953–69
            White House File, 1963–77
                Office File, 1968–73
                Officials, Staff, and Advisors, 1963–75
            Writings, 1962–80
        Paper of Neil Sheehan
            Vann-Sheehan Vietnam War Collection
                Research File, ca. 1920–91
                Individuals, 1957–91
    Microform Reader Services
    Serial and Government Publication Division
        Newspapers and Current Periodicals

Lyndon B. Johnson Presidential Library—Austin, TX
    Lady Bird White House Diary
    National Advisory Commission on Civil Disorders (Kerner Commission)
        Series I: Transcripts and Agendas of Hearings
    Oral Histories
        Joseph Alsop (Interview I)
        Keyes Beech (Interview II)
        Peter Braestrup (Interview I)
        William Bundy (Interview III)
        Ray S. Cline (Interview I)
        William J. Connell (Interview I)
        Cartha D. "Deke" DeLoach (Interview I)
        Robert Finch (Interview I)
        Mike Geissinger (Interview I)
        David Ginsburg (Interview II)
        Robert N. Ginsburgh (Interview I)
        Billy Graham (Special Interview)
        Bryce Harlow (Interview II)
        Lady Bird Johnson (Interview XXXII)
        Lyndon Johnson
        James R. Jones (Interview III)
        Arthur B. Krim (Interview V)
        Lawrence F. O'Brien (Interview XXVI)
        Benjamin H. Read (Interview II)
        John P. Roche (Interview I)
        James H. Rowe (Interview IV)
        Dean Rusk (Interview II)
        Robert E. Short (Interview I)
    Personal Papers
        Clark Clifford
            Vietnam Files
                Paris Negotiations—1968
        John Connally
            Democratic National Committee, 1968
        Democratic National Committee
            Series I
        George M. Elsey
            Notes of Secretary of Defense Clark Clifford's Morning Staff
                Conferences, May 1968—January 1969
        Curtis B. Gans
        Tom Johnson
            Notes of Meetings
        John W. "Jack" McNulty
        Drew Pearson

Papers of Lyndon Baines Johnson
    National Security File
        Country File
            Vietnam
        Files of Walt W. Rostow
        Head of State Correspondence
        Intelligence Briefings
        International Meetings
        Memos to the President
        Name File
        Special Head of State Correspondence
    Office Files of the White House Aides
        Joseph Califano
        James R. Jones
        Charles Maguire
        Harry McPherson
        Fred Panzer
        Ben Wattenberg
    Post-Presidential Papers
        Name File
        Ranch Files
    President's Daily Diary Collection
    Recordings and Transcripts of Telephone Conversations and Meetings
    Reminiscences of Lyndon B. Johnson
    Statements of Lyndon Baines Johnson
    White House Central Files
        Name File
        Speeches
        Subject File
    White House Confidential Files
Minnesota Historical Society—St. Paul, MN
    Hubert H. Humphrey Papers
        1968 Campaign
            Bill Connell Undated Notes
            Correspondence
                Coded Files
                Subject Files, 1968
            Democratic National Committee
                Lawrence O'Brien
                    Files, Correspondence, and Miscellaneous
            Democratic National Convention
            Personal Political Files
        Vice Presidential Files, 1965–68
            Trip Files
                Asia, 1967

National Archives Center II (Trung tâm lưu trữ quốc gia II)—Ho Chi Minh City,
    Vietnam
    Office of the President (Phòng Phủ Tổng thống Đệ nhất Cộng hòa)
        Activities of the President
        Foreign Affairs
        Organization
    Office of the Prime Minister, 1954–75 (Phòng Phủ Thủ tướng Việt Nam
        Cộng hòa)
        Activities of the Prime Minister
National Archives and Records Administration—College Park, MD
    Record Group 43: International Conferences, Commissions, and Expositions
        Paris Meetings on Vietnam
            Memorandums
            Plenary Session Files
            Subject Files
            Telegram Files
        Vietnam-U.S. Official Conversations
    Record Group 59: State Department
        Central Foreign Policy Files, 1967–69
            Political and Defense
                POL 7 US/HUMPHREY
                POL 7 US/LODGE
                POL 7 US/NIXON
        Files of Ambassador At Large Averell Harriman, 1967–68
        Office of the Executive Secretariat
            Paris Peace Conference Telegrams and Special Caption Messages,
                1966–72
                Todel Chrons
                Delto Chrons
        Office of the Secretary
            Executive Secretariat
                Conference Files, 1949–1972
                    Vice President's Asian Trip, October–November 1967
        Records of Ellsworth Bunker
        Records of Secretary of State Dean Rusk
            Speeches and Statements by the Secretary of State, 1961–69
            Transcripts and Telephone Calls, 1961–69
            White House Correspondence, 1961–69
        Subject Files of the Office of Vietnam Affairs (Vietnam Working Group),
            1964–74
    Record Group 65: Records of the Federal Bureau of Investigation
        Office of the Director, J. Edgar Hoover
            Official and Confidential Subject Files, 1924–72

Record Group 84: Records of the Foreign Service Posts
    U.S. Embassy—Saigon, Vietnam
        Files of Ambassador Ellsworth Bunker
            HARVAN Double Plus Telegrams
            Messages from Bunker in Saigon to the President
            Telegrams
            Working Files
      Unclassified Central Subject Files, 1964–71
        Embassy Saigon
National Law Enforcement Museum Foundation—Washington, DC
    Society of Former Special Agents of the FBI Oral History
        Cartha D. "Deke" DeLoach
Richard M. Nixon Presidential Library—Yorba Linda, CA
    National Security Council Files
        Henry A. Kissinger Office Files
            HAK Administrative and Staff Files—Transition
        For the President's Files—China/Vietnam Negotiations
        Name Files
        Paris Talks/Meetings
        Presidential/HAK MemCons
        President's Daily Briefs
        Vietnam Subject Files
    Personal Papers
        Thomas W. Evans
            Law Firm Oral Histories
                John Ehrlichman
                John Mitchell
                Richard Nixon
                Milton Rose
                Maurice Stans
                Rosemary Woods
    Oral Histories
        Richard Allen
        Dwight Chapin
        Deke DeLoach
        H. R. Haldeman
        Tom Charles Huston
        Raymond Price
    Returned Materials
        White House Central Files
            Martin Anderson
            Len Garment
                1968 Political Campaign File

Richard M. Nixon Pre-Presidential Papers
　　1968 Campaign
　　　　John C. Whitaker's Files
　　　　Research File
　　　　　　Special Files
　　Schedules and Appointment Books
　　Special Files
　　Speech File
　　Vice President
　　　　Country Files (Cushman Files)
　　　　General Correspondence
　　Wilderness Years
　　　　Name Files
Richard M. Nixon Post-Presidential Papers
　　Jonathan Aitken Collection
　　Post-Presidential Correspondence
　　　　Billy Graham
White House Central Files
　　Staff Member Office Files
　　　　Martin Anderson
　　　　Bryce N. Harlow
　　　　　　Memorandums
　　　　　　Public Correspondence
White House Special Files
　　Nixon Presidential Returned Materials Collection
　　President's Personal File
　　Staff Member Office Files
　　　　John D. Ehrlichman
　　　　　　Notes of Meetings with the President
　　　　H. R. Haldeman
　　　　　　Alpha Subject Files
　　　　　　Personal Files
　　　　　　Politics
Princeton University—Princeton, NJ
　　Seeley G. Mudd Manuscript Library
　　　　George W. Ball Papers
　　　　　　Series 1, Correspondence
　　　　　　Series 4, Public Statements
Ronald Reagan Presidential Library—Simi Valley, CA
　　David N. Laux files
Franklin D. Roosevelt Presidential Library—Hyde Park, NY
　　Alexander Sachs Papers
　　　　Chronological File
　　　　　　September 1968

        October 1968
        November 1968
Russian State Archive of Contemporary History [Российский Государственный Архив Новейшей Истории]—Moscow, Russia
    Fond (Ф.)
        Central Committee of the Communist Party of the Soviet Union (Ф. 5)
        Leonid Brezhnev Personal Files (Ф. 80)
Texas A&M University-Central Texas—Killeen, TX
    Central Texas Historical Archive
        Fritz and Sven Kraemer Papers
Texas Tech University—Lubbock, TX
    Southwest Collection/Special Collections Library
        Vietnam Center and Archive
            Chinh Luan
            Cong Bao VNCH
            Vietnam Bulletin
University of Georgia—Athens, GA
    Special Collections Libraries
        Walter J. Brown Media Archives and Peabody Awards Collection
        Richard Nixon/Frank Gannon Interviews
University of Kentucky—Lexington, KY
    University of Kentucky Libraries
        Louie B. Nunn Center for Oral History
        Bess Abell Oral History Project
University of Massachusetts—Boston, MA
    University Archives and Special Collections
        WGBH Educational Foundation Vietnam Project
        Interview Transcripts
University of Michigan—Ann Arbor, MI
    Bentley Historical Library
        George Romney Papers
        Sound Recordings
University of North Texas—Denton, TX
    University Libraries
        Oral History Collection
University of Oklahoma—Norman, OK
    Carl Albert Center
        James R. Jones Collection
        White House Records, 1965–69
University of Virginia—Charlottesville, VA
    Miller Center of Public Affairs
        Scripps Library
        Presidential Oral Histories
University of Southern California—Los Angeles, CA

USC Libraries Special Collections
    Herbert G. Klein Papers
        Richard Nixon's 1968 Presidential Campaign and Election
University of Texas—Austin, TX
    Dolph Briscoe Center for American History
        Ramsey Clark Papers, 1945–2015
            Legal Case Files Series
            Manuscript Series
        Walter Cronkite Papers, 1932–2010
        Richard N. Goodwin and Doris Kearns Goodwin Papers
WGBH Media Library and Archives—Boston, MA
    Vietnam Collection
        Vietnam: A Television History, America's Mandarin (1954–63)
            Interviews
Yale University—New Haven, CT
    Yale University Library
        Manuscripts and Archives
            Henry A. Kissinger Papers, Part II
                Series I. Early Career and Harvard University
                    Professional Files
                        Harvard University
                            Defense Studies Program
                                Administration
                                Government 259
                    Writings
                        Writings by Others
                Series II. Government Service
                    Correspondence
                        State Department Personal File
                        White House Personal File
                    Subject Files
                Series V. Photographs
                    Albums
                Series VI. Press Clippings
                    Chronological
                    Scrapbooks
                    Subject
            Henry A. Kissinger Papers, Part III
                Series III. Post-Government Career
                    Speeches and Writings
                        General
                Series IV. Telephone Conversation Transcript Copies
            Cyrus R. and Grace Sloane Vance Papers
                Series I: Government Service Papers

Kennedy and Johnson Presidential Administrations, 1960–77
Series III: Papers on Professional and Personal Activities,
1957–92
Series Accession 1996-M-152
Additional Material, 1946–93
Series Accession 2015-M-027
Additional Material, 1950–83

Original Interviews, Conversations, and Correspondence

President Lyndon B. Johnson / Johnson Administration

Joseph Califano	June 27, 2018—New York
Nash Castro	December 19, 2017—Williamsburg, VA, and email
Daniel I. Davidson	October 16, 2017—Washington, DC, and email
James Dobbins	October 18, 2017—Arlington, VA, and email
David Engel	November 25, 2017—email
Leslie Gelb	October 16, 2018—New York
Morton Halperin	August 23, 2017—Austin, TX, and email
Charles Hill	April 12, 2017—New Haven, CT, and email
Luci Baines Johnson	August 22, 2018—Austin, TX, and email
Tom Johnson	January 23, 2019—Atlanta, GA, and email
James R. Jones	October 17, 2017—Washington, DC, and email
Sergei Khrushchev	December 15, 2017, telephone
Richard Keiser	December 18, 2017—Williamsburg, VA, and email
Sven Kraemer	December 4, 2019—Washington, DC, and email
Walter J. McIntosh	December 11, 2017—email
Bill Moyers	May 8, 2017—email
John Negroponte	October 18, 2017—Washington, DC, and email
Merle Pribbenow	April 21, 2017—email
Robert Pursley	June 26, 2017—Stamford, CT
Lynda Johnson Robb	July 8–9, 2018—telephone
Peter Swiers	December 18, 2017—Williamsburg, VA, and email
Larry Temple	December 20, 2017—Austin, TX, and email
Mark K. Updegrove	May 8, 2019—Austin, TX
Katherine Westmoreland	December 30, 2017—Charleston, SC
Frank Wisner II	June 4, 2018—telephone and email
Steve Young	June 7, 2018—St. Paul, MN, and email

Vice President Hubert H. Humphrey / Humphrey Campaign

William Connell	November 11, 2017—email
Vic Fingerhut	January 29, 2021—telephone and email
Don and Arvonne Fraser	December 7, 2017—Minneapolis, MN, and email

Ken and Patricia Gray   July 3, 2018—telephone and email
Fred Harris   December 15, 2017—telephone and email
William Howard   December 7, 2017—Golden Valley, MN, and email
Thomas L. Hughes   August 5, 2017—Chevy Chase, MD, and telephone
Hubert H. Humphrey III   December 7, 2017—Golden Valley, MN
Walter Mondale   December 8, 2017—Minneapolis, MN
Rufus Phillips   March 18, 2017—Arlington, VA, and email
John Rielly   December 15, 2017—telephone and email
Norman Sherman   October 28, 2017—email
John Stewart   November 8, 2017—telephone and email
Ted Van Dyk   November 13, 2017—telephone and email

Former Vice President Richard Nixon / Nixon Campaign

Richard Allen   February 10, 2017—Yorba Linda, CA, and email
Pat Buchanan   November 8, 2018—Washington, DC, and telephone
Dwight Chapin   June 24, 2018—Riverside, CT, and email
Anna Chennault   April 25, 2017—Washington, DC
Edward Cox   October 15, 2018—New York
Tricia Nixon Cox   November 16, 2017—Washington, DC
David Eisenhower   July 22, 2017—telephone and email
Julie Nixon Eisenhower   November 7, 2018—Washington, DC
Alan Greenspan   June 11, 2018—email
Tom Charles Huston   November 22, 2017—Carmel, IN, and email
Kenneth Khachigian   September 5, 2018—San Clemente, CA, and telephone
Henry A. Kissinger   June 27, 2018—New York
Tom Korologos   December 2, 2019—Washington, DC, and email
Edward C. Nixon   October 14, 2016—Newport Beach, CA
John Price   December 12, 2018—Yorba Linda, CA, and email
Ray Price   May 29, 2018—telephone and email
Richard "Sandy" Quinn   September 5, 2018—Orange, CA, and telephone
John Sears   October 16, 2017—telephone

Governor George Wallace / Wallace Campaign

David Azbell   June 8, 2021—Montgomery, AL, and email
William "Billy" Joe Camp   January 31, 2019—telephone and email
John Paul DeCarlo   February 6, 2019—telephone
George "Ed" Ewing   January 25, 2019—Wetumpka, AL, and telephone
Joe Fine   March 14, 2019—telephone and email
Peggy Wallace Kennedy   June 10, 2021—Montgomery, AL, and email
  and Mark Kennedy

Alva Hugh Maddox	February 1, 2019—telephone and email
Charlie Snider	October 2, 2019—email
Tom and Judy Turnipseed	February 8, 2019—email
Cliff Wallace	December 16, 2020—telephone and email
George C. Wallace Jr.	June 8, 2021—Montgomery, AL, and email

Vietnamese

Bui Diem	August 7, 2017—Rockville, MD, and telephone
Hoang Duc Nha	May 22, 2017—Chicago, IL, and email
Tran Thien Khiem[1]	

Journalists

Peter Arnett	January 26, 2018—email
Marvin Kalb	January 28, 2020—Washington, DC, and email
Beverly Deepe Keever	January 22, 2019—email
Hedrick Smith	October 21, 2017—email
Evan Thomas	May 31, 2019—Washington, DC, and email

Books, Articles, and Other Resources

Abrams, Creighton. *Vietnam Chronicles: The Abrams Tapes, 1968–1972.* Edited by Lewis Sorley. Lubbock: Texas Tech University Press, 2004.

Abramson, Rudy. *Spanning the Century: The Life of W. Averell Harriman, 1891–1986.* New York: William Morrow, 1992.

Algeo, Matthew. *All This Marvelous Potential: Robert Kennedy's 1968 Tour of Appalachia.* Chicago: Chicago Review Press, 2020.

Alonso, Karen. *The Chicago Seven Political Protest Trial: A Headline Court Case.* Berkeley Heights, NJ: Enslow Publishers, 2002.

Ambrose, Matthew J. *The Control Agenda: A History of the Strategic Arms Limitation Talks.* Ithaca, NY: Cornell University Press, 2018.

Ambrose, Stephen E. *Nixon, Volume One: The Education of a Politician, 1913–1962.* New York: Simon & Schuster, 1987.

———. *Nixon, Volume Two: The Triumph of a Politician, 1962–1972.* New York: Simon & Schuster, 1989.

———. *Nixon, Volume Three: Ruin and Recovery, 1973–1990.* New York: Simon & Schuster, 1991.

Anderson, Martin. *The Federal Bulldozer: A Critical Analysis of Urban Renewal, 1949–1962.* Cambridge, MA: MIT Press, 1964.

Andrew, Christopher. *For the President's Eyes Only: Secret Intelligence and the American Presidency from Washington to Bush.* New York: HarperCollins Publishers, 1995.

Arnett, Peter. *Live from the Battlefield: From Vietnam to Baghdad, 35 Years in the World's War Zones.* New York: Simon & Schuster, 1994.

Asselin, Pierre. "Forgotten Front: The NLF in Hanoi's Diplomatic Struggle, 1965–1967." *Diplomatic History* 45, no. 2 (2021): 330–55.

———. *Vietnam's American War: A History.* New York: Cambridge University Press, 2018.

Baker, Bobby. *Wheeling and Dealing: Confessions of a Capitol Hill Operator.* New York: W. W. Norton, 1978.

Ball, George W. *The Past Has Another Pattern: Memoirs.* New York: W. W. Norton, 1982.

Barrett, David M. *Uncertain Warriors: Lyndon Johnson and His Vietnam Advisers.* Lawrence: University Press of Kansas, 1993.

Berger, Raoul. *The Fourteenth Amendment and the Bill of Rights.* Norman: University of Oklahoma Press, 1989.

Berman, Edgar. *Hubert: The Triumph and Tragedy of the Humphrey I Knew.* New York: G. P. Putnam's Sons, 1979.

Berman, Larry. *Lyndon Johnson's War: The Road to Stalemate in Vietnam.* New York: W. W. Norton, 1989.

Bernstein, Irving. *Guns or Butter: The Presidency of Lyndon Johnson.* New York: Oxford University Press, 1996.

Bloom, Alexander, and Wini Breines, eds. *Takin' It to the Streets: A Sixties Reader.* New York: Oxford University Press, 1995.

Blumenthal, Seth. *Children of the Silent Majority: Young Voters and the Rise of the Republican Party, 1968–1980.* Lawrence: University Press of Kansas, 2018.

Boot, Max. *The Road Not Taken: Edward Lansdale and the American Tragedy in Vietnam.* New York: Liveright Publishing, 2018.

Bowden, Mark. *Hue 1968: A Turning Point of the American War in Vietnam.* New York: Atlantic Monthly Press, 2017.

Bradlee, Ben. *A Good Life: Newspapering and Other Adventures.* New York: Simon & Schuster, 1995.

Braestrup, Peter. *Big Story: How the American Press and Television Reported and Interpreted the Crisis of Tet 1968 in Vietnam and Washington.* Vols. 1 and 2. Boulder, CO: Westview Press, 1977.

Branch, Taylor. *At Canaan's Edge: America in the King Years, 1965–1968.* New York: Simon & Schuster, 2006.

———. *The King Years: Historic Moments in the Civil Rights Movement.* New York: Simon & Schuster, 2013.

Brennan, Mary C. *Turning Right in the Sixties: The Conservative Capture of the GOP.* Chapel Hill: University of North Carolina Press, 1995.

Brigham, Robert K. *Guerrilla Diplomacy: The NLF's Foreign Relations and the Viet Nam War.* Ithaca, NY: Cornell University Press, 1999.

———. *Reckless: Henry Kissinger and the Tragedy of Vietnam.* New York: PublicAffairs, 2018.

Brinkley, Douglas. *Cronkite.* New York: Harper, 2012.

Brodie, Fawn M. *Richard Nixon: The Shaping of His Character*. New York: W. W. Norton, 1981.

Brokaw, Tom. *The Greatest Generation*. New York: Random House, 1998.

Brower, Kate Andersen. *First in Line: Presidents, Vice Presidents, and the Pursuit of Power*. New York: Harper, 2018.

Brown Jr., Lonnie T. *Defending the Public's Enemy: The Life and Legacy of Ramsey Clark*. Stanford, CA: Stanford University Press, 2019.

Buchanan, Patrick, J. *The Greatest Comeback: How Richard Nixon Rose from Defeat to Create the New Majority*. New York: Crown Forum, 2014.

———. *Nixon's White House Wars: The Battles That Made and Broke a President and Divided America Forever* (New York: Crown Forum, 2017), 9.

———. *Right from the Beginning*. Boston: Little, Brown, 1988.

Bui, Tin. *Following Ho Chi Minh: Memoirs of a North Vietnamese Colonel*. Translated by Judy Stowe and Do Van. Honolulu: University of Hawaii Press, 1995.

———. *From Enemy to Friend: A North Vietnamese Perspective on the War*. Annapolis, MD: Naval Institute Press, 2002.

———. *Vietnam, 1945–1999: Le Face Cachée du Régime*. Paris: Éditions Kergour, 2000.

Bundy, William. *A Tangled Web: The Making of Foreign Policy in the Nixon Presidency*. New York: Hill and Wang, 1998.

Califano Jr., Joseph A. *Inside: A Public and Private Life*. New York: PublicAffairs, 2004.

———. *The Triumph and Tragedy of Lyndon Johnson: The White House Years*. New York: Simon & Schuster, 2015.

Cannon, Lou. *Governor Reagan: His Rise to Power*. New York: PublicAffairs, 2003.

Carlson, Jody. *George C. Wallace and the Politics of Powerlessness: The Wallace Campaigns for the Presidency, 1964–1976*. New Brunswick, NJ: Transaction Books, 1981.

Carter, Dan T. *The Politics of Rage: George Wallace, the Origins of the New Conservatism, and the Transformation of American Politics*. New York: Simon & Schuster, 1995.

Carter, Paul. *Richard Nixon: Native Son*. Lincoln, NE: Potomac Books, 2023.

Chapin, Dwight. *The President's Man: The Memoirs of Nixon's Trusted Aide*. New York: William Morrow, 2022.

Chen, Jian. *Mao's China and the Cold War*. Chapel Hill: University of North Carolina Press, 2001.

Chennault, Anna. *The Education of Anna*. New York: Times Books, 1980.

———. *A Thousand Springs: The Biography of a Marriage*. New York: Paul S. Eriksson, 1962.

Cheshire, Maxine, with John Greenya. *Maxine Cheshire, Reporter*. Boston: Houghton Mifflin, 1978.

Chester, Lewis, Godfrey Hodgson, and Bruce Page. *An American Melodrama: The Presidential Campaign of 1968*. New York: Viking Press, 1969.

Christian, George. *The President Steps Down: A Personal Memoir of the Transfer of Power.* New York: Macmillan, 1970.

Clark, Ramsey. *Crime in America: Observations on Its Nature, Causes, Prevention, and Control.* New York: Simon & Schuster, 1970.

Clarke, Thurston. *The Last Campaign: Robert F. Kennedy and 82 Days That Inspired America.* New York: Henry Holt, 2008.

Clemis, Martin G. *The Control War: The Struggle for South Vietnam, 1968–1975.* Norman: University of Oklahoma Press, 2018.

Clifford, Clark, with Richard Holbrooke. *Counsel to the President: A Memoir.* New York: Random House, 1991.

Cline, Ray S. *Secrets, Spies, and Scholars: Blueprint of the Essential CIA.* Washington, DC: Acropolis Books, 1976.

Coffey, Justin N. *Spiro Agnew and the Rise of the Republican Right.* Santa Barbara, CA: Praeger, 2015.

Coffey, Thomas M. *Iron Eagle: The Turbulent Life of General Curtis LeMay.* New York: Crown Publishing, 1986.

Cohen, Adam, and Elizabeth Taylor. *American Pharaoh: Mayor Richard J. Daley; His Battle for Chicago and the Nation.* Boston: Little, Brown, 2000.

Cohen, Michael A. *American Maelstrom: The 1968 Election and the Politics of Division.* New York: Oxford University Press, 2016.

Cohen, Warren I. *Dean Rusk.* Totowa, NJ: Cooper Square Publishers, 1980.

Colby, William, and Peter Forbath. *Honorable Men: My Life in the CIA.* New York: Simon & Schuster, 1978.

Congressional Quarterly Almanac, 1968. Washington, DC: Congressional Quarterly, 1969.

Connally, John, with Mickey Herskowitz. *In History's Shadow: An American Odyssey.* New York: Hyperion, 1993.

Cooper, Chester L. *In the Shadows of History: Fifty Years behind the Scenes of Cold War Diplomacy.* Amherst, NY: Prometheus Books, 2005.

Critchlow, Donald T. *The Conservative Ascendancy: How the GOP Right Made Political History.* Cambridge, MA: Harvard University Press, 2007.

Cronkite, Walter. *A Reporter's Life.* New York: Alfred A. Knopf, 1996.

Daddis, Gregory A. *Westmoreland's War: Reassessing American Strategy in Vietnam.* New York: Oxford University Press, 2014.

———. *Withdrawal: Reassessing America's Final Years in Vietnam.* New York: Oxford University Press, 2017.

Dallek, Matthew. *The Right Moment: Ronald Reagan's First Victory and the Decisive Turning Point in American Politics.* New York: Free Press, 2000.

Dallek, Robert. *Flawed Giant: Lyndon Johnson and His Times, 1961–1973.* New York: Oxford University Press, 1998.

———. *Nixon and Kissinger: Partners in Power.* New York: HarperCollins Publishers, 2007.

Davis, Deborah. *Katharine the Great: Katharine Graham and the Washington Post.* New York: Harcourt Brace Jovanovich, 1979.

DeBenedetti, Charles. *An American Ordeal: The Antiwar Movement of the Vietnam Era*. Syracuse, NY: Syracuse University Press, 1990.

Dees, Morris, with Steve Fiffer. *A Season for Justice: The Life and Times of Civil Rights Lawyer Morris Dees*. New York: Simon & Schuster, 1991.

DeLoach, Cartha "Deke." *Hoover's FBI: The Inside Story by Hoover's Trusted Lieutenant*. Washington, DC: Regnery Publishing, 1995.

Del Pero, Mario. *The Eccentric Realist: Henry Kissinger and the Shaping of American Foreign Policy*. Ithaca, NY: Cornell University Press, 2010.

Dent, Harry S. *The Prodigal South Returns to Power*. New York: John Wiley & Sons, 1978.

Diem, Bui, with David Chanoff. *In the Jaws of History*. Boston: Houghton Mifflin, 1987.

DiLeo, David L. *George Ball, Vietnam, and the Rethinking of Containment*. Chapel Hill: University of North Carolina Press, 1991.

Dionne Jr., E. J. *Why Americans Hate Politics*. New York: Simon & Schuster, 1991.

Dobbins, James F. *Foreign Service: Five Decades on the Frontlines of American Diplomacy*. Washington, DC: Brookings Institution Press, 2017.

Dobrynin, Anatoly. *In Confidence: Moscow's Ambassador to America's Six Cold War Presidents (1962–1986)*. New York: Times Books, 1995.

Dommen, Arthur J. *Conflict in Laos: The Politics of Neutralization*. New York: Frederick A. Praeger, 1964.

———. *The Indochinese Experience of the French and the Americans: Nationalism and Communism in Cambodia, Laos, and Vietnam*. Bloomington: Indiana University Press, 2001.

———. *Laos: Keystone of Indochina*. Boulder, CO: Westview Press, 1985.

Drea, Edward J. *McNamara, Clifford, and the Burdens of Vietnam, 1965–1969*. Washington, DC: Office of the Secretary of Defense, 2011.

Edsall, Thomas Byrne, with Mary D. Edsall. *Chain Reaction: The Impact of Race, Rights, and Taxes on American Politics*. New York: W. W. Norton, 1991.

Ehrlichman, John. *Witness to Power: The Nixon Years*. New York: Simon & Schuster, 1982.

Eisele, Albert. *Almost to the Presidency: A Biography of Two American Politicians*. Blue Earth, MN: Piper, 1972.

Eisenhower, David, with Julie Nixon Eisenhower. *Going Home to Glory: A Memoir of Life with Dwight D. Eisenhower, 1961–1969*. New York: Simon & Schuster, 2010.

Eisenhower, Dwight. *The Eisenhower Diaries*. Edited by Robert H. Ferrell. New York: W. W. Norton, 1981.

Eisenhower, Julie Nixon. *Special People*. New York: Simon & Schuster, 1977.

Elliott, David W. P. *The Vietnamese War: Revolution and Social Change in the Mekong Delta, 1930–1975*. Concise edition. Armonk, NY: M. E. Sharpe, 2007.

Ellsberg, Daniel. *Secrets: A Memoir of Vietnam and the Pentagon Papers*. New York: Viking Press, 2002.

Elsey, George McKee. *An Unplanned Life*. Columbia: University of Missouri Press, 2005.

Endicott, Michael A. *Walking with Presidents: Stories from Inside the Perimeter*. BookSurge, 2009.

Engelmayer, Sheldon D., and Robert J. Wagman. *Hubert Humphrey: The Man and His Dream*. New York: Methuen, 1978.

Evans Jr., Rowland, and Robert D. Novak. *Nixon in the White House: The Frustration of Power*. New York: Random House, 1971.

Fall, Bernard B. *Anatomy of a Crisis: The Laotian Crisis of 1960–1961*. Garden City, NY: Doubleday, 1969.

———. *Last Reflections on a War*. Garden City, NY: Doubleday, 1967.

———. *The Two Viet-Nams: A Political and Military Analysis*. 2nd revised edition. New York: Frederick A. Praeger, 1967.

———. *Viet-Nam Witness, 1953–66*. New York: Frederick A. Praeger Publishers, 1966.

Farber, David. *The Age of Great Dreams: America in the 1960s*. New York: Hill and Wang, 1994.

———. *Chicago '68*. Chicago: University of Chicago Press, 1988.

———, ed. *The Sixties: From Memory to History*. Chapel Hill: University of North Carolina Press, 1994.

Farrell, John A. *Richard Nixon: The Life*. New York: Doubleday, 2017.

Felzenberg, Alvin S. *A Man and His Presidents: The Political Odyssey of William F. Buckley Jr*. New Haven: Yale University Press, 2017.

Ferguson, Niall. *Kissinger, 1923–1968: The Idealist*. New York: Penguin Books, 2015.

Flamm, Michael W. *Law and Order: Street Crime, Civil Unrest, and the Crisis of Liberalism in the 1960s*. New York: Columbia University Press, 2005.

Forslund, Catherine. *Anna Chennault: Informal Diplomacy and Asian Relations*. Wilmington, DE: SR Books, 2002.

Frady, Marshall. *Wallace*. New York: New American Library, 1968.

Frank, Jeffrey. *Ike and Dick: Portrait of a Strange Political Marriage*. New York: Simon & Schuster, 2013.

Frankel, Max. *The Times of My Life and My Life with the Times*. New York: Random House, 1999.

Fraser, Steve, and Gary Gerstle, eds. *The Rise and Fall of the New Deal Order, 1930–1980*. Princeton, NJ: Princeton University Press, 1989.

Frederick, Jeff. *Stand Up for Alabama: Governor George Wallace*. Tuscaloosa: University of Alabama Press, 2007.

Frederickson, Kari. *The Dixiecrat Revolt and the End of the Solid South, 1932–1968*. Chapel Hill: University of North Carolina Press, 2001.

Free, Lloyd A., and Hadley Cantril. *The Political Beliefs of Americans: A Study of Public Opinion*. New York: Simon & Schuster, 1968.

Freeman, Wilson C. "The Logan Act: An Overview of a Sometimes Forgotten 18th Century Law." Congressional Research Service, January 12, 2018.

Fursenko, Aleksandr, and Timothy Naftali. *Khrushchev's Cold War: The Inside Story of an American Adversary*. New York: W. W. Norton, 2006.

Gaddis, John Lewis. *Strategies of Containment: A Critical Appraisal of American National Security Policy during the Cold War*. Revised and expanded edition. New York: Oxford University Press, 2005.

Gaiduk, Ilya V. *Confronting Vietnam: Soviet Policy toward the Indochina Conflict, 1954–1963*. Washington, DC: Woodrow Wilson Center Press, 2003.

———. *Divided Together: The United States and the Soviet Union in the United Nations, 1945–1965*. Washington, DC: Woodrow Wilson Center Press, 2012.

———. *The Soviet Union and the Vietnam War*. Chicago: Ivan R. Dee, 1996.

Gallup, George H. *The Gallup Poll: Public Opinion, 1935–1971. Volume 3, 1959–1971*. New York: Random House, 1972.

Gardner, Lloyd C., ed. *The Great Nixon Turnaround: America's New Foreign Policy for the Post-Liberal Era*. New York: New Viewpoints, 1973.

Garment, Leonard. *Crazy Rhythm: My Journey from Brooklyn, Jazz, and Wall Street to Nixon's White House, Watergate, and Beyond*. New York: Times Books, 1997.

Gelb, Leslie H., with Richard K. Betts. *The Irony of Vietnam: The System Worked*. Washington, DC: Brookings Institution, 1979.

Gellman, Irwin F. *Campaign of the Century: Kennedy, Nixon, and the Election of 1960*. New Haven: Yale University Press, 2021.

———. *The Contender: Richard Nixon, The Congress Years, 1946–1952*. New York: Free Press, 1999.

———. *The President and the Apprentice: Eisenhower and Nixon, 1952–1961*. New Haven: Yale University Press, 2015.

Gibbons, William Conrad, ed. *The U.S. Government and the Vietnam War: Executive and Legislative Roles and Relationships, Part IV, July 1965–January 1968*. Princeton, NJ: Princeton University Press, 1995.

Gibbs, Nancy, and Michael Duffy. *The Preacher and the Presidents: Billy Graham in the White House*. New York: Center Street, 2007.

———. *The President's Club: Inside the World's Most Exclusive Fraternity*. New York: Simon & Schuster, 2012.

Gillon, Steven M. *Separate and Unequal: The Kerner Commission and the Unraveling of American Liberalism*. New York: Basic Books, 2018.

Goodwin, Richard N. *Remembering America: A Voice from the Sixties*. Boston: Little, Brown, 1988.

Goscha, Christopher. *Vietnam: A New History*. New York: Basic Books, 2016.

Gottlieb, Robert. *Katharine Graham's Washington*. New York: Alfred A. Knopf, 2002.

Goudsouzian, Aram. *The Men and the Moment: The Election of 1968 and the Rise of Partisan Politics in America*. Chapel Hill: University of North Carolina Press, 2019.

Gould, Lewis L. *1968: The Election That Changed America*. 2nd edition. Chicago: Ivan R. Dee, 2010.

———. *Grand Old Party: A History of the Republicans*. New York: Random House, 2003.

Graff, Garrett M. *Watergate: A New History*. New York: Avid Reader Press, 2022.

Graham, Billy. *Just As I Am: The Autobiography of Billy Graham*. New York: Harper-Collins, 1997.

Graham, Katharine. *Katharine Graham's Washington*. Edited by Robert Gottlieb. New York: Alfred A. Knopf, 2002.

Greenberg, David. *Nixon's Shadow: The History of an Image*. New York: W. W. Norton, 2003.

Greenhaw, Wayne. *Fighting the Devil in Dixie: How Civil Rights Activists Took on the Ku Klux Klan in Alabama*. Chicago: Lawrence Hill Books, 2011.

Gromyko, Andrei. *Memoirs*. Translated by Harold Shukman. New York: Doubleday, 1989.

Gross, Norman, ed. *America's Lawyer-Presidents: From Law Office to Oval Office*. Evanston, IL: Northwestern University Press, 2004.

Guan, Ang Cheng. *The Vietnam War from the Other Side: The Vietnamese Communists' Perspective*. New York: Routledge Curzon, 2002.

Gulley, Bill, with Mary Ellen Reese. *Breaking Cover*. New York: Simon & Schuster, 1980.

Hagopian, Patrick. "The 'Frustrated Hawks,' Tet 1968, and the Transformation of American Politics." *European Journal of American Studies* 3, no. 2 (2008): 1–13.

Haig Jr., Alexander M., and Charles McCarry. *Inner Circles: How America Changed the World, A Memoir*. New York: Warner Books, 1992.

Halberstam, David. *The Best and the Brightest*. New York: Random House, 1969.

———. *The Unfinished Odyssey of Robert Kennedy*. New York: Random House, 1968.

Haldeman, H. R., with Joseph DiMona. *The Ends of Power*. New York: Times Books, 1978.

Hall, Perry D., ed. *The Quotable Hubert H. Humphrey*. Anderson, SC: Drake House, 1967.

Hanhimäki, Jussi. *The Flawed Architect: Henry Kissinger and American Foreign Policy*. New York: Oxford University Press, 2004.

Harris, Fred, and Alan Curtis, eds. *Healing Our Divided Society: Investing in America Fifty Years After the Kerner Report*. Philadelphia: Temple University Press, 2018.

Harris, T. George. *Romney's Way: A Man and an Idea*. Englewood Cliffs, NJ: Prentice-Hall, 1967.

Hart, Richard R. *A Sense of Joy: A Tribute to Ted Moss*. Springville, UT: Bonneville Books, 2003.

Hastings, Max. *Vietnam: An Epic Tragedy, 1945–1975*. New York: Harper, 2018.

Hayes, Harold, ed. *Smiling Through the Apocalypse: Esquire's History of the Sixties*. New York: McCall Publishing, 1969.

Helgerson, John. "Intelligence Support for Richard M. Nixon: A Difficult Relationship." *Studies in Intelligence* 39, no. 4 (1995): 103–12.

Herring, George C. *America's Longest War: The United States and Vietnam, 1950–1975*. Philadelphia: Temple University Press, 1979.

———. *LBJ and Vietnam: A Different Kind of War*. Austin: University of Texas Press, 1994.

Hersh, Seymour. *Reporter: A Memoir*. New York: Alfred A. Knopf, 2018.

Herzog, Arthur. *McCarthy for President*. New York: Viking Press, 1969.

Hess, Stephen. *The Professor and the President: Daniel Patrick Moynihan in the Nixon White House*. Washington, DC: Brookings Institution Press, 2015.

Hess, Stephen, and David S. Broder. *The Republican Establishment: The Present and Future of the G.O.P.* New York: Harper & Row, 1967.

Hill, Clint, with Lisa McCubbin. *Five Presidents: My Extraordinary Journey with Eisenhower, Kennedy, Johnson, Nixon, and Ford*. New York: Gallery Books, 2016.

Hillings, Pat. *The Irrepressible Irishman, A Republican Insider: The Story of a Political Life*. Harold A. Dean, 1993.

Hoàng Văn Hoá. *Biên niên sự kiện: Bộ tổng tham mưu trong khang chiến chống Mỹ, cứu nước, tập V (1968)* [*Chronology of Events: General Staff During the Resistance War Against the Americans to Save the Nation, Volume V (1968)*]. Hanoi: People's Army Publishing House, 2005.

Hodgson, Godfrey. *America in Our Time: From World War II to Nixon, What Happened and Why*. New York: Doubleday, 1976.

———. *The World Turned Right Side Up: A History of the Conservative Ascendancy in America*. Boston: Houghton Mifflin, 1996.

Hoeh, David C. *1968, McCarthy, New Hampshire: "I Hear America Singing."* Rochester, MN: Lone Oak Press, 1994.

Hoffman, Abbie. *Revolution for the Hell of It*. New York: Pocket Books, 1970.

Holden, Charles J., Zach Messitte, and Jerald Podair. *Republican Populist: Spiro Agnew and the Origins of Donald Trump's America*. Charlottesville: University of Virginia Press, 2019.

Hughes, Ken. *Chasing Shadows: The Nixon Tapes, the Chennault Affair, and the Origins of Watergate*. Charlottesville: University of Virginia Press, 2014.

Hughes, Thomas. *Anecdotage: Some Authentic Retrievals*. Self-published, CreateSpace, 2014.

Humphrey, Hubert H. *The Education of a Public Man: My Life and Politics*. Garden City, NY: Doubleday, 1976.

———. *The Political Philosophy of the New Deal*. Baton Rouge: Louisiana State University Press, 1970.

Hunt, David. *Vietnam's Southern Revolution: From Peasant Insurrection to Total War*. Amherst: University of Massachusetts Press, 2008.

Immerman, Richard H. *The Hidden Hand: A Brief History of the CIA*. Malden, MA: Wiley Blackwell, 2014.

Ingle, H. Larry. *Nixon's First Cover-Up: The Religious Life of a Quaker President*. Columbia: University of Missouri Press, 2015.

Isaacson, Walter. *Kissinger: A Biography*. New York: Simon & Schuster, 1982.

Isserman, Maurice, and Michael Kazin. *America Divided: The Civil War of the 1960s*. New York: Oxford University Press, 2000.

Jeffries, John W. *A Third Term for FDR: The Election of 1940*. Lawrence: University Press of Kansas, 2017.

Jensen, Geoffrey W., and Matthew M. Stith. *Beyond the Quagmire: New Interpretations of the Vietnam War*. Denton: University of North Texas Press, 2019.

Jezer, Marly. *Abbie Hoffman: American Rebel*. New Brunswick, NJ: Rutgers University Press, 1992.

Johns, Andrew L. *The Price of Loyalty: Hubert Humphrey's Vietnam Conflict*. Lanham, MD: Rowman & Littlefield, 2020.

———. *Vietnam's Second Front: Domestic Politics, the Republican Party, and the War*. Lexington: University Press of Kentucky, 2010.

Johnson, Lady Bird. *A White House Diary*. New York: Holt, Rinehart and Winston, 1970.

Johnson, Lyndon Baines. *The Vantage Point: Perspectives of the Presidency, 1963–1969*. New York: Holt, Rinehart and Winston, 1971.

Johnstone, Andrew, and Andrew Priest. *U.S. Presidential Elections and Foreign Policy: Candidates, Campaigns, and Global Politics from FDR to Bill Clinton*. Lexington: University Press of Kentucky, 2017.

Jones, Clarence B., and Joel Engel. *What Would Martin Say?* New York: Harper, 2008.

Jones, Howard. *My Lai: Vietnam, 1968, and the Descent into Darkness*. New York: Oxford University Press, 2017.

Kabaservice, Geoffrey. *Rule and Ruin: The Downfall of Moderation and the Destruction of the Republican Party, From Eisenhower to the Tea Party*. New York: Oxford University Press, 2012.

Kalb, Marvin. *The Nixon Memo: Political Responsibility, Russia, and the Press*. Chicago: University of Chicago Press, 1994.

Kalb, Marvin, and Elie Abel. *Roots of Involvement: The U.S. in Asia, 1784–1971*. New York: W. W. Norton, 1971.

Kalb, Marvin, and Bernard Kalb. *Kissinger*. Boston: Little, Brown, 1974.

Kampelman, Max M. *Entering New Worlds: The Memoirs of a Private Man in Public Life*. New York: HarperCollins, 1991.

Karnow, Stanley. *Vietnam: A History*. New York: Viking Press, 1983.

Karthikeyan, Arjun. "The Logan Act—Did We Wake Up a Criminal Act 200 Years Dormant?" *Tulane Journal of International and Comparative Law* 6, no. 1 (Winter 2017): 211–27.

Kattenberg, Paul M. *The Vietnam Trauma in American Foreign Policy, 1945–1975*. New Brunswick, NJ: Transaction Books, 1980.

Kaufman, Jonathan. *The Last Kings of Shanghai: The Rival Jewish Dynasties That Helped Create Modern China*. New York: Viking Press, 2020.

Kearns, Doris. *Lyndon Johnson and the American Dream*. New York: Harper & Row, 1976.

Keeney, L. Douglas. *15 Minutes: General Curtis LeMay and the Countdown to Nuclear Annihilation*. New York: St. Martin's Press, 2011.

Keever, Beverly Deepe. *Death Zones and Darling Spies: Seven Years of Vietnam War Reporting*. Lincoln: University of Nebraska Press, 2013.

Kennedy, Peggy Wallace, and H. Mark Kennedy. *The Broken Road: George Wallace and a Daughter's Journey to Reconciliation*. New York: Bloomsbury Publishing, 2019.

Kennedy, Robert F. *To Seek A Newer World*. Garden City, NY: Doubleday, 1967.

Kennelly, Thomas A. *One More Story and I'm Out the Door: A Life, with Recollections about Jimmy Hoffa, the Mafia, G. Gordon Liddy, and Guardian Angels, among Others*. New York: iUniverse, 2006.

The Kerner Report: The 1968 Report of the National Advisory Commission on Civil Disorders. New York: Pantheon Books, 1988.

Kessler, Ronald. *The First Family Detail: Secret Service Agents Reveal the Hidden Lives of the Presidents*. New York: Crown Forum, 2014.

Khoo, Nicholas. *Collateral Damage: Sino-Soviet Rivalry and the Termination of the Sino-Vietnamese Alliance*. New York: Columbia University Press, 2011.

Kieninger, Stephan. *Dynamic Détente: The United States and Europe, 1964–1975*. Lanham, MD: Lexington Books, 2016.

Kiernan, Ben. *Viet Nam: A History from Earliest Times to the Present*. New York: Oxford University Press, 2017.

King Jr., Martin Luther. *Where Do We Go from Here? Chaos or Community?* New York: Harper & Row, 1967.

Kissinger, Henry A. *American Foreign Policy: Three Essays*. New York: W. W. Norton, 1969.

———. *Ending the Vietnam War: A History of America's Involvement in and Extrication from the Vietnam War*. New York: Simon & Schuster, 2003.

———. *Leadership: Six Studies in World Strategy*. New York: Penguin Press, 2022.

———. "The Viet Nam Negotiations." *Foreign Affairs* 47, no. 2 (January 1969): 211–34.

———. *White House Years*. Boston: Little, Brown, 1979.

———. *Years of Renewal*. New York: Simon & Schuster, 1999.

———. *Years of Upheaval*. Boston: Little, Brown, 1982.

Klein, Herbert G. *Making It Perfectly Clear: An Inside Account of Nixon's Love-Hate Relationship with the Media*. Garden City, NY: Doubleday, 1980.

Kleindienst, Richard G. *Justice: The Memoirs of Attorney General Richard Kleindienst*. Ottawa, IL: Jameson Books, 1985.

Kornitzer, Bela. *The Real Nixon: An Intimate Biography*. New York: Rand McNally, 1960.

Kotlowski, Dean. J. *Nixon's Civil Rights: Politics, Principle, and Policy*. Cambridge, MA: Harvard University Press, 2001.

———. "Nixon's Southern Strategy Revisited." *Journal of Policy History* 10, no. 2 (April 1998): 207–38.

Kozak, Warren. *LeMay: The Life and Wars of General Curtis LeMay.* Washington, DC: Regnery Publishing, 2009.

Kraemer, Sven F. *Inside the Cold War from Marx to Reagan: An Unprecedented Guide to the Roots, History, Strategies, and Key Documents of the Cold War.* Lanham, MD: University Press of America, 2015.

Kramer, Michael, and Sam Roberts. *"I Never Wanted to Be Vice President of Anything!" An Investigative Biography of Nelson Rockefeller.* New York: Basic Books, 1976.

Krock, Arthur. *Memoirs: Sixty Years on the Firing Line.* New York: Funk & Wagnalls, 1968.

Kruse, Kevin. *White Flight: Atlanta and the Making of Modern Conservatism.* Princeton, NJ: Princeton University Press, 2005.

Kuhn, David Paul. *The Hardhat Riot: Nixon, New York City, and the Dawn of the White Working-Class Revolution.* New York: Oxford University Press, 2020.

Kurlantzick, Joshua. *A Great Place to Have a War: America in Laos and the Birth of a Military CIA.* New York: Simon & Schuster, 2016.

Kusch, Frank. *Battleground Chicago: The Police and the 1968 Democratic National Convention.* Westport, CT: Praeger, 2004.

Kusnet, David. *Speaking American: How the Democrats Can Win in the Nineties.* New York: Thunder's Mouth Press, 1992.

Ky, Nguyen Cao. *Buddha's Child: My Fight to Save Vietnam.* New York: St. Martin's Press, 2002.

———. *How We Lost the Vietnam War.* New York: Cooper Square Press, 2002.

———. *Twenty Years and Twenty Days.* New York: Stein and Day, 1976.

LaFeber, Walter. *The Deadly Bet: LBJ, Vietnam, and the 1968 Election.* Lanham, MD: Rowman & Littlefield Publishers, 2005.

Laine, Evan Edward. *Nixon and the Dragon Lady: Did Richard Nixon Conspire with Anna Chennault in 1968 to Destroy Peace in Vietnam?* Champaign, IL: Common Ground Publishing, 2015.

Lansdale, Edward Geary. *In the Midst of Wars: An American's Mission to Southeast Asia.* New York: Harper & Row, 1972.

Larner, Jeremy. *Nobody Knows: Reflections on the McCarthy Campaign of 1968.* New York: Macmillan, 1969.

Lassiter, Matthew D. *The Silent Majority: Suburban Politics in the Sunbelt South.* Princeton, NJ: Princeton University Press, 2006.

Lawrence, Mark Atwood. *The End of Ambition: The United States and the Third World in the Vietnam Era.* Princeton, NJ: Princeton University Press, 2021.

———. *The Vietnam War: A Concise International History.* New York: Oxford University Press, 2008.

Leary Jr., William M. "Portrait of a Cold War Warrior: Whiting Willauer and Civil Air Transport." *Modern Asian Studies* 5, no. 4 (1971): 373–88.

Lee, Heath Hardage. *The League of Wives: The Untold Story of the Women Who Took on the U.S. Government to Bring Their Husbands Home.* New York: St. Martin's Press, 2019.

LeMay, Curtis E. *Mission with LeMay: My Story.* Garden City, NY: Doubleday, 1965.

LeMay, Curtis E., with Dale O. Smith. *America Is in Danger.* New York: Funk & Wagnalls, 1968.

Lesher, Stephan. *George Wallace: American Populist.* Reading, MA: Addison-Wesley Publishing, 1994.

Levy, Peter B. *The Great Uprising: Race Riots in Urban America during the 1960s.* New York: Cambridge University Press, 2018.

Li, Danhui, and Yafeng Xia. *Mao and the Sino-Soviet Split, 1959–1973: A New History.* Lanham, MD: Lexington Books, 2018.

Li, Victor. *Nixon in New York: How Wall Street Helped Richard Nixon Win the White House.* Vancouver: Fairleigh Dickinson University Press, 2018.

Li, Xiaobing. *Building Ho's Army: Chinese Military Assistance to North Vietnam.* Lexington: University Press of Kentucky, 2019.

Liebmann, George W. *The Last American Diplomat: John D. Negroponte and the Changing Face of American Diplomacy.* New York: I. B. Tauris, 2012.

Lipset, Seymour Martin, and Earl Raab. *The Politics of Unreason: Right-Wing Extremism in America, 1790–1977.* Chicago: University of Chicago Press, 1978.

Logevall, Fredrik. *Choosing War: The Lost Chance for Peace and the Escalation of War in Vietnam.* Berkeley: University of California Press, 1999.

———. *Embers of War: The Fall of an Empire and the Making of America's Vietnam.* New York: Random House, 2012.

Loi, Luu Van, and Nguyen Anh Vu. *Le Duc Tho–Kissinger Negotiations in Paris.* Hanoi: Gioi Publishers, 1996.

Longley, Kyle. *LBJ's 1968: Power, Politics, and the Presidency in America's Year of Upheaval.* New York: Cambridge University Press, 2018.

Lowitt, Richard. *Fred Harris: His Journey from Liberalism to Populism.* Lanham, MD: Rowman & Littlefield Publishers, 2002.

Lungren, John C., and John C. Lungren Jr. *Healing Richard Nixon: A Doctor's Memoir.* Lexington: University Press of Kentucky, 2003.

MacKenzie, G. Calvin, and Robert Weisbrot. *The Liberal Hour: Washington and the Politics of Change in the 1960s.* New York: Penguin Books, 2008.

Mailer, Norman. *Miami and the Siege of Chicago: An Informal History of the Republican and Democratic Conventions of 1968.* New York: Signet Books, 1968.

———. *Some Honorable Men: Political Conventions, 1960–1972.* Boston: Little, Brown, 1976.

Malek, Frederic V. *Washington's Hidden Tragedy: The Failure to Make Government Work.* New York: Free Press, 1978.

Manac'h, Étienne. *Mémoires d'Extrême Asie: La Chine.* Paris: Fayard, 1980.

———. *Mémoires d'Extrême Asie: La face cachée du monde.* Paris: Fayard, 1977.

———. *Mémoires d'Extrême Asie: Une terre traverse de puissances invisibles, Chine-Indochine, 1972–1973.* Paris: Fayard, 1982.

Mann, Robert. *A Grand Delusion: America's Descent into Vietnam.* New York: Basic Books, 2001.

Martin, William. *A Prophet with Honor: The Billy Graham Story.* New York: William Morrow, 1991.

Mason, Robert. *Richard Nixon and the Quest for a New Majority*. Chapel Hill: University of North Carolina Press, 2004.

Matusow, Allen J. *The Unraveling of America: A History of Liberalism in the 1960s*. New York: Harper & Row, 1984.

Mazo, Earl. *Richard Nixon: A Political and Personal Portrait*. New York: Harper & Brothers Publishers, 1959.

Mazo, Earl, and Stephen Hess. *Nixon: A Political Portrait*. New York: Harper & Row, 1968.

McCarthy, Dennis V. N., with Philip W. Smith. *Protecting the President: The Inside Story of a Secret Service Agent*. New York: William Morrow, 1985.

McCarthy, Eugene. *Frontiers in American Democracy*. Cleveland: World Publishing, 1960.

———. *Gene McCarthy's Minnesota: Memories of a Native Son*. Minneapolis: Winston Press, 1982.

———. *The Limits of Power: America's Role in the World*. New York: Holt, Rinehart and Winston, 1967.

———. *Up 'Til Now: A Memoir*. New York: Harcourt Brace Jovanovich, 1987.

McGhee, George C. *On the Frontline in the Cold War: An Ambassador Reports*. Westport, CT: Praeger, 1997.

McGinniss, Joe. *The Selling of the President, 1968*. New York: Trident Press, 1969.

McGirr, Lisa. *Suburban Warriors: The Origins of the New American Right*. Princeton, NJ: Princeton University Press, 2001.

McKean, David. *Tommy the Cork: Washington's Ultimate Insider from Roosevelt to Reagan*. South Royalton, VT: Steerforth Press, 2004.

McMaster, H. R. *Dereliction of Duty: Lyndon Johnson, Robert McNamara, the Joint Chiefs of Staff, and the Lies That Led to Vietnam*. New York: HarperCollins Publishers, 1997.

McNamara, Robert S., with Brian VanDeMark. *In Retrospect: The Tragedy and Lessons of Vietnam*. New York: Times Books, 1995.

McNamara, Robert S., James G. Blight, and Robert K. Brigham, with Thomas J. Biersteker and Herbert Y. Schandler. *Argument Without End: In Search of Answers to the Vietnam Tragedy*. New York: PublicAffairs, 1999.

McPherson, Harry. *A Political Education: A Washington Memoir*. Austin: University of Texas Press, 1972.

Mehta, Harish C. "The Secret Business Diplomacy of Anna Chennault as Nixon's Envoy in South Vietnam, 1967–1974." *International History Review* 42, no. 2 (2020): 235–59.

Middendorf II, J. William. *A Glorious Disaster: Barry Goldwater's Presidential Campaign and the Origins of the Conservative Movement*. New York: Basic Books, 2006.

Military History Institute of Vietnam. *Victory in Vietnam: The Official History of the People's Army of Vietnam, 1954–1975*. Translated by Merle Pribbenow. Lawrence: University Press of Kansas, 2002.

Miller, Robert Hopkins. *Vietnam and Beyond: A Diplomat's Cold War Education.* Lubbock: Texas Tech University Press, 2002.

Miller, Stephen P. *Billy Graham and the Rise of the Republican South.* Philadelphia: University of Pennsylvania Press, 2009.

Moïse, Edwin E. *The Myths of TET: The Most Misunderstood Event of the Vietnam War.* Lawrence: University Press of Kansas, 2017.

Mollenhoff, Clark R. *George Romney: Mormon in Politics.* New York: Meredith Press, 1968.

Mondale, Walter F., with David Hage. *The Good Fight: A Life in Liberal Politics.* Minneapolis: University of Minnesota Press, 2010.

Morrow, Lance. *The Best Year of Their Lives: Kennedy, Johnson, and Nixon in 1948, Learning the Secrets of Power.* New York: Basic Books, 2005.

Moynihan, Daniel P. *Maximum Feasible Misunderstanding: Community Action in the War on Poverty.* New York: Free Press, 1969.

———. *Miles to Go: A Personal History of Social Policy.* Cambridge, MA: Harvard University Press, 1996.

———. *The Politics of a Guaranteed Income: The Nixon Administration and the Family Assistance Plan.* New York: Random House, 1973.

Napolitan, Joseph. *The Election Game and How to Win It.* Garden City, NY: Doubleday, 1972.

Nelson, Justin. "Drafting Lyndon Johnson: The President's Secret Role in the 1968 Democratic Convention." *Presidential Studies Quarterly* 30, no. 4 (December 2000): 688–713.

Nelson, Michael. "Lost Confidence: The Democratic Party, the Vietnam War, and the 1968 Election." *Presidential Studies Quarterly* 48, no. 3 (September 2018): 570–85.

———. *Resilient America: Electing Nixon in 1968, Channeling Dissent, and Dividing Government.* Revised and expanded. Lawrence: University Press of Kansas, 2014.

Neufield, Jack. *Robert Kennedy: A Memoir.* New York: E. P. Dutton, 1969.

Nguyen, Lien-Hang T. *Hanoi's War: An International History of the War for Peace in Vietnam.* Chapel Hill: University of North Carolina Press, 2012.

Nguyen, Phu Duc. *The Viet-Nam Peace Negotiations: Saigon's Side of the Story.* Edited by Arthur J. Dommen. Christiansburg, VA: Dalley Book Service, 2005.

Nguyen, Tien Hung, and Jerrold L. Schecter. *The Palace File.* New York: Harper & Row, 1986.

Nichter, Luke A. *The Last Brahmin: Henry Cabot Lodge Jr. and the Making of the Cold War.* New Haven: Yale University Press, 2020.

Nitze, Paul H. *From Hiroshima to Glasnost: At the Center of Decision—A Memoir.* New York: Grove Weidenfeld, 1989.

Nixon, Edward C., and Karen L. Olson. *The Nixons: A Family Portrait.* Bothell, WA: Book Publishers Network, 2009.

Nixon, Richard. *Nixon on the Issues.* New York: Nixon-Agnew Campaign Committee, 1968.

———. *Nixon Speaks Out.* New York: Nixon-Agnew Campaign Committee, 1968.

———. *RN: The Memoirs of Richard Nixon.* New York: Grosset & Dunlap, 1978.

Oberdorfer, Don. *Tet! The Turning Point in the Vietnam War.* Baltimore: Johns Hopkins University Press, 1971.

O'Brien, Lawrence F. *No Final Victories: A Life in Politics—from John F. Kennedy to Watergate.* Garden City, NY: Doubleday, 1974.

O'Donnell, Lawrence. *Playing with Fire: The 1968 Election and the Transformation of American Politics.* New York: Penguin Books, 2017.

Offner, Arnold A. *Hubert Humphrey: The Conscience of the Country.* New Haven: Yale University Press, 2018.

Olsen, Mari. *Soviet-Vietnam Relations and the Role of China, 1949–64: Changing Alliances.* New York: Routledge, 2006.

Packer, George. *Our Man: Richard Holbrooke and the End of the American Century.* New York: Alfred A. Knopf, 2019.

Parmet, Herbert S. *Richard Nixon and His America.* New York: Smithmark Publishers, 1990.

Patterson, James T. *Freedom Is Not Enough: The Moynihan Report and America's Struggle over Black Family Life—from LBJ to Obama.* New York: Basic Books, 2010.

Pearson, Drew. *Washington Merry-Go-Round: The Drew Pearson Diaries, 1960–1969.* Edited by Peter Hannaford. Lincoln, NE: Potomac Books, 2015.

Perlstein, Rick. *Before the Storm: Barry Goldwater and the Unmaking of the American Consensus.* New York: Hill and Wang, 2001.

———. *Nixonland: The Rise of a President and the Fracturing of America.* New York: Scribner, 2008.

Phillips, Kevin P. *The Emerging Republican Majority.* New Rochelle, NY: Arlington House, 1969.

Phillips, Rufus. *Why Vietnam Matters: An Eyewitness Account of Lessons Not Learned.* Annapolis: Naval Institute Press, 2008.

Pierson, Paul, and Theda Skocpol, eds. *The Transformation of American Politics: Activist Government and the Rise of Conservatism.* Princeton, NJ: Princeton University Press, 2007.

Polsby, Nelson W. *The Citizens' Choice: Humphrey or Nixon.* Washington, DC: Public Affairs Press, 1968.

Powers, Thomas. *The Man Who Kept the Secrets: Richard Helms and the CIA.* New York: Alfred A. Knopf, 1979.

Prados, John. *The Family Jewels: The CIA, Secrecy, and Presidential Power.* Austin: University of Texas Press, 2013.

Price, John Roy. *The Last Liberal Republican: An Insider's Perspective on Nixon's Surprising Social Policy.* Lawrence: University Press of Kansas, 2021.

Price, Raymond. *With Nixon.* New York: Viking Press, 1977.

Putnam, Robert, with Shaylyn Romney Garrett. *The Upswing: How America Came Together a Century Ago and How We Can Do It Again.* New York: Simon & Schuster, 2020.

Radchenko, Sergey. *Two Suns in the Heavens: The Sino-Soviet Struggle for Supremacy, 1962–1967*. Washington, DC: Woodrow Wilson Center Press, 2009.

Rae, Nicol C. *The Decline and Fall of the Liberal Republicans from 1952 to the Present*. New York: Oxford University Press, 1989.

Rainwater, Lee, and William L. Yancey. *The Moynihan Report and the Politics of Controversy*. Cambridge, MA: MIT Press, 1967.

Reedy, George. *Lyndon B. Johnson: A Memoir*. New York: Andrews McMeel, 1982.

Reich, Cary. *The Life of Nelson A. Rockefeller: Worlds to Conquer, 1908–1958*. New York: Doubleday, 1996.

Reinhard, David W. *The Republican Right since 1945*. Lexington: University Press of Kentucky, 1983.

Report of the National Advisory Commission on Civil Disorders. Washington, DC: Government Printing Office, 1968.

Reston Jr., James. *The Lone Star: The Life of John Connally*. New York: Harper & Row, 1989.

Richardson, John H. *My Father, The Spy: An Investigative Memoir*. New York: HarperCollins Publishers, 2005.

Rieder, Jonathan. *Canarsie: The Jews and Italians of Brooklyn against Liberalism*. Cambridge, MA: Harvard University Press, 1985.

Robb, Chuck. *In the Arena: A Memoir of Love, War, and Politics*. Charlottesville: University of Virginia Press, 2021.

Roberts, Lawrence. *Mayday 1971: A White House at War, a Revolt in the Streets, and the Untold History of America's Biggest Mass Arrest*. Boston: Houghton Mifflin Harcourt, 2020.

Roberts, Priscilla, ed. *Behind the Bamboo Curtain: China, Vietnam, and the World beyond Asia*. Washington, DC: Woodrow Wilson Center Press, 2006.

Rohler, Lloyd. *George Wallace: Conservative Populist*. Westport, CT: Praeger, 2004.

Rosen, James. *The Strong Man: John Mitchell and the Secrets of Watergate*. New York: Doubleday, 2008.

Royko, Mike. *Boss: Richard J. Daley of Chicago*. New York, E. P. Dutton, 1971.

Rubin, Jerry. *Do It! Scenarios of the Revolution*. New York: Simon & Schuster, 1970.

———. *Growing (Up) at Thirty-Seven*. New York: M. Evans, 1976.

Rusk, Dean. *As I Saw It*. New York: W. W. Norton, 1990.

Rust, William J. *Before the Quagmire: American Intervention in Laos, 1954–1961*. Lexington: University Press of Kentucky, 2012.

———. *So Much To Lose: John F. Kennedy and American Policy in Laos*. Lexington: University Press of Kentucky, 2014.

Safire, William. *Before the Fall: An Inside View of the Pre-Watergate White House*. Garden City, NY: Doubleday, 1975.

———. *Safire's Political Dictionary*. Updated and expanded edition. New York: Oxford University Press, 2008.

Sainteny, Jean. *Histoire d'une paix manquée: Indochine, 1945–1947*. Paris: Amiot-Dumont, 1953.

Salisbury, Harrison E. *Behind the Lines—Hanoi: December 23, 1966–January 7, 1967*. New York: Harper & Row, 1967.

Sandbrook, Dominic. *Eugene McCarthy: The Rise and Fall of Postwar American Liberalism*. New York: Alfred A. Knopf, 2004.

Sander, Robert D. *Invasion of Laos, 1971: Lam Son 719*. Norman: University of Oklahoma Press, 2014.

Scammon, Richard M., and Ben J. Wattenberg. *The Real Majority*. New York: Coward-McCann, 1970.

Schäfer, Axel R., ed. *American Evangelicals and the 1960s*. Madison: University of Wisconsin Press, 2013.

Schandler, Herbert Y. *The Unmaking of a President: Lyndon Johnson and Vietnam*. Princeton, NJ: Princeton University Press, 1977.

Schlesinger, Andrew, and Stephen Schlesinger, eds. *The Letters of Arthur Schlesinger, Jr.* New York: Random House, 2013.

Schlesinger Jr., Arthur. *The Crisis of Confidence: Ideas, Power and Violence in America*. Boston: Houghton Mifflin, 1969.

———, ed. *History of American Presidential Elections, 1789–1968*. Vol. 4. New York: McGraw-Hill, 1971.

———, ed. *History of U.S. Political Parties: 1945–1972, The Politics of Change*. Vol. 4. Philadelphia: Chelsea House Publishers, 1973.

———. *Robert Kennedy and His Times*. Boston: Houghton Mifflin, 1978.

Schoenbaum, Thomas J. *Waging Peace and War: Dean Rusk in the Truman, Kennedy, and Johnson Years*. New York: Simon & Schuster, 1988.

Schulman, Bruce J., and Julian E. Zelizer, eds. *Rightward Bound: Making America Conservative in the 1970s*. Cambridge, MA: Harvard University Press, 2008.

Schultz, John. *The Chicago Conspiracy Trial*. Revised edition. Chicago: University of Chicago Press, 2009.

———. *No One Was Killed: Documentation and Meditation, Convention Week, Chicago, August 1968*. Chicago: Big Table Publishing, 1969.

Schulzinger, Robert D. *A Time for War: The United States and Vietnam, 1941–1975*. New York: Oxford University Press, 1997.

Schumacher, Michael. *The Contest: The 1968 Election and the War for America's Soul*. Minneapolis: University of Minnesota Press, 2018.

Schwartz, Thomas A. *Henry Kissinger and American Power: A Political Biography*. New York: Hill and Wang, 2020.

———. *Lyndon Johnson and Europe: In the Shadow of Vietnam*. Cambridge, MA: Harvard University Press, 2003.

Shafer, Byron E., and Richard Johnston. *The End of Southern Exceptionalism: Class, Race, and Partisan Change in the Postwar South*. Cambridge, MA: Harvard University Press, 2006.

Shaplen, Robert. *The Road from War: Vietnam, 1965–1970*. New York: Harper & Row, 1970.

Sharman, Nick. *The Chicago Conspiracy Trial and the Press*. New York: Palgrave Macmillan, 2016.

Sheehan, Neil. *A Bright Shining Lie: John Paul Vann and America in Vietnam*. New York: Random House, 1988.

———, ed. *The Pentagon Papers, as Published by the* New York Times. New York: Bantam Books, 1971.

Shen, James C. H. *The U.S. and Free China: How the U.S. Sold Out Its Ally*. Washington, DC: Aeropolis Books, 1983.

Sherman, Norman. *From Nowhere to Somewhere, My Political Journey: A Memoir of Sorts*. Minneapolis: First Avenue Editions, 2016.

Sherrill, Robert, and Harry W. Ernst. *The Drugstore Liberal*. New York: Grossman Publishers, 1968.

Shesol, Jeff. *Mutual Contempt: Lyndon Johnson, Robert Kennedy, and the Feud That Defined a Decade*. New York: W. W. Norton, 1997.

Sidey, Hugh. *A Very Personal Presidency: Lyndon Johnson in the White House*. London: Andre Deutsch, 1968.

Sieg, Kent G. "The 1968 Presidential Election and Peace in Vietnam." *Presidential Studies Quarterly* 26, no. 4 (Fall 1996): 1062–80.

Sihanouk, Norodom. *My War with the CIA: The Memoirs of Prince Norodom Sihanouk*. New York: Pantheon Books, 1972.

Small, Melvin, ed. *A Companion to Richard M. Nixon*. Malden, MA: Blackwell Publishing, 2011.

———. *The Presidency of Richard Nixon*. Lawrence: University Press of Kansas, 1999.

Small, Melvin, and William D. Hoover, eds. *Give Peace a Chance: Exploring the Vietnam Antiwar Movement*. Syracuse, NY: Syracuse University Press, 1992.

Smith, Anita. *The Intimate Story of Lurleen Wallace: Her Crusade of Courage*. Montgomery, AL: Communications Unlimited, 1969.

Smith, Richard Norton. *On His Own Terms: A Life of Nelson Rockefeller*. New York: Random House, 2014.

Solberg, Carl. *Hubert Humphrey: A Biography*. New York: W. W. Norton, 1984.

Sorley, Lewis. *A Better War: The Unexamined Victories and Final Tragedy of America's Last Years in Vietnam*. New York: Harcourt, 1999.

———, ed. *The Vietnam War: An Assessment by South Vietnam's Generals*. Lubbock: Texas Tech University Press, 2010.

———. *Westmoreland: The General Who Lost Vietnam*. Boston: Houghton Mifflin Harcourt, 2011.

Southwick, Leslie H., ed. *Presidential Also-Rans and Running Mates, 1788 through 1996. Volume 2, 1892–1996*. 2nd edition. Jefferson, NC: McFarland, 2008.

Stanley, Timothy. *The Crusader: The Life and Tumultuous Times of Pat Buchanan*. New York: Thomas Dunne Books, 2012.

Stans, Maurice H. *The Terrors of Justice: The Untold Side of Watergate*. New York: Everest House Publishers, 1978.

Stavis, Ben. *We Were the Campaign: New Hampshire to Chicago for McCarthy*. Boston: Beacon Press, 1969.

Steel, Ronald. *In Love with Night: The American Romance with Robert Kennedy*. New York: Simon & Schuster, 2000.

Steigerwald, David. *The Sixties and the End of Modern America*. New York: St. Martin's Press, 1995.

Stewart, John G. "When Democracy Worked: Reflections on the Passage of the Civil Rights Act of 1964." *New York Law School Law Review* 59, no. 1 (2014–15): 145–72.

Stockdale, Jim, and Sybil Stockdale. *In Love and War: The Story of a Family's Ordeal and Sacrifice During the Vietnam Years*. Revised and updated edition. Annapolis: Naval Institute Press, 1990.

Stout, Richard T. *People*. New York: Harper & Row, 1970.

Strober, Gerald S, and Deborah H. Strober. *Nixon: An Oral History of His Presidency*. New York: HarperCollins Publishers, 1994.

Sugrue, Thomas J. *The Origins of the Urban Crisis: Race and Inequality in Postwar Detroit*. Princeton, NJ: Princeton University Press, 1996.

Sullivan, Patricia. *Justice Rising: Robert Kennedy's America in Black and White*. Cambridge, MA: Harvard University Press, 2021.

Sullivan, William C., with Bill Brown. *The Bureau: My Thirty Years in Hoover's FBI*. New York: W. W. Norton, 1979.

Sullivan, William H. *Obbligato, 1939–1979: Notes on a Foreign Service Career, 1939–1979*. New York: W. W. Norton, 1984.

Summers, Anthony, with Robbyn Swan. *The Arrogance of Power: The Secret World of Richard Nixon*. New York: Penguin Books, 2000.

Summers Jr., Harry G. *On Strategy: A Critical Analysis of the Vietnam War*. Novato, CA: Presidio Press, 1982.

Suri, Jeremi. *Henry Kissinger and the American Century*. Cambridge, MA: Belknap Press of Harvard University Press, 2007.

Sweig, Julia. *Lady Bird Johnson: Hiding in Plain Sight*. New York: Random House, 2021.

Swift, Will. *Pat and Dick: The Nixons, an Intimate Portrait of a Marriage*. New York: Threshold Editions, 2014.

Taylor, K. W. *A History of the Vietnamese*. New York: Cambridge University Press, 2013.

———, ed. *Voices from the Second Republic of South Vietnam (1967–1975)*. Ithaca, NY: Cornell Southeast Asia Program Publications, 2014.

Tedford, Drew. "Silent No More: The Logan Act as a Constitutionally Enforceable Tool in Foreign Policy." *Houston Journal of International Law* 32, no. 3 (2010): 733–66.

Theoharis, Athan. *Chasing Spies: How the FBI Failed in Counterintelligence but Promoted the Politics of McCarthyism in the Cold War Years*. Chicago: Ivan R. Dee, 2002.

———, ed. *From the Secret Files of J. Edgar Hoover*. Chicago: Ivan R. Dee, 1991.

————. *Spying on Americans: Political Surveillance from Hoover to the Huston Plan.* Philadelphia: Temple University Press, 1978.

Thimmesch, Nick. *The Condition of Republicanism.* New York: W. W. Norton, 1968.

Thomas, Evan. *Being Nixon: A Man Divided.* New York: Random House, 2015.

————. *Robert Kennedy: His Life.* New York: Simon & Schuster, 2000.

Thomas, G. Scott. *Counting the Votes: A New Way to Analyze America's Presidential Elections.* Santa Barbara, CA: Praeger, 2015.

Thurber, Timothy N. *The Politics of Equality: Hubert H. Humphrey and the African American Freedom Struggle.* New York: Columbia University Press, 1999.

————. *Republicans and Race: The GOP's Frayed Relationship with African Americans, 1945–1974.* Lawrence: University Press of Kansas, 2013.

Thurmond, Strom. *The Faith We Have Not Kept.* San Diego: Viewpoint Books, 1968.

Tolles, Frederick B. "Unofficial Ambassador: George Logan's Mission to France, 1798." *William and Mary Quarterly* 7, no. 1 (January 1950): 1–25.

Tran Ngoc Chau, with Ken Fermoyle. *Vietnam Labyrinth: Allies, Enemies, and Why the U.S. Lost the War.* Lubbock: Texas Tech University Press, 2012.

Turner, Stansfield. *Burn before Reading: Presidents, CIA Directors, and Secret Intelligence.* New York: Hyperion, 2005.

Unger, Irwin. *The Best of Intentions: The Triumphs and Failures of the Great Society under Kennedy, Johnson, and Nixon.* New York: Doubleday, 1996.

Unger, Irwin, and Debi Unger. *Turning Point: 1968.* New York: Scribner, 1988.

U.S. National Advisory Commission on Civil Disorders. *Report of the National Advisory Commission on Civil Disorders.* Princeton, NJ: Princeton University Press, 2016.

Valenti, Jack. *My Life: In War, the White House, and Hollywood.* New York: Harmony Books, 2007.

Vance, Cyrus. *Hard Choices: Critical Years in America's Foreign Policy.* New York: Simon & Schuster, 1983.

VanDeMark, Brian. *Road to Disaster: A New History of America's Descent into Vietnam.* New York: Custom House, 2018.

Van Dyk, Ted. *Heroes, Hacks, and Fools: Memoirs from the Political Inside.* Seattle: University of Washington Press, 2007.

Vanden Heuvel, William. *Hope and History: A Memoir of Tumultuous Times.* Ithaca, NY: Cornell University Press, 2019.

Vanden Heuvel, William, and Milton Gwirtzman. *On His Own: Robert F. Kennedy, 1964–1968.* Garden City, NY: Doubleday, 1970.

Veith, George J. *Drawn Swords in a Distant Land: South Vietnam's Shattered Dreams.* New York: Encounter Books, 2021.

Vinen, Richard. *1968: Radical Protest and Its Enemies.* New York: Harper, 2018.

Vu, Tuong, and Sean Fear, eds. *The Republic of Vietnam, 1955–1975: Vietnamese Perspectives on Nation Building.* Ithaca, NY: Cornell University Press, 2020.

Walker, J. Samuel. *Most of 14th Street Is Gone: The Washington, DC Riots of 1968.* New York: Oxford University Press, 2018.

Wallace, George C. *Stand Up for America.* Garden City, NY: Doubleday, 1976.

Wallace Jr., George. *Governor George Wallace: The Man You Never Knew.* 2011.

Wallerstein, Immanuel, and Paul Starr, eds. *The University Crisis Reader: Confrontation and Counterattack.* Vols. 1–2. New York: Random House, 1971.

Walters, Vernon A. *Silent Missions.* Garden City, NY: Doubleday, 1978.

Wasow, Omar. "Agenda Seeding: How 1960s Black Protests Moved Elites, Public Opinion, and Voting." *American Political Science Review* 114, no. 3 (August 2020): 638–59.

Watson, W. Marvin, with Sherwin Markman. *Chief of Staff: Lyndon Johnson and His Presidency.* New York: Thomas Dunne Books, 2004.

Webb, Samuel L., and Margaret E. Armbrester, eds. *Alabama Governors: A Political History of the State.* Tuscaloosa: University of Alabama Press, 2014.

Weinstein, Allen. *Perjury: The Hiss-Chambers Case.* 3rd edition. Stanford, CA: Hoover Institution Press, 2013.

Weisman, Steven R., ed. *Daniel Patrick Moynihan: A Portrait in Letters of an American Visionary.* New York: PublicAffairs, 2010.

Wells, Tom. *The War Within: America's Battle over Vietnam.* Berkeley: University of California Press, 1994.

Westmoreland, William C. *A Soldier Reports.* Garden City, NY: Doubleday, 1976.

Whalen, Richard J. *Catch the Falling Flag: A Republican's Challenge to His Party.* Boston: Houghton Mifflin, 1972.

White, Theodore H. *Breach of Faith: The Fall of Richard Nixon.* New York: Atheneum Publishers, 1975.

———. *In Search of History: A Personal Adventure.* New York: Harper & Row, 1978.

———. *The Making of the President, 1968.* New York: Atheneum Publishers, 1969.

Wicker, Tom. *One of Us: Richard Nixon and the American Dream.* New York: Random House, 1991.

Wiener, Jon, ed. *Conspiracy in the Streets: The Extraordinary Trial of the Chicago Eight.* New York: New Press, 2006.

Wills, Garry. *Nixon Agonistes: The Crisis of the Self-Made Man.* Boston: Houghton Mifflin, 1969.

Witcover, Jules. *85 Days: The Last Campaign of Robert Kennedy.* New York: G. P. Putnam's Sons, 1969.

———. *Party of the People: A History of the Democrats.* New York: Random House, 2003.

———. *The Resurrection of Richard Nixon.* New York: G. P. Putnam's Sons, 1970.

———. *Very Strange Bedfellows: The Short and Unhappy Marriage of Richard Nixon and Spiro Agnew.* New York: PublicAffairs, 2007.

———. *White Knight: The Rise of Spiro Agnew.* New York: Random House, 1972.

———. *The Year the Dream Died: Revisiting 1968 in America.* New York: Warner Books, 1997.

Woods, Randall B. *LBJ: Architect of American Ambition.* New York: Free Press, 2006.

Xia, Yafeng. *Negotiating with the Enemy: U.S.-China Talks during the Cold War, 1949–1972.* Bloomington: Indiana University Press, 2006.

Young, Marilyn B., and Robert Buzzanco, eds. *A Companion to the Vietnam War.* Malden, MA: Blackwell Publishing, 2002.

Zhai, Qiang. *China and the Vietnam Wars, 1950–1975.* Chapel Hill: University of North Carolina Press, 2000.

Zubok, Vladislav, and Constantine Pleshkov. *Inside the Kremlin's Cold War: From Stalin to Khrushchev.* Cambridge, MA: Harvard University Press, 1996.

Index